EN AQUEL ENTONCES

To Armando Rendón —
Cordially,
Manuel
Mar. 25, 2010

EN AQUEL ENTONCES

[IN YEARS GONE BY]

READINGS IN MEXICAN-AMERICAN HISTORY

EDITED BY
MANUEL G. GONZALES
AND
CYNTHIA M. GONZALES

INDIANA UNIVERSITY PRESS · *Bloomington and Indianapolis*

This book is a publication of

Indiana University Press
601 North Morton Street
Bloomington, IN 47404-3797 USA

http://www.indiana.edu/~iupress

Telephone orders   800-842-6796
Fax orders   812-855-7931
Orders by e-mail   iuporder@indiana.edu

Library of Congress Cataloging-in-Publication Data

En aquel entonces : readings in Mexican-American history / edited by
Manuel G. Gonzales and Cynthia M. Gonzales.
    p.   cm.
  Includes bibliographical references and index.
    ISBN 0-253-33765-8 (alk. paper) — ISBN 0-253-21399-1 (pbk. :
alk. paper)
    1. Mexican Americans—History.   I. Gonzales, Manuel G.
  II. Gonzales, Cynthia M., date.

E184.M5 E45 2000
973'.046872—dc21
                                                    00-020340
1 2 3 4 5 05 04 03 02 01 00

To our parents,

MANUEL ESQUIVEL GONZALES
and
FRANCIS GARCÍA GONZALES

IRVING ROGERS MERRILL
and
VIRGINIA VANCE MERRILL

CONTENTS

◄◦►◄◦►◄◦►

ACKNOWLEDGMENTS

Many people contributed to this anthology. We are grateful to the authors who allowed us to reproduce their essays. Several of them were kind enough to either edit their own pieces or provide valuable suggestions that have been incorporated into our work. These collaborators deserve special recognition. We begin with Arnoldo De León, one of the most respected historians in the profession. In spite of a hectic schedule, Arnoldo, a model of efficiency, was willing to help at every turn. Other authors who should be singled out for special thanks include Armando Alonzo, Antonia Castañeda, Alma García, Richard García, Cynthia Orozco, and Frank de la Teja. Carlos Larralde was generous with advice and bibliographical materials.

As always, David Weber has been an inspiration. Moreover, he was kind enough to read our introduction and offer suggestions.

Not all our debts are owed to the "Sons—and Daughters—of Texas." The selection of essays for this anthology was facilitated by Rudy Acuña, who provided valuable suggestions. We also owe a profound debt of gratitude to Lillian Castillo-Speed of the Chicano Studies Library at UC Berkeley, a consummate professional; and Christine Marín, who heads the Chicano Studies Library at Arizona State University.

Manuel's colleagues at Diablo Valley College (DVC) have always been supportive. Friend and fellow historian Greg Tilles, in particular, has often provided encouragement. We should also single out James J. Rawls, who has been helpful in a multitude of ways through these many years. Moreover, his superb work on California history has been a true inspiration. Patrick Leong, Lisa Orta, David Vela, and Nancy Zink shared valuable comments on both style and substance. Isabel Izquierdo lent her linguistic expertise. DVC librarians Carol Bartlett and Lorrita Ford helped with permissions, as did Manuel's brother, Michael Gonzales. Another example of diligence is Francisco Arce, DVC Dean of Instruction, who has consistently backed our scholarly investigations. Jay Lesnansky, a student, helped unravel the mysteries of the computer.

Finally, the staff of Indiana University Press did a stellar professional job. We are grateful to all the staff members who lent their talents to the project.

INTRODUCTION
MANUEL G. GONZALES

–◀O▶–◀O▶–◀O▶–

En aquel entonces, "in those years gone by"—these magical words are etched in the memory of those of my generation who grew up in Spanish-speaking households. Our elders, our first and most respected mentors, often began their nostalgic recollections of the distant past, those unforgettable tales that held us wide-eyed youngsters spellbound, with this attention-grabbing preface. Thus, we received our first lessons in history. Our appetites whetted, many of us, the most intellectually curious, yearned for more. Unfortunately, as we grew older, knowledge of our Mexican-American past was largely limited to this oral tradition. Our ancestors were nowhere to be found in the American history textbooks we were asked to read in school. We truly were an "invisible minority."

All of this changed dramatically in the late 1960s with the advent of the Chicano (and soon after, the Chicana) movement. This struggle to secure justice for Mexican Americans through the acquisition of political power and the preservation of ethnic culture stimulated a passionate interest in the historical roots of "the children of the sun." Since that turbulent decade, the systematic study of the Mexican-American past has been so thoroughly dominated by movement scholars that the academic discipline is popularly referred to as "Chicano history," and is identified with the broader field of Chicano studies. However, the perspectives that inform historical investigation of ethnic Mexicans in the United States, both native-born and immigrant, are too varied and complex to be incorporated under a single rubric. Generally speaking, at least three distinct lines of inquiry can be distinguished today: Chicano, Mexican-American, and Anglo.

Chicano historians, in the special sense that I use the term here, are ethnic Mexicans (occasionally other Latinos) whose interpretations of the past are informed by the basic tenets of Chicanismo. The roots of Chicano historiography, of Chicano studies in general, are to be found in the *Plan de Santa Bárbara.*[1] This key document was the work of the young Chicano college students, professors, and administrators who met at the University of California at Santa Barbara in April 1969 to formulate a blueprint for higher education. Convened by the Chicano Coordinating Committee on Higher Education, the assembly was hosted by Jesús Chavarría, Guillermo Villa, and Fernando De Necochea. The most momentous consequences of the meeting, and the document it published, were the creation of a militant student organization, the *Movimiento Estudiantil Chicano de Aztlán* (MECHA), and the institution of Chicano studies, a new academic field of inquiry that would focus on La Raza (Mexican Americans). Committed to a multidiciplinary approach, Chicano studies from the very beginning put a special emphasis on history.[2]

Chicano historiography began as a reaction to traditional Anglo portrayals of Mexican Americans.[3] Writing in 1972, Matt S. Meier and Feliciano Rivera rightly noted, "Historians, for the most part, have neglected Mexican Americans both in broad historical coverage and in monographic detail; when they have been mentioned in general United States histories, typically the viewpoint has been negative."[4] Other social sciences were more willing to examine the Mexican-American experience, but their perceptions were equally deficient, resulting in a stereotypical and monolithic image of Mexicans as docile peons.

From the outset, the fledgling field of Chicano studies, born of a militant movement, indeed a product of the *movimiento* at its very zenith, sought to produce a "scholar-activist." The scholarship that was encouraged not only was supposed to demolish old stereotypes; it was also to ameliorate the plight of the *barrios* (Mexican neighborhoods). That is, the mission of the Chicano scholar was not simply to describe society, but ultimately to change it. Rodolfo (Rudy) Acuña, founder of the Chicano Studies department at California State University, Northridge, who best personifies the ideal, also expresses it most cogently:

> For me, Chicano studies is a public trust, and those who choose to teach it assume the duty of protecting the interests of Chicano students and the community. A Chicano studies scholar can't be solely academically committed to the discipline, she or he must also be politically committed.[5]

Chicanos in academia were expected to recruit, train, and mentor students who would return to and transform their communities.

Ideally, according to *El Plan,* this change was to be accomplished in Chicano Studies departments, where, working largely among themselves, Chicanos could control hiring, finances, and the curriculum, though research centers were also envisioned. (In fact, the first of these departments had already been created, in 1968 at San Fernando Valley State College, now California State University at Northridge.) However, given the small numbers of ethnic students and the conservative nature of educational institutions, militants often had to settle for what they could get. Consequently, courses came to be taught in a variety of academic settings. Some Chicano professors wound up in Chicano Studies departments; others in traditional academic departments, like History or English; and a few in non-traditional departments, like Women's Studies. Many received joint appointments.[6]

The tone of Chicano historiography was set in the decade of the seventies when, like militant colleagues in other non-traditional disciplines, Chicano historians began producing a body of works that was "counter-hegemonic." The dominant paradigm established at this time in Chicano studies was the internal colony model introduced to the field by University of California, Berkeley, political scientist Carlos Muñoz, Jr.[7] This theoretical model worked on the assumption that Mexican Americans were a conquered people subjected to the same oppression at the hands of whites as were people of color in the Third World. Widely adopted by ethnic scholars, especially in urban California, its foremost exposition is found in Rodolfo Acuña's *Occupied America: The Chicano's Struggle toward Liberation* (1972), a work widely recognized as the bible of Chicano studies.[8] Eventually, the internal colony model was abandoned; it did not seem to be particularly relevant to the twentieth century, when massive numbers of Mexicans immigrated into the United States of their own volition. But Chicano historians have never totally escaped the tendency to see their subjects as victims.[9] Nor have they really come to terms with the inherent contradiction of seeking historical objectivity while enhancing a community's self-esteem, the burden of being scholar-activists.[10] Brigham Young University historian Ignacio M. García, himself a sixties activist, has perceptively noted: "Their history often worked chronologically backward. Their premise was that Chicanos were a strong and courageous people who had survived conquest, colonization, and racial brutality. Working back from that premise meant interpreting the 'facts' to support the thesis."[11]

As Arthur F. Corwin, a specialist on Mexican immigration, pointed out in 1973, even at their inception, militant Chicano historians encountered a competing line of inquiry into their past by more moderate Latino scholars inclined to identify themselves as "Mexican American."[12] He labels the first group "La Raza school"; the second group is referred to as the "establishment school." The latter, Corwin argues, attempts to integrate its findings into national history, whereas the former prefers to work in isolation from mainstream history. While Corwin may have erred on particulars, as Rudy Acuña was quick to point out, he was essentially correct in identifying a group of *raza* (Mexican-origin) academics who were simply interested in analyzing the Mexican-American historical experience according to traditional canons without a firm commitment to social transformation.[13] Certainly there were Mexican Americans who studied their own history even before the advent of the movimiento. And although modern-day Chicano scholars have attempted to portray George I. Sánchez, Américo Paredes, Julián Samora, and other such pioneers as "precursors" of Chicanismo, their view is not completely convincing.[14] Carlos Muñoz concurs:

Sánchez, Paredes, and Samora were part of the Mexican-American Generation, whose ideology had been shaped by the politics of their youth during the 1930s and 1940s. As progressive as they were, they could not relate their own work to the task of building a Chicano consciousness in accordance with the cultural nationalist ideology of the Chicano Movement as a whole.[15]

And, of course, the same could be said of Carlos E. Castañeda, Jovita González, and other Mexican-origin scholars who did their work before 1965. Good examples of Mexican-American scholars who maintained their distance from the emerging Chicano orientation in the 1970s are political scientist Ralph Guzmán and historian Manuel Servín. The latter's views of Mexican Americans, and especially pachucos (zoot suiters), were roundly condemned by Chicano movement critics for being what today would be labeled "politically incorrect."[16] Likewise, Raúl Morín, who wrote a pioneering history in 1963 of Mexican Americans in the military service, could not be considered a Chicano scholar.[17] Indeed, there were ethnic scholars who were absolutely opposed to the Chicano perspective. No critic was more vehement than Manuel A. Machado, Jr., whose scathing attack on Chicano studies in *Listen, Chicano! An Informal History of the Mexican Americans* (1978) won him the enmity of many young scholars.[18] More recent historians whom I see as "Mexican American" rather than "Chicano" include Félix D. Almáraz, Jr., Adrian Bustamante, Lawrence A. Cardoso, Thomas E. Chávez, Gilbert R. Cruz, Bernardo P. Gallegos, Oscar J. Martínez, and Lorena Oropeza. These scholars have all been affiliated with traditional academic departments.

A third perspective on Mexican-American history is provided by Anglo scholars, whose work Richard Griswold del Castillo has labeled *historia Chicanesca,* defined as "interpretations of Chicano/a history by non-Chicanos."[19] These scholars are not ethnic Chicanos, but can they be called "Chicano historians"? There does not seem to be a consensus of opinion on this question among raza colleagues; however, most would probably reply in the negative, for even as the millennium draws to a close, there are Chicano scholars who feel that Anglos lack the sensitivity to write Mexican-American history.[20] While this exclusive perspective was relatively common among minority scholars in the 1970s, I am surprised that it still has currency today. Virtually everyone agrees that, say, white scholars Herbert G. Gutman and Leon F. Litwack can write valid accounts of the African-American experience. Why is ethnic origin an issue in "Chicano" historiography? After all, the seminal work in the field of Mexican-American history was *North from Mexico: The Spanish-Speaking People of the United States* (1949) by Carey McWilliams.[21] David J. Weber has also been a formidable presence in the field, as a mentor as well as a scholar. In fact, some of the very best work done in Chicano studies has been accomplished by non-Latinos. These include Leonard Pitt, Mark Reisler, Sarah Deutsch, Devra Weber, and Lisabeth Haas. It might be said, too, that many "Chicano" historians are themselves products of mixed marriages; Louise Año Nuevo Kerr, Douglas Monroy, Vicki Ruiz, and Neil Foley come readily to mind.

The three lines of inquiry I have outlined above can hardly be called "schools," since they are not rigid and mutually exclusive categories of scholars. In my own case, for instance, I fluctuate between the Chicano and Mexican-American perspectives. On the one hand, I was greatly influenced by the movimiento as a college student in the sixties. Furthermore, I completely endorse its basic goals: political power and cultural regeneration. As a resident of the west side of the San Joaquin Valley, working in the fields until the age of twenty-six, I experienced the poverty and oppression that Rudy Acuña describes so graphically in *Occupied America.* Indeed, when Marc Reisner made a PBS documentary based on his *Cadillac Desert: The American West and Its Disappearing Water* (1986), a well-researched exposé of environmental abuses associated with water and land use in the American West, he chose my hometown, Huron, California, as the prime example of the "sorry social impact agricultural monopoly can have."[22] On the other hand, I was always on the periphery of the movimiento. As a product of a Catholic upbringing stressing personal responsibility and a macho ethic calling for massive self-sufficiency, I am not temperamentally suited to affiliation with a movement, especially a protest movement. Moreover, it is difficult to be a "true believer" given my academic training in a traditional field, modern European history. I'm sure there are many Anglo scholars who are more "Chicano" than I am. Also, it should be recognized that even within each of the three categories of historians outlined above, there is significant diversity. For example, within the Chicano "school" (to use Corwin's term), there is a vast difference between the historical perspectives championed by Rudy Acuña, on the one hand, and by Mario García, on the other, the "conflictive" and "pluralist" views of Chicano history respectively.[23]

The research on the Mexican-American experience that has been done since the late 1960s, especially the work produced by Chicano scholars, many of them affiliated with Chicano Studies departments, programs, or centers, has always met with a chilly reception by non-Hispanic colleagues in academe. Such was the case in the past, and regrettably it remains largely true today among the old guard.[24] Like the eminent historian Arthur Schlesinger, Jr., many critics in traditional departments oppose "the notion that history and literature should be taught not as intellectual disciplines but as therapies whose function is to raise minority self-esteem."[25]

There is some truth to these charges. There are Chicano Studies departments where so much emphasis has been put on activism that scholarship has been neglected or even disparaged.[26] Thus, Chicano studies continues to fight to gain legitimacy as an area of scholarly inquiry. On the other hand, it needs to be said, too, that the quality of minority scholarship, in all academic disciplines, has steadily improved, markedly during the past decade. The discipline of history is a case in point. That academe is beginning to recognize their efforts is best reflected in the number of *Chicano* historians (defined in the narrow sense I have used above) who have won major prizes from prestigious regional and national professional associations. These include Vicki L. Ruiz, Ramón Gutiérrez, David Gutiérrez, David Montejano, George J. Sánchez, Neil Foley, and many more.

High quality Chicano/a scholarship, however, has not been confined to book-length manuscripts. There is a growing body of important periodical literature. Given the reluctance of major presses to publish ethnic scholarship in the past, as well as the constraints placed on their time by the demands of an activist orientation, many Chicanos and Chicanas have found that the only viable outlets for their investigations have been professional journals. Unfortunately, many of these publications are obscure and difficult to access, even within the academic community. It is not easy, for example, for scholars in California to find the *Journal of South Texas,* or, conversely, for Tejanos to gain access to the *Journal of San Diego History.* Our anthology of readings was conceived as a partial solution to the problem. With only two exceptions—essays by Armando Alonzo and Arnoldo De León—all were originally published in journals.

The essays reproduced here are meant to provide a scholarly overview of Mexican-American history and Chicano historiography. Most of these pieces were written by historians, but given the interdisciplinary orientation of Chicano studies, a variety of academic fields are represented among the chosen authors. Since another intent is to demonstrate the scholarly production of *Chicanos,* a group of men and women whose efforts have often been maligned by fellow academics, all the authors represented here are of Latino background. We have deleted notes and, with rare exceptions, heavily edited the selections in other ways. However, complete bibliographic citations of the sources are provided in footnotes preceding each piece. Readers are encouraged to consult the original essays for a better appreciation of the sources and methodologies the scholars employed. At the end of this volume, we have also provided a bibliographic essay on important historical works focusing on Mexican Americans in hopes of aiding readers who want to go beyond the periodical literature.

NOTES

1. See *El Plan de Santa Barbara: A Chicano Plan for Higher Education* (Oakland, Calif.: La Causa Publications, 1969). Several of the student participants would eventually pursue academic careers: Luis Arroyo, Gracia Molina de Pick, Ana Nieto-Gómez, Gilbert González, Ron López, Ysidro Ramón Macías, Carlos Muñoz, Juan Gómez-Quiñones, Rene Nuñez, Armando Valdez, and Eliezer Risco.

2. "As the concept of Chicano Studies evolves," noted Jesús Chavarría in the initial number of *Aztlán,* "history has clearly emerged as the discipline central to the concept." "A Précis and a Tentative Bibliography on Chicano History," *Aztlán: Chicano Journal of the Social Sciences and Arts* 1 (Spring 1970): 133.

3. David G. Gutiérrez, "Significant to Whom? Mexican Americans and the History of the American West," *Western Historical Quarterly* 24 (November 1993): 524–25.

4. *The Chicanos: A History of Mexican Americans* (New York: Hill and Wang, 1972), pp. 281–82.

5. "Chicano Studies: A Public Trust," in *Chicano Studies: Critical Connection between Research and Community,* ed. Teresa Córdova (Albuquerque: The National Association for Chicano Studies, 1992), p. 2.

6. The troubles and tribulations of these early years are the subject of Carlos Muñoz, Jr., "The Development of Chicano Studies, 1968–1981," *Chicano Studies: A Multidisciplinary Approach,* ed. Eugene T. García, Francisco Lomelí, and Isidro Ortiz (New York: Teachers College Press, 1984): 5–18. For a concise history of Chicano studies, see Carlos F. Ortega, "Introduction: Chicano Studies as a Discipline," in *Chicano Studies: Survey and Analysis,* ed. Dennis J. Bixler-Marquez et al. (Dubuque, Iowa: Kendall/Hunt, 1999), pp. v–xiv. See, too, Rodolfo F. Acuña's provocative *Sometimes There Is No Other Side: Chicanos and the Myth of Equality* (Notre Dame, Ind.: University of Notre Dame Press, 1998), especially Chapter 5, "Chicana/o Studies and the American Paradigm."

7. Carlos Muñoz, Jr., *Youth, Identity, Power: The Chicano Movement* (New York: Verso, 1989), p. 147.

8. *Occupied America: The Chicano's Struggle toward Liberation* (San Francisco: Canfield Press, 1972).

9. Alex M. Saragoza, "Recent Chicano Historiography: An Interpretive Essay," *Aztlán* 19 (1989–90): 10. The most compelling case against the internal colony model is found in Tomás Almaguer, "Ideological Distortions in Recent Chicano Historiography: The Internal Model and Chicano Historical Interpretation," *Aztlán* 18 (Spring 1987): 7–28.

10. A theme I explore in *Mexicanos: A History of Mexicans in the United States* (Bloomington: Indiana University Press, 1999).

11. *Chicanismo: The Forging of a Militant Ethos among Mexican Americans* (Tucson: University of Arizona Press, 1997), p. 67.

12. Arthur F. Corwin, "Mexican-American History: An Assessment," *Pacific Historical Review* 42 (August 1973): 300.

13. For Acuña's criticisms, see his "Mexican-American History: A Reply," *Pacific Historical Review* 43 (February 1974): 147–50.

14. Alluding to these "important individual intellectual precursors," one researcher observes: "These scholars, it could be argued, were 'doing' Chicano Studies as early as the 1930s." Raoul Contreras, "Chicano Movement Chicano Studies: Social Science and Self-Conscious Ideology," *Perspectives in Mexican American Studies* 6 (1997): 46.

15. Muñoz, *Youth, Identity, Power,* p. 142.

16. Servín's conservatism is reflected best in his oft-quoted article, "The Post–World War II Mexican Americans, 1925–65: A Nonachieving Minority," in *An Awakened Minority: The Mexican-Americans,* ed. Manuel P. Servín, 2d ed. (Beverly Hills, Calif.: Glencoe Press, 1974 [1970]), pp. 160–74.

17. *Among the Valiant: Mexican Americans in WWII and Korea* (Alhambra, Calif.: Borden Publishing Company, 1963).

18. *Listen Chicano! An Informal History of the Mexican Americans* (Chicago: Nelson Hall, 1978). See, too, Manuel A. Machado, Jr., "Mexican American History: Problems and Prospects," *Western Review* 8 (Winter 1971): 15–21. Ironically, Machado's major contention that heterogeneity rather than homogeneity characterized the Mexican-American community is now widely accepted by Chicano historians.

19. Richard Griswold del Castillo, "Chicano Historical Discourse: An Overview and Evaluation of the 1980s," *Perspectives in Mexican American Studies* 4 (1993): 2.

20. See, for example, Dennis N. Valdez's review of Craig Jenkins, *The Politics of Insurgency: The Farmworkers Movement of the 1960s* (New York: Columbia University Press, 1986), in *Chicano Discourse: Selected Conference Proceedings of the National Association for Chicano Studies,* ed. Tatcho Mindiola, Jr., and Emilio Zamora (University of Houston: Mexican American Studies Program, 1992), pp. 195–98.

21. *North from Mexico: The Spanish-Speaking People of the United States* (Philadelphia: J. B. Lippincott, 1949).

22. Marc Reisner, *Cadillac Desert: The American West and Its Disappearing Water,* rev. ed. (New York: Penguin Books, 1993), p. 377.

23. Griswold del Castillo, "Chicano Historical Discourse," p. 19.

24. "Mainstream U.S. historians tend to ignore Chicano history, apparently considering it the domain of specialists," lament Gilbert G. González and Raúl Fernández, "Chicano History: Transcending Cultural Models," *Pacific Historical Review* 63 (November 1994): 469. This sentiment is echoed by Rudy Acuña, who notes that in the field of history, "Chicana/o history is largely dismissed or devalued." *Sometimes There Is No Other Side,* p. 122.

25. Arthur M. Schlesinger, Jr., *The Disuniting of America: Reflections on a Multicultural Society,* rev. ed. (New York: W. W. Norton, 1998), p. 22.

26. This is essentially the point made by Adela de la Torre, Director of the Mexican American Studies Center at the University of Arizona, in "Perspective on Ethnic Studies: Activism Isn't Enough Any More; Scholarship and Intellectual Rigor Are Required If Programs Are to Move into the Academic Mainstream," *Los Angeles Times,* December 12, 1996.

◄○►◄○►◄○►◄○►EN AQUEL ENTONCES

PART I.
GENESIS OF A PEOPLE
1598–1846

While Chicano historians in the past have tended to begin their chronologies of the Mexican-American experience with the War of 1846–1848 and its aftermath, Mexican immigration into what is today the United States began in 1598, when Juan de Oñate led a group of *pobladores* (settlers) into New Mexico. Compared to the English presence, the impact of these fledgling Spanish settlements on American development has been relatively modest. The colonial legacy, however, is crucial to understanding the roots of the present-day Mexican-American population, especially in the Southwest.

The motives for Spanish expansion were complex. God, Gold, and Glory were undoubtedly factors, but perhaps the single most weighty consideration was frontier defense. By about 1600, both the French and the English were beginning to make serious incursions into North America. Nueva España, modern Mexico, with its lucrative mining industry, needed to be secured. Before too long, a series of *presidios* (forts) were set up on the northern perimeter.

Once established on the frontier, settler-soldiers had to contend with another threat—indigenous tribes. Needed primarily for labor, *indios* (Indians) had to be conquered and kept in submission. Moreover, given the crusading zeal of the Spaniards, a medieval legacy stemming from the Moorish crusades, a Catholic education was deemed essential. Hence, the mission would come to rival the presidio as the most important Spanish frontier institution. The threat posed by *indios bárbaros* ("savage Indians") meant that the colonists themselves would congregate in pueblos, a tendency fortified by the Iberian municipal tradition. As historian Antonia Castañeda reminds us in her essay, these early settlements were home to women as well as men.

The influence exerted by Native Americans on the northern frontier cannot be stressed enough. Their labor, of course, was absolutely essential. Equally significant was their contribution to the racial amalgam. As historian Ramón Gutiérrez indicates in his provocative essay, *mestizaje* (race mixture) was pervasive from the very outset, beginning in the Mexican interior immediately after the conquest of the Aztecs. Eventually, in marked contrast to English settlements, it came to be characteristic of Spanish frontier society. Finally, the nature of Spanish settlement was dictated not only by the availability of Indian labor, but also by the threat posed by indios bárbaros, a major factor in explaining Spanish failure to adequately populate the Far North. By 1800, as the colonial period approached its end, the frontier had advanced into North America at only three major points: Texas, where the modest settler population was to be found primarily in San Antonio; New Mexico, the heart of the borderlands, where a series of small villages along the Rio Grande extended from El Paso in the south to Santa Fe in the north; and California, occupied only after 1769, along a thin coastal strip. Isolated from the Mexican interior, these northern outposts played virtually no role in the struggle to win Mexican independence (1810–1821).

The most significant theme in the history of the short-lived Mexican period of Southwest history (1821–1848) was the arrival of *norteamericanos* (citizens of the United States) on Mexico's northern rim. The advent of the Yankees brought with it an expansion of trade and the prospects of wealth for the pobladores. In New Mexico, in fact, it was not long before Mexicans came to dominate the trade on the Santa Fe Trail, as historian David Sandoval relates in his essay. In California, too, as Federico Sánchez shows in his article, momentous socioeconomic changes occurred as the secularization of the missions and the initiation of the hide and tallow trade created a rancho aristocracy. The two frontier societies, as historian Frank de la Teja points out in his essay, had much in common. But as the two cultures came into contact, friction was inevitable. Many Yankees, particularly in Texas, soon developed a contempt for their Mexican hosts. These anti-Mexican sentiments, as cultural historian Raymund Paredes argues, were the product of an English legacy of hispanophobia and anti-Catholicism.

While the cultural clash is significant in explaining U.S. acquisition of the Southwest, it was ultimately economic factors that were most telling. The years between Mexican independence and the outbreak of the U.S.-Mexico War witnessed a gradual transformation of the Mexican frontier economy and the evolution of a more complex social system. Contrary to what some Chicano scholars have argued, incorporation into the global economy hardly signifies transformation into a capitalist system. Although here and there increased trade created the prospects of affluence for the first time—notably in northern New Mexico and coastal California—most pobladores continued making their living as humble peons and vaqueros, and living in pueblos which some Chicano historians liken to medieval villages. However, economic penetration did bring the Mexican North into the Yankee sphere of influence, paving the way for an armed conquest that was virtually inevitable.

1

PRESIDARIAS Y POBLADORAS
The Journey North and Life in Frontier California

ANTONIA I. CASTAÑEDA

Born in Crystal City, Texas, and raised in the Yakima Valley in Washington, feminist historian Antonia I. Castañeda is O'Connor Professor of Spanish Colonial History of Texas and the Southwest at St. Mary's University in San Antonio, Texas, where she is also Associate Professor in the Department of History. She has held positions at a variety of community and four-year colleges since earning her Ph.D. in U.S. history at Stanford University. Her research and teaching interests focus on gender, sexuality, and women of color in California and the Borderlands from the sixteenth century to the present. Her historiographical article "Women of Color and the Rewriting of Western History: The Discourse, Politics, and Decolonization of History" received the Joan Jensen/Darlis Miller Award from the Coalition for Western Women's History (1993), and the Louis Knott Kootz Award from the *Pacific Historical Review* (1993). Her current projects include a cultural history of native women in colonial Alta California, a bilingual critical edition of nineteenth-century Californiana narratives, and a cultural history of Tejana farm workers.

In the chilling, pre-dawn hours of December 21, 1773, Ana María Hurtado and her two daughters, 20-year-old Cipriana and 18-year-old María del Carmen, walked across shaky, torch-lit planks to board the *Santiago,* the supply ship that would carry them from San Blas to Alta California. Five other women boarded the *Santiago* that morning. Two of them, María Teresa Ochoa, a young servant girl, and María Josefa Davila, were also single and of marriageable age. The other three, Josefa María Góngora, María Arroyo Herrera, and Doña Josefa, came with their husbands. These eight women, wives, daughters, and kinswomen of blacksmiths, carpenters, a storekeeper,

From *Renato Rosaldo Lecture Series Monograph* 8 (1992): 25–46. The original text has been modified. Reprinted by permission of the author.

and a surgeon, were the first Spanish-speaking *mestiza* women to arrive in Alta California. . . .

From 1769 until 1774, when this first group of women and families that Father Junípero Serra recruited in Mexico City, Tepic, and Guadalajara to work in the missions arrived, the Spanish *entrada* [initial entry] to California was a militarized venture conducted exclusively by men. Sixty Spanish, *mestizo* and other *casta* soldiers, dispatched to defend the frontier against European incursions, to protect the missionaries, and to pacify the Indians, were garrisoned at the *presidios* (military forts) of Monterey and San Diego. In conjunction with nineteen Franciscan friars, the soldiers were to effect the temporal and spiritual conquest of Alta California, by peace if possible, by war if necessary. The friars, under the direction of Serra, staffed the two coastal and three inland missions that had been built by 1774. This contingent of soldiers and missionaries comprised the entire Spanish-speaking population on the 158,693 square miles of land that was home to an indigenous population of approximately 310,000 persons. . . .

Who were the women who settled Alta California during the height of the Bourbon reform era? Why were they and their families recruited and subsidized by the Department of War to colonize this frontier? Where and how did women fit within the imperatives of Spain's defensive expansion to this remote outpost of empire? Did the policy of *unidad doméstica* (domestic unity), which Spain employed throughout its American colonies, also extend to Alta California?

To answer these questions, as well as others, I examine the social history of mestiza women in Monterey, California, from 1770 to 1821. During these 51 years, Spain imposed its colonial hegemony on the Indians of California, and Spanish-mestizo soldier families established presidial society within the confines of the military forts while *poblador* (settler) families developed a nascent agro-pastoral society in the nearby *pueblos* (towns). Women, both the Amerindian women who lived on the land, and the Spanish-mestiza women who came to colonize, were central to developments on the frontier.

Incorporating non-European and racially mixed women into the concept of the frontier is essential to understanding the socio-political patterns that developed in the eighteenth and nineteenth centuries and that persist today in California and the Southwest. Therefore, in my work I seek to develop a theoretical approach to history that places gender, race, culture, class, and sexuality at the center of the historical inquiry, thus allowing me to examine and interpret the multiple roles of women in Spanish and Mexican frontier societies.

Gender as a category of historical analysis, and sex as a socio-political category, are fundamental to my theoretical approach and to my examination of the roles of women in frontier expansion and development of colonial Spanish society. As a Chicana feminist historian, I look closely at the intersecting dynamics of gender, race, culture, class and sexuality in the politics, policies, structures, and relations of conquest and social development in frontier California. I argue that these are pivotal issues in the historical process of Spanish expansion and the development of frontier society in California.

THE POLICY OF DOMESTIC UNITY

The arrival of Ana María Hurtado and the first group of Spanish-speaking women in 1774 may be attributed directly to the recruiting efforts of Junípero Serra, who acted within the framework of Spanish frontier politics and policies of sex-gender, conquest, and colonization. From the beginning of expansion to the Americas, Spanish authorities recognized sex-gender as a political issue in the conquest of Amerindian societies and in the imposition of permanent Spanish hegemony in the New World. That is, Spanish women were essential not only to the biological re-production of the species, but also to the reproduction of daily life, of the social institutions, and of the ideology that sustained them. Thus, sex-gender quickly be-came a pivotal issue in emigration and colonization policies under whose broad umbrella the Hapsburg rulers and their advisers incorporated substantive domestic and social policies that reunited spouses separated by the husbands' departure to the Americas or some other part of the colonial empire. These policies, which pro-moted the marriage of single men and facilitated the emigration of Spanish women, ensured the presence of women and families in the colonies.

The general policy, which scholars term a policy of domestic unity, or unity of residence, was initiated early in the sixteenth century. Spanish lawmakers consid-ered the voluntary long-term, long-distance separation of Spanish men from the connubial household as a serious political problem, and the king and his council responded to it with extensive legislation from the beginning to the end of the colo-nial enterprise.

First and foremost, the policy of domestic unity was based on the recognition that the economic exploitation of the New World was contingent upon the exist-ence of a permanently rooted, stable, and growing Spanish population and upon the establishment of the entire complex of Spanish institutions. Second, it was based on the perceived threats that the departure of single males to the expanding Ameri-can frontiers—where new, fluid social conditions were giving rise to unprecedented multiracial, multiclass societies and illicit sexual relations—posed for domestic and social institutions.

A serious consequence of this situation was the increasing number of Spanish wives and families, in both Spain and the Americas, whose husbands and fathers abandoned them, sometimes with no means of support. In addition to being highly concerned about the economic support of these abandoned families, ecclesiastical and civil authorities were equally concerned about the moral fabric of society and about the strength and development of social institutions.

Spanish officials especially feared that marriage, one of the principal structures sustaining patriarchal society, would crumble in the face of widespread concubi-nage, common-law marriages, polygamy, and other illegal unions that Spanish men entered into with non-Spanish women in the Americas. They were especially con-cerned that both women and men were contributing to the potential downfall of the institution. Cases of Spanish women abandoning husbands, forming illicit sexual relationships, and having multiple marriages were not unknown in the colonies.

To impose order and gain firm control of social development, the (Spanish) king decreed in 1505 that married men living in the colonies without wives and families had to either return to the woman or bring her to wherever he resided and be reunited with her in that location. The policy of domestic unity, elaborated in numerous royal edicts, decrees, and ordinances, was enforced by economic rewards and punishments. . . .

The colonization of California was thus informed by this extensive body of laws, which recognized the centrality of women to Spanish society in the Americas and incorporated sex-gender as a crucial element in the politics, policies, and strategies of frontier expansion and colonization.

SEX-GENDER AND THE COLONIZATION OF CALIFORNIA

When the first Spanish-mestiza women and families arrived in 1774, California was in a virtual state of war and the existence of the colony was in jeopardy due to the brutal sexual attacks that the soldiers perpetrated against Indian women. In fact, the first recorded acts of Spanish domination and aggression were acts of sexual violence against women. These acts included not only the hunting, rape, and abduction of native women, but also the beating and sometimes the killing of native men who refused to disclose the hiding places of women. Thus, the initial assertion of Spanish colonial power centered on women—on the violent extortion of sex.

In words reminiscent of the sixteenth-century chronicles, Junípero Serra, president of the California missions, described the depredations of the soldiers against Indian women, which began shortly after the founding of the presidio and mission at Monterey in June 1770. The despicable actions of the soldiers, Serra wrote Viceroy Bucareli in 1773, were severely retarding the spiritual and material conquest of California. The native people were becoming warlike and resisting missionization. Instead of pacifying and ensuring order in the colony, the soldiers were provoking the Indians to armed conflict. . . .

The Indian men who defended the women were shot. Sexual assaults on women were documented at all the missions. The soldiers, wrote Serra, "without any restraint or shame, have behaved like brutes toward the Indian women . . . and even children who came to the missions were not safe from their baseness."

Although Serra blamed the civil-military authorities in California for the sexual violence of the soldiers, his charges that Pedro Fages, Fernando Rivera y Moncada, and Felipe de Neve were lax about enforcing military discipline and punishing soldiers were not well-founded. The governor and commanders knew that the assaults against women established conditions of war on the frontier and each invoked military discipline, including incarceration, to restrain the soldiers.

During their respective administrations the military authorities enforced Spain's legal codes as well as the imperial policy of segregating Amerindians from non-

Indians. They prosecuted soldiers for major and minor crimes, including the rape and murder of Indian women, and issued numerous edicts to curb the soldiers' abuse of Amerindians in general and women in particular. The edicts had little effect.

In California, as throughout the Spanish empire, civil-military and ecclesiastical officials responded to the sex-gender issues with sex-gender policies defined and implemented in earlier colonization ventures. The response to both specific native-military problems and the more general need to populate the region was a dual strategy involving women.

First, drawing upon a colonial tradition of promoting intermarriage with Amerindian noblewomen in order to advance particular political, military, religious, or social interests, colonial authorities sought to induce single soldiers to remain in California by awarding the use of land in perpetuity to those who married neophyte Indian women. . . .

The second part of the strategy, the plan for colonization, involved major efforts to populate California with three groups of families recruited from other parts of New Spain's northern frontier: soldier, artisan, and poblador families. The idea was that soldier families would establish and reside at the new presidios planned for San Francisco and Santa Bárbara, thereby strengthening military defenses and increasing the population base.

The artisan group, husband and wife, would instruct the neophyte mission population in blacksmithing, carpentry, herding, cooking, sewing, and all other manual and domestic arts essential to the self-sufficiency of the missions. Agrarian poblador families would establish and reside in the three projected pueblos: San José de Guadalupe, Los Angeles, and La Villa de Branciforte. They would grow crops to feed themselves and to supply the presidios. . . .

The presence of women was also intended to convince Amerindians that Spanish soldiers would cease to depredate native women. Single women were encouraged to find husbands among the soldiers . . . The crown hoped that as marriage quelled their lustful behavior, the soldiers would choose to settle in the frontier once their military duty was completed. Thus the colony would prosper and be populated increasingly by *gente de razón* (people of reason), meaning Christians.

Thus, when Ana María Hurtado's family and the other families arrived, there was much rejoicing. However, this group, which constituted the first artisan, administrative, and professional classes recruited on six-year contracts to serve in the missions and the presidios of this remote colony, did not remain or settle in Alta California. . . .

Artisan wives, or women from what may be considered the middle strata of eighteenth-century colonial Mexican society, did not settle in California. The women who came to stay belonged instead to the lower socioeconomic classes of New Spain. They were the mothers, wives, daughters, and kinswomen of leather-jacket soldiers who staffed the frontier presidios of New Spain, of impoverished settlers who lived in the adjoining civilian pueblos, and of convicts from Mexico and Guadalajara sentenced to Alta California in lieu of other punishment. The women who settled Alta California were army wives and townswomen already living in the fron-

tier presidios and pueblos of northern New Spain. They came with the two colonizing expeditions led by Commandant Fernando Rivera y Moncada in 1774 and 1781,
and in the expedition led by Juan Bautista de Anza in the winter of 1775–76.

PRESIDARIAS Y POBLADORAS: THE JOURNEY NORTH

. . . Little information has survived about the women who came with the Rivera y
Moncada soldier-colonist recruits in 1774, but documents exist which chronicle
the Juan Bautista de Anza expedition of 1775–76 that colonized San Francisco with
women and their families from Sinaloa and Sonora. Although the personal views of
the women who made that overland journey and their individual motives for migrating are not recorded, the documents make three facts abundantly clear. As a
group the women were hardy and uncomplaining; they persevered on the trail; and
their families were migrating to improve their lot. . . .

In May 1775, de Anza and the 20 soldier-settler families began the 400-mile
march from Culiacán in Sinaloa to San Miguel de Horcasitas in Sonora, which they
reached in early August. Data on the age of the married women and their husbands
who came with de Anza, on how long they had been married, and on the size of
their families reveal that in general, these were not young or new families. Rather,
they were in the middle of their familial life. The average age was 28 years for the
women and 35 years for the men. The 20 couples for whom data were available had
been married an average of 12 years, and their families averaged four children,
whose median age was eight years.

While the women's daily routine on the journey was not recorded, their primary responsibilities, including child care and laundry, appear to have differed little
from their standard familial and household work. Women probably relied heavily
on their daughters who were over the age of 11 for help with younger children and
other responsibilities. Since girls married and started families as young as 12 years
of age, pubescent females were expected to assume adult responsibilities. Although
the average family traveling to California was in mid-cycle, the women's young age
at marriage and long years of childbearing meant that mothers brought both young
and old children. . . .

The intrepid women who rode, walked, and sometimes staggered across desert
sands and through snow-capped mountain passes shared their living space and
their lives intensely on the trek from Culiacán to San Francisco. Thirty families
shared ten tents, which they put up and took down daily. Within the confines of
this space, as well as on the open trail, the women confronted the vicissitudes, the
joys, and the sorrows of daily life, including becoming pregnant and giving birth.
Within a single week they witnessed three marriages and buried a woman who had
died in childbirth. . . .

Whether migrating by land or by sea, women were equally vulnerable to the
perils of pregnancy and childbirth, if not on the actual journey, then certainly in

their frontier destination. Pregnancy, miscarriage, and childbirth on the trail from Culiacán to California during the de Anza colonizing expedition were well documented. Eight persons, or 25 percent, of the 32 married women journeying north were pregnant at the start of the journey. Of the eight pregnant women, five had miscarriages, and three gave birth to children who survived the journey.

Births, of course, delayed the expedition. Normally women could not ride horseback for four to five days after giving birth, so after resting a day or two, they walked. Time was of the essence as supplies were limited and the animals were giving out. The expedition needed to move on as quickly as possible. . . .

Covering approximately 22 miles each day despite muddy terrain, heavy fog, and rain, the colonists arrived at the northern presidio of Monterey on March 10, 1776. . . .

Since leaving Culiacán in May of 1775, their migration from the *tierra caliente* (hot country) of Sinaloa over two thousand miles to the foggy, bone-chilling lands of the Pacific Coast had taken them 11 months. Manuela Ygnacia Pinuelas, who died in childbirth the first night out of Tubac, was the only fatality of the entire journey. Her children and the other *pobladoras* (women settlers) arrived safely and became the first *presidarias* and *pobladoras* of northern California beyond Monterey. As such, they extended Spanish colonialism to the northernmost tip of the empire.

WOMEN'S LIVES, AND SOCIETY IN FRONTIER CALIFORNIA

Creating new homes and families exacted a heavy toll on the time and energy of women. They had to manage limited resources and maintain households with rations sent from San Blas. The supply ships, if they came at all, were often late and delivered food that was spoiled and clothing that was inadequate for their families' needs.

Little information exists on how women dealt with the hardships of inadequate housing, crowded conditions in the presidios, and scarcity of clothing and essential supplies. In their oral histories, Apolinaria Lorenzana, Dorotea Valdez, and Eulalia Pérez describe the life of women who worked in the households of presidial officers or in the mission system. They relate how they supported themselves with the work of their hands by sewing, cooking, cleaning, nursing, midwifing, and working as *maestras* (teachers), *enfermeras* (nurses), and *llaveras* (keepers of the keys or matrons) in the missions. . . .

The harshness of life in Alta California did not preclude sociability and celebration. People gathered to celebrate births, marriages, and religious and national holidays with food, merriment, song, and dance. They also celebrated the beginning and end of the harvest season. In Monterey women and girls sang and danced at Los Aguajitos, where they washed clothes in the canyon's numerous hot springs.

Dance was especially important as a medium of individual and group expression and allowed both men and women to demonstrate their skill, talent, and grace.

Special dances were performed by children and adults, groups and couples, and married and single people alike. Women and men danced both together and separately. In the colonial period most of the dances were accompanied by songs with folk or peasant themes. . . .

WOMAN'S CONSCIOUSNESS, MAN'S WORLD

. . . The literature does not examine the experiences of women or their contributions to the culture of the frontier. The few that examine, briefly, the narratives of women take at face value the interviewers' interpretation of their material. Thomas Savage, who interviewed Apolinaria Lorenzana, stated, for example, that her memory was quite fresh, but that "she passed her life in the mission, and had but little opportunity of ascertaining what happened of a political nature around her." Savage was mistaken. Lorenzana worked in both the homes of presidial officials and in the mission, the political and economic hubs of Alta California. Her narrative, as well as those of all of the women interviewed for Bancroft's history, reveals a clear consciousness of the politics of the era and provides accurate, verifiable detail about political as well as other events. . . .

An examination of the lives and experiences of mestizas is necessary in order to establish a balanced description and analysis of society in colonial California. Women experienced the privations of frontier life differently, but no less harshly, than men. Women shared their experiences and spent much time in the company of one another. Women were midwife to one another, nursed each other through life-threatening and minor illness, celebrated together, served as godmothers to each other's children, taught their daughters to read and write, and served the church and the state in the mission system. They were knowledgeable of the politics of the day and conscious that their participation was circumscribed by the fact of their sex. . . .

Despite the structures that sustained gender hierarchies and circumscribed their lives, even on this remote frontier, women acted in their own behalf and empowered themselves in ways we are only now beginning to examine. They turned notions about women inside out and used their alleged "weakness" for purposes they deemed important. . . .

CONCLUSION

This examination of mestiza women in colonial California revealed the centrality of sex-gender to the politics of colonization and the establishment of Spanish hegemony on this frontier. Spanish authorities in California, like their predecessors in the early conquest of Mexico some two-and-a-half centuries earlier, were acutely aware that the biological and social reproductive power of mestiza women was absolutely critical to the establishment and survival of Spanish society on the frontier. Placing gender and its intersections with race and class at the center of historical inquiry about frontier expansion forces us to pose entirely new questions and to define new categories of research and analysis. As we examine and define the nature of the politics of gender, we perforce must reexamine the politics of race, class, culture and sexuality. . . .

We still know very little about the lives and realities of mestiza women during the eighteenth and nineteenth centuries in Alta California and the northern Spanish-Mexican frontier that became the core of the Chicana/o homeland. However, what becomes abundantly clear when we approach court, mission, civil, military, and other documents with gender-specific questions is the contentious nature of life and society on the frontiers of expansion, including California. The "unique northern culture" that social historians have been so wont to write about, if not to extol, was rife with conflict centering on sex-gender and racial issues in the eighteenth century. We have yet to examine not only the nature of these conflicts and the relations of power between women of different races and classes, but also the multiple contradictions of women's lives under the conditions and structures of colonialism. In brief, we have yet to describe and analyze both the hegemonic and counterhegemonic strategies, roles, and activities that women, depending on their position in society, employed in California as this region changed from Spanish to Mexican to Euro-American rule. . . .

2

HONOR IDEOLOGY, MARRIAGE NEGOTIATION, AND CLASS-GENDER DOMINATION IN NEW MEXICO, 1690–1846

RAMÓN A. GUTIÉRREZ

Ramón A. Gutiérrez is Assistant Professor of Latin American and Chicano History at the University of California, San Diego. He is the author of the prize-winning *When Jesus Came, the Corn Mothers Went Away: Marriage, Sexuality, and Power in Colonial New Mexico, 1500–1846* (1991). He was born in Albuquerque. He earned his Ph.D. at the University of Wisconsin, Madison, in 1980. Dr. Gutiérrez is the recipient of numerous awards, including fellowships from the MacArthur, Danforth, and Fulbright-Hays foundations. He has also been a Fellow at the Center for Advanced Study in the Behavioral Sciences in 1983–1984 and 1988–1989.

The ways in which societies organize marriage provide us an important window into how economic and political arrangements are construed. When people marry, they forge affinal alliances, change residence, establish rights to sexual service, and exchange property. Besides being about the reproduction of class and power, however, marriage is about gender. The marital exchange of women gives men rights over women that women never gain over men. This feature of marriage provides a key to the political economy of sex, by which cultures organize "maleness" and "femaleness," sexual desire, fantasy, and concepts of childhood and adulthood.

With these theoretical moorings in mind, I present here an essay on the history of marriage in a colonial setting, New Mexico between 1690 and 1846, an environment in which class domination was culturally articulated and justified through hierarchies of status based on race, ethnicity, religion, and gender. My major con-

From *Latin American Perspectives* 12 (Winter 1985): 81–104. The original text has been modified. Reprinted by permission of Sage Publications.

cern will be to examine the key role that control over marriage choice played in the maintenance of social inequality, focusing on changes in the mode of marriage formation during the period under study—a decline in the incidence of parentally arranged nuptials and an increase in those freely contracted by adolescents on the basis of love and personal attraction. . . .

HISTORICAL SETTING

. . . Spanish colonists . . . fashioned a society that they perceived as ordered hierarchically by honor, a prestige system based on principles of inherent personal worth. Honor was a complex gradient of status that encompassed several other measures of social standing such as descent, ethnicity, religion, profession, and authority over land. The summation and ordering of these statuses and the pragmatic outcome of evaluations of honor resulted in the organization of society into three broadly defined groups: the nobility, the landed peasantry, and the genízaros.

The status hierarchy did not completely encompass class standing as structured by relations of production. The Pueblo Indians on whose labor and tribute the colonists so heavily relied fell outside the groups to whom honor mattered and refused to accept, cherish, and validate the ideals by which Spanish society organized its interactions. From the colonists' point of view, the physical tasks the Pueblo Indians performed were intrinsically dishonorable and conquest by a superior power itself dishonoring. . . .

The nobility consisted of 15–20 families that intermarried to ensure their continued dominance. Their sense of aristocracy was rooted in the legally defined honor granted to the kingdom's colonizers by King Phillip II in their 1595 charter of incorporation. As the colony developed, nobility gained a broader social meaning and was claimed by individuals who acquired large amounts of land, by military officials, and by bureaucrats—wealth and power acting as the determinants of intra-group mobility. . . . Bearing Old Christian ancestry, harboring pretensions of purity of blood, and eschewing physical labor, it reveled in its rituals of precedence, in ostentatious display of lavish clothing and consumption of luxury goods, in respectful forms of address and titles. Needless to say, such habits were buttressed by force of arms, wealth, and a legal superstructure premised on the belief that the social order was divinely ordained.

Landed peasants who were primarily of mestizo origin but considered themselves "Spaniards" were next in the hierarchy of honor. They had been recruited for the colonization of New Mexico with promises of land, and in 1700 all enjoyed rights to *merced,* a communal land grant consisting of private irrigated farmlands, house plots, and commons for livestock grazing. By 1800, the progressive subdivision of private plots had resulted in parcels too small for subsistence. Under these circumstances, owners of morseled holdings increasingly turned to wage labor. Their ranks were swelled by persons who had not gained access to land as part of their patrimony. Though the land area of New Mexico may seem boundless, it was constrained by limited water sources, by the previous and competing water and land claims of the Pueblo Indians, and by the resistance to geographic expansion offered by hostile tribes.

Lowest in prestige, dishonored and infamous because of their slave status, were the genízaros, a diverse group of Indians who resided in Spanish towns and performed the community's most menial and degrading tasks. Between 1694 and 1849, 3,294 genízaros entered Hispanic households. Early in the seventeenth century, New Mexicans had been granted the privilege of warring against infidel Indians and retaining them in bondage for ten years as compensation for the costs of battle. Though many genízaros remained slaves much longer, they were customarily freed at marriage. Lack of access to land and the development of emotional dependencies on their masters, by whom in most cases they had been raised, meant that even after manumission genízaros had few options for social mobility. Remaining in the household and employment of their former owners was common. . . .

THE IDEOLOGY OF HONOR

Honor was a polysemic word embodying meanings at two different but fundamentally interrelated levels, one of status and one of virtue. Honor was first and foremost society's measure of social standing, ordering on a single vertical continuum those persons with much honor and differentiating them from those with little. Excellence manifested as territorial expansion of the realm was the monarchy's justification for the initial distribution of honor. Yet, "the claim to honor," as Julian Pitt-Rivers notes, "depends always in the last resort, upon the ability of the claimant to impose himself. Might is the basis of right to precedence, which goes to the man who is bold enough to enforce his claim." The children of the conquistadores gained their parents' honor through ascription and maintained and enhanced it through behavior deemed appropriate to a highly esteemed person.

The second dimension of honor was a constellation of virtue ideals. Dividing the community horizontally along prestige-group boundaries, honor-virtue established the status ordering among equals. Definitions of virtue were gender-specific. Males embodied honor (the sentiment of honor) when they acted *con hombría* (in a manly fashion), exercised authority over family and subordinates, and esteemed honesty and loyalty. Females possessed the moral and ethical equivalent of honor, *vergüenza* (shame), if they were timid, shy, feminine, virginal before marriage and afterwards faithful to their husbands, discreet in the presence of men, and concerned for their reputations. Infractions of the rules of conduct dishonored men and were a sign of shamelessness in women. Shamelessness accumulated around the male head of household and dishonored both the family as a corporate group and all its members.

The maintenance of social inequality was central to the way in which status and virtue were defined to interact, the aim being the perpetuation of the nobility's preeminence. An aristocrat of however low repute was always legally more honorable than the most virtuous peasant. Because precedence at the upper reaches of the social structure guaranteed more material and symbolic benefits, it was usually among the nobility and elites that the most intense conflicts over honor-virtue oc-curred. Family feuds and vendettas were frequently the way sullied reputations were avenged and claims to virtue upheld.

Consensus seems to have existed among New Mexicans of Hispanic origin regarding the behavior deemed virtuous and worthy of honor. Among the nobil-ity and the peasantry alike, men concerned for their personal and familial repute, judged by how well they resolved the contradictory imperatives of domination (pro-tection of one's women-folk from assault) and conquest (prowess gained through sullying the purity of other men's women), hoped to minimize affronts to their vir-tue, thereby maintaining their status. Female seclusion and a high symbolic value placed on virginity and marital fidelity helped accomplish this aim.

Yet only in aristocratic households, where servants and retainers abounded, could resources be expended to ensure that females were being properly restrained and shameful. The maintenance of their virtue was made easier because genízaro women could be forced into sexual service. As slaves they were dishonored by their bondage and could therefore be abused without fear of retaliation, . . .

. . . Among the peasantry, gender prescriptions undoubtedly had to be recon-ciled with the exigencies of production and reproduction of material life. The re-quired participation of all able household members in planting and the harvest meant that there were periods when constraints on females of this class were less rigorously enforced. Juana Carillo of Santa Fe admitted as much in 1712 when she confessed enjoying the affections of two men her father had hired for their spring planting. Again, in households where men were frequently absent, such as those of soldiers, muleteers, shepherds, and hunters, cultural ideals were less rigid. The fact that females supervised family and home for large parts of the year, staved off Indian attack, and cared for the group's public rights meant that it was difficult for them to lead sheltered and secluded lives. It was not uncommon for these women to lament that they had been assaulted, raped, or seduced while their husbands or fathers were away from home.

HONOR AND MARRIAGE

Marriage was the most important ritual event in the life-course, and in it the honor of the family took precedence over all other considerations. The union of two prop-erties, the joining of two households, the creation of a web of affinal relations, the perpetuation of a family's symbolic patrimony—its name and reputation—were transactions so important to the honor-status of the group that marriage was hardly a decision to be made by minors. The norm in New Mexico was for parents to arrange nuptials for their children with little or no consideration of their wishes. Filial piety required the acceptance of any union one's parents deemed appropriate or advantageous. . . .

From a father's point of view, a round of poker is an excellent metaphor for the way in which limited resources (the patrimony) were manipulated to maximize the gains associated with marital alliance. Pierre Bourdieu has applied this metaphor to the marriage of a family's children. Success at enhancing and perpetuating the family's status is based not only on the hand one is dealt (whether the nuptial candidate is an only child, the eldest of several sons, or the youngest of many daughters) but also the skill with which one plays it (bids, bluffs, and displays). The patrimony was the material resource a father had to apportion among its claimants at strategic moments to maximize reproductive success. Although legally every legitimate child in New Mexico was entitled to an equal share of this wealth, practice varied by class. Aristocratic holders of large landed estates preferred male primogeniture as a way of keeping their property intact. The eldest son, as the heir to the household head's political rights over the group and the person responsible for the name and reputation of the family, was the individual to whom a disproportionate amount of parents' premortem resources was committed. As first in importance, even if preceded by older sisters, he could not suffer a misalliance without lowering the entire family's public rating and diminishing the possibilities of securing honorable partners for his unmarried brothers and sisters. Therefore, he was the child of whom parents expected the most and the child disciplined most severely to ensure obedience but allowed the greatest excesses in other matters. He was also perhaps the most predisposed to bow to duty.

If the eldest son had married well and the family's position had thus been attended to, filial participation in the marriage process was tolerated in subsequent cases. Because younger sons were unlikely to fare as well in the acquisition of marital property and could expect only enough money and movable goods to avoid misalliance, fathers might be more open to their suggestions regarding eligible brides.

Daughters of the nobility were a potential liability on the marriage market, dissipating the material and symbolic patrimony by having their dowries absorbed into their husbands' assets. Every attempt would be made to dispose of nubile females as quickly as possible and at minimal expense. If a daughter experienced a prenuptial dishonor, such as the loss of her virginity, additional resources would have to be committed to secure her an appropriate mate. Thus large amounts of time and energy were spent ensuring that a maiden's sexual shame was being maintained. Undoubtedly, the result was that a woman's freedom to object to a marriage, to express her desires in spouse selection, was more limited than that of her brothers.

Peasants enjoying rights to communal land grants practiced partible inheritance. Sons were given their share of the family's land when they took a bride and were assigned a certain number of *vigas* ("beams"—a way of dividing the space in a house) in the parental home. If space limitations prohibited such a move, assistance was given in the addition of rooms to the house or the construction of a separate edifice in the immediate vicinity. For females, premortem dowries usually consisted of household items and livestock. Daughters seldom received land rights at marriage because parents fully expected the husband's family to meet the need. The authority relations springing from this mode of property division meant that parental supervision over spouse selection and its timing was as rigidly exercised as among the nobility.

For landless freed genízaros, the institution of marriage itself was of no consequence. Many preferred concubinage, as they held no property to transmit and the alienation from their Indian kin that accompanied enslavement made the issue of perpetuation of family name irrelevant. . . .

MARRIAGE AND THE CHURCH

. . . Acting as defenders of the Indians, as guardians of community piety and morality, and as a counterpoint to the power of the state, the church at one and the same time legitimated and buttressed the colonial system and challenged certain tenets of its rule. Nowhere was this tension among the authorities of God, of the family head, and of the state clearer than on the issue of marriage. . . .

. . . [T]he vexing question clerics were obliged to ask, in the case of marriage, was when paternal guidance and filial obedience simply became coercion. The issue was of some importance because forced marriages, or those contracted under duress, were invalid. Matrimony was the sacramental union of free will based on mutual consent. Ideally it was the work of God, and "what God has joined together, let no man separate." . . .

A mechanism for the determination that a person was marrying freely existed in canon law. If the slightest hint of coercion surfaced, the local priest had the power to remove the candidate from his/her home for isolation from parental pressures. Once the person's wishes became known, the priest was legally bound either to marry the person, even against parental wishes, or to prohibit a forced union. . . .

The freedom that the Catholic church might grant the sexes in the selection of conjugal mates formed the legal foundation for the subversion of parental authority, but, as the experience of all areas of the Spanish colonial empire testifies, the law and its execution were two very different matters. It was not uncommon for clerics charged with the interpretation and execution of canon law to enforce it selectively or to bend its dictates to avoid misalliances or subversion of the social order. If a friar believed an arranged marriage was a good match, he might uphold parental prerogatives and rationalize that the natural authority of a father over his children was in full accord with the will of God. . . .

From the evidence in the ecclesiastical archives, "absolute" legal liberty to choose a spouse meant, in fact, freedom to select a mate from *within* one's class and ethnic group. No examples exist in the Archives of the Archdiocese of Santa Fe of clerics' sanctioning a cross-class marriage over parental objections. The church might subvert the particular authority of parents, but it would not subvert the social order at large.

CULTURAL CONTRADICTIONS AND THE DIALECTICS OF SOCIAL ACTION

Marriage was a ritual event with meanings derived from several interrelated and interpenetrating ideologies. For the state, it was a way of perpetuating status and property inequalities in their hierarchical order. In Christian thought, it prefigured the love between Christ and the church and was of necessity the union of free wills. The sacrament preserved community morality by providing a sanctioned arena for the expression of sexual desires. The emotions of parents and children regarding affinity and connubiality figured in behavior, as did fertility histories and demographic realities. . . .

The tensions between external forces and personal desires symbolized as conflicts between the head and the heart, between reason and sentiment, between collective responsibility and individual will, provided Hispanics in New Mexico with a variety of options and explanations for their behavior. . . .

The individuals, be they clerics, family heads, or bureaucrats, who articulated the ideals of marriage formation that opposed arranged marriage to marriage choice, hierarchy to egalitarianism, had a vested interest in presenting the cultural system as rigidly circumscribed by these dichotomies. In reality, much behavior fell along a continuum of which these oppositions were the extremes. After all, our information on these prescriptions comes largely from litigation before the civil and ecclesiastical courts, which established the outer limits of proper conduct. In their daily lives, individuals negotiated their behavior pragmatically in dynamic relationships with one another using the ideals of the cultural system as anchors. Thus, for example, on the continuum between arranged marriage and marriage choice, children of the aristocracy may all have their marriages arranged; children of the peasantry may vary between the two forms depending on their sex and birth order; and genízaros, wage laborers, and landless peasants would be relatively free to choose their own partners. . . .

The bishop of Durango in 1823 attested to the fact that children, though constrained in their marital options, did not sit by passively and always accept parental will. They manipulated the symbols of marriage, of honor and love, to obtain a desired spouse. . . .

Parents and children negotiated with different amounts of power. The dynamics of the process were clearly skewed in favor of the elders in both conscious and unconscious ways. Sons and daughters were familiar with the options available to them in marriage formation and knew exactly what was expected to ensure property transmission, to satisfy the requirements of the family's symbolic patrimony, and to avoid scandal and ostracism. Norms and the authority of custom buttressed parental prerogatives, as did the socialization process. Personal "tastes" were learned in infancy and reinforced through avoidance of contact with certain persons. Thus a child's desire for a certain mate was just as much the result of interaction with persons of similar status, race, education, and subcultural traits as it was of "individualistic" urges.

SOCIAL CHANGE

. . . The Bourbon reforms [of the late 18th century] and the growth of a landless population dependent on wage labor for its reproduction had increased social differentiation. This in turn brought into open question the ideological consensus that had formerly existed between the nobility and the landed peasants regarding ascribed honor as a sign of social status premised on family origin and control over means and instruments of production. For free genízaros, mestizos who could not boast of "Spanish" origin, and landless peasants, honor was of little material consequence. Their social status was obtained primarily through individual achievement; under such circumstances patriarchal control over marriage formation was of no functional significance. After all, parental sanction for arranged marriage was effective because familial honor carried with it property and social privileges. Once children were able with their own wages to accumulate the necessary resources to establish a household, and could not in any way count on significant inheritance of property, generational relations were placed on a new footing.

Examining the period from 1690 to 1848, the major change that occurred in marriage formation was an increased preference for unions based explicitly on romantic love over those arranged by parents pursuing economic considerations. This change was not sudden; it was an on-going process. Love matches were possible from the earliest days of Spanish settlement but occurred infrequently among the landed classes concerned for the perpetuation of their patrimonies. Children had plenty of parental counsels, ballads, folktales, laws, and sermons to make them realize the disastrous consequences of placing desires over reason.

The history of marriage in a colonial social formation such as New Mexico reveals the centrality of patriarchal control for generational, gender, and class forms of domination. Arranged marriages that enhanced honor provided the nobility and the landed peasantry with a tool by which to protect their status in an unequal society. The various ideologies by which gender and class hierarchies were comprehended and legitimated, however, were not monolithic and static. The partnership between the church and state so instrumental in the conquest of Latin America created distinct views on the meaning of marriage. Though the positions of church and state frequently converged, differences between them enabled children to challenge parental authority without danger to the social order. Similarly, the meanings attached to the system of status and prestige varied by class and changed in response to larger economic forces that themselves transformed relations of production and the power relations between church and state. By the 1800s, the material underpinnings of the honor code had been eroded, creating the conditions that allowed individual urges such as romantic love to exert greater influence on marriage formation.

3

GNATS, GOODS, AND GREASERS
Mexican Merchants on the Santa Fe Trail

DAVID A. SANDOVAL

David A. Sandoval is Professor of History and Chicano Studies at the
University of Southern Colorado in Pueblo. Educated at the University
of Utah, Southern Methodist University, and Eastern New Mexico Uni-
versity, he is an authority on the history of Chicanos in the Borderlands.
Dr. Sandoval, an ex–co-chair of the Santa Fe National Historic Trail
Advisory Council, is a member of the Board of Directors of the Santa Fe
Trail Association. He regularly presents papers at scholarly conferences
and has written many articles, especially in the journals *La Luz* and *El
Progreso*.

As American merchants and settlers pushed against a moving western frontier, Mexican society reached across a northeastern frontier in 1821: and both societies would
inextricably and synergetically be altered. The beginning of legal trade with the
United States not only heralded freight-wagon Manifest Destiny for Americans; it
signaled social and cultural changes within both Mexican and American societies.
Mexican frontier society expanded into new settlements along the trail routes, as
new occupations and opportunities became available, and the relative isolation of
New Mexican society was abruptly changed as Santa Fe became the hub of international trade and multinational political intrigues.

 While the umbilical *cordón* along the Camino Real (Royal Road) had led to
virtual monopolization of New Mexican commerce by Chihuahua merchants in the
past, New Mexican involvement in the Santa Fe trade transformed New Mexican
society from a Spanish imperial outpost to the gateway of international economic
activity. New patterns of settlement soon expanded to the eastern slope of the Rockies, while new occupations, basic necessities, and luxuries influenced and transformed New Mexican frontier society.

From *Journal of the West* 28 (April 1989): 22–31. The original text has been modified. Reprinted by
permission.

Within a generation, New Mexicans became masters of the mercantile trade through traversing the plains, and they maintained the Santa Fe route as the conduit for the multispoked international trade. New Mexican merchants, along with interior Mexican merchants, combined to achieve economic dominance of the trade by the early 1840s, and the New Mexican sphere of trading expanded to tributaries throughout the Great American Desert.

Mexican needs determined the essence of trail goods, just as Mexican *arreiro* (muleteer) experience on the Camino Real shaped the nature of the caravans. Even an American military overland manual commented on Mexican abilities: "No people . . . are more familiar with the art of packing than the Mexicans. . . . [They] understand the habits, disposition, and powers of the mule perfectly, and will get more work out of him than any other men I have ever seen. The mule and the donkey are to them as the camel to the Arab. . . . Spanish Mexicans are, however, cruel masters, having no mercy upon their beasts. . . ."

Mexican specie insulated the American frontier from economic fluctuations; freight wagons were built for the Santa Fe trade in Pittsburgh; and Mexican livestock as well as material culture flavored the American frontier. While binational partnerships became common, the Anglo-Hispanic historical conflict continued on the frontier; and, despite common cause or interest, the legacy of conflict was exacerbated throughout the period as economics dominated the relationships. Nineteenth-century cultural conflicts and value differences made for fascinating reading in the United States, but merchants remained interested in Mexican women's attire, for example, because of marketplace considerations, not because of the moral observations of their contemporaries. Demand for American products was often determined by the fashion desires of Mexican women, and competition seemed to demand a psychological-political borderland, as even the choice of citizenship was determined by its value in the overland trade.

A pathway of commerce and conquest, the Santa Fe Trail led to experiences rivaling Gulliver's for the many Mexican merchants, packers, and families who set out toward an eastern frontier. American families were late in traveling the trail compared to Mexican families, who took children to eastern schools. Caravans from the east freighted American material culture, while those toward the east conveyed not only Mexican products but Mexican families as well. The route was used by Spanish families exiled by the Mexican government in 1829, and by 1830 New Mexican children were sent over the trail.

Involvement in the trade ranged from the sending out of troops (to defend the caravans as well as the tax coffers) to civilian travel and retail and wholesale mercantile operations, including merchants who lobbied in Washington and traded in New York, Pittsburgh, and Europe. Mexicans assumed every possible role within the Santa Fe trade, and they achieved dominance, seemingly bound for virtual monopolization, during the early 1840s. The Mexican War, however, led to American annexation of Mexico's northern territories and abruptly altered the pattern of Mexican mercantile interests. New Mexicans, with few exceptions, were less numerous or successful on the trail after the war.

The 1820s, characterized by saturated markets and expansion into the interior of Mexico, provided the stimulus for Mexicans to begin to carve out more important roles in an expanded trading system. The nature of the caravans, from wagons to pack mules, changed in Santa Fe, and governmental regulations could be most easily observed by extensive trading families who served their country as customs officers or as government officials.

While it appears that Ramon Garcia from Chihuahua and an unnamed "Spaniard" in the employ of William Anderson were in 1823 the first Mexicans to be robbed on the trail, by 1824 government officials as well as merchants were active in the United States. Concerned with protection for the caravans, a delegation of 26 had been sent by New Mexico Governor Bartolomé Baca to trade as well as to negotiate a treaty with the Pawnee Indians, and Mexicans planned to place 1,500 soldiers on the trail for protection. As American products saturated New Mexican markets, a river of goods began to flood downstream toward interior markets. Mexican merchants sent by Governor Baca reached the United States, and Mexican proprietorship began in earnest.

By 1825 Americans were proving imaginative in beginning a litany of pejorative characterizations of Mexicans. They were characterized in "The Book of the Muleteers" as Montezumans "[living in] tabernacles of clay and they be miners and shepherds. . . . And they have among them gold and silver and precious furs . . . and they be moreover a barbarous people and heathen idolators . . . [with] skin of Ethiope."

The 1830s saw a continuation of the consolidation of capital, the marketing of native goods (particularly sheep) into the interior, and the embryonic development of a merchant class that traded within the United States. 1830 also saw a new route opened to California more directly from Santa Fe. As a constant trickle of Mexican caravans eastward-bound across the rolling Kansas plains during the 1820s and 1830s conveyed specie, native goods, and travelers, Mexican merchant influence would become particularly threatening to American merchants in the 1840s.

As early as 1838 Mexican merchants may have transported the bulk of New Mexico–bound goods on the trail. An attempt by Chihuahua merchants to bypass Santa Fe in 1839 was successfully stopped by New Mexican merchants through the national legislature. *La Luna* noted the success of the 1839 caravan of Mexicans which used a shorter route to the United States, complete with requisite water, for trade with the departments of Chihuahua, Durango, and even Zacatecas. Authorities from New Mexico pointed to the obligations and responsibilities of a frontier buffer state and demanded, in the national interest, that Santa Fe remain the primary route of commerce. The rattling of sabers accentuated New Mexico's continued role as a first line of defense, and New Mexican merchants retained control of the primary trade route. New Mexico's exposed frontiers and relative isolation had often brought military expeditions to the plains, and besides donating funds and supplies, Mexican merchants routinely served in official or military capacities during times of national threat.

The nineteenth-century reporter Matthew Field was a better poet than prophet, when he observed that Mexicans would not be able to compete with Americans. "Señor Campo" noted that "the Americans despise the Spaniards, and are jealous of seeing attempts made by the natives to share in the trade, hitherto monopolized by traders from the States." He inaccurately observed that "the simple Mexicans are subject to such disadvantages, and are so much exposed to imposition from their want of knowledge of our customs and method of dealing, that the probability is they will soon abandon the trade."

Rather than abandonment, significant components of the various branches of the trading system were under New Mexican control by the following year, 1840. The centuries-old system of Indian-settler trading fairs was institutionalized and adapted to the Santa Fe Trail system. A consistent market for merchants involved in the Santa Fe Trade was the fair at San Juan de Los Lagos. A duty-free period meant increased profits, and the fair began on 10 December each year and continued for 10 days. During that time, one merchant wrote, "Immense amounts of goods of all descriptions are disposed of, all merchandise sold here being exempt from all other duties except those attendant upon their first introduction into the country. . . ."

The trade had always been influenced by danger, and in the early 1840s Texas became a major threat. Ceran St. Vrain wrote to Charles Bent that a party of Texan bandits were hidden near the crossing of the Arkansas River and that 300 Texans were poised to attack along the Cimarron. Texans warned Americans "not to allow any Mexican trader to cross in your company, and there [sic] safest route would be by way of the Platte river. . . ." As early as 1835 another estrangero (stranger; used for Americans) had written of threats. "Anglo-Americano" wrote of danger on the trail, asserting that all strangers are enemies of the country.

American participation in the trade dropped sharply after the unsuccessful Texan invasion in 1841–1842; several resident American traders were accused of conspiracy and suffered at the hands of angered New Mexicans. The American consul and merchant, Manuel Alvarez, reported numerous allegations of injustice but yet found time to repeat a theme often found in his correspondence, asserting that economic relationships might be stronger than national affinity:

> It cannot be doubted that a more extensive intercourse between the inhabitants of Missouri and those of the neighboring states of Santa Fe and Chihuahua, would . . . greatly promote and strengthen those feelings of mutual amity and confidence which from their relative geographical position and the intimate connection of their interests it is for the welfare of all parties to cultivate.

Development of the trade meant more than the accumulation of capital to be invested with the New York branch of the Spanish firm of Harmony, Nephews, and Company. It meant facing the Cossacks of the Plains, other natives, bandits, Texan military men, as well as spring blizzards and windstorms. The wind often provided relief from gnats and mosquitos, but more than one traveler saw his investment lost to the elements.

Marketing of American goods also required personal knowledge of northern Mexican roads from Santa Fe to Acapulco and Vera Cruz, and many foreigners headed for Santa Fe and the United States from the interior of Mexico. William Henry Glasgow kept a journal in 1842 and 1843 on his journey from New Orleans to Santa Fe via Tampico. He noted that European merchants seemed to dominate the region where Mexican merchant J. Calistro Porras conducted business. Porras was a merchant and mine-owner from Aguiles Serdan who had interests throughout Chihuahua and often went to California as well as to eastern states, and it is not surprising that other merchants located near this particular millionaire. It became common for Chihuahua merchants to ally themselves with Americans, Europeans, and New Mexicans engaged in the Santa Fe trade, and it was not unusual for New Mexicans to receive manufactured goods from coastal port cities such as Tampico or Mazatlan.

In 1842 the June caravan to Santa Fe from the United States included Juan Perea and Juan Otero, who carried numerous items for the Mexican marketplace. While 1842 saw a decline in American participation in the overland trade due to the recent Texan debacle, New Mexicans arrived in Independence with an entourage of 80 and about $200,000 in specie intended for investment. Regional newspapers reported that six of the Mexican traders had traveled to Pittsburgh in order to contract for wagons and products, and they reportedly carried 17 boxes of specie valued at $350,000.

The year brought a significant blow to Governor Manuel Armijo, who lost an investment of $20,000 when a third of the goods bound for Santa Fe (valued at $80,000) in the fall caravan were lost on the steamboat *Lebanon*. . . .

American soldiers and businessmen noted the dominance of the Mexican merchants in 1843, as economic interests solicited a Drawback Act from the American Congress to enable Americans to better compete with Mexicans. Newspapers continued to record tremendous fortunes brought to the United States, and the Latinization of American speech began the genre of literature eventually known as the American Western. Santa Fe was exotic, profitable, and entrancing to Americans.

New Mexican merchants increased in number. While one brother would be on the trail from the United States, another would be headed toward Zacatecas or California, with American and native products or livestock. For Mexican merchants from Chihuahua, Durango, and the El Paso region, Santa Fe signaled only a phase of international commerce. The *guias* (customs records) in 1844 indicate that New Mexico remained the hub of activity, and New Mexicans' homes often became way-stations for goods bound for the duty-free trade fairs at San Juan de Los Lagos or El Paso del Norte.

To protect their investments, Mexican merchants continued military service and financial contributions. Interior Mexican merchants often responded to patriotic appeals for money or weapons when threatened by Texans or Indians. They responded in similar fashion when threatened by American invasion, despite the fact that their wares were being "protected" by Kearny's army. *La Restauracion* included a patriotic call to arms on 16 June 1846 that was signed by merchants such as Luis Zuloaga, Juan B. Escudero, Pedro Olivares, Estanislao Porras, and Estevan Ochoa.

Characterized by contemporaries as "greasers" and by many historians as patriots of the purse as well as traitors to their nation, New Mexican merchants in the Santa Fe trade and within the context of the American conquest remain little understood. The year 1846 began with [a] prophetic circular distributed on 10 January by

Governor Armijo warning of impending war with the United States. That warning was followed by another circular from interior officials about the probability of war.

War was declared, and on 3 June 1846 Secretary of War W. L. Marcy wrote Col. S. W. Kearny that if his conquest was successful he should establish a temporary civil government, continue the trade between the two countries "as far as practicable," protect the Mexican merchants with his army, and continue Mexican employment "at a rate as may be barely sufficient to maintain the necessary officers, without yielding any revenue to the Government."

Before crossing the notorious 70-mile desert on his way to defend Mexican territorial integrity, the military commander of the state of Chihuahua, Mauricio Ugarte, recorded his initial impressions of the American invasion of Santa Fe. Ugarte organized settlers to resist American troops and advanced with a small contingent of soldiers to Santa Fe, arriving on 7 August. On 14 August Governor Armijo assembled "dos mil hombres de todas classes" (two thousand men of all classes) at Cañoncito for the purpose of defending New Mexico from Kearny's Army of the West. Faced with dissension among leaders of the auxiliaries, and after meeting with several merchants sent by Kearny, including Thomas Gonsales, Armijo abandoned the defenses; and, with an entourage of 70, including 12 or 13 regular cavalry as well as Mauricio Ugarte, he traveled south by way of Galisteo. Ugarte and his command would have to await a different time, the battle at Sacramento, to defend the Mexican nation; but he would not postpone condemnation of Armijo as a traitor.

While Ugarte erroneously reported that a merchant and naturalized Mexican citizen, Don Santiago Magoffin, had been appointed American governor, he also noted that the Santa Fe caravan following Kearny's invading army was valued at a million pesos. Ugarte would use Mexican merchants' observations, written in Independence, Missouri, for information on the strength of American troops, as well as on the rather strange wartime circumstance of Americans protecting Mexican merchandise.

Mexican merchants became involved in organized attempts to combat the American invasion, and even Manuel Armijo complained to his former secretary, Donaciano Vigil, that New Mexican merchants opposed the conquest as well as besmirched his reputation.

> I believe it to be very certain that this territory at this hour belongs to the United States. . . . I fear, for having expressed our opinions, Tomas Ortiz, Diego Archuleta, Manuel Pino and others are traveling in Mexico. . . . Don Jose Chavez and Don Juan Cristoval Armijo have just left; imagine to yourself what all this faction will do there. . . . You are the first to be brought out to dance to the Oteros . . . and it is certain that I will not remain without my slice. . . . I am not like the Rich of New Mexico who become frightened at the idea of losing their wealth.

Even as Armijo noted the partisan position of New Mexican merchants, Dr. J. N. Dunlap of Santa Fe found it ironic that the wealthy did not seem to have to pay the same price paid by other classes. He wrote in 1847, "In spite of the flogging we gave the natives in January and February symptoms of revolt still manifest themselves, . . . while the wealthy . . . implicated in the late rebellion escape." A. B. Dyer observed on 17 February 1847 that "the clergy, and ricos or wealthy men, were inimical to the change from motives of interest and . . . the lower classes . . . (indeed nearly the whole population) wholly under the influence of the two higher classes were too degraded and ignorant to appreciate or understand the advantages to be derived from the changes."

The Santa Fe Trail continued to be used after the war until Santa Fe Railroad steel made it obsolete, but the level of New Mexican participation in the Santa Fe trade declined, even though the most successful mercantile houses during the American period included the Chaves, Otero, and Manzanares families. There should be no doubt that the American invasion was not beneficial to Mexican merchants.

4

RANCHO LIFE IN ALTA CALIFORNIA
FEDERICO A. SÁNCHEZ

Federico A. Sánchez is Professor Emeritus of Mexican American Studies at California State University, Long Beach (CSULB). Born in Los Angeles, he began his studies at California State University, Los Angeles, where he earned his B.A. He received his Ph.D. in 1983 from the University of Southern California, specializing in the history of the American frontier. Later, his particular interest shifted to the history of Chicanos in the Southwest during the nineteenth century. Dr. Sánchez was chair of the Chicano Latino Studies Department at CSULB for many years.

SETTLEMENT

The initial military and mission settlement of Alta California was quickly followed by the colonization of this seemingly remote territory. The new settlers soon developed a way of life based on cattle raising and subsistence agriculture. In time, these settlers would evolve an economy and a lifestyle in Alta California that would remain unique within the context of United States history.

The colonization of Alta California was planned by the *Visitador General* (Inspector General) José de Galvez and carried out by Captain Gaspar de Portolá and Father Junipero Serra. It was a wholly military-clerical venture comprised of two maritime and two land contingents, which set out from Baja California. The packet boat *San Carlos* sailed first on January 9, 1769; by July 1, 1769, the last of the four parties had finally reached San Diego, where all were reunited. . . .

Women were not included in the first expedition, and the men who comprised it were not colonists in the true sense. They were clerics destined to establish missions; soldiers sent to staff the presidio garrisons and to protect the missionaries;

From *Masterkey: Anthropology of the Americas* 60 (Summer/Fall 1986): 15–25. The original text was slightly modified. Courtesy of the Southwest Museum, Los Angeles, California.

and civilian craftsmen and Christianized Indians, who were to supply the labor and perform the specialized tasks needed to construct and maintain the missions and presidios.

The first true colonists arrived in Alta California in 1775, as part of Captain Fernando de Rivera y Moncada's expedition. These 51 colonists were joined the following year by 240 men, women, and children, under the leadership of Captain Juan Bautista de Anza. They were sent to Alta California for two principal reasons: to solidify Spain's hold on Alta California by introducing permanent settlers and to reduce the number of desperately poor settlers in northwestern Mexico. The colonists were also expected to raise crops and livestock in support of the missions and presidios.

The first private land grant in Alta California, a small tract of land near Mission San Carlos in present-day Carmel, was awarded in 1775 by Governor Rivera to Manuel Butrón and his Indian wife. . . .

. . . Only about twenty-five grants were awarded during the Spanish period from 1769 to 1821; the others—about eight hundred—were awarded during the Mexican period, from 1821 to 1848. . . .

In California the land grants devoted to stock raising were known as *ranchos,* unlike the rest of Latin America where they were usually called *haciendas* or *estancias.* To obtain a rancho grant, the applicant was required to submit a petition containing his name, religion, residence, occupation, family size, and number of livestock. The petition included a description of the vacant lands and a *diseño* (map) of the property. Next, the petitioner presented his document to the appropriate granting authority, and an appointed commissioner was sent to ascertain that all the required conditions had been met. After securing the necessary approval, the grant was issued to the petitioner as either a marginal note on the petition, signed by the granting official, or as a separate document. The grantee was required to remain on the land for at least four years and to make certain improvements on it, including a house, corrals, and garden, in order to receive title in fee simple.

DAILY LIFE

Life on an Alta California rancho in the late eighteenth and early nineteenth centuries was arduous and lonely. The work day began before sunrise and was preceded by morning prayers. While the women cooked breakfast, the men caught and saddled their horses, and rode out to inspect the ranch and livestock. They returned at about eight or nine in the morning for a hearty breakfast, usually consisting of *carne asada* (meat broiled on the spit), beefsteak with a rich gravy or with eggs, onions, beans, chili, tortillas or bread, and coffee.

After breakfast, the men rode off to inspect or perform the many ranch tasks that required attention. Around noon, they returned for lunch, which was similar in menu to breakfast. The remainder of the day was spent performing additional ranch chores and, at times, visiting with neighbors. About six in the evening, they returned for the dinner meal, which was also similar to breakfast. Most sources confirm that although there was little variety from one meal to another, the food was invitingly prepared, with the matron of the house giving her personal attention to every detail.

In addition to cooking three large meals, women performed a variety of other tasks and chores, including house cleaning, tending of the family garden, making soap, carding wool, and weaving cloth for the family's clothing. Women paid particular attention to the knitting, crocheting, and fine needlework that adorned the family's best apparel. This apparel was worn only on special occasions such as baptisms, birthdays, weddings, and important patriotic and religious holidays. The women also gathered medicinal herbs and locally available wild fruits and nuts. Since Californio women generally had very large families, often as many as ten to sixteen children, much of their day was absorbed by the exhausting job of childcare.

Rancho homes were generally constructed of adobe walls, dirt floors, and tile roofs, although many Alta California families could only afford thatch roofs. The homes were comfortable and roomy; warm in winter, cool in summer. All cooking was done outside the main house, usually in a small adjoining room built specifically for that purpose. Whatever furniture they possessed—tables, chairs, benches, and beds—were largely handmade and roughly finished.

Most rancho homes were built on open hilltops overlooking wide stretches of surrounding countryside. This gave ranchero families an unobstructed 360° view of their surroundings. In this way rancheros were able to check their cattle and gardens and, most importantly, to spot raiders who might be after their cattle and horses. Raiding Indians were a continual problem for the rancheros. During the period of Mexican rule in Alta California and the first decade after the takeover by the United States, a variety of cattle and horse thieves—renegade French trappers, Mexican bandits, and Anglo American miners, settlers, and outlaws—were to cause the rancheros great losses in lives, livestock, and destroyed property.

Work implements, including ranch equipment and agricultural tools, were fashioned from whatever materials were available. *Carreta* (wagon) wheels were made by cross-cutting large tree trunks; saddles and bridles were fashioned out of woodstock, leather and horsehair; and *reatas* (lariats) were braided out of thin strips of soft cowhide. Leather stirrup covers, large cowhide covers to protect horses from briars and cactus, and leather forage bags, used to carry provisions when camping out, were handmade and continually repaired or replaced as they wore out. Whatever tools the rancheros were unable to manufacture they obtained in trade from a presidio or mission and, on rare occasion, by trading contraband with passing British or Yankee ships.

THE HIDE AND TALLOW TRADE

Alta California's rancheros were economically put at a great disadvantage by Spain's closed mercantile system. The Spanish Crown required all its citizens to sell agricultural products and livestock to army quartermasters at set prices and to purchase scarce and over-priced supplies from the same source. To their great dismay, the rancheros were caught in an economic squeeze that required them to sell low and purchase high. Also, to protect her own industries and merchants, and to maximize tax revenues, Spain required that all trade be conducted solely within the empire, thus prohibiting foreigners from interacting with her colonies. Monopolies and price-fixing were fostered as a result of this exclusionist policy and prices were driven up throughout the colonial system. Little wonder that the rancheros entered into contraband trade with British and Yankee ships whenever possible!

Following Mexican independence from Spain in 1821, the Mexican government ended the closed Spanish mercantilist system and instituted a form of limited free trade. Ports which had once been closed to all foreign trade were now opened. Alta California's impoverished rancheros were to benefit greatly by the change in governments and economic policies, primarily due to the soon-to-be-developed hide and tallow industry.

In June of 1822, the British ship *John Begg* anchored at Monterey and William Edward Petty Hartnell and Hugh McCulloch, British merchants operating out of Callao, Peru, disembarked. They had sailed to the Californias to explore the possibilities of establishing their own hide and tallow trade company. Hartnell and McCulloch presented their trade venture to Governor Pablo Vicente de Solá and Father Mariano Payeras, prefect of the missions. Hides and tallow would be exchanged for needed European, South American, and Asian manufactured goods and luxuries. The trade was to be organized by supercargos or company representatives, who would contact the missions and rancheros, buy their products, and arrange for their purchase from the ship captains. Ships were to be allowed to enter all California ports in order to conduct their trade. In return, customs duties would be paid on all trade goods carried by the ships. A fixed price was set of 1 peso per hide and 2 pesos per *arroba* (25 pounds) of tallow. Secondary trade items included soap, horsehair, horn, hemp, beef in brine, *manteca* (cooking fat), *aguardiente* (brandy), and wheat. The sale price for each item would be arranged on an individual basis at the ports.

As a result of Hartnell and McCulloch's successful efforts, the hide and tallow industry became of vital importance to the rancheros, and Monterey became a link in an international trade system that stretched from Liverpool to Rio de Janeiro, Montevideo, Santiago, and Lima. . . .

In order to transform their hitherto subsistence ranchos into more efficient producers of hides and tallow, the rancheros relied on a varied labor force, including their offspring, hired *mestizos* (of mixed Spanish and Indian parentage), laborers from the local pueblos, and newly converted mission Indians. As the only large, easily available labor pool, Indians from the missions and *rancherías* (free villages) were quickly utilized for expansion of ranchero enterprises.

The missions profited from the new hide and tallow industry. Because their cattle herds were larger and they had more extensive lands under cultivation, the missions were able to enjoy even greater success than the rancheros. Their organizational structure permitted them to help one another by providing loans and supplies, as well as the labor of hundreds of Christianized Indians. Although each mission was a separate institution, they could, when necessary, act in concert. The rancheros were simply unable to compete with the well-organized and well-directed missions.

The unexpected but profitable development of the hide and tallow trade and the subsequent connection with world markets revolutionized ranchero life in Alta California. Ranching, which had generally been a subsistence life style, was irreversibly changed by the wealth derived from the new trade.

SECULARIZATION OF THE MISSIONS

One of the immediate effects of the new industry was the demand it created for more land to be brought into stock raising; however, all the best lands along the coast were already taken—and jealously guarded—by the missions. For example, Mission San Fernando, located in Los Angeles' San Fernando Valley, sat on 350 square miles of fine agricultural and range land. The only other good lands available were in the interior valleys, away from the ports and settled coastal areas and inhabited by aggressive Indians. Rancheros in Alta California and interested parties in Mexico soon began to lobby for the enactment of mission secularization.

There had been talk in Alta California of secularizing the missions prior to Mexican independence; however, little was done until Mexico took control of the territory in 1822. José María Echeandía, a Mexican-appointed governor, attempted to secularize some of the missions in 1826, in 1830, and again in 1831. Each time he was vigorously opposed by the mission fathers, but supported by the *Diputación Territorial* (a body of elected and appointed officials with quasi-legislative authority). On August 17, 1833, the Mexican Congress passed its mission secularization decree and on August 9, 1834, Governor José Figueroa issued Alta California's provisional regulations that called for proceeding with the secularization program. The mission fathers continued to oppose secularization in spite of Figueroa's decree. Their efforts were partially successful until the first of the native Californio governors, Juan Bautista Alvarado, assumed control of the territory in 1836.

As might be expected, the mission padres fought a tenacious battle to defeat secularization, at times succeeding, at other times simply delaying secularization efforts, but, finally, losing the fight to California governors and the Diputación Territorial. Several alternative plans for secularization were put forth by Mexico and the Californios. Mexico's plan was to secularize the missions and distribute mission lands and livestock among Mexican and Indian colonists on an equal basis.

The Californios, however, were unwilling to see the best lands of the territory go to newly arrived immigrants from Mexico. Although they masked their arguments with concern for the Indian neophytes, their intent was to retain some of the missions as productive haciendas for the benefit of the territory and to free selected Indians who were to receive lands from the missions. The rancheros fully expected to divest the freed neophytes from whatever property they were given. In this manner, the rancheros, over time, intended to increase their rancho acreage and utilize the newly available Indian laborers.

The period from 1831 to 1850 marks the high point of ranchero life and of the hide and tallow trade. While the secularization battle continued, the rancheros were prospering, expanding their holdings by acquiring new lands and herds from the declining missions. New settlers, arriving in the territory as part of the Híjar-Padrés colonization project of 1834, were also being awarded land grants. It was during this time that the rancheros organized their herding, slaughter, and hide-drying techniques, and transportation operations, into efficient systems, as they filled the orders of the merchants and supercargos.

RANCHING

The organization of the ranchos was extensive and complex, with traditions and rules governing almost every aspect of rancho work. Regulated branding and ear marking to indicate ownership took place during the cool months from February to May. The intensive activities associated with *matanza* (slaughter) took place in July and generally lasted until October. From the end of matanza to the beginning of the next branding and marking period, rancho life took on a more leisurely pace. This was the time for repairing rancho tools and property and for families to visit each other.

Alta California cattle were descended from northern Mexican stock and, like their forebears, were rangy, long-horned, tough animals, well-adapted to Alta California's semi-desert climate. They were allowed to run free, although the *vaqueros* (cowboys) trained the cattle to gather when called at specific *rodeo* (roundup) locations. Vaqueros, hooting and shouting, would drive small groups of cattle to the rodeo area two or three times a week, until the cattle became thoroughly accustomed to the routine. As the cattle moved to the rodeo grounds, strays were cut from the herd and returned to their owners. . . .

Rancho horses were carefully trained by vaqueros to perform specialized tasks during matanza and marking time. When Anglo Americans first observed Californios on horseback, they reacted with disapproval at the sight of the large, cruel-looking Mexican bits used on the horses, failing to understand that California riders did not control their horses by pulling hard on the reins. Ranchero horses were trained to react to the feel of the rein on the neck and the pressure of the rider's knees, for firm yet gentle control.

At the rodeo grounds, the cattle were cut from the herd one at a time by a pair of vaqueros called *apartadores* (separators) and taken to a *parada* (standing ground), an open area about 100 yards from the rodeo, near a stream. There, they were mixed with six to eight *cabestros* (tame cows) until a group of fifty to seventy-five was gathered. Then the matanza began. Generally, steers three years and older were selected for slaughter. A vaquero would toss his reata over a steer's horns, while another would lasso its hind legs.

As the vaqueros quickly tied their reatas to the saddle pommels, their ponies reared back, causing the steer to tumble to the ground. The vaquero who had lassoed the hind legs would dismount and slit the steer's throat, while his well-trained pony kept the reata taut by reacting to the fallen animal's movements. As the steer died, its legs were tied, the reatas removed, and the skinning process begun. Altogether, it took the skilled vaqueros about half an hour to complete the entire operation.

Once the steer was skinned, about 200 pounds of meat was cut and dried for future consumption. About 75 to 100 pounds of *sebo* (tallow) and 40 to 50 pounds of manteca were taken from each animal. Manteca was collected from the fat close to the hide, while sebo was collected from the interior fat. The tallow was rendered in large pots bought from Yankee whalers, boiled, and poured, while still warm, into sewn leather sacks. Each sack, made from two hides, held from 500 to 1000 pounds of tallow.

The hides from the slaughtered steers were scraped clean, then dipped in brine, and stretched out to dry. After drying, they were piled in stacks to await transportation to the nearest harbor, where they would be exchanged for goods and merchandise. Much of the butchering, tallow boiling, and hide cleaning and drying was performed by mission Indians. . . .

As ranching became more profitable in the years following the establishment of the hide and tallow trade, the rancheros were able to afford new material comforts. The wealthier rancheros built better homes, furnished them with articles purchased from the Boston merchant ships that regularly plied Alta California's coastline, and began to adopt European dress styles.

THE ANGLO AMERICAN PERIOD

The war between Mexico and the United States, from 1846 to 1848, however, brought about another drastic change in rancho life. . . .

The signing of the Treaty of Guadalupe Hidalgo on February 2, 1848, which ended the war with Mexico, obligated the United States government to protect the Californios in the free enjoyment of their liberty, property, and religion. It also bound the U.S. government to recognize property titles in the ceded territories. However, events in California during the hectic period of the Gold Rush, which followed on the heels of the ending of hostilities, soon caused the government to abandon its initial intent. . . .

The Gold Rush was an economic boom for the rancheros, who supplied beef to the hungry miners. Within three or four years, however, disillusioned miners began leaving the gold fields in search of more certain and more familiar forms of economic endeavor. They descended on the lands of the Northern California rancheros, destroying houses, garden plots, and orchards; killing or stealing cattle; and generally exhibiting complete disregard for property rights. With the aid of unprincipled politicians, lawyers, judges, and other local authorities, they squatted on ranchos and pressed for legislation that would permit them to legally possess Californio lands.

In 1851 squatters were able to bring about the passage of a land law that established a three-man commission to validate land titles as defined by Spanish and

Mexican law, the Treaty of Guadalupe Hidalgo, and United States common law. Of approximately eight hundred ranchero titles reviewed over a period of six years, more than six hundred were found to be legitimate. But the drawn-out and expensive legal process usually bankrupted rancheros and forced them to sell parts or all of their lands—often to the unscrupulous lawyers who had defended them in court and to their land-speculator friends. Many economically solvent rancheros lost their property because they had co-signed loans for relatives and close friends—a familial obligation among the traditional and closely knit Californios—who were unable to repay them. Competition from Mexican and Anglo ranchers added to the rancheros' woes, as livestock was driven west from New Mexico and Texas, and north from Mexico, to provide beef, sheep, and mules for the gold miners. . . .

Nature struck the final blow against the rancheros. On November 4, 1861, it began to rain, never really stopping until late the following spring. By May, 1862, it had rained 50 inches! When the rains finally halted, most of the state had been devastated by floods. Adobes had been washed away, roads and bridges had disappeared, and thousands of livestock had drowned. The rains had wrought havoc throughout the state.

Cattle recovered rapidly throughout the summer of 1862 because of the lush grasses made available by the heavy rains. Unfortunately, the floods were followed by three years of severe drought, resulting in the death of even more stock. . . .

The few ranchos that survived the devastations of flood and drought in the 1860s were unable to survive the next two major assaults on ranch life. Throughout the 1860s, 1870s, and 1880s, ranch land was gradually being converted to agriculture, particularly wheat and citrus, but the rancheros refused to abandon their pastoral way of life. Rancheros who still had large holdings, particularly in Southern California, retained their lands until the 1880s by taking loans and selling portions of their ranchos for agricultural and urban development.

The coming of the railroads in the 1880s, however, brought a final end to ranchero life and industry. Agriculture, California's new major industry, needed more land, and the railroads brought waves of settlers from the eastern and midwestern states who built towns and cities where Californio rancheros once herded long-horned, long-legged, rangy Mexican cattle.

CONCLUSION

The passing of the Californio rancheros thus brought to an end a unique period of California history. The lifestyle of the rancheros during the early years meant long, hard days in the saddle for the men and equally long, arduous, and lonely days for the women; beyond that, there is little information available about the everyday life of the rancheros who were not members of the landed gentry. The gracious lifestyle of the elite that has come down to us, particularly from the accounts of Californio descendants, travelers, and the literature of the west, has presented a highly romanticized, distorted view. Few Californios were wealthy enough to afford ostentatious homes; most rancheros still lived austere lives, rising early to work their ranchos, and using their families and Indians (usually paid in goods rather than coin) as a labor force.

Hard work, an extended family, and love of a pastoral way of life were traditions that the rancheros brought to Alta California from Spain and Mexico. Certainly these values were not unique, but their special mix of Spanish and Mexican heritage was. Over time the Alta California frontier transformed the mix into a singular regional society, rich in folkways and important in the political and economic history of Spain, Mexico, and the United States.

5

DISCOVERING THE TEJANO COMMUNITY IN "EARLY" TEXAS

JESÚS F. DE LA TEJA

Born in Cienfuegos, Cuba, Jesús F. de la Teja came to the United States as a child and grew up in northeastern New Jersey. He attended Seton Hall University, where he obtained a B.A. in political science and an M.A. in history. He went on to pursue a doctoral degree at the University of Texas at Austin, where he had the good fortune to become research assistant to the novelist James A. Michener, an experience which turned his attention to Texas and Borderlands history. After a five-year career as an archivist at the Texas Land Office, he joined the history faculty at Southwest Texas State University in 1991, where he is now an associate professor. His professional activities include being book review editor for the *Southwestern Historical Quarterly* and managing editor for *Catholic Southwest: A Journal of History and Culture*. His major work is *San Antonio de Bexar: A Community on New Spain's Northern Frontier* (1995).

Most Anglo-American writers refer to the Texas of the 1820s, 1830s, and 1840s as early Texas, and in one sense they are right. The transformation of Texas into a member state of the American Union began in those years. Most of the country that the Anglo-American colonies and later the republic occupied was wilderness, as that term was defined by Euro-American concepts of wilderness and civilization. Unquestionably, however, there was an even earlier Texas; a Texas that existed within a Hispanic historical context and responded to Spanish-Mexican social, economic, political, and religious norms. Before that, there had been no Texas. To the Indian peoples who inhabited the coastal prairies, the piney woods, the high plains, and the mountains and basins of the extreme southern Rockies, there were very different economic and political geographies, most of which remain a mystery to us

From the *Journal of the Early Republic* 18 (Spring 1998): 73–98. Copyright 1998 Society for Historians of the Early American Republic. Reprinted by permission. The original text has been modified.

today. Nevertheless, in this essay "Early Texas," denotes the span between the 1820s and 1850s, during which Texas in its modern form came into being.

The foundations of this work are based on what other scholars have had to say about everyday life in nineteenth-century Texas. Fifty years ago, William Ransom Hogan published *The Texas Republic: A Social and Economic History,* a path-breaking work that remains unsurpassed in breadth of scope and depth of understanding. Not surprisingly for his time, Hogan was primarily interested in the immigrant white population, not the preexisting Hispanic one. His references to the Tejanos (Texans of Spanish-Mexican heritage) are few and most often incidental. For instance, in six pages devoted to Republic-period housing, there is only one paragraph on Tejano architecture. In the six pages devoted to clothing there is one paragraph on how slaves were dressed, but not one line on Tejano fashions. . . .

About a dozen years ago another path-breaking work in Texas social history appeared, Arnoldo De León's *The Tejano Community, 1836–1900.* Although encompassing a much broader time span than *The Texas Republic,* De León's book dealt with many of the same issues. He looked at how Mexican Texans, the Tejanos, went about constructing and reconstructing their communities to meet the exigencies of the environment, both physical and social. De León's most important contribution was his description of a complex economic, political, and social life among people usually dismissed simply as Mexicans. Curiously, many of Hogan's descriptions of republic-era customs, practices, and material culture among Anglo-American settlers bear considerable resemblance to ones described by De León for the Tejano community.

The purpose of this essay is to make some of these connections—to point out how the two "early Texases," one largely descended from southern United States colonial and early national experiences, the other from Mexican colonial culture, compared, focusing primarily on Tejanos. The evidence demonstrates that despite suspicions, and sometimes overt racism and antipathy, there existed between early Texans and Tejanos much common ground. In what they ate, how they lived, what they enjoyed, and what they suffered, Tejanos and Texians [Anglo Texans] had more in common than they realized. How the two groups drifted increasingly apart is another story, however, and comment on the political and legal status of Tejanos is beyond the scope of the present work.

Corn—*maiz* to the Spanish world—was easy to grow under a variety of conditions; could be consumed before ripening; and was the most important gift of the New World to the Old. It was already being grown in Texas when the first Hispanic settlers arrived in the early eighteenth century to establish permanent residence. For hundreds of years the Caddoan people of East Texas, part of the Mississippian culture group, had raised corn, as had the Jumanos of the trans-Pecos and, perhaps, even the ancestors of the Lipan Apaches. What the Spanish colonial settlers and missionaries introduced was the application of Spanish technologies—plowing, *acequia* irrigation, and new varieties of the staple. . . .

The importance of corn to both the Anglo-American population and the Tejanos cannot be overstated. Boiled ears of corn and mush kept many a family from starving on both the Anglo-American and Mexican frontiers. In the *Texas Republic*

William Hogan writes that "newly arrived pioneers always hastened to plant patches of corn, a grain distinctly adapted to its role as a fundamental factor in the conquest of the wilderness." Yet Hogan does not draw the connection between Tejanos and Anglos with regard to this fundamental aspect of frontier life. For both Mexican and Anglo-American frontier farmers, corn was the first crop in the ground; its hardiness, versatility, and quick consumability making it much more popular than wheat. . . . As a matter of fact, from Spanish-colonial times until the last days of the republic wheat remained an imported luxury.

If the Republic-era Tejana used a *metate* and *mano* while the Anglo-American frontierswoman used an Armstrong mill, the result was the same, a coarse meal that could be used in numerous ways. In the absence of American grinding tools, some Anglo women adopted Mexican methods, as Mrs. Dilue Harris reminisced: "Mrs. Roark had a Mexican utensil for grinding corn, called a *metate*. It was a large rock which had a place scooped out of the center that would hold a peck of corn. It had a stone roller. It was hard work to grind corn on it, but the meal made good bread." The *tortilla* may have had its counterpart in cornbread, but the *tamale* stood alone as the one Mexican item that appears to have won universal approval (other than silver) from Anglo-Americans otherwise quick to disparage everything Hispanic. . . .

Livestock provided food, clothing, transportation, and entertainment not only for Tejanos, but Indians and Anglos as well. From an early date Texas acquired a reputation as prime ranching country, and Tejanos as natural pastoralists. . . . Frederick Law Olmstead, who was quite condescending in his remarks about Tejanos, described them as "excellent drovers and shepherds." . . .

Tejanos, moreover, had learned to make as much use of cattle as Comanches did of buffalo. . . . Tejanos made soap and candles from the tallow and jerky from the dried beef, just as did Anglo-American frontier folk. . . .

The first commercial cattle drives from Texas took place by the early 1770s. From that time forward, what little export earnings, legal and illegal, Tejanos experienced came from the livestock trade. Cattle drives to Coahuila, while legal, were not as lucrative as drives to Louisiana, where the booming frontier market created a steady demand. Picking up on Tejano tradition, Texan stockmen continued to take their herds into Louisiana, more often than not breaking the same kinds of laws which had been passed in colonial Texas for similar reasons. . . .

It should come as no surprise that Tejanos and Texans shared the concept of utility in their fashions. Once again, the frontier environment intruded into the choices people made. That the results could be strikingly dissimilar in outward appearance has obscured the underlying similarity of function. In the absence of an efficient commercial network and a stable and sufficient money supply, people made do with few garments and created their own fashion trends. Hogan makes clear that homespuns, home-tanned, and home-sewn were the order of the day for most people in the republic era. Furthermore, a considerable number of people went barefoot or made use of home constructed shoes. . . .

The Mexican, or Saltillo, blanket, aside from tamales, seems to have left the most unequivocally positive impression on observers. Lieutenant George Mead of the United States Army, camped at Corpus Christi, noted the quality and colorfulness of the blankets. In her memoirs, Annie Harris recounted the impression left by a band of Karankawas returning the horses and goods taken from a group of Mexican traders they had assaulted near Matagorda: "The Indians presented a formidable array, riding into town on the gayly caparisoned horses of the Mexicans, made still more showy by the brilliantly colored Mexican blankets." . . .

Whether picket hut or *jacal* [modest stick and adobe home], form and function were similar—simple, labor-saving, inexpensive, easy to abandon and rebuild. In the absence of sawmills, or money with which to purchase dressed lumber, early Tejanos continued to employ the building techniques of their Mesoamerican forebears. The *jacal* may have been crude, but it served its purpose well from the time of the earliest Spanish colonial settlement in the region until the end of the nineteenth century. John Leonard Riddell, passing through San Antonio in September 1839, found the population at work throwing up a new subdivision, most probably what became known as La Villita, and described the *jacal* quite elegantly. . . . This common structure in which the poor lived could be found masquerading behind a clapboard façade in Houston about the same time. And, according to Hogan, the "picket huts" abounded among the Anglo-American settlers of central Texas during the first decades of settlement. . . .

Everyday life in Republic-era San Antonio was also marked by the visible reminders of warfare. Travelers commented on the evidence that San Antonio continued to be a hostile frontier, a boundary between contending forces—Indian, Mexican, Anglo-American. . . .

Gonzales and Harrisburg, burned to the ground during the war for independence, experienced brief moments of tragedy compared with San Antonio. As the gateway between the interior of Texas and Mexico, it had been invaded numerous times, not to mention almost constantly harassed by Indian raiders. . . .

Indian hostilities constituted the single most important factor in the development of Texas until the 1870s. From its permanent settlement in the early eighteenth century, Spanish Texas was a magnet for Lipan Apaches, Comanches, and other Plains peoples who, rather than breed their own horse stock, participated in an elaborate round of expropriations. One Indian group took from the Spanish, and promptly lost their equine booty to a second group, which would then ride into a Spanish settlement to barter the animals back to the frontiersmen for trade goods. . . .

Despite numerous references to the superiority of Anglos to Mexicans and Indians, the former group was not immune from the same kinds of losses experienced by the Tejanos. Mary Maverick's brief account of her family's efforts to farm in the area just north of the Alamo is instructive. "This year our negro men plowed and planted one labor above the Alamo and were attacked by Indians," she wrote. "Griffin and Wiley ran into the river and saved themselves. The Indians cut the traces and took off the work animals and we did not farm there again." . . .

Consistent with the marginal inclusion of Tejanos in the rest of his text, Hogan presents them in regard to general violence only in passing, as victims of a gang of rustlers known as the "Band of Brothers." Yet Tejanos were affected by the lawlessness endemic to the republic. Prince Carl of Solms-Braunfels, who was in Texas in the mid–1840s, noted that homicides were common in the republic. He singled out the relationship of Tejanos to violence, not as perpetrators, but rather as its victims. "Burglary and violent theft are rare occurrences and happen mostly to the unfortunate Mexicans," he declared, "and then they are always connected with murder." . . .

A rough and dangerous frontier life could hardly be expected to be the medium in which "high" culture would develop. As in other aspects of life, a great deal of similarity can be found in the pastime pursuits of Tejanos and Texians. Hogan writes that "dancing and horse racing were among the most common amusements." And, as for games of chance: "A fever for gambling ran in the blood of the age. It was a chronic social ailment in the South and reached even higher virulence in Texas." He also mentions that theater was popular wherever the resources made it possible. Yet, as in most other areas of life during the republic, he has little to say about Tejano pursuits in this regard. . . .

Tejanos had as rich a social life as Texans, however. Their vices were the same, and their entertainments were similar in form and often in function. Perhaps it was the town-centered living pattern of Tejanos that appeared to Anglo observers to indicate a more desultory and dissolute way of life. Anglo Americans often became converted to the new ways they discovered among the Tejanos, however, suggesting that Mexican ways may not have been as strange as some of the writings might indicate.

The daily siesta and regular bathing were features of Tejano life that, according to some writers, symbolized the population's "unconcerned indolence and ease." William Bollaert made quick work of the Tejano's work-day, stressing the portion of leisure over strenuous activities among Béxar's town population. "Early in the morning they go to mass, work a little on the *labores,* dine, sleep the *siesta,* and in the evening amuse themselves with tinkling the guitar to their *dulcinea,* gaming, or dancing," he scorned. . . .

In the Tejano's way of life, however, "loafing" seemed to be a good adaptation to the environment. W. Steinert, the meticulous German observer, had the following advice for would-be settlers: "you should never ride horseback during the noon hours; from eleven to three o'clock you should look for a shady place." Mary Maverick's memoirs make equally clear that the Tejanos' behavior was rational. "During this summer [1841], the American ladies led a lazy life of ease," she remembered. "We fell into the fashion of the climate, dined at twelve, then followed a siesta, until three, when we took a cup of coffee and a bath." . . .

After the bath, dances and gambling were the norm. Superficially, these events proved for Anglos the indolence of the Tejano population. Immediately following his description of the lazy characteristics of Tejanos, the unnamed traveler who visited San Antonio in 1837 commented, "The evening is spent by a large portion of the population at the fandango, a kind of Spanish waltz. There are seldom less than three or four of this description of dances during the night in different portions of the city." . . .

Fandangos were typically associated with gambling, a pastime that seems to have captivated the attention of all manner of people. William Kennedy described games of chance as "one of the prominent vices of the South." He went on to add that "among all ranks and classes in Mexico, the mania for gambling ruinously prevails." A decade later William McClintock made similar observations. Gamblers had by then descended on San Antonio in order to profit off the United States Army personnel stationed there, and "day and night, with unremitting zeal and application they ply their infamous trade." The Mexican population was also consumed in this gaming frenzy. So much so, McClintock added, that "yesterday saw (and the like may be seen on any Sabbath) many Mexicans leave chapel even before mass was concluded, and repair to the gaming table; where they spent the remainder of the day, and perhaps the whole night." To this sin may be added the sacrilege observed earlier by another traveler. "So strong is this passion," this outsider commented, "that even the priests sometimes forget their sacred office and are seen dealing monte, the favorite game of the Mexicans." . . .

Horse racing was one activity that Anglos, Indians, and Tejanos had in common. Although Mexican frontier horse racing differed in form from the Anglo-American pastime, it served similar functions. Races meant opportunities for social interactions, for showing off of personal skills and mastery of good horse flesh, and for gambling. . . .

Secular and religious events of various kinds are used by people, consciously and subconsciously, to celebrate their common bonds. The calendar of holidays was somewhat fuller than Hogan described it in *The Texas Republic*. Although he mentions the anniversaries of the battle of San Jacinto, the Texas declaration of independence, the Fourth of July, and Christmas as those holidays generally celebrated, he neglects commemorations important to Tejanos. Yet, in the 1840s Mexican Texans continued to celebrate feasts, some old and some recent, analogous to Anglo-American holidays.

In the early 1840s Tejanos still commemorated Mexican independence on September 16, according to Mary Maverick. At San Antonio, the celebration as early as the 1820s contained processions, speeches, Catholic Mass, and dancing—a ball for the town's prominent families and dances for the general population. . . .

Tejanos also continued to commemorate the feast of Our Lady of Guadalupe, a holiday that since colonial days had marked the beginning of the Christmas season. Mary Maverick's description of the event in the early 1840s suggests that Tejano society continued to exercise internal cohesion, despite the Anglicizing forces at work. . . .

The public and communal character of Catholicism was certainly lost on most writers, even those who avoided calling the Tejanos' faith superstition. J. C. Duval, who escaped the execution of Fannin's force at Goliad, claimed that it would have been "very easy" for him to have "passed" for Catholic, as "Catholicism (at least among the lower class of Mexicans) consists mainly in knowing how to make the sign of the cross, together with unbound reverence first, for the Virgin Mary, and secondly for the saints generally—and the priests." The somewhat harsher terms of the 1837 informant nonetheless convey the same sense of public religiosity: "every Mexican professes to be a Catholic and carries about his person the crucifix, the rosary, and other symbols of the mother church. But religion with him, if one is permitted to judge of the feelings of the heart by outward signs, is more a habit than a principle or feeling." . . .

Everyday life in Republic-era Texas was rough and violent. For Tejanos, it was marked by uncertainty about the future and a great deal of disconnectedness from the past. The rapid improvement of the country largely bypassed them. Still, evidence exists that Mexican Texans did not necessarily view their position in society as inferior; nor did antagonism color all relations with Anglo Texans. Among the many negative depictions of Tejanos as a group, sympathetic comments appear. Mrs. Teal reminisced that in the Refugio County area southeast of San Antonio, the settlers, "surrounded by Mexicans and Indians, . . . learned to fear neither, as they were never harmed during all the long years they lived among them." Auguste Fretéllièr, a Frenchman and friend of the artist Gentilz, was very positive about getting to know the Tejano population of San Antonio. He noted approvingly, "my mentor spoke Spanish very well, so I made rapid progress and in a little while I understood much better the Mexican character which pleased me infinitely—they were very polite, always gay and very obliging."

At the same time, Texans, in regarding Tejanos as "Mexicans," that is foreigners, were in the process of dissolving that uneasy partnership that had been created during the Mexican era. Promises that the laws would be published in Spanish went unfulfilled. Manipulation of the legal system led to land loss. Association with the enemy—Mexico and Indians—licensed indiscriminate violence against them. Identification with Catholicism made them the enemies of progress and enlightened thinking.

The history of Texan-Tejano relations in the second half of the nineteenth century is, therefore, one of increasing intolerance and segregation. Even as they accepted words into their vocabulary, livestock practices and equipment into their economy, legal principles into their system of law, and a number of dishes into their cuisines, Anglo-Texans increasingly excluded the Tejanos themselves. Even so, the work of a growing body of scholars of Mexican Texans makes clear, Tejanos managed to retain much of the culture they inherited from "early Texas," and continued to participate in Texas society, whether or not that participation was fully recognized and appreciated.

6

THE ORIGINS OF ANTI-MEXICAN SENTIMENT IN THE UNITED STATES

RAYMUND A. PAREDES

A native of El Paso, Texas, Raymund Arthur Paredes received his B.A. from the University of Texas at Austin in 1964. He served in the U.S. Army for two years, spending fourteen months in Vietnam. After earning an M.A. at the University of Southern California, he returned to his alma mater, where he was awarded his Ph.D. in American civilization in 1973. Dr. Paredes initiated a distinguished teaching career at the University of California, Los Angeles (UCLA) in 1973 as a member of the Department of English. Chair of the César Chávez Center for Chicano Studies in 1996–1998, he has served as editor of *Aztlán: A Journal of Chicano Studies,* and on the editorial boards of several other scholarly journals. At present, Dr. Paredes is Associate Vice Chancellor, Academic Development, at UCLA. Also, he is currently co-chair of the Committee on Educational Research of the Inter-University Program on Latino Research, a national, multi-campus research initiative based at the University of Texas at Austin.

Traditionally, when scholars have treated the development of anti-Mexican sentiment in the United States, they have focused on the first large-scale encounters between Mexicans and Americans in the early 19th century as the source of bad feelings. The cultures of the two peoples, goes the conventional wisdom, were so dissimilar that misunderstanding and resentment grew rapidly and hardened into a tradition of prejudice. Samuel Lowrie, in his study of Mexican-American relations in Texas, found that a "culture conflict" developed immediately after American colonists entered Mexican Texas in 1821 while Cecil Robinson, the well-known scholar of American literary images of Mexico, describes the "inevitable collision" between two nations competing for the same stretches of land. The weakness of these stud-

From *The New Scholar* 6 (1977): 139–65. The original text has been modified. Reprinted by permission.

ies, and others of their type, is that they have little to say about the attitudes American travelers and settlers carried into Mexican territory that largely determined their responses to the natives. The enmity between the two peoples may well have been inevitable but not exclusively for reasons of spontaneous culture conflict and empire building.

Rather, American responses to the Mexicans grew out of attitudes deeply rooted in Anglo-American tradition. Americans had strong feelings against Catholics and Spaniards and expected their evils to have been fully visited upon the Mexicans; after all, had not the Mexicans been subjected to nearly three hundred years of Catholic-Spanish oppression? The logic may have lacked a certain finesse but the fact of its application is inescapable. Secondly, although Americans in the early 19th century knew little about the contemporary people of Mexico, they held certain ideas about the aborigines—and the natives of Latin America generally—that affected their judgments.

The purpose of this essay is to trace the nature and history of those attitudes and images that shaped early American assessments of the Mexicans. Anti-Catholic sentiment and hispanophobia will be considered first, inasmuch as these prejudices operated in Anglo-American culture from the earliest days and exerted the most immediate influence on American attitudes. Next, I will discuss the more desultory career of the Mexican aborigines in early American thought. Finally, I will consider how these notions merged, in effect forming a mode of perception which rendered unlikely the possibility that 19th-century Americans would regard the people of Mexico with compassion and understanding.

The English settlement of America commenced at a time when hatred of Catholicism and Spain had been building for over fifty years. Widespread dissatisfaction with the Roman Church, based on charges of corruption and complacency, appeared in England shortly after 1500, crystallized during the Reformation, and intensified as Protestantism drifted leftward. Propagandists denounced the Mass as blasphemous, indicted the clergy for the encouragement of superstition and ignorance, and assailed the Pope as the anti-Christ. Eventually, resentment of Catholicism transcended religious issues. Englishmen came to regard the Roman Church as a supra-national power which sought to overthrow their government. . . . It was in the context of this fear that English anti-Catholicism intersected and merged with a nascent hispanophobia. As every Englishman knew, Spain was the most powerful of Catholic nations and the self-proclaimed champion of the Roman Church. The Spanish military forces—the "popist legions"—were the very instruments of Catholic tyranny. The Catholic-Spanish alliance was regarded by many Englishmen as a partnership conjured by Satan himself and thus one that possessed an unlimited capacity for mischief. Englishmen were well aware of the most notorious product of this collaboration, the Spanish Inquisition.

Although Englishmen disliked Catholics in the lump, the Spaniard was considered the worst of the breed for reasons not altogether related to the religion. The spirit of nationalism surged in the Elizabethan era and England's attempts to assert itself as an international power placed it directly across the gun barrel from Spain. Countless military engagements, the most spectacular of which was with the Armada in 1588, maintained animosities at a high pitch until well into the 18th century. During the Revolt of the Netherlands (1555–1609), an event closely followed in England, Dutch nationalists conducted an impassioned "paper war" against their Spanish rulers, vilifying them for their cruelty, avarice, arrogance, and immorality. In 1583, *The Spanish Colonie* by Bartolomé de Las Casas appeared in England and reported how the Spaniards, in an astonishing display of brutality, managed to reduce the native population of America by twenty million souls. By the end of the decade, the "Black Legend" had been firmly planted in the English mind and the Spaniard had displaced the Turk as the greatest of English villains. . . .

The colonial record provides ample evidence that prejudices against Catholics and Spaniards traveled across the Atlantic intact. Indeed, they may have been more intense among the immigrants than in the general English public. After all, many of the colonists derived from the most anti-Catholic element in England, the radical Puritans, and to a man the settlers were ardent nationalists who regarded their role in the struggle with Spain with high seriousness. They saw themselves as guardians against Spanish penetration into the northern regions of the New World, its economic rivals intent on undermining the fragile structure of Spanish mercantilism, and as Protestant missionaries who would carry the Gospel unperverted to the American savages.

Always in contact with their homeland, the colonists received a steady influx of anti-Catholic and hispanophobic literature from England. One of the most popular works among the settlers was John Foxe's *Book of Martyrs,* a study of Catholic persecution which described vividly the numerous outrages of the Spanish Inquisition. The collections of Richard Hakluyt and Samuel Purchas, the two great literary champions of English imperialism, were also well known to the settlers. By the late 17th century, the denunciation of Spanish activity in the New World by Las Casas and Thomas Gage had appeared in colonial booklists. . . .

The settlers themselves produced a conspicuous body of anti-Catholic and hispanophobic literature. . . .

The literary campaign against Rome and Spain continued throughout the colonial period and beyond, engaging some of the most able and influential figures in the settlements. Cotton Mather inveighed eloquently against the traditional enemies of the Puritans while publishers of popular almanacs such as Nathaniel Ames (both father and son) and Nathaniel Low issued a stream of anti-Catholic and anti-Spanish materials. . . .

Colonial resentment of Rome and Spain was not confined to the printed page but found expression in a number of statutory and military actions. As the settlers desired to see Catholicism removed from the continent, many of the colonial legislatures passed exclusionary and restrictive laws. . . .

It is no exaggeration to characterize the 18th century as a period of incessant military and political conflict between English-Americans and Spain. . . .

The political and military conflicts combine with the mass of literary evidence to reveal that prejudices against Catholics and Spaniards, transported to the New World at the end of the Elizabethan era, persisted among Anglo-Americans for two centuries without significant modification. The colonists believed the Roman

Church to be corrupt and ostentatious, an institution that demanded blind allegiance and thus fostered ignorance and superstition. As for the Spaniards, they were the perfect adherents of Popery, cruel, treacherous, avaricious, and tyrannical, a people whose history was an extended intrigue. As Americans gazed southward with increasing interest, they saw yet another episode of that history unfolding and they could not but believe that the Mexicans had been blighted by their participation in it.

Concerning their impressions of the Mexican aborigines, the early English-American colonists had virtually nothing to say but such notions as they held were unquestionably those of their contemporary home-bound compatriots. Although questions related to the character and culture of the Mexicans—and of all the American Indians—were not issues of pressing concern to 17th century Englishmen, information on these subjects had been accumulating since the 1550s. . . .

. . . The major breakthrough came in 1589 with the publication of Richard Hakluyt's *Principall Navagations* . . . , a collection of travel narratives touching on English exploration. Hakluyt, as indicated earlier, was the greatest literary champion of English imperialism and as he urged his compatriots across the Atlantic, he described what to expect on the other side. The "Voyages" (as Hakluyt's work was generally known) was extremely popular and undoubtedly provided many Englishmen with their first glimpse of Mexico and other American regions. Samuel Purchas, Hakluyt's successor as literary imperialist and hispanophobe, issued two works, *Purchas his pilgrimage* (1613) and *Hakluytus Posthumus* . . . (1625), which circulated widely and provided new information on Mexico. By the time their program of colonization was well underway, Englishmen had access to as much general information about Mexico as any people in Europe with the possible exception of the Spaniards.

The image of Mexico that emerges from these works is marked by a distinctive cleavage characteristic of general European responses to the Mexicans. On the one hand, European writers expressed admiration for the relatively advanced civilization of the Mexicans as compared with other New World aborigines. . . .

. . . A number of Europeans noted that the Mexicans lived according to a body of laws while the learned Jesuit, José de Acosta, found that they selected their rulers through democratic elections.

. . . The greatest champion of the Mexicans, as for all the Indians, was Las Casas, who particularly admired the aborigines of Yucatan for their prudence and the general "uprightness" of their lives.

Las Casas' diligent, indeed obsessive, campaign notwithstanding, the preponderance of European and, consequently, English opinion weighed heavily against the Mexicans. Virtually every writer declaimed on their indolence, while others reported that the Mexicans were given to drunkenness, polygamy, and incest. The Mexicans were vilified for their hostility to the Spaniards and their refusal to acquiesce promptly in the moral and cultural superiority of their conquerors. Their rapid degeneration under colonial rule also adversely affected European judgments. Ultimately, the Mexicans were regarded as a depraved race whose defects were only slightly mitigated by the grandeur and opulence of their cultures. . . .

No European writer on Mexico failed to note the terrible forms that heathenism had assumed in that land. Witches, sorcerers, and other agents of Satan fairly overran the countryside and held the natives in thralldom. Believing that their deities lived on human blood, the Mexicans had devised elaborate rites of sacrifice. Sullen priests led children, virgins, and prisoners of war to altars where they ripped open the chests of their victims, removed the still-beating hearts, and smeared blood on the marble lips of their idols. The priests would next burn the entrails in the belief that their gods enjoyed the smoke from such offerings. Finally, the priests ate various parts of the victims' bodies, including the arms and legs. English readers learned that human sacrifices in Mexico sometimes reached the astonishing total of fifty thousand a year. . . .

As I have said, English images of Mexico derived largely from general European notions, mainly Spanish. There was, to be sure, a small irony in Englishmen accepting rather uncritically the views of their greatest enemies. But Englishmen had little experience in Mexico themselves and they took information where they found it. A small number did travel and live in Mexico, however, and a few even wrote about their experiences. Some of these early reports were collected by Hakluyt; together they provide a somewhat different perspective on the Mexican situation from the Spanish.

These early accounts form a tissue of fantasy, distortion, and occasionally acute observation. . . .

As to the character of the natives, the English travelers had little good to report. Miles Philips came to regard the aborigines as pleasant and compassionate, but none of his compatriots shared his affection. More typical was the reaction of Henry Hawks who described the Indians as "void of all goodness." More than one writer found the Mexicans to be cowardly and drunken. John Chilton observed that for a bottle of wine, an Indian would sell his wife and children. But the most persistent charge against the Mexicans was indolence. English travelers were appalled that the natives had so little exploited their land. . . .

Within a span of three-quarters of a century, English translators, scholars, and propagandists had presented to their countrymen a substantial body of literature on Mexican subjects. The images that emerged from these works were not distinctively English but belonged to a broader European tradition. In any case, they did little to enhance appreciation of the Mexicans, grounded is they were in distortion, fantasy, and simple confusion. As Europeans passed through Mexico, they carried ideological equipment which essentially precluded true understanding of the natives. . . .

The evidence regarding early colonial images of the Mexicans is primarily inferential. As indicated earlier, the collections of Hukluyt and Purchas were well-known to many colonists, perhaps even a majority. Probably the same percentage was acquainted with Thomas Gage's *The English-American,* the first book-length treatment of America by an English eyewitness and a work which managed to excoriate simultaneously the Spanish conquerors, the Catholic missionaries, and the hapless aborigines of Mexico and Guatemala. Gage added nothing new to available knowledge about Mexico except his pervasive malice but his work was quite popular in England and the colonies nonetheless. Las Casas was also known to many colonists while the works of other major Spanish historians, notably Acosta, were read by a few intellectuals. Two other considerations should be borne in mind here. As a group, the colonists—particularly the New Englanders—were unusually well-educated and alert to intellectual fashions in England and on the Continent. Secondly, given their powerful hatred of Catholicism and Spain, they were unlikely to disregard completely so important an area of activity for their enemies. It seems reasonable to conclude, therefore, that the early settlers held images of the Mexicans such as were circulating in contemporary England. Unquestionably, these images were not so clear, widespread, or fixed as those of Catholics and Spaniards, but still they lived in the minds of the colonists and grew more vigorous as time passed. . . .

With the advent of local newspapers, word of contemporary Mexican affairs began to circulate more actively among the colonists. Mostly, it treated mundane issues and shed little light on the Mexicans themselves. . . .

The significance of these newspaper accounts is threefold. First, the willingness of newspapers to publish Mexican items, no matter how trivial, inaccurate, or fanciful, suggests a considerable curiosity among colonists about the country. Secondly, the nature of the reports reflects the abiding Anglo-American interest in the economic exploitation of Mexico. . . . Finally, and most importantly, the information received by the colonists contained nothing to challenge traditional images of Mexico as established by Spanish and English writers in the Elizabethan and Jacobean ages.

Actually, traditional images of Mexico underwent a period of revitalization after the mid–18th century. . . .

By all odds the most important study of Mexico to reach English-Americans in the 18th century was William Robertson's *History of America.* This work, originally issued in London in 1777, remains with William Prescott's books the classic treatment of the Spanish Conquest in the English language. The "History" made an immediate impact in Britain and was soon transported to the United States where its influence was enormous.

Robertson gracefully recounted the historical episode which he regarded as one of the greatest of human adventures. He chronicled the exploits of the heroic Columbus, the ambitious Cortés, and the villainous Pizarro, all the while condemning what he perceived as the tragic flaw of Spanish character, an avarice so boundless that it compelled the conquerors to an unprecedented succession of outrages. . . . Robertson's low estimate of the American performance of the Spaniards was no surprise, coming as it did from a Scottish Presbyterian and a licensed minister at that. More interesting, and ultimately of greater importance, were Robertson's comments on the Mexican aborigines.

Robertson moved to his assessment of the Mexicans from a broader consideration of the character of the New World aborigines. Writing in an age when the idea of the noble savage had gained wide currency, he vigorously rejected the concept. He found nothing in his researches to conclude that the Americans were innocent and generous, a race that had luxuriated in a western paradise before the intrusion of the Spaniards. Instead, Robertson argued that their pre-Columbian way of life was less an example of dignified repose than a case of extraordinary indolence. . . .

[A]s a group, the Americans were brutal, treacherous, and cruel: in a word, "savages" without any mitigating adjectives. They were given to drunkenness and cannibalism and the only activity likely to shake them from their indolence was war. In sum, the Americans exhibited few of the traits that distinguish man from beast. . . .

While Robertson characterized the Americans as altogether a bad lot, some were worse than others and the supreme villains, by any measure, were the Mexicans. Unlike earlier writers such as Acosta, Robertson did not soften his denunciations with concessions to the cultural achievements of the Mexicans. He argued instead that their institutions "did not differ greatly from those of other inhabitants of America." They fought incessantly, were vengeful, and never learned to temper their rage, a certain sign of savagism. Robertson concluded that "we cannot but suspect their degree of civilization to have been very imperfect." . . .

Ultimately, Robertson presented an extremely gloomy assessment of the Mexicans, greatly underestimating their cultural achievements while exaggerating the uniqueness of their barbarism. In his mind, the Mexicans stood as the fiercest and most detestable of the New World peoples, inferior culturally to the Incas and in qualities of character to the North American natives. By also arguing that the Spaniards who were attracted to America were the most undesirable elements of their society, Robertson offered to his readers a Mexico populated by two extraordinary breeds of scoundrels already mixing their bloods. In an era when revolutionary movements in Latin America were at last beginning to gather real support, Robertson's Mexico seemed an unlikely setting for the flourishing of humane, republican institutions. To those readers acquainted with traditional portraits of Mexican life, Robertson's depictions were all too familiar; his claims of objectivity and originality notwithstanding, he essentially took old images and couched them in a variety of 18th-century scientism. . . .

The popularity of Robertson's "History" served to bring into play the final component necessary to form an ideological prism through which Americans would view contemporary Mexicans in the 19th century. As we have seen, anti-Catholicism and hispanophobia were clearly defined and pervasive in Anglo-American culture long before 1777; more than any previous event or literary work, *The History of America* helped to codify and disseminate anti-Mexican sentiment and raise it to a more nearly equal level of importance. These various antipathies eventually linked and merged as Americans came to recognize the phenomenon of cultural and racial fusion between Indian and Spaniard which had been proceeding since the Conquest.

When Americans began actually to encounter Mexicans in Texas, Santa Fe, and other Mexican territories after 1821, their initial responses were conditioned primarily by the traditions of hispanophobia and anti-Catholicism. Many American travelers in Mexico called the natives "Spaniards" and assigned to them, almost reflexively, the familiar defects of the Black Legend. Josiah Gregg, a trader on the Santa Fe Trail, observed that the New Mexicans "appear to have inherited much of the cruelty and intolerance of their ancestors and no small portion of their bigotry and fanaticism." Other travelers called the Mexicans "priest-ridden." Richard Henry Dana, a visitor to California, attributed Mexican indolence to their Catholicism which subordinated work to the celebration of an interminable series of religious holidays. The primacy of hispanophobia and anti- Catholicism in early American treatments of the Mexicans was partly the result of their sheer tenacity in the national consciousness but it was also a function of the traditional European belief that advanced cultures (which is to say their own) invariably overwhelmed primitive ones. Robertson lent support to this view when he contrasted the awesome hegemony of the Spaniards with the languid acquiescence of the Mexicans.

About 1840, racialist thought emerged to focus attention on the "inherent" characteristics of the Mexicans rather than those acquired during their long subjugation to the Catholic Spaniards. Here again, we note a natural line of development and the force of traditional images. The core of Anglo-American notions about the Mexicans had always been an assumed depravity and certainly the racialists retained this idea. It is striking how closely their depictions of contemporary Mexicans resemble Robertson's portrayal of pre-Conquest aborigines: there is the same indolence, duplicity, melancholy, violence, and cruelty. I am not suggesting that racialists generally bore the direct influence of Robertson but that his views of the Mexicans represent a traditional mode of perceiving them that persisted into the mid–19th century with only slight modifications. . . .

Of all racialist theories, the doctrine of miscegenation, which held that the progeny of racially different parents inherited the worst qualities of each, had the greatest impact on American views of Mexicans. Racialists regarded mixed-breeds as impulsive, unstable, and prone to insanity. The Mexicans, as the most conspicuous products of mass miscegenation, inevitably were assigned these qualities. . . .

PART II.

GRINGOS VERSUS GREASERS
1846–1900

As a result of the Texas revolt in 1835–1836 and the U.S.-Mexican War in 1846–1848, the United States acquired about half of its neighbor's territory. Thanks to the Treaty of Guadalupe Hidalgo, some 80,000 Mexicans, mostly *Hispanos* (New Mexicans), found themselves citizens of a new country. The next half century witnessed chronic strife between the two peoples, as is reflected by the pejorative terms they used to refer to one another: "gringos" and "greasers."

Even under the best of circumstances, the relationship was bound to be strained, given the bitterness engendered by the armed conflict. The Lone Star State was the worst case. Texans had played a prominent role in the invasion of the south under General Zachary Taylor. By all accounts, the fighting in northeastern Mexico was intense. Despite being undermanned and poorly led, Mexican patriots put up a fierce resistance to protect home and hearth. Moreover, the memory of the Alamo ensured a xenophobic reaction among the Texans. Racism also heightened tensions. That most of the early Anglo immigrants to Texas were Southerners, and many were slaveholders, helps to explain the particularly strident discrimination encountered by Tejanos. The ferocity of reprisals by Texas Rangers during the Mexican campaign was condemned even by General Taylor himself. Racism, however, was not confined to Texans; the historian Reginald Horseman has shown that it permeated U.S. society at mid-century.

The dominant tendency in Chicano historiography is to characterize the nineteenth century as a period of cultural conflict, with race being the key factor. Typical is the work of historians Raymund Paredes, cited earlier, and Arnoldo De León, whose views are presented in this section. More recently, however, the economic aspect of the conflict has gained greater attention. Sociologist David Montejano, another scholar who focuses on Texas history, best represents this perspective.

Rather than replacing them, the Montejano interpretation augments race-centered views of conflict. There are a number of scholars, however, who are clearly revisionist in the sense that they deemphasize the amount of racial prejudice and discrimination in the late nineteenth century. The work of these scholars, particularly sociologist Tomás Almaguer in California and historian Armando Alonzo in Texas, has yet to gain a large audience. Alonzo's essay, focusing on Anglo acquisition of Mexican lands in South Texas, reflects his more modest assessment of the amount of racial discrimination suffered by Mexicanos.

Another recent trend in nineteenth-century historiography that attempts to move beyond the notion of conquest and resistance focuses on demographic shifts, especially immigration and urbanization. There is some evidence that migration from Mexico to the United States *did* begin to increase in the 1880s. By this time, the *Porfiriato* (the dictatorship of Porfirio Diaz) had restored political stability to Mexico, but at a huge cost to the nation's agrarian working class. On the other hand, across the border, particularly in Arizona, the mining industry started to expand. The result was the emigration of disaffected Mexican peasants and miners, who were joined by a small group of middle-class émigrés. By 1900, there were 100,000 Mexican immigrants in the United States.

Less convincing is the argument by urban historians that international migration was accompanied by significant internal migration to cities during the late nineteenth century. Given the difficulty in acquiring their own lands, some Mexicans and Mexican Americans undoubtedly did move to fledgling cities like Los Angeles, Tucson, Albuquerque, El Paso, and San Antonio. Here, in competition with Anglo newcomers, they increasingly found themselves residing in ethnic enclaves (*barrios*), the subject of the essay by historian Antonio Ríos-Bustamante, and, as historian Richard Griswold del Castillo notes in his essay, developing a variety of lifestyles. By 1900, though, the great majority of Mexicans either continued to live as they had before, in rural villages, or they were reduced to residing in isolated labor camps. To apply the term "urbanization" at this point in Mexican-American history would be premature.

Whether in rural settings or in urban settings, there can be no doubt that the Mexican population throughout the Southwest was beleaguered. Having lost their economic and political power by the end of the century—the Hispanos were the sole exception—they were reduced to second-class citizens. To make matters worse, as church historian Albert Pulido demonstrates in his essay, the Catholic Church failed to provide much-needed spiritual care, for Anglo priests were unable to understand the popular religious beliefs and practices of their Mexican flocks.

Mexicans were forced to rely on their own resources. The family was first and foremost. Another institution that proved invaluable was the *mutualista* (mutual benefit society). These service-oriented associations proliferated by the turn of the century. The *Alianza Hispano-Americana* (Hispanic-American Alliance), as historian Manuel Gonzales indicates in his essay, was particularly significant. Established in Tucson in 1894, the Alianza became the most influential Mexican-American organization before World War I.

7

IN RE RICARDO RODRIGUEZ

An Attempt at Chicano Disfranchisement in
San Antonio, 1896–1897

ARNOLDO DE LEÓN

Arnoldo De León is C. J. "Red" Davidson Professor of History at Angelo
State University in San Angelo, Texas. Possibly the most prolific of Chicano historians, De León has published a great number of works, both
articles and books. His best-known studies include *The Tejano Community, 1836–1900* (1982), *They Called Them Greasers: Anglo Attitudes toward Mexicans in Texas, 1821–1900* (1983), and *North to Aztlán: A History of Mexican Americans in the United States* (1996), an excellent survey
co-authored with Richard Griswold del Castillo.

When Ricardo Rodríguez filed application for naturalization papers before United
States Circuit Court, in and for the district of Texas at San Antonio, May of 1896,
two San Antonio politicians, T. J. McMinn and Jack Evans, inveighed before Judge
T. S. Maxey that Rodríguez did not qualify for citizenship on the grounds that he
was not "a white person, nor an African, nor of African descent, and is therefore not
capable of becoming an American citizen." Their pleas, explained the two attorneys,
sought to ask judgment of the court on the matter of individual naturalization, the
issue never having been satisfactorily adjudicated since the Treaty of Guadalupe
Hidalgo (1848). Their intent was not malicious, but simply, "to prevent newly arrived Mexicans from voting." Yet, they acknowledged that this attempt to disfranchise Mexican voters threatened the political rights of native-born Mexicanos and
those of Anglo-Mexican parentage as well.

Historically, whites in Texas had expressed reservations about granting Mexicanos voting privileges. In San Antonio, a so-called Reform Club organized in the
late 1880s to bring about political improvements in the city seriously discussed the
notion of disfranchising the Mexican American population. According to one mem-

From a book of the same title (San Antonio: Caravel Press, 1979). The original text has been slightly
modified by the author. Reprinted by permission of the author.

ber, there existed a "finely drawn legal distinction" disqualifying those of Mexican blood from the franchise. The pronouncement quickly incurred the challenge of a dissident signing himself "Quiet Observer." Inquiring first as to McMinn's qualifications on law, then arguing strenuously that the Fourteenth Amendment protected Mexicans from disfranchisement, "Quiet Observer" contended that the Amendment made no distinction as to color or race, and, until Congress disallowed Mexicanos from naturalization as it had done in the case of the Chinese, then the constitution insured Tejanos the franchise. McMinn, persistent in his legal argument, countered that the word "person" in the Amendment was ambiguous: "A mongolian is not a 'person'; an Indian is not a 'person'; a woman is not a 'person'; is an Aztec a 'person' from the suffrage standpoint?" Since the question had already been considered and passed upon in the case of the Chinese, it stood *res adjuticata.*

McMinn continued to raise the issue before every subsequent election. Then, when Rodríguez came before Maxey's court with affidavits containing the requirements of naturalization laws in hand, McMinn and Jack Evans resisted, and brought the case for legal ruling.

Locally, the case caused much comment and political ado. Anglos speculated that a verdict against Rodríguez might mean calling upon every Mexican applicant to show suitability for citizenship papers, a procedure that would keep out illegal voters who tended to inundate the eligible voters in San Antonio and surrounding districts at election time. Others claimed that such a decision, even if it did not favor the applicant, would affect only a small number, as Mexicanos could still vote on their intention papers. To the contrary, argued those opposed to the Mexican voter, a ruling against Mexicans meant an end to the practice of using papers of intent, and thus a nullification of their right to vote. Compounding the matter, explained the San Antonio *Express,* a decision against the Mexicans might determine the standing of others who had already taken out their first and final papers. Not only would it disfranchise them, but would leave them a people without a country.

The potential outcome provoked speculation as to its significance in local and state politics. The court action caused concern among politicians who considered Mexican Americans a meaningful force in local politics. A ruling to the effect that a Mexican could not cast a ballot in the United States could conceivably reduce the total number of votes in San Antonio alone by about one-fifth, and perhaps by a larger percentage in the counties south and west. Political observers generally agreed that it would weaken the Democrats, and even transform the political complexion of southern and western Texas.

A few days following the introduction of the briefs against Rodríguez, Judge Maxey pled lack of preparation and, because of the importance of the case, thought it more prudent to submit the question to a committee of friends of the court and have it investigated thoroughly before rendering a decision. Following the judge's remarks, Rodríguez was sworn in and asked about his past and current status. His testimony and proofs submitted to the court showed him to be in his late thirties, born in Ojuelos, Guanajuato, that he had moved subsequently to Laredo in 1883 before coming to San Antonio the same year, and now worked for the city cleaning the streets and river. An illiterate man unable to read or write English or Spanish, he spoke his native tongue "as it is spoken by others of his class and humble condition in life." He had dark eyes, straight black hair, and high cheek bones, and observers described him as the "peon type, very dark" and associated him with the "copper-colored or red man." As to ancestry, Rodríguez claimed to be a "pure-blooded Mexican." He knew nothing of pre-Columbian Mexican civilizations, maintained that he did not belong to the Aztecs nor other native races of Mexico or the Spaniards, and felt strongly that no African blood coursed through his body.

Queried as to his motive for wanting citizenship, he replied that he now made the United States his home. Conceding lack of familiarity with American political institutions when asked about the U. S. form of government, he conjectured that the United States was a Republic. He could not name the American President but knew that Don Porfirio Díaz now served as president of Mexico. When asked to whom he would be loyal should war break out between his country of origin and his adopted nation, he replied that as a peaceful man he did not wish to fight, but considered the question too serious to render an impromptu decision.

James Fisk, a character witness, testified that on the basis of his ten-year acquaintance with the applicant, Rodríguez was a good man, of sound moral character, a hard worker, a peaceful law-abiding citizen, and his ignorance of the Constitution notwithstanding, would dutifully uphold its principles if he knew them. The supporting affidavits of L. G. Peck and Lorenzo Galván further showed that Rodríguez had resided in the United States for five years and was "attached to the principles of the Constitution of the United States and well disposed to the order and happiness of the same."

Among Mexicanos, the feeling that whites sought infringement upon their civil liberties led to an indignation meeting in October 1896, and a denunciation of the responsible parties attempting to prevent their naturalization and enfranchisement. At a site that served as a cockpit, some 200 Bexareños [Mexicanos from San Antonio] met to discuss the matter they considered fraught with serious and important consequences. A. L. Montalbo, the apparent force behind the assembly, addressed the "Texas-Mexicans" in Spanish, admonishing them that the upcoming November election included platforms that could be detrimental to the civil rights of Mexican Americans. He urged his followers to mass behind the Democratic Party, the only political group which had "heretofore recognized the rights" of Mexican Americans. Mexicanos, he said, had been instilled with Democratic principles and been faithful to that camp. Despite this, he continued, a number of them had defected into opposition parties. He denounced the Populists for seeking to pass state legislation designed to dilute Mexican rights and accused it along with McMinn of desiring to reduce Texas-Mexicans "to the category of pack animals, who may be good enough to work, but not good enough to exercise any civil rights." Concerning the Republican Party (and Evans), Montalbo emphasized that the Republicans had made common cause with the Populists and that both parties expressed anti-Mexican attitudes. Calling upon the audience to renounce McMinn and Evans, he adjourned the meeting and all Mexicans present, reports said, endorsed their name to the address.

Meanwhile, the members of the committee to whom Maxey had referred the Rodríguez case studied the question. Four of those constituting the six-man committee responded. The most lengthy, and seemingly the more persuasive observations came from Thomas M. Paschal, a local attorney with a long career in jurisprudence. Turning to the question at hand after some prefatory remarks, he declared that citizenship could be acquired only by birth; adherence to the naturalization laws; constitutional amendment; and by blanket naturalization, as when the United States annexed a region by conquest or purchase. Mexicans acquired by the Treaty of Guadalupe Hidalgo of February, 1848, and the Gadsden Purchase of June, 1854, had become citizens by collective naturalization once swearing allegiance to American principles. The last two examples, Paschal indicated, showed how the government, through its power to negotiate treaties, could interpret or apply the naturalization laws when non-white peoples were involved.

Paschal then cited *In re* Ah Yup, which purportedly ruled that only the Caucasian and African races qualified for citizenship. But the Ah Yup decision demonstrated unquestionably that Congress inserted the word "white" in that statute to exclude the Chinese. Consequently, Congress never displayed an attempt to refuse citizenship to Mexicanos.

The brief then turned attention to race. The copper-colored Indian races of Mexico had long abandoned their tribal condition in the process of merging with their Spanish conquerors, Paschal noted. Mexicans of pure Indian and Aztec ancestry had led the independence movement of 1810 in Mexico and now Porfirio Díaz, more of an Indian than Caucasian, occupied the presidential chair. No reason existed, Paschal thought, for excluding a Mexican not living in a "savage" state and long residing as a law-abiding citizen in the United States. Legally, Paschal declared, Rodríguez met the test that he be "a man of good moral character, and that he is attached to the principles of the constitution of the United States, and that he is well disposed to the good order and happiness of the same."

Paschal then posed a question. Was there anything in the law which deterred naturalization for an American Indian if such an individual had severed relations with his tribe and surrendered himself completely to the jurisdiction of the country? Paschal could see nothing for such an assumption. If that be the case, Paschal ended, Rodríguez, an Indian citizen of Mexico who no longer owed allegiance to any tribe, was eligible. But his ignorance of American government certainly made it impossible for him to declare true allegiance to the United States. But such questions remained for the court to judge, he decided.

The brief of Floyd McGown encouraged the court to rule against Rodríguez. Departing from Paschal's view of the Ah Yup case, McGown argued that the decision held that American citizenship extended to whites only and subsequent cases confirmed its meaning. According to authorities on the matter, McGown said, applicants qualified for naturalization only if Caucasian and Rodríguez' appearance indicated him to be a Mexican Indian. In seeking the racial classification of Mexicans, McGown examined the writings of a number of experts, of whom he considered the French anthropologist Dr. Paul Brocas the most eminent. In Brocas's scheme, the ethnologist could "follow the varieties of the human skin from the fairest hue of the Swede, and the darker tint of the Provencal, to the withered leaf brown of the Hottentot, the chocolate brown of the Mexicans, and the brown black of the West

African." The applicant, McGown insisted, did not meet the standards of "white-ness," either by scientific definition or by understandings white society had of the term. Moreover, even if accepted as white, Rodriguez' total unfamiliarity with con-stitutional principles invalidated his petition.

A. J. Evans' brief sharply challenged Rodriguez' right to citizenship. Under the law, argued Evans, the applicant qualified for naturalization if an alien, if of the Caucasian race, or if of African nativity or descent. Without doubt, he was of alien status, but neither white nor black. From the appearance of the applicant, the evi-dence submitted to the court, and the findings of students of ethnology, Rodríguez clearly belonged with the six million pure-blooded Mexican Indians and plausibly with the several Indian tribes. If that was the case, could he be considered a white person? If of the Indian race, naturalization was not possible.

Taking up naturalization treaties, Evans declared that Congress had the sole power of naturalization, and he knew of no legislation passed applying the United States naturalization laws to Mexicans, nor of the President consummating a treaty permitting such an action. But this was not even of great importance, he main-tained, for the sovereign state of Texas could decide a people's eligibility for the vote, and if the state government opted to do so "could make the wildest Indian of Mexico a voter upon one hour's arrival."

According to the fourth brief, that of T. J. McMinn, all Mexicans fell outside the pale of eligibility, except Lorenzo de Zavala and other loyalists of the Texas war for independence (1836); the children of patriots; Mexicans who lived in the province on Texas Independence Day and those who descended from them; and Mexican citizens considered white. What factors rendered the rest ineligible? First, the Texas Revolution intended to remove Tejanos "unfit to be free, and incapable of self-gov-ernment." Second, members of the first convention in 1835 directed that Anglos and only those Mexicans resisting the central government qualified for the fran-chise. Third, Sam Houston had confided to Provisional Governor Henry Smith that he had "no confidence in them." Fourth, a person of Mexican descent was racially an Indian, and as such was ineligible. Fifth, the United States had seriously consid-ered prohibiting Mexicans from citizenship, an intention made evident in congres-sional debates and in the opinions advanced by leading politicians. Last, McMinn asserted, discussions in Extra Sessions of the Senate revealed that the Treaty of Guadalupe Hidalgo exempted Mexicans from having the rights of citizens, and Mexico's representatives had so understood that disqualification despite wishing it otherwise.

A year following Rodriguez' application, District Judge Maxey pronounced judgment on the case. Acknowledging the receipt of statements by Paschal, McGown, Evans, and McMinn, Maxey assured that the briefs had received full study as necessitated by the case with such serious implications.

Concerning the Ah Yup case, Maxey stated, the Chinese presence preoccupied the people on the West coast when the issue came before the courts, but no longer was this a debatable point in 1896, as the Act of May 1882 clearly stipulated that no American court could grant citizenship to the Chinese. The Ah Yup opinion, Maxey cautioned, in no way decided the present question.

The judge found no need to delve meticulously into Rodríguez' racial classi-fication. By the definition of the anthropologist, Maxey argued, Rodríguez was not a white person. But if the meaning and intent of the law embraced him, Maxey went on, he should receive his application for naturalization, even if the letter of the statute excluded him.

Leading toward the final verdict, Maxey began citing precedents. Over the past several decades, he commenced, both the Republic of Texas and the United States had by various acts addressing naturalization given Mexicans rights and privileges enjoyed by white citizens. The Texas Constitution of 1836 granted citizenship to Mexicans living in the Republic on Independence Day. By Article VIII of the Treaty of Guadalupe Hidalgo, he continued, Mexicans who stayed in the U.S. Southwest automatically became Americans after opting not to retain Mexican citizenship. Similarly, provisions accompanying the Gadsden Purchase granted citizenship to Mexicans who remained within the Mesilla Valley after one year. The Fourteenth Amendment, continued Maxey, extended all the rights of citizens to those born or naturalized in the United States, regardless of race or color. As the courts held that the provisions of the Amendment applied even to the Chinese who could not be-come naturalized, it followed that Mexicans born in the United States were Ameri-can citizens and of the state wherein they made their home.

Taking into account all the body of laws, treaties, and constitutional principles which gave Mexicans the status of citizenship or in some way extended them the right to acquire naturalization, Maxey rendered the following verdict:

> After a careful and patient investigation of the question discussed, the court is of opinion that, whatever may be the status of the applicant viewed solely from the standpoint of the ethnologist, he is embraced within the spirit and intent of our laws upon naturalization, and his application should be granted if he is shown by the testimony to be a man attached to the principles of the constitution, and well disposed to the good order and happiness of the same. It is suggested that the proof fails in this respect; and the objection appears to be based upon the ground, intimated in the briefs, of his inability to understand or explain those principles. That the applicant is lamentably ignorant is conceded, and that he is unable to read and write the testimony clearly discloses. Naturally enough, his untrained mind is found deficient in the power to elucidate or define the principles of the constitution. But the testimony also discloses that he is a very good man, peace-able and industrious, of good moral character, and law abiding "to a remarkable degree." And hence it may be said of him, notwithstanding his inability to undergo an examination on questions of constitutional law, that by his daily walk, during a residence of ten years in the city of San Antonio, he has practically illustrated and emphasized his attachment to the principles of the constitution. Congress had not seen fit to require of applicants for naturalization an educational qualification, and courts should be careful to avoid judicial legislation. In the judgment of the court, the applicant possesses the requisite qualifications for citizenship, and his applica-tion will therefore be granted.

In employing the power at their disposal to weaken the voting capability of Mexicanos, whites had failed. While directed at the practice of illegal voting, the attempt at disfranchisement still represented a form of legal discrimination against Chicanos, for—as Maxey noted—it sought to curb privileges clearly guaranteed by the law. Such experiences, indeed, explain the relative political powerlessness among nineteenth-century Tejanos. Repeated intimidation produced discouragement, distrust, and doubt as to the futility of their participation. Abrasive gestures politicized them negatively to a political order that espoused democracy but practiced exclusion. Psychologically, the contact estranged them to the point of minimal involvement, a behavior that came not from apathy, lack of leadership, factionalism, culture or socioeconomic factors, but from external conditions stifling their political potential.

8

MEXICAN-AMERICAN LAND GRANT ADJUDICATION

ARMANDO C. ALONZO

Armando C. Alonzo, a product of Edinburg in South Texas, graduated from the University of Notre Dame with a B.A. in American government and continued his studies at the University of Texas–Pan American, where he earned an M.A. in history. He received his Ph.D. in history from Indiana University in 1994. Three years later, he was the recipient of a Ford Postdoctoral Fellowship to do research on the northeastern provinces of New Spain in the seventeenth and eighteenth centuries. At present he teaches in the Department of History at Texas A&M University. A specialist on the Borderlands, he is the author of *Tejano Legacy: Rancheros and Settlers in South Texas, 1734–1900* (1998).

The Mexican War brought not only soldiers to the lower border country, but also a host of Anglo-Americans who began almost immediately to challenge the Mexicans for control of the land. Spanish and Mexican land grants, some of long standing, became the focus of competition, controversy, and conflict. Despite what Mexicans believed to be specific guarantees to their property and civil rights under Articles VIII and IX of the Treaty of Guadalupe Hidalgo, the older Mexican landholders on the north bank of the Rio Grande often found themselves uncertain about their rights to lands granted by Spain and Mexico. The treaty provided no standard for validation of land grants. Land grant adjudication proceeded in a piecemeal fashion with the federal government determining the procedures in the new American Southwest, except that, by virtue of its prior claim to the trans-Nueces, the state of Texas controlled the process in the annexed lands. Because the federal government never challenged this position, the state determined the manner of settling the titles to lands in the annexed territory. Contrary to popular belief, however, Texas acted

From *The New Handbook of Texas,* Vol. 4 (Austin: The Texas State Historical Association, 1996): 656–59. The original text has been slightly modified. Reprinted by permission of the Texas State Historical Association.

equitably by making available several opportunities for adjudication. Still, the validation of Hispanic land grants opened the gates to Tejano land loss, an event that involved complex dynamics beyond the range of this article. Anglos ultimately took advantage of their growing economic power, used new laws to gain land, and occasionally resorted to devious means to subvert the Mexicans' position as dominant landholders.

At the end of the war, some soldiers and other Anglo adventurers stayed in the area as well as several scores of Anglo and European merchants who had moved to Matamoros in the 1820s and 1830s. While the latter were content merely to restart the Mexican trade, many newcomers had loftier economic and political ambitions. Some of them were interested in the delta farmlands and rich pastures upon which large numbers of livestock grazed. They often manifested an anti-Mexican bias that stirred up trouble and widened the chasm between Mexicans on the one hand and Anglos and Europeans on the other. For example, Judge Rice Garland, who sold lands and bought land certificates in Matamoros, advertised in the Brownsville *American Flag* on June 2, 1847, that "Mexican law and authority are forever at an end" in the Nueces territory and that "by the laws of Texas no alien can hold real estate within its limits." In the same ad he declared in Spanish that all original owners of land must have their lands surveyed and possess deeds. He warned Mexican owners that "preparations are being made to locate other claims on the land covered by such titles." Despite such threats, Mexicans were not about to relinquish their claims so easily. But before adjudication, Anglo legal challenges against Mexican claimants resulted in newcomers acquiring rights to lands in the Espíritu Santo grant and to a tract containing La Sal del Rey, a dry salt lake mined since the late seventeenth century, in the San Salvador del Tule grant. In the first case, Charles Stillman's economic and political power forced Rafael García Cavazos to sell his rights, even though the court had ruled in the latter's favor by voiding squatters' claims to property acquired by Stillman. In the second case, the courts ruled against the Hispanic claimants to the grant in favor of Anglos who had received land certificates from the Republic of Texas. One can only surmise that the Mexican claimants' anxiety must have increased instead of lessened as a result of these actions. Those in the middle of the controversy over land grants included rancheros who were concerned about their property rights and newcomers who during the Mexican War had acquired *derechos* or undivided interests in the land. The latter were mostly merchants who had sought out grantees or heirs as well as previous purchasers of the grants and for a few dollars bought the undivided rights or *derechos* from them. They must have anticipated that the lands along the Rio Grande frontier would be more valuable once the war was over. In fact, during the conflict some merchants located stores and warehouses on the north bank of the river. Others desired the new lands for purposes of speculation. Thus, those claiming vested interests and those interested in the acquisition of land grants insisted that public policy would best be served if the state took rapid steps to validate the grants.

Governor Peter H. Bell responded energetically. Writing to the Texas legislature on December 26, 1849, he noted the urgency of "settling upon a secure and permanent basis the land titles of the country" and recommended that the legislature establish a board of commissioners to investigate titles. It soon became apparent that some people did not like the idea of a special commission and particularly objected to the governor's recommendation to limit investigation of claims to those where evidence of title was already in Texas. This would effectively bar the claims of those who lacked original records but whose titles were longstanding. Another concern was a belief that Article 8 of the Texas constitution, which allowed for the confiscation of land if the owner had left or refused to participate in the Texas Revolution, or aided the Mexicans, would be used against claimants. The intent of this article was to punish Texans of Mexican descent who had sided with General Santa Anna or who had remained neutral. However, an amendment requiring an affidavit that a claimant or person under whom he claimed title had not borne arms or aided the enemy during the revolution was voted down in the House of Representatives by a vote of 23 to 19. The bill's opponents argued that it was unfair to demand the allegiance of Mexicans to whom no protection had been offered.

While these proceedings were under way in Austin, a movement emerged to establish a Rio Grande territory separate from Texas. Meeting at Brownsville on February 2, 1850, the leading territorialists included a motley group of Anglos and, at least initially, Mexican rancheros, although the role played by the latter is unclear. Perhaps they, too, were perplexed by the motives of Texas officials of whom they had always been suspicious since the revolution. These lower Valley men asserted that Texas never had jurisdiction over the region and warned that the state government might annul land titles in the Nueces Strip or impose on residents there "expensive and ruinous lawsuits" to defend their property. They proposed that Congress be petitioned to allow the formation of a territorial government that would quickly and fairly adjudicate land titles, arguing that land with clear titles might then be purchased for less money than it would cost to obtain under a certificate from the state. The separatists concluded with a call for a convention to form a provisional government until the United States Congress could be petitioned. The separatists' meeting precipitated a countermovement whose supporters expressed confidence in the state of Texas and who denied the separatists' charges that Texas had neglected and acted in bad faith with regard to the interests of the lower Rio Grande valley. On February 5, 1850, they adopted resolutions that recognized state sovereignty over the Trans-Nueces territory and denied that they had ever submitted to the jurisdiction of Texas previous to its statehood. The assembly also urged the state to establish one or more tribunals to investigate "legal and just titles to land situated between the Nueces river and the Rio Grande," and applauded Governor Bell's previous proposal calling on the legislature to institute a commission for such purpose. On February 8, 1850, the state legislature passed an act providing for the appointment of a special commission to investigate claims to all Spanish and Mexican grants west of the Nueces River. On February 22, Governor Bell again addressed the people of the new counties in south Texas, stating that the commissioners would investigate and recommend for confirmation to the state legislature claims that originated in equity and fairness. He also assured them that the work of the commission would promote the prosperity of the area. Before the work of the commission got underway, the separatist movement was entirely bankrupt. Cognizant of the lingering legacy of conflict between Mexicans and Anglo-Texans, Senator Thomas J. Rusk told the United States Senate on March 11, 1850, that the Mexicans had been duped by individuals who only recently came to the area and that they had exploited the prejudices of "Mexicans who were originally and always adverse to Texas." Texans generally condemned the separatists for engaging in dirty politics and for currying the support of Northerners, whose motives Texans detested. Despite the demise of the territorialists' cause, the commission was hampered in some localities by the suspicions aroused by the separatists.

Under this law, the commission was to consist of two commissioners and an attorney who were to "take cognizance of all claims [that] . . . originated in good faith." William H. Bourland and James B. Miller, experienced public officials in Texas, were appointed commissioners, and Robert Jones Rivers, a well-known lawyer and judge, served as the board's attorney. Claimants were required to submit a full written description of the land claimed, along with all the evidence of title and rights on which the claim was based. They also had to provide an affidavit that documents submitted were not forged or antedated. Witnesses could be summoned to testify before the commission. Once this phase of the investigation was complete, the commissioners were to report where the titles were perfect. In case of an imperfect claim, the commission could recommend confirmation if it concluded that all requirements for perfecting the title would have been met had there not been a change in national sovereignty. The board was required to prepare an abstract on each claim together with a recommendation on whether it should be confirmed or rejected. The abstract and supporting evidence would then be submitted to the governor who, in turn, would give the documents to the legislature for final action.

After several delays the three members of the commission opened for business at Laredo on July 15, 1850. Laredoans, suspicious of the commissioners, did not want to present any claims. Upon being assured by Webb county clerk Hamilton P. Bee of the board's honest intentions, however, rancheros submitted fifteen claims. Sensing the urgency of showing good faith to the Mexican people, Bourland felt it wise to present the claims for immediate confirmation, although the board had a year to report. Bourland returned to Austin and submitted the list to Governor Bell on August 24, 1850. On September 4, 1850, the legislature confirmed the rancheros' fifteen claims. In the meantime, Miller and Rivers had proceeded to Rio Grande City, county seat of Starr County. There, Miller and Rivers received an inhospitable welcome from the Mexican residents, who refused to submit a single claim. In frustration Rivers resigned from the commission, and Miller resolved that he would not return to Rio Grande City. He moved on to Brownsville, where a letter from Bourland found him, requesting him to return to Rio Grande City. As a result of this unfavorable stay, no claims were presented at Rio Grande City. From Austin Bourland proceeded to Brownsville, where Miller was taking testimony. From there, Bourland wrote to the governor that because of the demise of the separatists' movement they were being treated with respect, and that he was confident no trouble would arise. When the board finished its work in Brownsville, Miller decided to make the voyage from Port Isabel to Galveston on the steamer *Anson* before going overland to Austin. Two days out, the *Anson* sank fifteen miles from Matagorda. Miller lost his trunk, the original titles, and about $800 in fees from claimants. Because of this loss, he urged the governor to amend the law to make the commissioners' decision final. Miller's suggestion was not accepted, however, and as a result the commission had to redo all of its work by procuring duplicates and other evidence. Following an adjournment of several months in the early part of 1851, Bourland went on his own to Eagle Pass, Laredo, and Rio Grande City in April. He then traveled to Corpus Christi, where he held his last session in late summer of 1851. In accordance with the law, on November 20, 1851, the governor sent a report on the work of the commission to the legislature, where a select committee examined the testimony. On February 10, 1852, the legislature, closely following the commissioners' recommendation, confirmed 234 claims in the names of the original Spanish and Mexican grantees, including those transferred to heirs and purchasers. The claims confirmed included those to 31 tracts in Webb County, 144 in Starr County, 56 in Cameron County, 21 in Nueces County, and 2 in Kinney County.

What is the significance of the legislative confirmations of 1852? Evidently, the validation of land grants satisfied not only rancheros but anyone claiming an interest in or desiring to acquire land. Clearly, the way was now open for additional transactions as well as for lawsuits between parties claiming title to the same lands. On another level, as David Montejano asserts, confirmation of title ostensibly incorporated the landed elites into the new political fabric of the region so that at least the old conflicts between Mexicans and Anglo-Texans were temporarily set aside.

Several of the claims that the commissioners refused to recommend were nonetheless confirmed by the state legislature in 1852. These included the claims to Llano Grande (1790) and Las Mesteñas (1794), both located in Hidalgo County. It is interesting to speculate why the legislature overrode the commission. Perhaps the facts that the two grants were well settled and that they belonged to the influential Hinojosa and Ballí families may have persuaded the legislature to confirm them. Besides, the confirmation of these two grants facilitated acquisitions by other interested parties and served to ease suspicions on the part of the old settlers and those wanting to purchase the land from them.

The important work of the commission and subsequent confirmation by the state, however, did not entirely bring an end to the issue of settling Spanish and Mexican land grants, mainly because seventy grants were not adjudicated either in 1851 or in 1852. In addition, the commission had rejected a small number of claims. Since the Bourland Commission had completed its work, Texas responded by allowing claimants the right to sue in the district courts for validation and confirmation, and by making individual legislative confirmations. Of these two methods, the first was by far more commonly used. Special state laws enacted in 1860, 1870, and 1901 provided the manner and time limitations under which claims could be presented. Under the first act, suit had to be brought in the state district court in which the grant was located. The second and third acts permitted the bringing of suit in the district court of Travis County. Sixty-eight land grants ended up in the courts under the three legislative acts. Of these, fifty-three were approved by the courts without having to resort to any other adjudication procedure. Except for seven grants adjudicated under the 1901 act, all of these claims were presented under the 1860 and 1870 acts. Thus, the claimants acted relatively quickly. Only two grants were rejected by the courts.

Among the more important claims that the Bourland Commission had denied but that were later approved by the district courts was that to San Salvador del Tule (1797), one of the largest land grants in south Texas. This claim had a history similar to those the commissioners rejected in 1851 in that the grant was occupied by the grantees and other purchasers, who made improvements on the land, vacated it temporarily, and subsequently reoccupied it. In the second half of the 1800s Mexican landholders in the San Salvador del Tule grant raised considerable livestock. When this claim was first presented to the Bourland Commission in 1852, it had been rejected on the basis of abandonment of the grant in 1811 due to Indian attacks. Yet, James B. Miller, in a dissenting opinion to the governor's, recommended confirmation. Miller asserted that the grantees and descendants soon returned to the grant, that the cattle had greatly increased, and that "the amount of land now in cultivation, owning to the long continuity of settlement, and the great number of occupants is very considerable." He urged that the grant be recognized, since rejection would work a great hardship on the settlers. He said that he did not favor depriving them of their homes or annulling "their titles, which, for three quarters of a century have been respected and considered valid." In 1904 the district court in Austin ruled in favor of the claimants, forty-seven landowners, most of whom were well-known Tejano rancheros.

The courts also confirmed another seven grants that had been recommended initially by the commissioners but not confirmed by the state legislature in 1851 and 1852. Due to the loss of the original records of the Bourland Commission, the loss of the legislative committee report which examined the commissioners' recommendations, and a lack of social or legal histories of these grants, it is impossible to explain why confirmation did not take place in 1851 and 1852. A possible hypothesis is that the original Mexican claimants and subsequent buyers vacated the grants, and evidently Anglo newcomers squatted on the land. Interestingly, six land grants had to be adjudicated and validated by both the courts and the legislature. The Ballís' claim to Padre Island suffered this fate. It is not clear why this double confirmation took place in these cases. Perhaps the claimants did not hold the grant as original grantees, but rather as purchasers of undivided interests or as holders under the legal doctrine of adverse possession. Consequently, their rights were not as secure. Further study would be necessary to determine the status of their holdings.

Texas courts ultimately rejected only two claims. One of these, the claim for the *ejidos* or commons of Reynosa in Hidalgo County, had been rejected outright by the Bourland Commission in 1851. The courts agreed with the commissioners' judgment that the *ejido* lands reverted to the Mexican government when the old town of Reynosa was broken up, and that Mexico claimed the land in October of 1836 when Mexicans bought it. But as a result of winning its independence in March 1836,

Texas claimed the land so that the Mexicans had no right to it. Obviously, this case was a travesty of justice because Texas never had effective control over the Trans-Nueces before 1848. A claim for a *porción* [tract of land] in the jurisdiction of Revilla (Guerrero), downriver from Laredo, became only the second claim to be rejected by the courts. The reason for this decision is unknown.

Long after the completion of the work of the Bourland Commission, the state legislature, and the courts, fifteen *porciones* were approved by the state legislature on March 31, 1921. Only one of these grants had originally been recommended by the commissioners in 1851. Because of the limited information in the General Land Office files and in the *House of Representatives Journal,* where the bill (H.B. No. 496) originated, it is not clear why these *porciones* had not been adjudicated earlier. However, the notes on *porciones* 34 and 57 state that these grants had been vacated. This ground evidently was used by the commissioners to refuse to recommend validation. It is likely that the other grants had a similar history and determination. Why were they finally confirmed in 1921? It would appear that equity dictated this result in view of the fact that people continued to hold onto the land into the twentieth century. After 1921, four other *porciones* received legislative adjudication and confirmation. *Porciones* 39 and 40 in the jurisdiction of Guerrero had evidently never been adjudicated, despite the fact, noted earlier by the Bourland Commission, that they were "older and [longer] subsisting grants" than those of 1767. They were approved by the legislature on March 25, 1927. The third *porción,* also in Guerrero, had been recommended in 1855, but evidently the legislature took no action. As a result it, too, was validated and confirmed at a late date—March 11, 1930. The last *porción* to be validated and confirmed by the legislature was *porción* 69 in the jurisdiction of Mier. It received confirmation on June 16, 1965. Again, it is likely that as the lands in these grants were held by either descendants or others in good faith, equity demanded their approval.

Despite the availability of the Bourland Commission, the state courts and the legislature, twenty-four land grants in south Texas, such as Juan Garza Díaz's grant, Vargas, and Joseph Antonio Cantú's *porción* 55 in Hidalgo County were never adjudicated. The reasons are unknown. However, a few theories can be advanced. It is possible that the holders of the grants temporarily vacated the land, and therefore they missed the commissioners. It is also possible that the expense of hiring a lawyer to seek confirmation through either the courts or the legislature was too prohibitive. Some claimants might not have wanted to pursue adjudication, believing or knowing that the grant was subject to challenge. It is important to note that in these cases people continued to hold land and to make and record transactions in the county where the land was located, so that while the state of Texas has no knowledge of the land because no record of title and patent exists in the General Land Office, the lands are of record in the county to this very day.

Contrary to popular history among Tejanos, the adjudication process in the Trans-Nueces was quick, and it favored Mexican land tenure. Thus by 1852 the legislature confirmed 209 claims with only a handful of outright rejections. The state courts then proceeded to validate sixty-seven additional claims, all but seven of them before the act of 1901. The courts rejected only two claims in the 1920s. As noted above, special circumstances prevailed in the Laredo area, resulting in this late adjudication. Equity, however, favored Mexican landholders for the most part. In the end only twenty-four land grants were never adjudicated for sundry reasons. Stephen Powers, Edward Dougherty, and other lawyers evidently profited from the validation proceedings by receiving land as a fee for representing claimants before the commissioners. Therefore, except for individual cases in which very few new-comers acquired interests in land grants and in which Anglo lawyers profited from defending land grant claimants, Mexicans maintained control of the land at least in the initial period of incorporation of the Trans-Nueces under the sovereignty of Texas and the United States. It was a different story after confirmation.

9

THE BARRIOIZATION OF NINETEENTH-CENTURY MEXICAN CALIFORNIANS
From Landowners to Laborers

ANTONIO RÍOS-BUSTAMANTE

Antonio Ríos-Bustamante is Director of the Chicano Studies Program at the University of Wyoming. He has been Visiting Lecturer in Chicano History, University of California, Santa Barbara; Senior Staff Research Associate, Chicano Studies Research Center, University of California, Los Angeles; and Director of the Chicano Studies Research Center at the University of Arizona. He received his Ph.D. in history from the University of California, Los Angeles, and has authored numerous publications concerning Mexicans and Latin Americans in the United States. Dr. Ríos-Bustamante is co-author (with Pedro Castillo) of *An Illustrated History of Mexican Los Angeles, 1781–1985* (1986), and co-editor (with Christine Mari) of *Latinos in Museums: A Heritage Reclaimed* (1998).

. . . In the nineteenth century a false dichotomy was drawn between *Californios,* the California-born Mexican residents of Alta and Baja California, and other Mexicans, said to be separate and mutually distinct peoples. Thus misused, the term "Californio" was also a convenient euphemism through which a small minority of the elite within the larger Mexican population, having ties of intermarriage with prominent Anglo Americans, could be accommodated as "Spanish Californians" and hence members of "respectable white society." At the same time the majority of Californios, other Mexicans, and Latin Americans could be conveniently lumped together and given no historical recognition or civic status.

Certainly most Californios, other Mexicans, and Latin Americans were not the only groups in California excluded from full participation in nineteenth-century Anglo American society. . . .

From *Masterkey: Anthropology of the Americas* 60 (Summer/Fall 1986): 26–35. The original text has been modified. Courtesy of the Southwest Museum, Los Angeles, California.

But Mexicans (including both Californios and later Mexican immigrants), like the California Indians, were also different from other groups in being perceived as a "conquered race" and in being subject to racial as well as cultural and economic discrimination.

As "conquerors," a widespread attitude held by many Anglo Americans in the years after 1848, the common perception was that Mexican Californians and, by extension, other Latin Americans had no rights that should not yield to the superior rights of "white American men." Thus it is not surprising that the period from 1848 to 1880 has been described by Alberto Camarillo as "the crucial period of transition in the formation of the set of unequal relationships which have characterized the social, economic, political and cultural subordination of Mexicans" in California and the United States.

The growth of the "Spanish" Californian myth and the denial of historical continuity of Mexican Californians was both a result of and a contributing factor to the rise of systematic inequality for California's Spanish-speaking population, which, before the end of the nineteenth century, had made the word and nationality "Mexican" a pariah term and identity.

POPULATION AND ORIGINS, 1800–1900

What then was the actual nature of the Spanish-speaking experience in nineteenth-century California? The identity and origins of the Spanish-speaking population were much more complex than previously supposed. Spanish-speaking Californians were a predominantly, although not exclusively, Mexican-origin population and included Californios, descendants of the mainly Mexican *pobladores* or first generation settlers; more recent Mexican emigrants, primarily from the northwestern Mexican states; and smaller numbers of Mexicans from Arizona, New Mexico, and Texas. Also present were other Latin Americans, including Chileans, Peruvians, and some Central Americans.

According to the 1793 census of colonial New Spain, Alta California's population of *gente de razón*—the Spanish-speaking Christians of all ethnic backgrounds—was 1,066 persons, of whom only 30 (or 3 percent) were European Spaniards. The remaining 1,036 were soldiers, settlers, and artisans born in Mexico. A small but continuing number of individuals from other areas of the Spanish Empire were also present as soldiers, settlers, artisans, and sailors. Thus the majority of Alta California's Spanish-speaking population were of Mexican origin and of various ethnic mixtures.

To the extent that California has a Spanish heritage, it is due to the Mexicans, *criollos* of Spanish descent, *mestizos* of part Indian and part European descent, *mulatos* of European and Black descent, and Indians who established it. Theirs was a new culture, a new identity—more than a composite of Spanish, Indian, and African cultures—and it was uniquely Mexican. The original influences were blurred, merged, and reformed into the west coast variant of Norteño Mexican culture. Their language was Spanish but included many Indian words. Their customs, modes, traditions, and beliefs reflected a strong generalized Spanish influence, but they had become distinctive from those of Spain. The settlers were Catholic, but their Virgin was the Virgin of Guadalupe, and their religious ambience reflected its Mexican origin.

Ironically, a large proportion of the settlers were the descendants of Indian peoples from the western coast of Mexico, who had themselves undergone a similar process of colonization and missionization only a century or so before. They were the product of the northern Mexican frontier experience and most important of all, they brought with them their culture, influenced by Spain but not simply Spanish. Their language was Spanish, but not exclusively; many of the settlers still retained a portion of languages of their Indian forebears. Many settlers were Indian, including José Vanegas, the first *alcalde* (mayor) of Los Angeles. It is also possible that some of those of African descent—and they were numerous—still retained some vestige of African traditions and modes.

The Mexican society of the region also had strong and complex links to the Indians of California. In fact, the Mexican community descended in part from members of the indigenous population who had been incorporated into their community through intermarriage, casual unions, and transculturation. The pobladores and their descendants interacted in all spheres with California Indians, including the economic and cultural, as well as the social. This interaction was on an unequal basis, however; Mexicans considered themselves culturally (not racially) superior to native peoples, whom they sought to incorporate into the community primarily as laborers. Indians were economically exploited, subjected to cultural domination, and militarily coerced, but they were also regarded as human beings who could become members of the community by the adoption of the language, culture, and the religion of the settlers. . . .

By 1848, the year California became part of the United States, the Mexican population of Alta California had grown to 7,500. The Gold Rush also stimulated a movement of Mexican emigration, composed primarily of gold seekers from the state of Sonora. It is variously estimated that from 7,000 to 15,000 *Sonoreñes* emigrated to California during the Gold Rush, with about half that number remaining permanently in California. The 1850 census showed a Mexican population of 14,150 persons, including 6,454 born within the post–1848 territory of Mexico.

From 1860 to 1900 the level of Mexican emigration remained low, reflecting the declining fortunes of the community and the arrival of Chinese and Japanese immigrants who met the demand for low-paid manual labor. California's total Latin American population in 1900 was probably in excess of 50,000 persons, of whom about 90 percent were of Mexican descent, with probably at least 40 to 50 percent native-born Californians. Contrary to nineteenth-century prophecies of their ultimate disappearance, the Mexican and Latin American population was beginning an upward cycle of increase, which would reach new highs in the 1900s.

MEXICAN CALIFORNIA, 1800–1848

The original presidios, established at San Diego, Santa Barbara, Monterey, and San Francisco, and the pueblos at Los Angeles, San Jose, and Santa Cruz developed into self-sustaining agricultural settlements and embryonic urban centers. Mexican settlers introduced the *zanja* system of irrigation, whereby canals were fed by gravity flow from a dam, as well as the concept of community ownership of riparian rights. With irrigation, both subsistence and commercial agriculture were able to develop as the sustaining economic base of the society; and without water, there could be no urban society. . . .

In 1822 Alta California became part of independent Mexico. The period from 1821 to 1848 was the high point of development of the pastoral Californio variant of Norteño Mexican regional culture. Mexican population growth advanced at a relatively rapid rate of natural increase, and a low but continuing level of Mexican emigration served to maintain cultural continuity and to introduce new fashions in dress, dance, and politics. There was also a limited but continuous movement of individuals and families from neighboring Baja California and Sonora, where most Californios had near relatives.

ALTA CALIFORNIA CULTURE, 1800–1848

The transition from Spanish colony to Mexican territory was also reflected in significant development and changes in popular culture and ideology. The Alta California pobladores and their Californio children possessed rich and vigorous traditions. As the gente de razón were primarily rural country people, the most characteristic expressions of their culture were oral in form. . . .

The oral culture of the Californios was based in the family. Ideally this was an extended patriarchal family, but because of death or internal migration it was more likely to be a somewhat smaller unit at any given time. The family included not only direct relatives but extended to fictive kinship relationships, including godparents and family friends. Kinship, real and fictive, was a fundamental organizing principle of Mexican society which influenced all dimensions of life in Alta California. . . .

Popular culture in Alta California included modes of family conduct; religion, such as *alabados* or religious chants sung each morning by the head of the family and the veneration of the Virgin of Guadalupe and particular saints; popular ideology; the modes, lores, and skills of the ranchero; the traditions and skills of the *labrador* (farmer), including irrigation technology; specific female skills such as embroidery and cookery; and forms of entertainment and recreation, including music, dance, songs, tests of horsemanship, and public entertainment during *fiestas*.

Women possessed their spheres of special knowledge, especially in the popular healing arts. They acted as *curanderas* (herbal curers) or administered *sobadoras* (a type of massage or chiropractic). In their role as healers the most skillful women could recognize and process hundreds of natural herbs. Much of the knowledge associated with curandería was handed down by California Indians to their Mexican descendants. Unfortunately, because of its associations with female power and pagan knowledge, curandería was, of necessity, kept secret from male missionaries and officials who might be antagonistic.

Mexican women enjoyed the legal rights conferred by tradition and law, such as community property (a legally protected interest in property owned jointly or in her husband's own property). Women also had the right to independently own and, if they desired, manage their property. A few ran their own ranchos and almost all were excellent horsewomen. Interestingly, contemporary Anglo American women, viewed as legal minors, lacked these rights and were considered economic wards of their husbands, fathers, or court-appointed guardians.

After Mexican independence, Alta California society entered a dynamic period of change. The transition from Spanish domination to Mexican independence introduced innovations in popular culture and ideology. Most dramatically, independence resulted in a revolutionary change in the participation of large numbers of people in the political process and other public events. Unlike the colonial period, the gente [people] no longer viewed themselves merely as subjects of the Spanish Crown, but rather as participating *ciudadanos* (citizens). If political life was mainly the province of a growing elite, that was equally true of the other new American republics, including the United States.

THE TRANSITIONAL PERIOD, 1848–1880

The period from 1848 to 1880 was a difficult time of transition for Mexicans in California. The ultimate political question facing their political leaders was the threat and finally the actuality of invasion, conquest, and annexation by the United States. . . .

. . . In the end, Mexican Californios chose to resist. The Californios rose in arms after the initial occupation of the territory, and numerous battles and skirmishes were fought from Santa Clara in the north to San Pasqual in the south. Their resistance, while massive for the small population of the territory, collapsed under overwhelming United States military power and the defeat of the entire Mexican nation in the war of 1846–1848. . . .

For the majority of the Mexican population, Californios and more recent immigrants alike, the period from 1848 to the 1880s was to signal a turning inward to their own community. There were many exceptions, as Mexicans, whenever possible, sought to exercise the rights guaranteed them as citizens or as immigrants entitled to elementary protection of the law. The Mexican community in cities such as Los Angeles, San Diego, San Francisco, and others, developed new types of institutions, including Spanish language newspapers and mutual aid societies. Unfortunately, even when they addressed the Anglo community through the courts and other institutions, they met an increasingly deaf ear.

Although California's Mexican and other Spanish-speaking population was growing through both natural increase and immigration during the period from the 1850s to the turn of the century, massive Anglo American and European immigration dwarfed the Spanish-speaking population. In Northern California, with the exception of Monterey and a few rural areas, Mexicans and Latin Americans formed ethnic enclaves or *barrios* within predominantly Anglo-European cities, towns, and their surrounding countryside. This phenomenon has been called barrioization by urban historians, which denotes both the negative aspect of segregation and the response of the Mexican community in its rising ethnic consciousness. Also part of the phenomenon has been the development of new types of ethnic and cultural institutions emphasizing Mexican and Latin American identity.

By the 1870s Monterey, Alta California's one-time capital, was eclipsed as the county seat by the new Anglo American town of Salinas. . . .

By 1880 several thousand Mexicans, Chileans, and other Latin Americans formed an enclave or barrio near Broadway between Mason and Taylor Streets in San Francisco.

Mexican vaqueros formed a predominant or substantial part of the workforce on cattle ranches in Central California, and from the 1870s Mexicans and small numbers of other Latin Americans formed small but visible semi-rural barrios in the San Joaquin Valley. These were sometimes known as "Spanishtowns" to local Anglos and visitors and were found in predominantly Anglo towns like Visalia, Stockton, and Bakersfield.

Growing social and political trends in Southern California prior to 1860, which would be significant for the remainder of the century, included initial hostility and passive political resistance of the Mexican elite and general population; a growing accommodation between a sector of the Mexican elite and the new Anglo elite of public officials, attorneys, and merchants; an economic boom resulting from high Gold Rush prices for beef; an increasing Anglo-European settlement; increasing commercialization resulting in land loss for a growing number of rancheros; monopolization of new occupations by skilled Anglo workers; a period of lawlessness from 1854 to 1857 caused by an influx of Anglo-European outlaws, gamblers, and prostitutes; increasing violence between Mexicans and Anglo outlaws prompting vigilantism of Anglo and Mexican elite; and the collapse of the cattle boom and beginning of a period of economic depression.

In Los Angeles, the period from 1850 to 1880 was a time of almost continuous change, tension, and challenge for the Mexican community. In the most general sense, Los Angeles went from being a principally Mexican community dominated by a mixed Mexican-Anglo-European elite to a multicultural community marked by declining Mexican and increasing Anglo-European population and economic and political dominance.

A major increase in population shifted from a Mexican to a slight Anglo-European majority. Of the population of Los Angeles in 1850 more than 75 percent were Mexicans; by 1860 Mexicans formed only about 47 percent of the population. In contrast, the population of Los Angeles County (which then included present Orange, San Bernardino, and Riverside Counties) was to retain a largely Mexican majority population until the late 1860s.

While by 1860 the non-Mexican population had become the majority population in the city, Los Angeles was, in reality, a multi-ethnic community, with about half of the non-English speakers as yet unassimilated European immigrants. Indeed, into the late 1860s, Spanish was the common language of the community and Anglos and Europeans frequently communicated with each other in that language rather than in English, which had yet to become predominant.

Occupational discrimination tended to restrict the Spanish-speaking to menial jobs and further eroded the economic status of native California Mexicans and later Mexican and Spanish-speaking immigrants. As in other California communities, this unequal status also took the form of residential segregation in Los Angeles. By 1870 most urban Mexicans in Los Angeles were concentrated in the segregated area around the original Pueblo de Los Angeles. This area, known in Spanish as "Sonora" and called by Anglos "Sonora Town," became an economically depressed and increasingly blighted ghetto. As jobs became increasingly unstable for the Spanish-speaking population, individuals and families moved back and forth from the city to rural agricultural employment, often on a seasonal basis.

Contrary to past misconceptions, these economic conditions applied to most of the native-born Californios, as well as to more recent immigrants. Once impoverished, few bothered to distinguish the native-born descendants of the rancheros from more recent immigrants when they were engaged in such menial tasks as bailing [sic] hay or washing laundry. With few exceptions, the native-born and more recent immigrants merged into a common community.

THE END OF THE CENTURY, 1880 TO 1900

The period from 1880 to 1900 in many ways marked the low point of Mexican presence in California. The proportion of the Spanish-speaking population of Los Angeles, for example, had shrunk to 19 percent in 1880 and to about 6 percent in 1900. California Mexicans were in the process of rapidly losing the last of their political representation. The few Mexican politicians left at the state level were primarily men who depended upon their long-standing Republican affiliations and now faced a majority Anglo American electorate. With the growth of the Spanish myth they were no longer even called Mexicans, but rather Spanish Americans or Californians. The last of these men included Reginaldo del Valle and Roumaldo [sic] Pacheco, Lieutenant Governor of California, who was called upon in 1875 to serve a one-year term as Governor of the state.

Following Pacheco, a handful of other persons of Mexican descent were to hold positions in the California State Assembly and Senate. But these individuals were heavily assimilated and not representative of a Mexican constituency. The last elected representative of Mexican descent in the state legislature (until the early 1960s) served in 1909.

Deprived of political representation and economic clout and demographically outnumbered, the California Mexican community was largely a matter of indifference to the Anglo majority, except for the continuing manifestations of discrimination. It is important to realize that the Mexican community never lost its interest in the larger Anglo society. At any given time during this period, twenty or more Spanish-language newspapers existed in the major cities and towns of California, most of which reported exclusively on public affairs. Nor did Mexicans cease participation in the political process; they were simply reduced to the role of local ward politicians and their constituents in areas of significant citizen Mexican population. Highly significant was the fact that Mexican emigrants as non-citizens were disenfranchised.

Changes in the economic circumstances, occupational stability, and residence patterns of Spanish-speaking Californians exercised significant influences on their cultural life. As cities, towns, and even rural areas became urbanized or influenced by nearby urbanization, many of the older customs of the pastoral era fell into disuse. By the 1880s there was increasing access to primary education, but this varied greatly according to urban or rural residence and economic status. Most Spanish-speaking children had access at best to a few years of primary instruction, frequently in a segregated "Spanish" or Mexican school or, if urban, in a ghetto or barrio school attended by Latin Americans and European immigrants. Research on literacy appears to indicate that more recent Mexican and Latin American immigrants tended to have a higher literacy level than native Mexican Californios who generally had a more rural heritage and lifestyle.

Despite the increase of Anglo American population to the majority status, opportunities for cultural interaction and English acquisition by Mexicans were significantly limited to the more affluent members of the Latin American community. The families of the urban and rural poor interacted with Anglo Americans primarily in the sphere of work, where socialization was limited. Acquisition of English or partial bilingualism was therefore uneven and would not become predominant even among the native-born until the twentieth century when compulsory school attendance and the growth of the electronic media penetrated Spanish-speaking homes.

Barrioization stimulated a sense of ethnic consciousness expressed as "Mexicanidad." A growing Spanish-language press was both a result and a means of increasing ethnic awareness through a new medium of communication. Urbanization facilitated the emergence of new types of community organizations and institutions which complemented older types of familial-based community interaction. Civic and fraternal organizations were organized in most Spanish-speaking communities in California and other states with large Mexican and Spanish-speaking populations. Significant among these were *mutualistas,* or mutual benefit societies which provided burial insurance, assistance in times of illness, and other self-help services.

Thus California's Mexican and Latin American community prepared to face the new century, a century which would signal not its demise or disappearance but a new period of unparalleled growth. While faced with social and economic adaptation for survival, California's Mexican and Latin American community neither continued to decline nor marked a totally new departure from its origins in the eighteenth and nineteenth centuries.

10

TUCSONENSES AND ANGELENOS

A Socio-Economic Study of Two Mexican-American Barrios, 1860–1880

RICHARD GRISWOLD DEL CASTILLO

Richard Griswold del Castillo is chair of the Chicana and Chicano Studies Department at California State University, San Diego. A native of Los Angeles, Professor Griswold received his Ph.D. in history from the University of California, Los Angeles, in 1974. His field of specialization is Mexican American history in the nineteenth century, although recently he has begun to investigate more contemporary developments. He has published extensively. His publications include *La Familia: Chicano Families in the Urban Southwest, 1848 to the Present* (1984); *César Chávez: A Triumph of Spirit* (1995), co-authored with Richard A. García; and *North to Aztlán: A History of Mexican Americans in the United States* (1996), co-authored with Arnoldo De León.

In 1775 Captain O'Connor, an Irishman in the service of the King of Spain, ordered that the entire garrison of Tubac be moved some 12 miles north to found the royal presidio of San Augustín de Tucson. The next year a company of troops marched north to the site located near the Santa Cruz river next to an already existing Indian pueblo that had been established by Jesuit priests a decade earlier. Five years had passed when another soldier, Captain Fernando de Rivera y Moncado, led a small expedition of soldiers and settlers into the walled presidio at Tucson. He was bound for California under orders to establish a new settlement on the banks of the Rio Porciúncula. After enlisting a few Tucsonenses, he set out across the desert following De Anza's trail. Rivera was fated to die in a revolt of Yuma Indians but the settlers, mostly married men, escaped to help establish the presidio of Nuestra Senora la Reina de Los Angeles de Porciúncula on 4 September 1781.

From *Journal of the West* 18 (January 1979): 58–65. The original text has been modified. Reprinted by permission.

The founding of the settlements of Los Angeles and Tucson, along with the establishment of outposts in Texas and upper California in the 18th century, marked the final northern thrust of Spain's colonial power in the New World. For the next 80 years the centralizing and organizing energies of Spain and Mexico would decline so that Tucson and Los Angeles, along with other scattered outposts along the northern frontier, would share in what Miguel Leon Portilla has called the main themes of the Mexican American West—isolation and insecurity. Isolation, due to the vast wasteland separating these settlements from administrative centers in Mexico, and insecurity, due to the constant threats of Indian attack and foreign invasion.

Accidents of geography gave the settlers of the Los Angeles pueblo relief from Indian depredations. Although not too far to the south and east, Mojave Indians occasionally raided ranchos and killed travelers. But this was as nothing compared to the long and bloody war waged between the Tucson settlers and the Apache, a conflict that took hundreds of lives and lasted well into the late 19th century.

The histories of Tucson and Los Angeles are linked by their common origin in a defensive Spanish imperial policy. Tucson was established to defend the wealthier towns and settlements in northern Mexico against Indian attack just as Los Angeles was part of an effort to defend the Californias from foreign encroachment. Yet the social history of these two pueblos has been very different. The purpose of this study is to examine, in a comparative way, the Mexican populations in these towns after 1850 and to evaluate their development in the American era. In an earlier study, I traced the social, economic, familial, cultural and political history of the Mexican-Americans in Los Angeles during the period 1850–1880. Comparing the data gathered for this project with similar information on the Tucsonenses, I have been able to test generalizations which I made regarding the urban evolution of the Mexican-American people during the first four decades of American domination. The results, I think, emphasize the diversity of the 19th century Hispanic population of the Southwest.

The sources used for this longitudinal comparative study are primarily the manuscript returns of the United States Federal censuses. For Tucson, one of the earliest counts taken in the American era was the territorial census of 1864, followed by the decennial censuses of 1870 and 1880. The 1890 returns for both California and Arizona Territory were destroyed by fire and the 1900 returns are not freely available to researchers. The City of Los Angeles had censuses taken in 1850, 1852, 1860, 1870, [and] 1880. For purposes of convenience and economy, I chose to use the 1860 and 1880 censuses for Los Angeles and compare them with the 1864 and 1880 censuses for Tucson.

The data used for Los Angeles in 1860 and 1880 and that for Tucson in 1864 is a complete listing of the Mexican-American population in those two towns, subject, of course, to a 10 to 15 percent underenumeration error. The 1880 Tucson data is a systematic sample of 1,327 individuals out of a total estimated Mexican-American population of over 3,300. In all cases the criteria for determining membership in the ethnic group was a combination of surname and place of birth. Mixed families, those with a non-Mexican or non-Spanish surnamed mother or father, were counted as part of the Mexican-American group. Although the 1880 Tucson and Los Angeles censuses were comparable, the 1864 Territorial and 1860 Los Angeles censuses were not because there were some categories that were mutually exclusive in each. In addition, the 1880 censuses did not have information on property holdings.

A summary of population statistics for both *barrios* show that, in relation to the nineteenth-century Anglo-American population, the Mexican-Americans of Tucson were always in the majority while the Mexican-Americans of Los Angeles were not.

In 1880 the Tucson Spanish surnamed population was still about two thirds of the total while in Los Angeles they were only about one fifth of the city's population.

Although there are many dimensions of comparison possible, I have chosen to start with systematic differences in the socio-economic development of the two *barrios*, since changes in this sector most certainly influenced changes in other areas of community life. The two most commonly agreed upon indices of socio-economic status are occupation and wealth. In both these areas there were progressively widening differences between the Tucson and Los Angeles Spanish-speaking populations.

Mexican-Americans in Los Angeles enjoyed a greater diversity of jobs than in Tucson. The census-taker listed Angelenos employed in 86 different jobs in 1860 while Tucsonenses were listed in only 47. In Los Angeles, laborers were in the majority, constituting 62 percent of the total work force while in Tucson only 42 percent worked as laborers . . . The types of jobs listed in both *barrios* were, of course, indicative of the different economics of the regions. The occupational structure may also be viewed as the degree of colonization experienced by Mexican-Americans in these two areas. Tucson, where the Anglo population was much more of [a] minority in the 1860s, seemed to offer Mexican-Americans more of a chance of independent or unsupervised work. There were no servants listed for Tucson in 1864, but it was the second most common occupation listed for Mexican-Americans in Los Angeles. In Tucson the occupations of farmer, teamster, miner and merchant were important ones, comprising almost 45 percent of the Mexican-American force. These were jobs which required a minimum of employer supervision and indeed were probably self-employed. In contrast, the most common occupations listed for the Spanish-speaking in Los Angeles after that of laborer were minor in importance in terms of the work force, accounting for less than 18 percent of all those employed. Of this number only shopkeepers, miners and saddlers probably had a degree of job autonomy and these occupations were less than 8 percent of the total work force.

A breakdown of occupations grouped in larger categories only emphasizes the differences in occupational structure between the two *barrios* in the 1860s. In terms of both the total population and the work force the Tucsonenses had a more favorable occupational outlook and most probably a higher standard of living. In Tucson about 36 percent of the work force earned their living in "white collar" occupations while in Los Angeles only 13 percent of the work force was in that category. With the notable exception of ranching and farming occupations, the two *barrios* were about equal in terms of the numbers in high status jobs (professional and mercantile occupations), but owing to the different sizes of the populations, the economic impact of those in non-manual jobs was more pronounced in Tucson than in Los Angeles.

There were more than twice as many farmers and ranchers in Tucson as in Los Angeles during the 1860s, and this alone accounts for much of the variation in occupational structure. More than one quarter of employed Tucsonenses worked their own farms and ranches while this was true for only 8 percent of Angelenos. This difference in occupational stratification is, of course, a comment on the differential impact of Anglo-American immigration, squatterism, laws and taxes. It is one indication that, by 1864, the farmers and ranchers had not yet experienced a decline in rural land tenure but this was definitely the case in Los Angeles.

This hypothesis as to the better socio-economic position of Tucson's *barrio,* at least in terms of occupations, can be further tested by turning to the 1880s to see if these patterns were long term and indeed they were, as twenty years later the general differences remained. Los Angeles continued to offer a greater diversity of employment (95 occupations listed versus 64 for Tucson) and Tucson's Mexican-American population continued to be better represented in non-laboring jobs, although for both groups unskilled laborers remained the majority. Comparing the 1860–1864 data with the 1880 shows that the Tucsonenses' occupational participation in professional and mercantile callings was still higher than that of the Angelenos. By 1880 about 26 percent of the work force in Tucson's *barrio* could be classified as "white collar" and 23 percent of the Los Angeles *barrio* work force was in this category. The difference of change between 1860 and 1880 indicates that the Tucsonenses were improving their lot in these "white collar" occupations faster than the Angelenos. Tucson's proportion of mercantile and professional workers increased by 15 percent while the Angelenos increased their representation in the same categories by only 6 percent.

On the other hand, the Californio landholders, while declining in wealth and acreage, did not decline as fast as did the Tucsonenses. From 27 percent of those employed in 1864, Tucson's ranchers and farmers almost disappeared by 1880, with only 4.5 percent of all occupations in that year. The decline of farmers among Tucson's Spanish-speaking was probably more evidence of a voluntary shift of occupational structure than of increased Anglo-American pressure. As will be explained later, Indian warfare forced many to abandon outlying ranches during the intervening 20 years. At the same time the Californios, ranchers and farmers who experienced other kinds of difficulties, mainly drought and depression, managed to hold their own, actually increasing to 11 percent of those employed.

In terms of the five most common occupations, already analyzed for 1860–1864, a large portion of the Tucson Mexican-Americans continued to work in semi-independent jobs and the Angelenos continued in more dependent ones. Relative to the total work force, almost twice as many men in Los Angeles were classified as laborers, but owing to the increased specialization of laboring occupations in Tucson the total proportion of unskilled workers was almost equal.

This analysis of occupational distributions in the two pueblos indicates that the Spanish-speaking were better off, at least in terms of probable job mobility, in Tucson than in Los Angeles. It further implies that the Tucsonenses were more successful in adjusting their traditional job skills to the technological and commercial changes wrought by the Anglo-American conquest.

Another index that shows the higher standard of living for the Spanish-speaking of Tucson in comparison to Los Angeles is the differences in the dependency ratios for both towns. This ratio of persons employed to non-working population to provide a source of income for women, children and aged family members [sic]. Conversely, the lower the ratio, the greater the number of individuals dependent on working men's pay checks. In Tucson, the ratio of employed to non-employed dropped slightly between 1864 and 1880, from 46 per 100 to 45.6 per 100. During the same period Los Angeles' dependency ratio for the Spanish-speaking population dropped even more—from 42.1 per 100 to 34.2 per 100. This meant that, during the 20-year period, more and more Angelenos were becoming dependent on employed persons.

This comparison of the dependency ratio depends for its validity on the relative wages paid workers and the distribution of income and wealth in both communities. Lockwood reported that Charles D. Poston's Sonora Mining and Exploring Company paid between 50 and 75 cents a day plus rations for miners during the 1860s. A comparable laborer's wage in Los Angeles for the same period was between one and two dollars. A chronic shortage of currency in Tucson accounts for much of this difference. During the 60s Tucsonenses used *boletas* or scrip money and engaged in barter and trade in kind. Detailed data [on] wages and the cost of living for both cities is hard to find, but it appears that although wages were higher in Los Angeles than in Tucson, laborers in the latter town probably had a comparable standard of living.

There are some difficulties in making generalizations about wealth based on property-holding data in the censuses. Besides a probable under enumeration factor referred to earlier, the respondents may have made errors in reporting the value of their personal and real property. This was probably more true for the Spanish-speaking than for Anglo-Americans, since the former had reason to distrust federal officials and suspect that the census was a pretext for further taxation. Another variable making the property data hard to analyze is the fact that land was worth more in Los Angeles than in Tucson. The average value of a parcel of land in Los Angeles was 1,228 dollars in 1860 while in Tucson the average was only slightly more than 176 dollars. Owing to differences in climate, population and location, dollar for dollar a settler could buy more acreage in Tucson than in Los Angeles. Hence, it is dangerous to make assumptions about the comparative size of parcels in both *barrios* based on stated values in the census.

An analysis of the distribution of real and personal property among the Tucsonenses and Angelenos adds more evidence to support the hypothesis that the Tucson Spanish-speaking had a better standard of living. Table 4 [omitted] clearly indicates that, while the absolute numbers of property holders were comparable (164 for Tucson and 154 for Los Angeles), differences in the size of the population and work force along with the differences in the distribution of wealth gave the Tucson population the edge in socio-economic well being.

Relative to the total population, comparatively more Tucsonenses were property-holders than Angelenos. Fourteen percent of the Spanish-speaking held parcels in Tucson while only 8 percent were land owners in Los Angeles. Using the *barrio* work force as a base, almost twice as many of Tucson's employed were property owners as in Los Angeles. The distribution of property conformed to an inverted pyramid pattern for Tucson, with many more modest holdings than wealthy ones. In Los Angeles the distribution was skewed towards the upper economic levels; more than half of all property-holders had land worth more than 500 dollars. Less than 5 percent of all Tucson's population was in this affluent class. This meant that the landed aristocracy counted for less of the wealth of the community than in Los Angeles where the Californio *hacendados* held clear sway.

An analysis of the distribution of personal property—holdings including cash, furniture, horses and livestock and other moveables—shows the same tendency: there was a more equitable distribution of this kind of property in Tucson than in Los Angeles. In terms of the employed population, a very large number, more than 88 percent of the employed Tucsonenses, held personal property while this was true for only about 60 percent of the Angelenos.

All this is not to say that Tucson's Spanish-speaking did not have their share of economic difficulties which made life less than comfortable. Indian raids, prior to the Mexican war, had devastated the cattle herds and forced many *hacendados* to abandon their lands and seek protection behind the walls of the pueblo. The intensification of Apache wars in the 1860s and 1870s kept the Tucsonenses from expanding their agriculture and from stock-raising. Captain John G. Bourke, who served in Arizona and New Mexico from 1869 to 1875, reported that travel on the main roads into and out of the pueblo was suspended between sunset and daybreak, and at night, packs of dogs were set loose to roam the streets. The residents of Tucson and outlying farms posted sentries every night and farmed only during the day with cocked revolvers on their hips and loaded rifles slung over their shoulders. Pete Kitchen, a colorful character of old Tucson, once remarked that if the victims of the Indian massacres of this period were laid side by side, their bodies would have stretched from Nogales to Tucson.

By 1880 the Indian wars were drawing to a close and the Federal government withdrew many of its troops from nearby Camp Lowell, which had served as a depot for military supplies bound for the Gila River. For decades, since the end of the Mexican War, the merchants, freighters, stock raisers and farmers, both Anglo and Mexican, had depended on the military trade for their livelihood. Their departure, along with the arrival of the railroad in 1880, threw many out of work and by 1883 Tucson entered a depression.

Still, in comparison to the sister *barrio* of Los Angeles, Tucson's economic environment appears to have offered more promise to the Spanish-speaking. There are several general explanations for this. The Civil War and Indian depredations forced Anglo-Americans in southern Arizona to postpone their ambitions for economic and social dominance. During times of danger, they cooperated with their Mexican neighbors. Joint mercantile ventures, such as the one formed by Estevan Ochoa and Frank Tully, along with many instances of mutual political support were common till the 1880s. Tucson was much more a Mexican village than Los Angeles, by the 1860s. Throughout the period studied, the Tucsonenses remained the numerical majority increased by immigration from Sonora and in this environment the Anglo-

American population became Mexicanized. Bourke reported that in 1873, the official language of commerce and politics was Spanish and that frequent Mexican *teatro* performances were well attended by both groups. Contrasted to the Mexican *barrio* of Los Angeles, Tucson was a quiet town with a slow pace of mercantile and commercial development. Traditional patterns of culture, laid down in the Spanish and Mexican eras, were more enduring.

The conclusions of this study emphasize the heterogeneous characteristics of the urban development of the nineteenth-century Mexican-Americans—a population that, in the popular imagination, appears to be a fairly recent addition to the urban scene. But the town-dwelling Hispano has a long history stretching from Spanish colonial times to the present. Another implication is that the economic decline of the Mexican in the Southwest followed a different time-table outside of California. This has been observed by other historians, but has never been substantiated in great detail.

In terms of the larger discussion of the creation of dependent relationships in the Southwest, it is important to note that the timing and causation of the Mexican-American decline varied according to locale. In California, due to the gold-rush migrations, the Mexican-Americans were quickly relegated to a minority status. This was less true in Arizona, where the slow pace of population growth moderated the clash of cultures. While racial discrimination and prejudice may have underlain Anglo-Mexican relations in the 19th century Southwest, variations in geographic, economic and historical conditions seem to have produced qualitatively different social relations, as the examples of Tucson and Los Angeles *barrios* seem to suggest.

11

MEXICAN AMERICAN CATHOLICISM IN THE SOUTHWEST
The Transformation of a Popular Religion

ALBERTO L. PULIDO

Alberto López Pulido was born in East Los Angeles in 1959. He is currently Associate Professor of American Studies at Arizona State University West and is a Research Associate with the Hispanic Research Center. He teaches courses in American studies, Chicano/a studies, and religious studies. Professor Pulido's current research focuses on the relationship between religion and ethnicity in the Americas. He is particularly interested in understanding how people construct and create cultural and sacred expressions through the telling of their own stories, and the stories that are told about them. This is the focus of his forthcoming book, *The Sacred World of the Penitentes: Religious Memory and Storytelling in New Mexico* (Smithsonian Institution Press).

INTRODUCTION

. . . Past research by the author has established that religious symbols, beliefs and practices, and, in a larger sense, the interpretation of what is considered sacred, emerge out of specific racial/ethnic traditions. These traditions represent the source of intergroup conflict, as diverse groups mobilize to control symbolic resources, and mold "official" religious symbols, representative of religious institutions.

The purpose of this research is to trace the history of such conflict between Mexican American Catholics and the dominant Catholic hierarchy, and to assess its

From *Perspectives in Mexican American Studies* 4 (1993): 93–108. *Perspectives* is published by the Mexican American Studies and Research Center at the University of Arizona. The original text has been modified. Reprinted by permission.

impact on Mexican American religiosity in the American Southwest. It is assumed that Mexican American Catholicism is molded and structured by history, and is best understood through an interpretive historical sociological analysis. Mexican American religious symbolism, it is argued, is best described as "non-official" or "popular" religiosity that originated from within the laity, separate from the hierarchy of the Roman Catholic Church, and remains outside the structures of institutional Catholicism. The marginalization of this religious form has been accentuated ever since the United States' occupation of the Southwest and the formal establishment of the American Catholic Church. In sum, the marginalization of Mexican American Catholicism in contemporary society is the outcome of historical processes and relationships. . . .

TRANSFORMATION OF MEXICAN CATHOLICISM

The end of the Mexican-American War in 1848 brought with it major changes to Mexican Catholicism in what had been Mexico's northern frontier. Prior to the war, Mexican Catholicism was preserved by a popular and informal base, and reproduced without the imprint of the official Catholic hierarchy. For example, as early as the 18th century, *Los Hermanos Penitentes* (Confraternity of Our Father, Jesus the Nazarene) were vital for the maintenance of community unity in Northern New Mexico. They flourished in the early 19th century as a result of spiritual neglect by Catholic clergy. As a mutual-aid society, they functioned as a civil and ecclesiastical organization, leading the community in prayer, worship, and catechism. At the same time, they made sure everyone had the basics for a decent quality of life through collective irrigation and the harvesting of the lands. *La Hermandad* included an official *rezador* (prayer leader), and *cantor,* who led in song and public prayer at rosaries and wakes. They spiritually consoled and offered material aid for the dying and their families. This form of popular religion expressed the lifestyle, beliefs, and values that were interwoven with Mexican culture throughout the northern frontier. It was largely created in a Catholic atmosphere that lacked the presence of a religious clergy.

With the establishment of the American Catholic Church after 1848, this type of "self-reliant" religion was transformed from a popular to a marginal and deviant religious tradition, because ecclesiastical authority was now controlled and structured by a new European clergy. Whereas Mexican religiosity and the Spanish language were once considered normative dimensions of Catholicism along the northern frontier, they were now replaced by new languages and traditions in the new American Southwest. Traditional Mexican *peregrinaciones* (pilgrimages) and special religious days were forgotten or terminated and replaced with French, and later, Irish canons of institutional Catholicism. This new official Catholicism, imported by a foreign clergy, disrupted a "way of life" in Mexican communities at both civil and religious levels throughout the Southwest. . . .

TEXAS

The French clergy was instrumental in restructuring the Catholic Church in South Texas. After the official signing of the Treaty of Velasco, declaring Texas independent from Mexico, the Republic of Texas was established in August of 1836. To determine if the ecclesiastical administration should remain in the hands of the Mexicans, the Prefect of the Sacred Congregation of Cardinals de Propaganda Fide empowered Bishop Antonio Blanc of New Orleans to send delegates to inspect Texas in January of 1838. Father John Timon, rector and president of St. Mary of the Barrens College, along with a Spanish priest, were ordered on March 30 to go to Texas on a special ecclesiastical visit.

Having visited only two Texas municipalities, Timon received word from San Antonian representatives (an area he had been dissuaded to visit) that religious instruction had been absent from their city for years. These representatives signed sworn affidavits about the laxity and religious neglect of Fathers Refugio de la Garza and José Antonio Valdez, priests at the Church of San Fernando. It was stated that these two prelates did not hear confessions, did not distribute communion, and did not attend to the dying. Timon referred to them as "two plagues who were destroying the region with their scandalous behavior," even though he had never met them.

On July 18, 1840, the Republic of Texas was granted official recognition by the Vatican. Rome designated it a prefecture of the New Orleans diocese, with Father John Timon as its Prefect Apostolic of Texas. Bestowed with the power to act as bishop, he appointed Father Jean Marie Odin from New Orleans as his Vice-Prefect Apostolic. Soon after arriving in San Antonio in July of 1840, Odin decided to exercise his newly acquired power. On August 6, 1840, Odin's first official act as Vice-Prefect Apostolic was to remove de la Garza as pastor of San Fernando. Four days later he defrocked José Antonio Valdez.

The arrival of a European clergy in South Texas began to transform the "normative" religious structures as perceived by the Mexican/Mexican American community. Certain Oblate priests assigned to the Texas valley harbored strong anti-Mexican sentiments that typified ethnocentric and racist views of the time. Father Florent Vandenberghe, a Frenchman who became Superior of the Oblate priests in 1874, for example, felt repugnance towards his new assignment. He would have preferred to receive a mission "amongst civilized people" in Northern Texas, or in Louisiana if the opportunity arose. A more blatant hatred was expressed by Dominic Manucy, a clergyman of Italian and Spanish descent who, in 1874, was named Apostolic Vicar of Brownsville, Texas. Manucy made the following comment regarding his recent appointment:

> I consider this appointment of Apostolic Vicar of Brownsville the worst sentence that could be given me for any crime. . . . In the Brownsville district . . . the Catholics are exclusively greaser-Mexican-hunters and thieves. You cannot obtain money from these people, not even to bury their parents. . . .

Mantucy's perception of the "cheap" Mexican would remain with him throughout his tenure in the Valley of Texas and served to rationalize the new "judgement" rendered upon Mexican Catholics by the French hierarchy.

Yet, as the institution sought to control and eventually routinize the sacred, the Mexican American community embraced a religiosity interlaced with their everyday life. Hence, popular religion played an important role in sustaining Mexican Catholics in South Texas, functioning as a strategy to cope with a foreign hierarchy that sought to discredit their religious world-view. It gave Mexicans a nominal allegiance to the new American Catholicism, and simultaneously provided them with the " . . . psychic margin to circumvent the proscriptions of institutional Catholicism." Furthermore, popular religion provided a sense of order and stability in an otherwise chaotic and senseless world. It also gave a voice to a unique type of Catholicism, set apart from the controls of the Catholic hierarchy. . . .

In summary, the Mexican religious experience in South Texas is characterized by beliefs and practices that were maintained and survived outside the institutional Catholic context. The Mexican Catholic laity constructed places for prayer close to the community. The use of *altarcitos* (religious altars), and home devotions were common practices to keep the spirit of religion alive among a community without a clergy. It was the job of parents and grandparents to inculcate and provide religious instruction to their children and grandchildren. José Roberto Juárez provides an interesting example of a self-described hierophant who guided the Mexican community in Sunday prayer, and presided in funeral services during the 1830s in Nacogdoches. On *días de fiesta,* this individual draped himself in an alb and chasuble and recreated his version of the mass in neighborhood *jacales* (modest homes).

It is important to underscore that the relationship between the French clergy and the Mexican laity was not always antagonistic. There exist historical examples of the clergy's support of Mexican religious practices in Texas. However, history reveals that the French hierarchy made no attempt to understand and build its institution on the traditions initiated by Mexican Catholicism in Texas. As the new institution of American Catholicism began to unfold in the American Southwest, Mexican Catholics found their "community of memory" ignored, and absent from the institutional vision of the American Catholic Church.

NEW MEXICO

The history of Mexican Catholicism in New Mexico is one of an ethnic community which is deeply rooted in its Indo-Hispano-Mexican religious traditions. As discussed above, religious traditions such as those of Los Hermanos Penitentes firmly established their roots in Northern New Mexico. However, unlike the *Tejanos,* New Mexicans had adopted a strong religious identity and received dynamic leadership from a native clergy that included Padre Antonio José Martínez and Padre Mariano de Jesús Lucero. But with the arrival of French clergy after the Mexican-American War, New Mexican Catholics found themselves challenged and confronted by an insensitive, ethnocentric clergy led by Jean Baptiste Lamy.

On July 19, 1850, the Holy See of the Roman Catholic Church acted favorably on a request from the VII Council of Baltimore, and established the New Mexico Territory, which included present-day Arizona and Southern Colorado as a vicariate. Jean Baptiste Lamy, a recently ordained priest from France, was named Vicar Apostolic "*in partibus infidelium*" ("in the region of the infidels"), and sent from the Ohio Valley to take over the Santa Fe diocese. Within a short period, conflict erupted between Lamy and the native clergy. By the end of the conflict, five native priests were expelled by Lamy, the most famous being Padre Antonio José Martínez of Taos.

Padre Martínez is a major figure in New Mexican history. He was the scholastic father for native clergy, and highly influential among the citizenry of Taos. His life encompassed three distinct epochs of Mexican history. He was born on January 17, 1793, in Abiquiu when New Mexican property was under the control of the Spanish Crown. In 1822, Antonio Martínez was ordained a priest, one year after Mexican independence. The ideals of liberation offered by Mexico's first revolutionary hero, Padre José Miguel Hidalgo y Costilla, deeply influenced the life of Padre Martínez and his views on civil and ecclesiastical authority.

In 1826, Padre Martínez was assigned the pastorship of Nuestra Señora de Guadalupe in Taos, New Mexico. Soon after, he created schools for children at the Indian pueblos, and the nearby Hispano villages. By 1834, Padre Martínez had established a "preparatory seminary" out of which 16 native priests were ordained. In 1835, he began to publish books and newspapers with the first manual press (*imprentia manualita*) west of the Mississippi. In 1846, Padre Martínez, now 53, experienced the cession of New Mexico to the United States. Conflict between the native priest and the new French bishop ensued, and the accomplishments of Padre Martínez were soon forgotten.

On January 1, 1853, Bishop Lamy wrote his first pastoral letter to the laity. It introduced new rules for re-instituting tithing, something banned in Mexico by the Law of San Felipe in 1833. Lamy ordered sanctions for those who did not comply. The pastoral letter stated:

> . . . if anyone persisted in ignoring the obligation he would "with great pain and regret" deny him the sacraments and such a person would be considered outside the fold.

From Lamy's perspective, a good flock was one that remained " . . . devoted to right order and legitimate authority," and hence, the mark of a "successful" church was one that adopted the official practice of tithing.

However, for Padre Martínez, tithing was considered a burden for the laity. He had consistently opposed inflexible taxation because of the burden it placed on the poor. As a young priest, he was at the forefront of abolishing church tithing imposed by Mexican civil law in 1833. In a local newspaper, Padre Martinez expressed his opposition to Lamy's recently imposed sanctions. For Bishop Lamy, Martínez's actions were interpreted as a boycott to force him out of the diocese.

Lamy retaliated with a more severe church policy. In a second pastoral letter issued on January 14, 1854, Bishop Lamy incorporated church dogma on the Im-

maculate Conception to underscore the importance of tithes and the consequences
for those who failed to comply:

> Any family which does not fulfill the fifth precept of the Church (to support the
> church materially) will not have the right to receive the holy sacraments. Let us
> again inform you that we consider those as not belonging to the Church who do
> not observe this precept; and we like-wise would take away all faculties to say
> Mass and administer the sacraments from all pastors who fail to sustain and pro-
> vide for the maintenance of religion and its ministers. . . .

Church fees related to services provided by the church were as follows: marriages, eight dollars; burials, six dollars; burial of a child under seven years of age,
two dollars; and baptisms, one dollar. The bishop did allow for "those of meager
resources" to pay only one-half of these fees. Such church fees were a major burden
for a community dependent on a barter economy. A wage economy did not exist in
the area until the 1870s, when the railroad arrived in Southern Colorado.

On May 5, 1856, a Basque priest by the name of Damasio Taladrid was named
to replace Padre Martínez, who had written to Lamy indicating his desire to retire.
Unfortunately, the relationship between Talidrid and Martínez proved confronta-
tional. On July 23, 1856, Taladrid reported to Lamy that Padre Martínez was working on an article for the *Gaceta,* a local newspaper, and was often seen together with
his friend Padre Lucero of Arroyo Hondo. When an article calling for the abolition
of tithes appeared in the *Gaceta* on September 3, Padre Lucero was suspended by
Bishop Lamy on the grounds that he had close associations with Martínez.

On October 23, Taladrid informed Bishop Lamy that Martínez was celebrating
Mass in his private oratory, and was taking over some parish functions. The following day Lamy suspended Padre Martínez. Lamy deprived him of canonical faculties
because Martínez had celebrated Mass in the oratory. His suspension would remain
in effect until he retracted his article from the *Gaceta.*

As a person who had studied canon and civil law extensively, Martínez protested these actions. On November 12, 1856, he wrote to Lamy, arguing at length
that his suspension was null and void as prescribed by canon law. He stated that his
publication of letters on the matter of tithes were protected by guarantees of "republican free speech." He stated:

> I beg your excellency to respect my viewpoint for what I am about to say. . . . The
> diocesan statutes invite the faithful to enter into mercantile agreements making
> the parish priests appear like hucksters or traders. They also make the sacraments,
> Masses, and other spiritual gifts as so much merchandise in a warehouse by order
> of Your Excellency. . . . Compare this way of acting with the account of Simon
> Magus in the Acts of the Apostles. . . .

This, plus five additional pleas, were ignored by Lamy. In June of 1857 formal
excommunication procedures against Padre Martínez were set in motion. A native
Mexican priest, Eulogio Ortiz was sent to Taos to replace Taladrid. Within five
months, Padre Antonio José Martínez was formally excommunicated by the Santa
Fe diocese.

The salient issue in the Lamy-Martínez conflict revolves around differences in religious expression and interpretation. History reveals that Lamy was prejudiced and biased against New Mexican Catholicism prior to setting foot on New Mexican soil. In 1851, en route to New Mexico from Ohio, Lamy traveled by way of New Orleans and Galveston. French bishop Jean Marie Odin, head of the Galveston Vicariate, did not hesitate to offer his interpretation of the native people and clergy of New Mexico.

He warned Lamy that it would be a mistake to go to Santa Fe without the support of six to a dozen zealous and entirely devoted newly imported priests. According to Odin, Lamy would encounter

> . . . scandalous native clergy, and a public, especially among the Anglo Americans, who were waiting for reforms with the arrival of the new bishop. What could Lamy do alone and without support? If he should have occasion to banish a recalcitrant priest, without having someone to replace him, might not the people protest and perhaps insist on keeping the excommunicated priest in defiance of their bishop?

Bishop Odin continued to counsel Lamy, advising him to go immediately to France, instead of New Mexico, and recruit a number of priests. While in France, he could better prepare himself in the Spanish language, and procure new vestments to replace the old rubbish he would encounter in all the New Mexican churches.

Even though Lamy proceeded with his travel west, it is clear that Odin biased Lamy, who had not set eyes on the people of New Mexico. Recall that Odin's first assignment as Vice-Prefect Apostolic of Texas was to remove the two remaining Mexican priests. By 1868, Lamy boasted in letters back to his home province of Auvergne, that he had created a "little Auvergne" in New Mexico. By this date, Lamy's two assistants and three fourths of his priests were natives of Auvergne.

As an area with deeply rooted religious traditions, New Mexico presents a history of conflict between a native and foreign clergy that adversely affected the native people of New Mexico. Unlike Texas, New Mexico had a firmly established religious community with leaders who challenged and confronted the new religious system imposed upon them by a European clergy. However, like their Texan counterparts, Mexican Catholics in New Mexico found themselves marginalized and segmented from the new American Church. The Penitentes, for example, maintained the stronghold of traditional Mexican Catholicism in Northern New Mexico during the 19th century. As one who clearly disapproved of Penitente religious practices, Lamy sought to control and redefine their traditions. Lamy instituted the practice of verification before administering the sacraments in order to stop Penitentes from receiving communion unless they renounced their membership in the brotherhood. La Hermandad was driven into a position of protest and self-defense that profoundly affected their collective expressions as a civil and ecclesiastical organization.

ANALYSIS

The transformation of Mexican American Catholicism in the American Southwest is best understood from a historical and sociological perspective that is sensitive to the popular, non-official elements of Mexican American religiosity. What emerges is a self-reliant religious tradition, representative of an integrative world-view of a specific ethnic group, which, with the incorporation of the American Southwest, comes into conflict with a "legitimate," and ethnically distinct clergy. Mexican American Catholics become unorthodox Catholics, " . . . uninstructed in the faith and deficient in their adherence to the general norms of church practices," transforming their religion from a popular to a marginal tradition. Accordingly, a historical analysis establishes the patterns and structures of Mexican American Catholicism by which its sociological significance can be interpreted.

For example, the transformation of Mexican Catholicism in the history of the American Southwest helps address the "problems" of leadership formation and collective action in the Mexican American community. The change, from a popular to a marginal belief system, has brought forth a group of believers who have few, if any, leadership roles within the American Catholic Church. For the most part, they have remained inactive within the formal structures of the institution because of the neglect and misunderstanding of the hierarchy. Whereas other disenfranchised groups like African Americans have developed social movements and leaders through their religious structures and traditions, Mexican American Catholics have been discouraged from taking an active leadership role in the church and community. In fact, there are numerous examples in the history of the Chicano Movement where the American Catholic hierarchy has been diametrically opposed to collective action for economic and political change in the Mexican American community. Consider that the Roman Catholic hierarchy did not collectively support Cesar Chávez and the United Farm Workers until eight years into the movement. This despite the fact that official Roman Catholic teachings in the *Rerum Novarum* supported a worker's right to unionize in the 19th century. In 1973, the National Conference of Catholic Bishops presented a farm labor resolution stating their support for free and secret ballot elections.

On the other hand, what becomes very apparent in examining the history of Mexican and Mexican American religiosity in the Southwest are the collective forces at work in its popular, non-official beliefs and practices. Mexican American popular religion emerges out of an economic, political, linguistic, and cultural reality that is representative of the everyday life experiences of a people. Hence, in the history of Mexican Americans, popular religion has functioned to establish and provide community, and create collective action as people coalesce around religious symbols that possess no institutional imprint. Throughout history, the American Catholic hierarchy has not recognized this important contribution.

From a methodological standpoint, more historical research is needed to capture the informal structure provided by popular religion utilized by Mexican Americans and other disenfranchised groups in the United States. The religious symbols, beliefs and practices used by powerless communities to mobilize change need to be documented. Additional research, for example, on the histories of the Black church, ghost dance religions, and popular religious expressions in the United Farm Workers movement, is needed to identify the empowering elements of religion for these groups. Yet such an approach cannot rely solely on secondary documents. Rather, it requires a methodological approach that will incorporate primary historical documents and oral histories in order to discover the actual experiences of Mexican and Mexican American religiosity. Feminist scholarship, for example, has enhanced our understanding of the Latina religious experience from this perspective. Since Mexican religiosity originated outside the canons of Roman Catholicism, one need not begin an analysis from a structural perspective, but instead, from the everyday life experiences of the community. This will help us rediscover and validate the Mexican American religious experience.

12

CARLOS I. VELASCO AND THE DEFENSE OF MEXICAN RIGHTS IN TERRITORIAL ARIZONA

MANUEL G. GONZALES

Manuel G. Gonzales received his Ph.D. in history from the University of California at Santa Barbara in 1972. He is an instructor at Diablo Valley College in Pleasant Hill, California, where he has been teaching courses in American and European history since 1971. He has also taught in both the University of California and the California State University systems. Born in Fresno, California, and raised in the San Joaquin Valley, Dr. Gonzales and his family spend much of their time in northern Italy. His publications include *Andrea Costa and the Rise of Socialism in the Romagna* (1980), *The Hispanic Elite of the Southwest* (1989), and *Mexicanos: A History of Mexicans in the United States* (1999).

When the United States acquired the Southwest as a result of the Mexican-American War, it also gained some 80,000 *mexicanos*. As is common knowledge, this population was greatly augmented after the beginning of the 20th century, when Mexicans entered the United States in large numbers, driven from their country by the revolution and attracted to the Southwest by the rapid growth of the regional economy. Unfortunately, historians have left us with the impression that between 1848, when the Mexican War ended, and 1910, when the Great Migration was initiated, little movement occurred between Mexico and its northern neighbor, save for a few miners entering California early in the period. Such was not the case. Mexicans moved north in significant numbers in the late 19th century, and some of them left a lasting mark on their new homeland. This was true of Carlos I. Velasco, an immigrant who was to become one of Arizona's leading citizens by the turn of the century.

From Manuel G. Gonzales, "Carlos I. Velasco," *Journal of Arizona History* 25 (Autumn 1984): 265–84. The original text—including the title—has been modified. Reprinted by permission.

In 1894 Velasco founded the *Alianza Hispano-Americana* in Tucson. This mutual aid society represents the first Mexican-American association able to organize effectively throughout the Southwest. Despite the lofty significance attributed to the *Alianza,* little is known about its founder. For example, in the most complete study of the association, "Alianza Hispano-Americana, 1894–1965: A Mexican American Fraternal Insurance Society," only one paragraph is devoted to Velasco. The man, and his ideas, merit further examination.

The Velascos were among the most prominent families in Sonora during the mid–19th century. Don Jose Francisco Velasco, the father, apparently had few financial worries and dedicated his life to public service. He was the first mayor of Hermosillo and subsequently held many other positions of responsibility, among them the offices of secretary to the governor of Sonora and deputy to the federal Congress. . . .

The Velasco family made its home in Hermosillo (then called Pitic), which is where Carlos Ignacio Velasco first saw the light of day on June 30, 1837. Born into a society of privilege, young Carlos received the best education available in the struggling frontier town. When the time came to choose a profession, upon the completion of his secondary schooling, he opted for law, as had his father and his older brother Francisco . . . Carlos did not disappoint his family's expectations. Upon graduating from law school in Hermosillo, he set up his own practice. Thereafter, his career advanced spectacularly: in 1857 he was appointed superior court judge for the district of Altar and two years later he was elected to the Sonora legislature representing the district of Arizpe. His star rising, young Velasco looked forward to a long and rewarding life in his native state.

In fact, the future lay not in Sonora, but across the border, in the Territory of Arizona, which is where we find Carlos Velasco in 1865. How is it that this most unlikely of candidates wound up an immigrant in the United States?

The answer is to be found in Mexico's turbulent history during these years. After achieving independence in 1821, the unhappy Mexican Republic underwent a series of revolutions as Conservatives and Liberals struggled to acquire and maintain power. The miseries created by civil war were compounded by two other traumatic events: the war with the United States and the French Intervention of 1862–67. The resulting political instability and economic destruction continued unabated until the establishment of the Porfirio Diaz regime (the *Porfiriato*) after 1876.

The situation in the state of Sonora mirrored that in the rest of Mexico: there too political and economic chaos reigned. Sometimes these conditions were the consequence of national issues; at other times (and usually the case) the questions were local in scope. In any event, civil strife was endemic in Sonora by mid-century, when the competing factions were those championed by the *caudillos* Manuel María Gándara (1801–1878), a Conservative, and Ignacio Pesqueira (1820–1886), a Liberal.

Carlos Velasco, in keeping with his liberal principles, backed Pesqueira, although his older brother Francisco had served under Gándara. When the *pesqueiristas* triumphed over their opponents in the mid–1850s, he was rewarded handsomely. . . .

During the French invasion of Mexico, Gándara, hoping to regain power in Sonora, aligned himself with the imperial cause. Once again local conditions deteriorated. In early 1865 the *gandaristas* and their French allies succeeded in inflicting a crushing defeat on Pesqueira, forcing the general and "a small group of faithful followers" to flee north into the United States. They found sanctuary in Tubac, a village about fifty miles south of Tucson. Velasco was probably among these emigres; it was in this year that he first came to Arizona.

Pesqueira returned to Sonora a year later, and when his opposition was routed shortly thereafter he became the *jefe político* of the state, a position he retained during the next decade, albeit with considerable difficulty. . . .

Velasco did not accompany General Pesqueira back to Sonora in 1866. Instead he migrated north, to Tucson. . . .

The Velasco family grew rapidly. Eventually Carlos and Beatríz, married in 1859, had ten children, and although six of them did not survive infancy, the family took in five orphans. . . .

Despite growing family responsibilities, Velasco longed to return to his motherland. Clearly it had never been his intention to reside in the United States permanently. Shortly after 1870, therefore, as the political situation at home took a turn for the better, the Velascos went back to Sonora. Resuming his political activities, Carlos served as a deputy in the state legislature in 1872 and 1873, where he faithfully supported General Pesqueira. . . . The Pesqueira regime, however, became increasingly arbitrary and unpopular, and when the pesqueiristas were overthrown in 1877, Carlos Velasco left Sonora, a political refugee. He arrived in Tucson on November 2, 1877.

Velasco's change of residence at this time was not an isolated incident. As historian and ethnologist James Officer has discovered, Mexican immigration to Tucson, mostly from Sonora, in the decade of the 1870s exceeded "both in percentage increment and in actual numbers the immigration touched off by the Mexican Revolution." Like the Velascos, many of these newcomers were relatively prosperous people. Such was true, for example, of Estevan Ochoa (1831–1888) from Chihuahua . . . , and Mariano G. Samaniego (1844–1907), a Sonoran. These two men exerted a powerful and benign influence on the affairs of the city during the next few years.

Carlos Velasco must have felt reasonably at home in the Tucson of the 1870s. The Old Pueblo and the rest of Arizona south of the Gila River had been incorporated into the United States as a result of the Gadsden Purchase of 1853. Twenty years later, though, the settlement was still essentially a Mexican town. The 1870 census indicates that of the 3200 residents, most were Mexicans. And many of those Tucsonans with Anglo names were in fact products of mixed marriages. Anglo men —several of them prominent citizens—readily married Mexican ladies, a state of affairs to be expected as it was only in 1872 that the first Anglo women came to live in Tucson on a permanent basis.

. . . The mixed marriages helped to establish amiable relations between the two communities (though a minority, Anglos already had firm control of the town's political and economic life). Then, too, both peoples were united by now in a common hatred. The Apache, after a period of comparative inactivity, had risen up again at the time of the American Civil War and continued to terrorize northern Mexico and the American Southwest, the *apachería,* into the 1880s.

For a brief period Velasco tried his hand at retail merchandising, but given his legal training he was probably not completely happy as a businessman. . . .

Velasco's real passion was journalism, and he had had some experience in the field. Now he determined to take up the profession in earnest. Selling his store, he invested the money on a printing press, and at the age of forty-one he embarked on what was to be a highly successful career as a newspaperman.

The first issue of *El Fronterizo* appeared on the streets of Tucson on September 21, 1878. Written in Spanish, the four-page weekly was aimed primarily at the Hispanic peoples of southern Arizona and northern Sonora. Its columns dealt particularly with politics, industry, and commerce, but no subject of interest was neglected. The emphasis was on local news, though some attention was given national and even international developments.

The publication was received with enthusiasm, and it maintained its appeal. Initially the paper was put together entirely by its editor-publisher, but in time the staff was expanded to include eight workers. Another measure of success was its thirty-seven-year existence, a remarkable achievement given the difficulties of publishing on the frontier. Part of the reason for the newspaper's popularity can be attributed to the quality of the publication. Moreover, it did not simply describe events; ideas loomed large, especially those of its editor, who perceived the paper as a vehicle for public instruction.

Velasco clarified his editorial position in the second issue of *El Fronterizo*. His paramount concern was "the social improvement" of the peoples of the Territory of Arizona and the Republic of Mexico, especially Sonora. His paper, he pledged, "would work unremittingly to improve the good relations which exist at present between the two frontier communities, attempting to inculcate in their inhabitants the best sentiments of mutual respect and sincere fraternity." "Finally," the editor concluded, "the *Fronterizo* will establish itself as a zealous defender of the interests of the Mexican people in both countries, expressing their point of view, and directing their initiative along the path leading to their moral perfection and material progress."

The language used by Velasco in his newspaper suggests the influence of Positivist philosophy, which dominated the intellectual climate of Mexico during the late 19th century. (Positivism in its narrow sense constituted a system of thought developed in the latter half of the 19th century by Frenchman Auguste Comte and "held that human thought had passed inevitably through a theological stage into a metaphysical stage and was passing into a positive or scientific stage.") In fact, Velasco was critical of Comte's Mexican followers at the outset, calling them "false apostles who corrupt and lead us astray."

As his thought evolved, though, Velasco came to espouse a Positivist point of view—a trend evident among most Mexican Liberals. They had grown weary of the chaos brought on by years of revolution and consequently were drawn to the conservative ideology advocated by the French thinker. The change in Velasco's orientation occurred in early 1880. In January he noted a growing apathy in Mexico and wondered if perhaps this condition was the product of sixty years of convulsions. Two months later he was more succinct: liberty, he declared, was impossible without peace. Finally, in May, disturbed by news of a possible uprising in northern Mexico, he insisted that "the epoch of revolutions has passed." Thereafter *El Fronterizo* devoted little space to discussions on liberty, emphasizing instead the ideals of order and progress. . . .

Like the Positivists, Velasco came to stress peace, prosperity, and progress, while deemphasizing freedom. And like Comte's Mexican disciples, as he embraced this new point of view he came to discover the incarnation of these ideals in the *Porfiriato*. Before long he had become an enthusiastic partisan of Porfirio Diaz. This personal devotion proved to be a lifelong passion.

. . . As was true of almost all frontier newspapers, *El Fronterizo* was a strong supporter of law and order. Violence, after all, was a chronic problem, and Tucson attracted its share of the criminal element, especially in the 1880s when it became "a mecca for rowdies." It would be a mistake, however, to assume that crime was the exclusive province of these rowdies. Lack of respect for the law extended to some of the town's most respected citizens, and even Velasco, under certain circumstances, was capable of modifying his views on the subject. In 1871, for example, J. M. Elias and William Oury, two "pillars" of local society, led a band of disgruntled Tucsonans—Anglos, Mexicans, and Indians—in an attack upon the Apache village near Camp Grant, slaughtering over 140 men, women, and children.

Velasco's views on the Camp Grant massacre have not been recorded, but it is almost certain that he condoned the attack. When New Mexico's citizens began arming in early 1880, threatening to move against the Apache themselves because of the government's reluctance to deal with the problem (a situation not unlike the one nine years before), Velasco gave his wholehearted support. In an article entitled "The Indian Question," he defended the New Mexicans against criticism from eastern newspapers. These outsiders, he asserted, were misguided. As long as white men continued to protect the Indians, he warned, "not only will there be no hope of civilizing them, but not even the possibility. He who believes otherwise has no understanding of the arrogant and unconquerable nature of the savage." These views were identical to those of the Positivists, who saw in the Indian an impediment to progress. . . .

Up to this point Velasco's thinking could best be described as conservative. There was one area, however, in which militancy was retained: the defense of the rights of fellow Mexicans in Arizona. The relations between Anglos and Mexicans in Tucson began to deteriorate . . . after 1880. One reason stems from Mexican fears that the United States meant to annex more territory south of the border. The Spanish-speaking community in the pueblo was outraged. More significant in explaining the turn of events, though, was the arrival of the Southern Pacific Railroad on March 20, 1880, which drastically altered the proportions between the Anglo and Mexican populations to the detriment of the latter. In 1878, when the publication of *El Fronterizo* was initiated, Mexicans made up sixty-seven percent of the town population of approximately 4500 people; in 1881 the total had grown to about 10,000, with Mexicans constituting only forty-three percent. . . . [T]he railroad weakened the bargaining position of Tucson's Mexican freighters and merchants, as it redirected the main trade routes from Mexico to Texas and California. Dependent on Sonoran commerce, many Mexican tradesmen found it difficult to survive, particularly in the midst of the general depression. . . .

Reviewing the history of the American Spanish-language press in 1930, Manuel Gamio found that its "principal characteristic" had been its defense of the Mexican population from Anglo abuse. *El Fronterizo* was no exception. As was true of Mexican editors in other parts of the Southwest, Velasco employed his newspaper to combat negative stereotypes of his people. He was also concerned with their treatment. Unprovoked attacks by Anglos were exposed, and the Mexican consul was urged to investigate allegations of physical violence. Velasco's concern for the welfare of local Mexicans was manifested in his campaign to have Tucson city council resolutions published in Spanish as well as English.

It was not enough simply to protest; Velasco felt that it was necessary that the Mexican community, those members who were eligible, unite politically to safeguard their rights. Time and again he appealed to those of his people who possessed American citizenship to vote. In local elections, he urged, they should support Mexican candidates, or—at the very least—Anglos who were sympathetic to the Mexican cause, regardless of party affiliation. Spanish-speaking voters, he claimed, while weak in numbers, had sufficient power to swing the vote toward either Democrats or Republicans. They should make use of this lever to gain concessions. . . .

Don Velasco's efforts in defense of the Spanish-speaking community were not confined to his journalistic activities. Also related to these labors was the foundation of the *Alianza Hispano-Americana,* certainly the best-known of his achievements.

During the course of the 1880s, the status of the Mexican in Tucson and throughout Arizona declined. The decade witnessed "increasingly overt discrimination" against the minority community. This oppression was described in the summer of 1889 by a correspondent for *El Fronterizo,* who concluded that there was no justice for Mexicans in Arizona and recommended voluntary repatriation of Sonorans living in the Territory. Anti-Mexican feeling in Tucson peaked during the depression following the panic of 1893, and about this same time the American Protective Association established a local chapter. People of Mexican descent in Tucson were "beginning to suffer the same prejudice and discrimination as the . . . Mexican Americans in other parts of the Southwest." Ignacio Calvillo, one of the organization's charter members, later recalled this deterioration of Anglo-Mexican relations and placed the creation of the *Alianza* in that context.

Their civil liberties threatened, the Mexicans in Tucson were stirred to action. Following Velasco's initiative, some forty-five of the most distinguished representatives of the Hispanic community assembled on January 14, 1894, and thus the *Alianza Hispano-Americana* came into being, with Carlos Velasco, appropriately enough, serving as first president.

At the outset the *Alianza* functioned as a mutual aid and benefit society catering to the social and cultural needs of the ethnic community and providing death benefits. Primarily, however, the *Alianza* was a defense organization: "It has, so far as can be learned," the *Daily Citizen*, Tucson's Republican newspaper, commented on January 15, "the sole object of a mutual protection of the interests of its members."

The society was composed of diverse elements. Some members were well-to-do, others common laborers; some were Republicans, others Democrats; some were immigrants, others were native-born. Not surprisingly, dissension surfaced from the very beginning, as Velasco disclosed in a speech celebrating the organization's first anniversary in January, 1895. Still, much was accomplished. The most immediate concern, Anglo hostility, diminished significantly as is clear from an 1896 publication which describes the ethnic relations in Tucson in these glowing terms: "Side by side the American, Mexican and Indian pursue the tenor of their way, smoothly, peacefully and successfully, and illustrate the progressive stages of modern civilization."

Encouraged by these early successes, the *Alianza* grew more ambitious. Lodges (from its inception the society was organized along Masonic lines) began to spring up throughout the Southwest and, by the turn of the century, in Mexico as well. In these years the *Alianza* was gradually transformed from a local association into a regional confederation. Paralleling this trend was its greater emphasis on insurance against illness and unemployment, a focus which predominated after the organization's incorporation in 1907. Now best described as a fraternal insurance society, the *Alianza* continued to expand until 1939, the year of its maximum strength.

The proliferation of lodges at the turn of the century was largely due to the efforts of Pedro C. Pellon (1852–1911) and Carlos H. Tully (1853–1923), who now became the driving forces behind the movement. Velasco's eclipse was inevitable. Age was a factor. . . . Moreover, an ideological gulf now separated him from many of his colleagues, for he continued to support the *Porfiriato* in Mexico at a time when the dictatorship was becoming increasingly unpopular both at home and abroad. . . .

Carlos I. Velasco played a secondary role in the *Alianza* after its inception, but his contribution should not be underestimated. Years later the grateful society would honor its founder as the "brain" of the organization (Pellon was the "heart" and Tully "the right arm"), a fitting tribute.

Velasco continued to lead a busy life right up to the end. He passed away in Tucson, his adopted hometown, on October 6, 1914. As was appropriate for a man who dedicated his life to serving others, Don Carlos died in poverty. Buried at Holy Hope Cemetery, he was joined there by his wife, Beatríz, eighteen years later.

The history of Mexican Americans between 1848 and 1910 is popularly interpreted as the story of two distinct classes of people: the old Spanish Dons, on the one hand, wealthy *rancheros* who dominated the Southwest before Anglo-Americans divested them of their power; and Mexican *cholos* on the other, impoverished and illiterate peons who began to arrive in this country about the turn of the century. While there are areas in the Southwest where such an analysis might apply in a very general way, this perception is not very useful in explaining the development of the Spanish-speaking community in southern Arizona. Certainly it does not apply to Tucson, where significant numbers of Mexican immigrants, mostly Sonorans, arrived in the aftermath of American occupation, many of them neither destitute nor ignorant. Some of them were or became prominent men. This group included Estevan Ochoa, Mariano Samaniego, and Carlos Velasco, but there were others too —Leopoldo Carrillo, Federico Ronstadt, and Carlos Jacome among them. Together, these individuals provided sorely needed leadership in the beleaguered Mexican community. They did it by example and by standing up for the rights of their people. If, as many observers claim, the relations between Mexicans and Anglos have been healthier in Tucson than in other places, some of the credit can be assigned to these Mexican pioneers.

PART III.
THE GREAT MIGRATION
1900–1940

Migration is the most significant theme of Mexican-American history in the twentieth century. This was particularly true in the period between 1900 and 1940: the first three decades witnessed unprecedented Mexican immigration into the United States, and the thirties saw a massive exodus back to Mexico. Life in the Mexican *colonias* (colonies) during this halcyon period, undoubtedly the most researched era by ethnic scholars during the 1990s, is the subject of the essays in this section.

Anywhere between 500,000 and 2,000,000 citizens of the Mexican Republic may have journeyed north in 1900–1930. The number is problematic given the paucity of data, which reflected the nature of immigration from the south: Mexicans continually crossed and recrossed the 2,000-mile border, as many as two-thirds without appropriate documents. While even the most liberal estimates made for that period have been eclipsed during the past thirty years—there were an estimated 4.4 million Mexican nationals residing in the United States in 1990—the initial wave continues to be known as the Great Migration by Chicano scholars.

Discontent and opportunity—these two words sum up the motivation of the uprooted immigrant population. Unrest mounted steadily during the thirty-year period. Popular dissatisfaction was fanned by the autocratic policies of the Porfiriato during the first ten years, the economic and political chaos associated with the Great Revolution (1911–1917) during the second decade, and the agrarian and religious policies of President Obregón and the triumphant Sonoran faction in the twenties. Meanwhile, the economy of the American Southwest boomed, especially during the Great War, creating a multitude of jobs in mining, railroad construction, agriculture, and other lines of work requiring unskilled labor. The Mexican diaspora was not confined to the Borderlands. The wartime need for labor was so severe that some Mexicans, as the essays by historians Louise Año Nuevo Kerr and Dennis Nodín Valdés demonstrate, were even able to enter the Midwest, where jobs were to be found in industry as well as agriculture.

The 1920s witnessed continuing urbanization, the subject of the essay by historian Ricardo Romo, as Mexicans, like the rest of the U.S. population, flocked to cities to take advantage of better economic opportunities. By 1930, Los Angeles had over one million Mexican-origin residents, making it the third-largest Mexican metropolitan area in the world after Mexico City and Guadalajara. For the first time the ranks of the middle class were sufficient to sustain more substantial organizations than the mutual benefit societies that had catered to the immigrants. Increasingly the newcomers' children, labeled the Mexican American Generation (1930–1960) by Mario T. García and like-minded scholars, came to identify with the country of their birth rather than that of their parents. This assimilationist orientation is under-scored by the creation of the League of United Latin American Citizens (LULAC) in 1929, which, as historian Cynthia Orozco shows in her essay, quickly expanded beyond its Texas birthplace.

Joining the American mainstream proved difficult, however, especially for the mestizo lower class. Postwar xenophobia combined with an upsurge of racism in the twenties to make life difficult for "meskins." No longer an invisible minority, Mexicans now came to be defined as a problem. Cries for the restriction of Mexican immigration were heard from many quarters, including welfare agencies, nativist organizations, and labor unions. Only the Great Depression prevented the imposi-tion of government sanctions.

The Great Depression made life in the United States precarious for Mexicanos, a group of people who were doubly damned as non-whites and aliens. A govern-ment-sponsored campaign to deport the immigrants resulted in massive repatria-tions. As many as 500,000 Mexicans returned to their homeland, perhaps half of them against their will. That many deportees were U.S. citizens seemed immaterial. Moreover, Mexican efforts to improve working conditions through strikes, espe-cially in the fields of California—where their livelihood was further jeopardized by the arrival of Dust Bowl immigrants in the mid-thirties—came to naught, as law enforcement officials openly supported employers. While showing that Mexican workers actively struggled to improve their lives, the essays by historians Ramón Chacón and Gilbert González make clear the insurmountable obstacles they faced. The same held true in Texas, according to the essay by historian Irene Ledesma. The collapse of the labor unions under the pressure exerted by agribusiness was the final iniquity. For many Mexicans and Mexican Americans, this ill-treatment confirmed the suspicion that American government and society were something to fear and mistrust, a legacy of bitterness that had widespread repercussions. Unlike other second-generation Americans, most Mexican Americans would maintain sentimen-tal ties with the old country, increasingly embraced as *México lindo* ("Beautiful Mex-ico," the nostalgic image of their homeland). For the next generation, at least, they continued to identify themselves as *mexicanos*.

13

CHICANO SETTLEMENTS IN CHICAGO
A Brief History

LOUISE AÑO NUEVO KERR

The product of a mixed marriage—her father was Filipino and her mother Mexican—Louise Año Nuevo was born in Denver and raised in California, where she received her education, graduating from UC Berkeley with a B.A. in sociology in 1960. Three years later she married Howard H. Kerr, and the growing family eventually moved to the Midwest when he was offered a teaching position at the University of Chicago. After attaining a Ph.D. in history from the University of Illinois in 1976, Dr. Año Nuevo Kerr taught at both Loyola University and the University of Illinois in Chicago, where she eventually became Associate Vice-Chancellor of Academic Affairs. The Kerrs now reside in California.

The migration of Mexicans and Mexican-Americans to Chicago began during World War I and, with the exception of the 1930s, has continued steadily and increasingly ever since. From the beginning, Chicago's Chicanos tended to settle in three distinct neighborhoods—the Near West Side, South Chicago, and Back of the Yards. First noticed in the 1920s, this tripartite settlement pattern was reflected in the census of 1930, which showed 20,000 Mexicans, most of them immigrants. Despite the drain of repatriation during the 1930s, by 1950 the number of Chicanos had grown to nearly 24,000, many of them born in Chicago. Growth was proportionately slower until 1965, but since then there has been a sharp increase in Chicano in-migration on the part of both Mexican immigrants and Mexican-Americans. Half a century after such migration began, the 1970 census reported 106,000 Chicanos in Chicago. Although Chicanos could now be found in almost every census tract in the

From *Journal of Ethnic Studies* 2 (Winter 1975): 22–32. The original text has been modified. Copyright by Bureau for Faculty Research, Western Washington University. Reprinted by permission.

city and in most of its suburbs as well, the three neighborhoods persisted with one significant change. South Chicago and Back of the Yards remained intact, while under the pressure of urban renewal half of the Near West Side community had moved a few blocks south, where it was undergoing enormous expansion. In-migration continued to flow primarily to these three areas. The purpose of this essay is to suggest some of the ways in which differences among these neighborhoods have led to diverse patterns of urban experience for Chicanos.

Well before the first Mexicans came, other Catholic immigrants had moved into these same neighborhoods to work in nearby industries. By 1920, therefore, each of them had already developed distinctive patterns of employment, ethnicity, and neighborhood identity. It was the railroads, the steel mills, and the packing houses which originally drew Mexican immigrants to the neighborhoods. Starting in 1916, unskilled Mexican workers recruited from Texas border towns were brought to the Near West Side to work on the nearby railroads and, later on, in factory and miscellaneous service jobs in the central city. The steel mills of South Chicago began bringing in Mexican laborers in 1919. In the same year the packing houses of Back of the Yards recruited Mexican workers from elsewhere and also sought to attract disaffected railroad and migrant agricultural labor.

By the end of the 1920s almost 20,000 Mexicans lived in Chicago—7,000 on the Near West Side with Italians, Russians, Greeks, and Poles as neighbors; 4,300 with Poles, Slovaks, and Germans in South Chicago; and 3,000 in Back of the Yards, primarily with Poles and Irishmen. The Mexicans immediately recognized these neighbors as European rather than "American," and although there was a tendency to think in terms of "we" and "they," there was also a clear understanding that some European ethnic groups were friendlier than others. At the same time it was understood that interaction with other ethnic groups could vary from neighborhood to neighborhood. The Poles who were just beginning to dominate South Chicago were the most openly antagonistic, successfully imposing and enforcing housing restrictions against Mexican newcomers. Perhaps as a result, the 1930 census tract most densely populated with Mexican aliens was found in South Chicago. On the other hand, the Poles of Back of the Yards, themselves often unfavorably compared to Mexicans by the neighborhood's Irish majority (which owned most of the housing), were less openly hostile. But it was the Italians of the Near West Side who were seen by the Mexicans as the most friendly, or more accurately, as the least unfriendly. No doubt physical and cultural similarities had something to do with this relative benevolence: a few lighter-skinned Mexicans of the Near West Side were allowed (and allowed themselves) to be thought of as Italians, operating Italian-owned businesses and adopting Italian names. Perhaps as pertinent, however, was the mutual recognition that the Italians had already consolidated political control over the area and had little to fear from such numerically and politically insignificant newcomers.

It was within the context of the three neighborhoods, with their economic and ethnic differences, that Mexican settlement took shape. Mexican businesses, social organizations, and religious affiliations developed primarily along neighborhood lines. Like other ethnic groups, the Mexicans were quick to form mutual aid societies, political and recreational clubs, and labor unions. Much of this activity took place in the settlement houses which served each neighborhood—Jane Addams's Hull House on the Near West Side, Mary McDowell's University of Chicago Settlement House in the Back of the Yards, and the Congregational Church's Bird Memorial Center in South Chicago. They provided athletic facilities, meeting rooms for labor and political as well as social organizations, along with instruction in English and other subjects. From 1920 through 1940, in all three neighborhoods, such activities were for the most part doubly segregated—by ethnic group within the neighborhood, by neighborhood so far as Mexicans elsewhere in the city were concerned.

Since almost all ethnic groups in the three neighborhoods were Roman Catholic, parish structures reinforced both neighborhood-centeredness and ethnic separatism. Indeed, the time it took each Mexican settlement to gain its own Spanish-speaking parish was a measure of its internal cohesion and of its recognition by the Archdiocese. In 1924, eight years after Mexicans first came to Chicago, Cardinal Mundelein requested that a Spanish-speaking clerical order be assigned to serve them, and in 1925 three priests from the Spanish-based Claretian order were sent to a Catholic chapel in South Chicago built by the Illinois Steel Company expressly for its Mexican workers, who had been excluded from Polish and Slovakian parishes. Three years later, the chapel was replaced by Our Lady of Guadalupe, the first permanent Spanish-speaking Catholic church in Chicago. On the Near West Side, St. Francis of Assisi, which had previously served Italians, received its first Spanish-speaking priest and officially became a Spanish-speaking parish in 1928. On the other hand, until 1945 the Mexicans of Back of the Yards had only a store-front church served by priests brought in by car every week from South Chicago or the Near West Side by parishioners.

During the formative period, then, the Chicano settlements in Chicago had undergone parallel yet different development in employment, housing, social organization, interethnic relationships, and parish organization. The hardships of the depression years exaggerated economic competition with other ethnic groups in the neighborhoods, especially as United States citizenship was increasingly required for jobs and relief. The Immigrant Protective League, located at Hull House on the Near West Side, sought to deal with the latter problem by stepping up its traditional efforts to naturalize alien immigrants, including Mexicans. And in Chicago as in the Southwest, Mexican immigration officials and the Mexican Consulate cooperated with U.S. Immigration authorities and local welfare agencies in the repatriation process which saw Mexicans as well as other immigrants returned to their homelands as a relief measure. As a result of repatriation and the halt in immigration during the 1930s, Chicago's Mexican population fell from 20,000 in 1930 to 16,600 in 1940.

The hardships of the 1930s did not lead to solidarity among Chicago's Mexicans. From time to time, it is true, there were such cooperative ventures among the settlements as the celebration of Mexican national holidays and the establishment of a speakers' bureau, but there were few attempts to discuss common problems or to represent those problems to the city at large. Instead, many of those who remained in the city in industrial employment sought economic survival by participating—on a multi-ethnic, neighborhood basis—in the unionization of their industries. In South Chicago, along with the Poles and other European ethnics in the steel mills, they enthusiastically took part in the formation of the United Steel Workers Union and in the great steel strikes of the late 1930s. The organizers of the packing-house unions in Back of the Yards solicited Mexican membership. In the Near West Side community, too, Mexican workers joined existing unions.

During World War II several thousand Mexican nationals and Mexican-Americans were recruited to Chicago for industrial labor. Many of the *braceros* were quartered in or near the three neighborhoods, but they appear to have kept more or less to themselves. Recruited under Public Law 45, they were of course required to return to Mexico after the war. Nonetheless, as a result of natural growth and in-migration from elsewhere in the United States, between 1940 and 1950 the Chicano population grew from 16,000 to 24,000. As a whole the 1950 population was younger and better off economically than it had been before the war, and considered itself more Mexican-American than Mexican.

While the Chicano population was changing in the post-war years, the neighborhoods themselves were changing too. In South Chicago the Mexicans, like most of the mill workers who had taken part in the steel strikes of the late 1930s, had become fairly ordinary union members, undeterred by the fact that there was still "no Mexican American on the staff of the union in the entire Calumet area with the exception of a single office girl." Housing barriers began to fall as White ethnics contemplated moving to the southern suburbs and as Chicanos began to make enough money to buy or rent homes in the better-off western part of South Chicago. Social distance and ethnic separation remained as the groups continued to maintain their own parishes and associations within neighborhood boundaries. But open antagonism had diminished, and a form of coexistence had emerged with the realization that union solidarity in the steel mills was essential.

Back of the Yards had witnessed a different sort of change. The unionization of the packing houses under the CIO in the late 1930s stabilized the economic lives of the packing house workers to some extent, just as the steelworkers' union had done in South Chicago. But ever since its immortalization in Upton Sinclair's *The Jungle* (1906), Back of the Yards had been considered the area of particularly serious social problems—housing, sanitation, delinquency, and official neglect. And when the Back of the Yards Neighborhood Council was formed with the help of Saul Alinsky in 1939 to deal with such problems, the Mexicans, who had been ignored by everyone but settlement house workers, became a necessary component of the multi-ethnic coalition, even more so when in 1945 they achieved a Spanish-speaking parish by funding a new church building themselves to replace their old storefront. In South Chicago, Mexicans could live entirely within the neighborhood, at best coexisting with, but separate from, their ethnic neighbors. In Back of the Yards, where they could also live wholly circumscribed by neighborhood boundaries, they took some part in the Council's attempt to break down ethnic separatism and create a new allegiance to the neighborhood at large.

Although the railroads had originally brought the first Mexicans to the Near West Side, the neighborhood was too close to the central city for a single industry ever to dominate. Relatively diverse unskilled employment therefore attracted Near

West Side Mexicans, as reflected by some of the unions to which they belonged in the late 1940s: the Brotherhood of Maintenance of Way workers; the Food, Tobacco, and Agricultural Workers; the Farm Equipment Workers; and the Hotel Service Employees. Probably this diversity in jobs had something to do with the fact that the Near West Side was always the major port of entry for Mexicans and contained the largest Mexican community in Chicago. But because it *was* the major port of entry, and because these jobs offered lower wages and less security than did the steel mills or packinghouses, the Mexicans of the Near West Side were more transient than those of the other neighborhoods.

On the other hand, the Chicano experience in the Near West Side seems to have been less parochial than in the other settlements. If ethnic separatism was stronger than in Back of the Yards, so was ethnic diversity. Simply by virtue of having to work outside the neighborhood, moreover, many Near West Side Mexicans had broader contact with the city at large than did those elsewhere. At the same time, insofar as public and private agencies and individual Chicagoans took any interest in the city's Chicanos, they tended to focus on the Near West Side neighborhood. As contrasted with the other settlements, then, there was greater mutual awareness, however skewed, on the part of Near West Side Chicanos and the city beyond the neighborhood.

For whatever reason, it was in the Near West Side neighborhood after World War II that new leadership, distinctly Mexican-American rather than (as in pre-war days) Mexican, began to try to unify the neighborhoods and to make their existence and needs known to the city. Much of this leadership came from the ranks of World War II veterans who were either born or raised in the United States. They generated groups like the Mexican Civic Committee and the Mexican Chamber of Commerce in the Near West Side, and took leadership in at least five AFL and CIO shop locals. Progress appeared possible, if not actual, as city agencies, the Catholic Archdiocese, and private groups seemed willing at least to help identify areas of pressing need: housing, employment, civil rights, and education. The prestigious Metropolitan Welfare Council formed a planning committee for Spanish-speaking people in 1948, and in 1949 the Illinois Federation of Mexican-Americans came into existence. Finally, in 1956, the research proposal sponsored by the Metropolitan Welfare Council and the Cardinal's Committee on the Spanish-speaking was submitted to the Chicago Research Group at the University of Chicago. An ambitious project which would study the problems of the "Spanish-speaking Community," the proposal got no further than an initial report. That the study itself was never completed was symbolic of the abortive efforts of the late 1940s and early 1950s. For though some light had been shed on the problems of Chicanos in Chicago, and an energetic leadership was looking for ways to solve them, no headway was made against one obstacle—the lack of Chicano unity.

Meanwhile important changes were taking place which would delay recognition and solution of those problems. Perhaps most significant from the Chicano point of view was the rapid increase of Puerto Rican in-migration. Puerto Ricans generally did not settle near the Chicanos, but they forced them into competition for the attention of the city which, increasingly aware of its "Spanish-speaking" citizens, regarded them as just that—a "Spanish-speaking" unit. Where the two groups did live together, as in parts of the Near West Side neighborhood, there was some conflict. With an increase in Puerto Rican population from 8,000 for the Midwest in 1950 to 32,000 for Chicago alone in 1960, the task of unifying the three settlements seemed insignificant alongside the clearly growing need to clarify the relationships among and to unify the "Spanish-speaking"—the Latinos of Chicago. One organization which did make such an attempt was the Pan American Council, composed of Anglos, Mexican-Americans, Puerto Ricans, and other Latin Americans. Intense internal strife, however, has prevented the Council from doing much more than providing an opportunity for the development of leadership skills.

The decade of the 1950s, which had begun so promisingly, ended on a note of confusion not only among Chicano leadership but at the grass roots in the three neighborhoods. By 1960, when there were officially 45,000 Mexicans and Mexican-Americans in the city, two of the three neighborhoods were faced with major internal changes, and all three felt vulnerable to the growing Black and other Latino populations. Urban renewal displaced over half of the Near West Side's 16,000 Chicanos. The stockyards were closing in Back of the Yards. The constrained Black ghetto on the city's South Side, bordered on the north, west, and south by the neighborhoods in which the Mexicans lived, expanded inexorably, creating fears among Mexican-Americans, as well as other ethnic residents. Meanwhile, during the 1960s, increasing numbers of Chicanos came from Mexico, from the Southwest (especially Texas), and from elsewhere in the Midwest, many of them continuing to settle in various proportions in the established communities.

South Chicago was least affected by these changes. Interethnic efforts to resist increasing pressure from Blacks was successful for the time being. Puerto Ricans seldom chose to live in the community, and even during the great influx of the late 1960s Chicano in-migration was relatively light. In 1970 only 7% of the neighborhood's 12,000 Chicanos had come from Mexico in the preceding five years, only 2% from the Southwest. Chicanos here were older on the average than elsewhere in the city, and less mobile: 45% had lived in the same house since 1965, 17% since 1959. Expansion of the Chicano population during the 1960s had consisted primarily of second and third-generation Chicagoans remaining to raise families, and, like most of the community, to work in the mills and related industries. Newcomers normally came only if they had friends or relatives with "clout" in the union or in the mills. Older residents departed for neighborhoods and suburbs to the south which were still within reach of the mills. And although the Chicano population in South Chicago had grown over the course of half a century, it had also dispersed throughout the neighborhood and in 1970 still comprised only 26% of the total population of South Chicago. Its leaders continued to concentrate primarily on union activities and ward politics, campaigning for non-Chicano candidates who would represent the neighborhood. Not surprisingly, South Chicago was (and is) perceived by Chicanos elsewhere in the city as the most stable, and the most static, of the three settlements.

The closing of Chicago's stockyards during the 1960s led to gradual changes in the Back of the Yards Chicano settlement. Though in-migration continued at a higher rate than in South Chicago, growth was by no means as dramatic as in the geographically shifting Near West Side area. By 1970, 15% of Back of the Yards' 8,000 Chicanos had come from Mexico since 1965, 2% from the Southwest. Probably in part as a result of the dwindling number of jobs in the once-dominant meatpacking industry, only 2% of the Chicanos had lived in the same place since 1959, though many long-time residents remained in the neighborhood. With only a small business district, with relatively few Chicano organizations of its own, and without a Spanish-language newspaper, Back of the Yards had become the most numerous of the settlements. Our Lady of Mary Vicariate Parish—La Capilla—was the only visible symbol of Chicano "community," though Chicanos now attended other neighborhood parishes too. The Back of the Yards Neighborhood Council remained intact, however, and boasted of the fact that its recently retired president was a Chicago-born Chicano. Increasing intermarriage between young Chicanos and people of other ethnic groups accompanied a partial exodus of first and second-generation, Chicago-born Chicanos to the neighborhood's periphery and to nearby suburbs. If South Chicago was perceived as the most stable Chicano neighborhood, Back of the Yards was seen, favorably or unfavorably, as having moved the farthest toward interethnic assimilation, and as having served as a staging ground for dispersal, even disappearance, into the larger metropolitan area.

Change was greatest during the 1960s in the Near West Side community. Urban renewal had displaced more than half of the community's Chicanos. Where all the refugees went is not accurately known. But many left the old neighborhood entirely—especially some of the younger and more affluent families. Others moved west within the neighborhood, hoping to maintain long-standing parish and social ties but fearful of future urban renewal. Of the 9,000 forced to leave Hull House, it is estimated that over half moved south to an extension of the old neighborhood centered around 18th street, which until the 1950s had been a Bohemian and Czech colony called "Pilsen." With the closing of the Near West Side, Pilsen became the chief "port of entry" for Chicano in-migrants just as that in-migration underwent enormous expansion. Immigrants from Mexico and migrants from the Southwest and Midwest joined the refugees in such numbers after 1965 that by 1970, 26,000 made up 55% of Pilsen's total population. So sharply and quickly had they increased that 2,000 more of them spilled westward beyond Pilsen and towards the city's border.

For the first time, Chicanos now constituted a majority in a Chicago neighborhood, neither bound to a single industry nor outnumbered locally by competing ethnic groups. As earlier in the Near West Side, they were less well off economically than in the other settlements in the city. Indeed, Pilsen has recently been ranked eighty-fourth out of eighty-five Chicago neighborhoods in terms of education and job levels, incomes, rents and home values. But as a new generation of leaders pressed for solutions to these problems, the new majority's dramatic growth gave it a political potential to which both city and state responded somewhat with programs operated by Chicanos. New schools were designated, and Chicanos began to run for office. Despite the new aggressiveness with which Pilsen demanded a voice in shaping its own destiny, however, there was still little sense of common purpose with South Chicago and Back of the Yards. Indeed, with its mixture of native-born Chicagoans and both old and ever-more-numerous new immigrants from Mexico, the Southwest, and elsewhere in the Midwest, Pilsen itself contained the most diverse Chicano population in Chicago, and together with its western spillover now contained over 40% of the city's 106,000 Chicanos. That some young people were moving there from South Chicago to be "where the action is" was perhaps evidence that, whatever its problems, Pilsen was perceived by Chicanos elsewhere in the city as the most dynamic of their settlements.

However underrepresentative the census figures may be, they do tell us that Chicano migration to Chicago between 1920 and 1970 went through essentially the same chronological stages which have marked it in the Southwest. Without inquiring here into the migration process itself, I have rather tried to show how Chicanos in Chicago have adapted to and participated in the further evolution of the three major neighborhoods in which they settled. I have also tried to show how distinctive neighborhood patterns have at least partially determined the variable development of Chicano identity within the three settlements. Many questions remain, not the last of which is: What future significance is there for Chicanos in Chicago in the fact that they now constitute only 40% of Chicago's total Latino population of one quarter million people?

14

SETTLERS, SOJOURNERS, AND PROLETARIANS

Social Formation in the Great Plains Sugar Beet Industry, 1890–1940

DENNIS NODÍN VALDÉS

Dennis Nodín Valdés, born in Detroit, received his Ph.D. in Latin American history from the University of Michigan in 1978. He has taught at the University of Wisconsin and at Lund University in Sweden, where he taught the first Chicano history course in Scandinavia. At present he is an associate professor in the Chicano Studies Department of the University of Minnesota. He has published many articles on agricultural labor in the West and several books, among them *Al Norte: Agricultural Workers in the Great Lakes Region, 1917–1970* (1991) and *Barrios Norteños: St. Paul and Midwestern Mexican Communities in the Twentieth Century* (2000).

The sugar beet industry was in the forefront of the opening of the northern Great Plains to commercial agriculture. At the end of the nineteenth century, massive expanses of cheap land with ideal climatic and soil conditions were available on the Plains, but the sparse population afforded few farmers or field workers to block, thin, hoe, and top the sugar beets. Between 1890 and World War II, the sugar corporations devised three labor recruitment strategies that created classes of settlers, sojourners, and proletarians on the Great Plains. This essay examines the interaction between the sugar beet industry and its field workers on the northern Plains in the early twentieth century.

The sugar beet industry had a hesitant start in the United States. Following a number of experiments in different locations, two factories were established in California: at Alvarado in 1870 and at Watsonville in 1888. A third factory was built in 1890 at Grand Island, Nebraska. . . .

From *Great Plains Quarterly* 10 (Spring 1990): 110–23. The original text has been modified. Reprinted by permission of *Great Plains Quarterly*.

The Great Plains states quickly led in national sugar beet production, as the industry took advantage of government-sponsored research and the construction of irrigation systems in the 1880s and 1890s. . . . Because of the sparse settlement, the industry had to lure workers as well as farmers, and in the process it helped transform the human geography of the region. . . .

SETTLERS

As production expanded at the turn of the century, haphazard recruitment mechanisms were no longer adequate. The settled population near the eventual heart of the Great Plains beet growing area, along the North and South Platte rivers, was much more sparse than around Grand Island, while the demand for field labor was greater than before. With cheap land available, the sugar companies frequently purchased tracts of land near their factories and then recruited workers. At the turn of the century they had two nearby sources of labor available—Germans from Russia to the east and United States citizens of Mexican descent to the south. They chose the former, whom they lured with promises of settling and opportunities to purchase land soon after arrival. The companies often built homes for prospective tenants in the early years. In southern Colorado, Holly Sugar set up the Amity Land Company to sell irrigated land at 10 percent down and payment over seven years. The companies also advanced Russian-German tenants money to buy food and supplies, teams of horses, and other farm necessities. They provided tools and technology, advice on planting and cultivation, cheap rental, and easy terms of purchase. The European workers faced many problems in establishing themselves, including erratic weather, but during emergencies, including droughts, the companies frequently advanced special loans to the German-speaking worker-farmers to make sure that they did not lose their land and homes.

Other inducements also made it possible for the early field workers to settle. The companies employed them in the higher-paying beet factories, affording extra months of income, a relative luxury seldom extended their successors. Furthermore, wages were very high during the first and second decades of the century. As a result, the Germans from Russia quickly purchased farms of their own, often within three years. Originally recruited into the Arkansas Valley of Colorado as laborers in 1899, they owned a third of the properties in the district by 1909. In Minatare, Nebraska, the immigrants whom Great Western had originally recruited as workers owned most of the land south of the city by the early 1920s.

The European immigrants who acquired lands in the beet districts did not remain isolated, as they had on the Volga. They quickly formed working-class neighborhoods in the beet towns, and although local Anglos referred to these neighborhoods as "Russiantown," "St. Petersburg," or "the Jungle," they were not segregated. Children, often despite the wishes of their parents, were compelled to attend English language schools with other Euro-American children. Furthermore, as they became land owners, Germans from Russia adopted the ways of other farmers and refused to perform stoop labor. For those who did not continue in agriculture, many quickly found employment as industrial workers, frequently rising to white collar positions. Their occupational mobility freed children for school, and attendance seldom was a significant problem among the European children after the earliest years of the century. Although they often built their own Protestant churches and formed a number of social and cultural organizations, they were gradually assimilated into the Euro-American culture of the Great Plains. . . .

A second group of settlers to be recruited were the Japanese. They represented a transition between settlers and sojourners. Many were initially recruited as single men to compete against the European families. Others were lured by the corporations to grow beets after they had already arrived in the sugar beet districts. Some came directly from California, while others came from work in nearby railroad gangs, coal mines, and smelters.

Many of the Japanese were experienced farmers, and they had a keen knowledge of, and appreciation for, intensive agriculture. They soon brought their families and quickly became tenants. Although they were less numerous than the Germans from Russia, they became victims of a much sharper anti-foreign hostility than the Europeans. As a result of the rising national anti-Japanese sentiment by the middle of the decade, immigration from Japan soon was cut off and many states passed laws prohibiting the Japanese from purchasing land. While many were able to buy farms through their United States–born children, more left the area. A generation later many former Japanese beet workers still owned farms and grew beets in scattered locations in Colorado, Nebraska, Wyoming, and Montana.

SOJOURNERS

The beet corporations also turned to Spanish-speaking workers, who appeared in the fields of southern Colorado in 1900 and in northern Colorado by 1903. By the early 1910s they were employed in the beet growing zones of Nebraska, and they moved north as the beet culture spread into the Yellowstone and Big Horn river valleys. Unlike the Europeans and Japanese, the workers of Mexican descent were not encouraged to settle. They were hired as sojourners, to remain for the season and leave the area after beet topping ended.

The corporations adopted the sojourner strategy for the Spanish-speaking workers both as a means of keeping wages down and in response to Euro-American fears of settlement in their midst. Euro-Americans asserted that these workers were "not a land-acquiring people" because they had roots deep in the villages of northern New Mexico and migrated only to earn enough to sustain their communities in the south. The sojourner strategy applied only for the period before World War I when single men came without their families.

The notion popularized by many observers, including historian Sarah Deutsch, that these workers came principally from the New Mexican villages is not accurate. The earliest recruitment of Mexicans as sojourners took place in southern Colorado for employment in the nearby Arkansas River Valley. Recruitment for northern Colorado first took place from Trinidad and Dry Creek, Colorado. The companies also sent agents to Las Vegas and other villages in northern New Mexico. By 1909, recruitment extended not only to Las Vegas and the northern New Mexico villages, but also to Albuquerque and places further south in New Mexico, and to Arizona and El Paso, where most of the workers recruited were born in Mexico. Many were small landowners who did seasonal migrant work to eke out survival, while others supplemented beet earnings with work as railroad section hands or in shops, coal mines, and foundries. Even in the first decade of the century, New Mexican villagers were a minority among the workers of Mexican descent on the Great Plains, and over time, their proportion continued to decline.

Many Euro-Americans argued that, unlike Europeans and Japanese, Mexicans were natural sojourners who did not want to settle down and were further held back by "the mañana attitude," lack of ambition, and by being "notoriously improvident." The arguments were consistent with company efforts to rationalize why Mexicans, unlike Germans from Russia or Japanese workers, did not acquire land. They do not explain why the companies at this time hired Europeans as families but Mexicans as single men. Nor do they account for the intense hostility of Anglo residents to the initial arrival of Mexican workers in new towns and the fear that they might settle permanently. The arguments also contradict the tremendous company success in the 1920s in converting these same workers to permanent residents eager to purchase houses.

PROLETARIANS

With the onset of World War I, the sugar beet industry faced a field labor crisis. Production expanded sharply, requiring more workers, but higher wages in competing industries drew immigrants out of the fields or enabled them to purchase and work on their own farms. Consequently, the companies intensified recruitment in Colorado, New Mexico, Texas, and Mexico. Company recruiters set up agencies in border towns and even went into Ciudad Juarez and the Mexican interior to find workers. Mexican nationals were particularly attractive. . . .

As late as 1919, the companies hired Mexican *solos* (single men) as sojourners, but the new strategy focused on recruiting entire families for the fields. By 1922 Great Western officially stopped hiring single workers because families offered a more abundant and controllable labor supply. The corporations recruited families from established centers in southern Colorado, New Mexico, Texas, and Mexico. During the course of the 1920s, often with the help of the United States Employment Service, they also turned to recently settled Mexican immigrants who worked in railroad and industrial centers on the Great Plains. While there was no sharp geographic distribution pattern distinguishing the old and New Mexicans, United States citizens were predominant in the beet colonies of southern Colorado, while Mexican citizens were concentrated in northeastern Colorado, Nebraska, Wyoming,

Montana, and Kansas. By the middle of the decade, families of Mexican immigrants dominated hand labor in the beet fields of the Great Plains.

In an effort to reduce recruitment costs, the companies offered these families opportunities to settle in the towns of the beet sugar region but not, as had been the case with the Germans from Russia, on farms of their own. American Beet Sugar and Holly Sugar constructed housing and made it available to workers, who paid rent indirectly, as they received lower wages in exchange for housing. Those workers who remained in the sugar beet districts during the winter could rent the housing cheaply. Great Western, which dominated production in the region, also arranged for workers to construct and purchase houses on lots of their own. It furnished free straw, lime, sand, and gravel, and offered workers credit to purchase lumber, doors, and cement. Company employees also supervised the laying of walls and other phases of construction. These corporation strategies created permanent worker colonias of from ten or twenty to one hundred fifty families in almost every factory district of Nebraska, Colorado, Wyoming, and Montana. More than one hundred of these settlements were constructed in the region by 1927. The sugar beet companies established the colonias "primarily for the purpose of building up a local labor supply," "to keep their workers from being drawn away" by competition, and to allay Euro-American perceptions that beet workers were a welfare burden on the community. Apparently the companies considered the colony cheaper than migrant labor.

The contrasting fates of European and Mexican workers were partly the consequence of decreasing earnings. Income between 1900, when Germans from Russia first came, and 1920, when Mexicans began to dominate the region, had already fallen sharply. Wages continued to slide, and were halved again by the nadir of the Depression in the mid-1930s. As a result the gap between the Mexicans' wages and the cost of a farm or even the equipment to become a tenant was too great for the Mexicans to advance in economic status. After many years in the region, very few Mexicans became renters and, as United States Department of Labor investigator George Edson reported in 1927, "none, so far as known, owns a farm." In contrast, Richard Sallet estimated that by 1910, "probably seventy-five percent of all the farms between Sterling and Denver were operated by Volga Germans."

Mexican beet workers' settlement patterns on the Great Plains also differed sharply from those of their European counterparts. A first, relatively affluent, generation of Germans from Russia had arrived in the early 1870s. They were immediately able to purchase farms and even, according to Norman Saul, "fine horses hitched to the best Studebaker wagons." Their presence softened Euro-American antagonism toward later and poorer Germans from Russia. The later arrivals had to accept proletarian work in the mines, on the railroads, and in the beet fields. As laborers they, like the Mexicans, initially resided in slum districts near the beet fields, but most quickly moved to more stable and higher-paying employment in the rapidly growing cities and towns in the region, or to rent and eventually purchase farms. In towns and on farms they lived, worked, and socialized as equals among United States-born Euro-Americans. As Bertram Hautner and W. Lewis Abbott of the National Child Labor Committee concluded: "Russian-Germans are considered members of the community. . . . Spanish Americans and Mexicans are looked upon as outsiders." . . .

THE FORMATION OF A CHICANO WORKING-CLASS CULTURE

. . . A comparison of the historical process of Germans from Russia and Mexican colonization challenges the argument posed by Richard Sallet that the former are an ethnic minority whose fate parallels that of Blacks and Chicanos. Despite numerous difficulties, especially in the early years, the European immigrants quickly settled and purchased farms, with abundant assistance from the sugar beet companies. The employers offered free tools, assistance in planting, and easy terms of rent and land purchase. As a result, the Germans from Russia were quickly absorbed into the Euro-American population. Throughout the period Mexicans were accepted and stereotyped only as proletarians. Holly Vice President J. C. Bailey of Colorado Springs testified in 1928: "Thinning and chopping beets is not the easiest work in the world—it is certainly a work that the white labor will not perform." As R. W. Roskelley later observed, unlike the Germans from Russia, the "Mexican is a different caste." . . .

The singling out of Mexicans went beyond work to public places. Constables and judges harassed Mexicans, who lacked political influence. In many counties the officials' earnings were based on a fee system, so they had "a financial interest in conviction." One observer noted that "for a Mexican to be arrested and accused is to be convicted." Police even raided adjoining counties to get workers, then set up "jack rabbit courts."

The discrimination affected old and New Mexicans alike. . . .

Segregation not only excluded old and New Mexicans, it forced them to share public places and to reside in the same parts of town. Their children attended the same public schools, and were taught that, despite the protests of those who were United States citizens, they were all Mexicans. They worked and played together and developed a common identity. A school teacher in Torrington, Wyoming, reported that the school they attended together "resembles a big family." Many residents recall that despite occasional friction, "the relationship[s] between native and non-native people were generally good." They attended common social events, and both old and New Mexicans shared the *Cinco de Mayo* and *Diez y Seis de Septiembre* holidays. Eventually organizations like the *Comision Honorifica,* created originally only for Mexican-born immigrants, admitted people from both groups. Furthermore, workers and their children from New Mexico, Colorado, and Mexico intermarried freely throughout the beet region.

. . . The common lives of *betabeleros* (beet workers) as workers served as a basis for unity within this developing working-class culture. The experience in the fields and confrontations with Euro-American farmers and corporation employers enhanced a common identity. As workers and settlers *betabeleros* often boycotted stores and public places that discriminated against them on the basis of Mexican ancestry. Organizations like the *Comision Honorifica* protested discrimination as a group. Beet workers sometimes achieved redress through the police or the Mexican consulate. On occasion they convinced farmers to remeasure fields that workers considered larger than they had been originally told. More often they had to accept the farmers' ultimatum, take it or leave it. Such failures resulted primarily from the fact that the lower class unskilled workers lacked highly schooled, well-placed, and politically influential voices within the dominant Euro-American community.

Yet their weakness as workers was also their greatest strength. Encouraged by the IWW during World War I, *betabeleros* organized and engaged in a handful of strikes for higher wages. . . .

. . . In 1929, a group of Mexican beet workers from Colorado were present when the Communist-led Trade Union Unity League (TUUL) formed in Ohio and established the Agricultural Workers Industrial League. Mexican and United States-born workers also created the *Asociación de Betabeleros* (Beet Workers' Association), an independent ethnic-oriented union that briefly affiliated with the American Federation of Labor. . . .

In 1935 many surviving beet-worker locals that had been affiliated with the AFL formed the Colorado Conference of Beet Field and Agricultural Unions, associated with the AFL's new national, the Agricultural Workers Union (AWU). They immediately demanded higher wages and asserted the rights of beet workers to relief and WPA employment.

By 1937, independent locals of the old *Asociación de Betabeleros* and the AWU, disenchanted with the lack of support from the AFL, bolted en masse to the United Cannery, Packing, and Agricultural Workers of America (UCPAWA) of the CIO. At its peak this Communist-led union claimed between 18,000 and 20,000 settled and migratory dues-paying members in the Great Plains states. The membership was estimated at 60 percent Mexican born and 40 percent United States born, proportions probably representative of the composition of the adult beet labor force in the region. . . . With at best modest success in organizing agricultural workers, UCPAWA barely survived in the beet fields beyond the end of the decade, and its failure supported the widespread criticism that the Anglo CIO leaders "don't know the first thing about beets."

The beet workers, organized and willing to challenge their employers, represented a self-conscious working class culture in the late 1930s. They were united by work, language and cultural similarities, and common alienation from the dominant Euro-American culture that included their neighbors and employers on the Great Plains, the Germans from Russia.

CONCLUSION

The labor demands of the sugar beet industry and the responses by its employees led to a stratified society of farm owners and proletarian field workers in the northern Great Plains. At the turn of the century, the industry adopted two simultaneous recruitment and employment strategies. To lure Germans from Russia, it encouraged their settlement as farmers. . . .

As production increased, the corporations had to develop a second strategy of hiring without the lure of land ownership. In the early 1900s, they brought in some Japanese workers as competition to the Germans from Russia. . . .

The companies adopted a different strategy for workers of Mexican descent whom they hired initially as single male sojourners in the early years of the century. . . . The sojourners represented a transitional phase in beet labor, a step toward permanent proletarianization of Mexicans as beet workers.

With the coming of World War I, expanded production, higher earnings, and alternative opportunities for Euro-Americans forced a field labor crisis on the companies. They adopted a new and less costly strategy of hiring more workers directly from Mexico and of bringing in entire families to settle. They thus could take advantage [of] the labor of women and children, who had not worked earlier as sojourners. The tactic was aimed at creating not a new class of farmers but rather a class of hired workers tied permanently to the industry.

Mexicans born in the United States and in Mexico worked and lived together and were segregated from the dominant Euro-American society. As Paul Taylor noted, "migratory labor is a proletarian class, not a people with a developed culture." As sojourners, the beet workers could not create a place for themselves in the beet fields, but once they settled their lives changed. The beet workers came to work, not to replicate the culture of the New Mexican homelands, which would have been impossible in any case because the beet communities were part of the recently formed rural industrial world whose residents came from several homelands. This new proletarian culture included elements of the old cultures and of the new environment the workers encountered during the settlement process on the northern Great Plains.

15

THE URBANIZATION OF SOUTHWESTERN CHICANOS IN THE EARLY TWENTIETH CENTURY
RICARDO ROMO

Born in San Antonio, Ricardo Romo received his Ph.D. in history from the University of California, Los Angeles, in 1975. He has taught at both the University of California at San Diego and the University of Texas at Austin, his alma mater. A college athlete, he was inducted into the Longhorn Hall of Fame in 1987. In 1992 he received the Educator of the Year Award from the League of United Latin American Citizens. He has also served as Vice President and Director of the Tomás Rivera Center at Trinity University, located in his hometown. Dr. Romo was named President of the University of Texas at San Antonio in 1999. His best-known work is *East Los Angeles: History of a Barrio* (1983).

. . . What follows is a discussion of the urbanization process of Chicanos in the Southwest during the period of greatest urbanization in the area, 1900–1930. For the purpose of this essay, three major components of urbanization—structural, demographic, and behavioral—will be considered. Among the questions underlying this discussion are: Is the widely expressed belief correct that Mexican population in this country is composed of "late arrivals?" Is the current popular image of the Chicano population as largely rural accurate? What factors accounted for the differential in urbanization between areas such as Los Angeles and El Paso? What were some of the cultural consequences of 20th century urbanization?

STRUCTURAL URBANIZATION

Structural urbanization concerns the organization of communities and society. In the American West, the extensive employment of modern technology, expanding

From *The New Scholar* 6 (1977): 183–207. The original text has been modified. Reprinted by permission.

capital investment, and the creation of a labor surplus, together with the improvement in communication and transportation, contributed to the emergence of urban-industrial communities. Of course, within the states of Texas, New Mexico, Arizona, and California which make up the Southwest, there existed regional variations in economic development and consequently, growth differentials among the principal cities. Three variables that will be discussed under the concept of structural urbanization are: economic development, specialization of labor or division of labor, and the internal spatial structure of cities (functional specialization of people and places).

ECONOMIC DEVELOPMENT

. . . The population of the Southwest grew slowly during the late 19th and early 20th century as it attracted only a small number of European immigrants and other migrants. With the exception of Los Angeles and San Francisco, this region in 1900 had no cities with a population of over 100,000. The population of the entire Southwest area at this time composed less than 10% of the national total. Overall urban growth in the southwestern states had reached only 50% of the level found in eastern and midwestern regions. The larger cities of this region—Los Angeles, San Antonio, San Francisco, El Paso, and San Diego—did not experience rapid urbanization until after 1900. Furthermore, it was in the 1900–1930 era that these cities attracted Chicanos in record numbers.

The urban areas that attracted the greatest number of Chicanos in this period were those which generally shared these common characteristics: diversified economic structure, proximity to the Mexican border, and labor distribution capabilities (favorable transportation and communication facilities). . . .

The explosive population growth of Los Angeles and simultaneous industrial expansion in the years between World War I and the Depression have been often described as nothing less than "miraculous." From 1900 to 1930 the population grew by ten times and the city added some 4,000 new factories. The construction of a major port in San Pedro, the completion of a 230 mile-long aqueduct that brought badly needed fresh water to the city, and the discovery of major oil deposits in the county assured the city's prosperity and growth potential. With the arrival of the first ships through the newly completed Panama Canal at the onset of the World War I, the city became a world trade center. Excellent inter-urban and inter-regional rail networks also gave Los Angeles a command of regional trade distribution thus enhancing its advantages over its old rivals, San Diego and Santa Barbara, in the crucial manufacturing sector. . . .

In 1929, southwesterners could look back with pride at twenty years of extraordinary growth and development. With the admission of New Mexico and Arizona to statehood in 1912 and the completion of deep water port facilities in Los Angeles and Houston, the rest of the nation no longer thought of the Southwest as an underdeveloped frontier region. Improved transoceanic trade after World War I spurred economic activity in southern California, while the increase in automobile travel contributed to regional and national integration. Not surprisingly, Southwest cities attracted thousands of newcomers as the economy of the urban communities experienced unprecedented expansion. Chicanos participated in the economic transformation of the region; in substantially large numbers they manned machines, constructed new railroad lines, and extracted mineral wealth from the earth.

SPECIALIZATION OF LABOR

A consequence of urbanization in this country has been the growing specialization of the work force. In the Southwest, as in every region of the country, the introduction of new sources of energy and raw materials, new supplies of labor and industrial skills, new machines and techniques of production eroded the 19th century pre-industrial class and occupational structure. After 1890, new employment patterns, based on the requirements of capital accumulation in areas such as steelmaking, automobile assembly, and textiles, began to play a larger role in the economy of the Southwest region. With the introduction of factory production came increased concentration of workers in urban areas.

For the Southwest, the transition from extractive industry and agriculture to capital intensive manufacturing and service activities came slowly. From 1890 through 1910, the Southwest (excluding California) had the lowest proportion of workers employed in manufacturing of any region in the United States. . . . Not surprisingly most Chicanos living in the Southwest in 1910 held jobs primarily in agriculture, ranching, mining, and transportation.

The most dramatic changes in the post 1910 urbanization process in the Southwest occurred within the Chicano community. As has been noted, prior to 1910 the majority of Chicanos living in the Southwest labored outside the urban-industrial job market. Even when they lived in cities, steady factory employment was scarce, forcing thousands to rely on casual agricultural employment in surrounding rural communities. In Texas, for example, many Chicanos who lived in the cities of San Antonio, Austin, Houston and Dallas migrated to work the crops in southern Texas, and some often ventured as far north as Wisconsin and Minnesota. . . .

Chicanos entered more specialized urban employment as cities became less dependent on trade and commerce with their hinterlands and more dedicated to manufacturing industries. The opening of several new military bases in San Antonio during World War I, which had spurred urbanization, also created a flood of new specialized jobs in construction, shipping, and manufacturing. A study in which 1,282 Chicano workers were surveyed in San Antonio showed that in less than a decade the majority of the Chicano labor force had shifted to the industrial sector. Although the largest number of Chicanos surveyed in that study (47%) held jobs as laborers, a sizable number worked in semi-skilled and skilled positions such as carpentry, masonry, tailoring, and baking. Some earned their living as storekeepers and clerks, while more than one hundred worked for the City of San Antonio mostly in unskilled and semi-skilled work such as street construction, sanitation, and building maintenance. . . .

In Los Angeles, Chicanos probably had greater opportunities to engage in specialized types of work than other urbanized Chicanos in the West. Already by 1890, manufacturing and mechanical industries employed 25% of the city's labor force. Although Los Angeles ranked behind San Francisco and Denver at the turn of the century in terms of the proportion of the labor force employed in industrial work, Los Angeles is important because by 1930 its Chicano population was ten times greater than either of the other two western cities. A survey of the Mexican work force in Los Angeles during World War I indicates that while a disproportionately high number of this group worked in unskilled labor, the majority of them earned their living in such industries as building trades, steel and iron, meatpacking, interurban transportation maintenance, and street-paving.

By 1930, industrial establishments in California with 100 or more workers on their payroll employed the majority of Chicano laborers in non-agricultural work. That year the United States Census showed that 30% of the Chicano labor force in California worked in manufacturing-related jobs, the highest proportion for any state in the Southwest. Indeed, 5,500 Chicanos in California held jobs in iron, steel, and clay-glass industries. Another 5,000 Chicanos labored in service related jobs. By 1930 only 37% of the Chicanos in the state worked in agriculture, and the majority of those agricultural workers lived in urban areas, commuting to rural areas to work. . . .

INTERNAL SPATIAL STRUCTURE

Cities have changed tremendously in size and complexity over the past hundred years, but many of the spatial patterns associated with urbanization and distribution of human activities during this initial period have persisted. . . .

In cities throughout the Southwest, residential patterns of Chicanos varied. During the early 20th century, some lived in segregated enclaves or barrios, while others lived in ethnically mixed neighborhoods. . . . The selection of housing proved one of the most difficult ordeals faced by the Mexican migrant to an urban area. In many cases the search did not begin until family members had a firm commitment of employment. The housing unit itself was of primary importance, since many of the Mexicans had sizable families. For example in the large cities, Los Angeles, San Antonio, and San Francisco, Mexicans often found housing units that had been converted from single family dwellings to multiple family type apartments or boarding houses. At the same time, the neighborhood had to be appraised. Basically, the main factor governing the selection of a neighborhood, other than a desire among most of the Chicanos to live in an area of similar social class and ethnic characteristics, was not its intrinsic value but its nearness to the economic activities of the user. . . .

Mexicanos, like Blacks and Asians, were severely limited in their selection of housing units by widespread discriminatory practices. A Chamber of Commerce brochure used to attract outside industries to southern California typified prevailing exclusionary policies of the period stating: "Lynwood, being restricted to the white race, can furnish ample labor of the better class." . . . In other southwestern cities, Mexicans found that real estate brokers used restrictive covenants to channel their movement into certain sections of the city.

In all southwestern metropolitan communities, newly arrived and longtime residents competed with industry and commerce for space. In some cities, industrial and commercial establishments proved more effective, however, than residential users in acquiring control of accessible sites. Chicanos often found that they had no alternative but to move into more crowded quarters away from the central district. In Los Angeles, some 40% of the Mexican population maintained its residential location near the central area until the middle 1920s largely because the city had sufficient land available in the more industrially desirable harbor area. Commercial development of central Los Angeles intensified as dozens of new banks and department stores located there. By the end of the decade, the majority of Mexican residents had moved eastward into a relatively inexpensive, but very poorly situated residential area near the Los Angeles River. Belvedere, the largest of the Chicano working class suburban communities in Los Angeles, had a Mexican population of almost 21,000. The extension of Henry Huntington's "red cars" to Belvedere contributed to its rapid growth. A number of new industries, such as the B.F. Goodrich plant, located their new facilities near Belvedere during this period, as did other industries from the old central business district. South of Belvedere, meatpacking companies, iron and steel plants, cement and tile factories, the major employers of Mexican workers in the city, sprouted up along a path several miles long. More extensive use of the automobile and improvements in the city's inter-urban transit system made it possible for eastside residents to live in the Los Angeles periphery and continue to work in the central area.

In other large cities of the Southwest, Chicanos constituted the greater proportion of the population. In El Paso, Chicanos comprised 56.9% of the population in 1930, and Mexican residents in Laredo formed 72% of the population. (Other than Belvedere, 60.9% Mexican, no California city registered a Chicano population higher than 18%.) In cities such as El Paso, with its very high Mexican concentration, segregation by socio-economic factors was more prevalent than ethnic segregation. Thousands of Mexicans clustered around the smelters and railroad yards of El Paso's southside. . . .

In San Diego, California's principal border community, Mexicans lived adjacent to the canneries and warehouses associated with intercoastal shipping. The Mexican population of this port city was relatively small during the 1900–1930 era. While the city had a population of 147,997, it included only 9,266 Mexican residents, or 6.3% of the population. Here Chicanos lived in small segregated enclaves. Constantine Panunzio found that the Mexican residents of the city, although socially and politically segregated, lived under "favorable" conditions in 1930. Panunzio noted the presence of moderately good sanitation facilities, wide streets and no serious housing congestion in the Mexican *colonia*. The area had a number of Mexican stores, churches, and pool halls, without, according to Panunzio, the "slum tenements" often found in eastern and midwestern cities.

In contrast to the more complex internal spatial patterns that developed in El Paso and San Diego during the early 20th century, Laredo, a small border community in Texas, had only minor socio-economic and ethnic variations in its residential districts. . . .

Each of the large southwestern cities where Chicanos lived in sizable numbers had unique features and all grew at different rates. The factors that appear most crucial to understanding differential patterns of spatial structure are the rate of urbanization, the quality of inter-city transportation, and the degree of suburbanization during the period under consideration. . . .

DEMOGRAPHIC URBANIZATION

. . . Chicanos in the southwestern states lived in hundreds of towns, although roughly from 25% to 35% of the total Chicano population was concentrated in four or five large cities in each state during the period 1900–1930. Twenty-five percent of the Mexican population of Texas, for instance, lived principally in four cities: San Antonio, El Paso, Laredo, and Houston. In California, more than a third of the Mexican population lived in Los Angeles, San Diego, and San Francisco. The percentage of Chicanos living in each of these cities also varied. In San Antonio, Chicanos constituted 35.6% of the total population in 1930, but in Houston and San Francisco, they represented less than five percent of the total population.

In contrast with later developments, there was nothing spectacular about the urbanization of the Mexican population in the United States prior to 1900. Indeed, it had taken until 1920, 310 years after the first settlement by Mexicanos in the Southwest, for the Chicano population to reach 500,000. A decade later, more than 700,000 Chicanos in the United States lived in urbanized communities. During the 1920s the Chicano population more than tripled, increasing by twice as much as it had grown in the previous 300 years. The urban trend during the turn of the century focused mainly on Texas and California, with Texas having a higher number of urban residents. El Paso, for example had a Mexican population of 39,571 by 1920, some 10,000 more than the officially recorded Mexican population of Los Angeles and only 2,000 less than San Antonio. . . .

The Mexican immigration era of 1900–1930 qualifies as one of the most important population shifts in southwestern annals. Slightly more than 10% of Mexico's population—approximately 1,500,000 people—emigrated to the United States during these years. The significance of this period is shown by the fact that 94% of the foreign born Mexican population in the United States in 1930 had arrived after 1900. Some 62% of them arrived after 1915.

Prior to 1920, better rail connections from Mexico to Texas made it possible for a greater number of Mexicans to settle in Texas than in other states. Emigrants leaving Mexico before World War I had a choice of several Texas ports, including

Matamoros, Laredo, Eagle Pass, and El Paso. New Mexico and California had no direct lines to Mexico, while Arizona had only Nogales as an inland port city. Thus between the years 1900 and 1920, 70% of the Mexican migrants crossing the border departed for Texas, while only 6.5% initially migrated to California. . . .

. . . [A]fter 1920 more Mexicans settled in Los Angeles than in any other city in the United States and the city's Mexican population more than tripled. By comparison San Antonio's Chicano population doubled. By 1930, more Mexicans resided in Los Angeles than lived in either New Mexico or Arizona.

Chicanos living in the Midwest and East were even more urbanized than Chicanos in the Southwest. Of the Chicanos who migrated to Indiana, for instance, 91% settled in either East Chicago or Gary. Some 67% of the Chicanos in Illinois lived in Chicago; and 61.7% of the Chicanos settling in Wisconsin preferred the state's largest city, Milwaukee. Thus in areas where there were few Chicanos, most tended to settle in large cities which offered greater economic opportunities.

During the early periods of heavy Mexican immigration, many of the immigrants came without their families, partly because so many of them were employed seasonally, and partly because of the high cost of bringing entire families across the border. A general pattern seems to have been that the greater the distance from the Mexican border, the lesser the presence of Chicano women, and consequently of Chicano families. . . .

BEHAVIORAL URBANIZATION

Behavioral urbanization can be seen as the changes in life styles and individual behavior associated with structural and demographic urbanization. When large numbers of individuals are concentrated in cities of different size and density, daily routines and sequences of activities change radically through progressive differentiation. The effects of urbanization on human behavior are profound, for people change their ideas, behavior and social values. . . .

. . . Ernesto Galarza concluded that living in urban areas presented the newcomer with many different problems. . . . An example cited by Galarza concerned the credit system in the Mexican urban communities. In cities, he noted, the migrants could not rely on "the traditional system of borrowing money," a variant of the traditional money lending at usury of rural Mexico, and "borrowing—since the poor must borrow—has presented an entirely new set of subtleties which baffle[d] the Mexican-American." . . .

One of the traits that most clearly distinguished urbanized Chicanos from rural Chicanos and Mexicanos was the inclination to join and participate in voluntary associations. Manuel Gamio, a noted Mexican anthropologist writing in the 1920s, commented on the popularity of mutual benefit societies among the Mexicans in the United States. The immigrants found that clubs and societies especially served members in areas where collective action was necessary, or where they as individuals could not be as effective. In the southwestern cities, Chicanos had a variety of clubs and societies from which to choose. It was not uncommon to find an individual who belonged to several organizations—including a trade union (Mexican and/or non-Mexican), a political party, and still another to accommodate leisure interests (athletic association, social club, etc.). . . .

Another consequence of urbanization for Mexican families in the United States was the large scale entrance of women into the industrial labor force, especially after World War I. Although many Mexican women could find employment only in domestic work, thousands of women in Los Angeles, El Paso, and San Antonio found jobs in manufacturing and service industries. Fully a third of the California Mexican female labor force was employed in manufacturing by 1930. Nearly 2,000 Mexican women held jobs in the garment industry, the vast majority in the Los Angeles area. In states where manufacturing jobs were less numerous and agricultural labor dominated the economy, the greater proportion of employed Mexican women were found in non-industrial jobs. While only 14% of the Mexican women in California were in the labor market, in three midwestern states, Minnesota, North Dakota, and Montana, the percentage of Mexican women in the labor market was the highest in the nation, ranging from 20% in Montana to 51.3% in North Dakota. Mexican women migrating that far north were generally migrant laborers. While few of these field-workers remained for more than two or three months, it was not uncommon for them to work as family units. . . .

CONCLUSIONS

The data presented here contests the notion that Chicanos are recent immigrants to the United States. A continuity clearly exists between those Spanish-Mexican settlers who first occupied the Southwest in the 17th century and Chicanos who now live in the cities of the same region. While immigration from Mexico has been intense in the 20th century, especially in the years between World I and the Depression, almost every community in the Southwest had Mexican *colonias* dating back to the 19th century or earlier. The *colonias* survived the influx of Anglo settlers and served as a haven for later Mexican immigrants.

Mexicans immigrating to the Southwest in the early 20th century came during a period of intensive economic development. Yet, as the evidence presented in this essay demonstrates, there were differential growth patterns in various southwestern cities. . . .

The belief that Chicanos have only migrated in large numbers to urban areas since World War II has little substance. The unremitting influx of Chicanos to cities during the period 1900–1930 undoubtedly makes it difficult to support the thesis expressed recently by one scholar that Chicanos "have been grossly unprepared by anything in their past experience" to meet the challenges of our "highly organized, predominantly urban and industrial" society. While the rate of urbanization varied from city to city due to economic development and regional industrialization, by 1930 more than 50% of Chicanos, both regionally and nationally, lived in cities. . . .

The urbanization of residents of Mexican ancestry in the United States under-mines certain stereotypes. Much of the labor history by Chicano historians centers on rural farmworkers. Only recently have some historians begun to examine the role of Chicanos in urban industries. Urban Chicano labor leaders have been all but ignored, while labor scholars have taken a greater interest in the union activities of agricultural labor organizer Cesar Chavez and his predecessors. As has been sug-gested in this essay, economic development and urbanization prompted geographic mobility and occupational differentiation among Chicanos. Only when researchers examine the experiences of the Chicano urbanite can we expect to explain other larger historical issues such as the contradictions of assimilation and social mobility.

16

REGIONALISM, POLITICS, AND GENDER IN SOUTHWEST HISTORY
The League of United Latin American Citizens' Expansion into New Mexico from Texas, 1929–1945

CYNTHIA E. OROZCO

Cynthia E. Orozco, currently Visiting Assistant Professor in History and Chicano Studies at the University of New Mexico, received her Ph.D. at the University of California, Los Angeles. She was born in Cuero, Texas. Among her recent accomplishments are 80 encyclopedia entries for the *New Handbook of Texas,* including the Selena Quintanilla Pérez biography. Dr. Orozco has been among the leading members of the National Association of Chicana and Chicano Studies (NAACS), where she founded the Chicana Caucus. Forthcoming books include *No Mexicans, Women, or Dogs Allowed: The Rise of the Mexican American Civil Rights Movement* and *Mexicans in Texas History,* co-edited with Emilio Zamora and Rodolfo Rocha.

In 1929, Mexican American men in Corpus Christi, Texas, founded the League of United Latin American Citizens, the first major Mexican American civil rights association. By 1940 LULAC expanded into New Mexico and from there, to Arizona, Colorado, and California. In 1946, when LULAC reorganized after World War II, these southwestern states helped constitute the LULAC fold.

In this essay I contend that scholars have treated LULAC as a Tejano organization, ignoring LULAC in states other than Texas, and neglecting to study regional differences in the league's politics. Because of this oversight, I examine LULAC in New Mexico and assess the role of regionalism in defining Chicano and Chicana politics, and I raise the following questions: How did the social, economic, and political status of Hispanos and Hispanas in New Mexico compare with Tejanos and

From *Western Historical Quarterly* 29 (Winter 1998): 459–83. The original text has been modified. Copyright by Western History Association. Reprinted by permission.

Tejanas in Texas? How did issues of class, race, gender, and identity compare in Texas and New Mexico, and how did LULAC in these two states mirror these differences? Finally, how does our analysis of LULAC change when regionalism is considered? To answer these questions I will address the men's and women's councils of the Albuquerque LULAC and issues they considered—including the Coronado Cuarto Centennial Commemoration, the creation of Latin American/Hispano studies at the University of New Mexico, and the founding of the Barelas Community Center. . . .

New Mexico proved significant to LULAC's evolution: 1) New Mexico was the first state incorporated outside of Texas, 2) the league organized significant numbers of men's and women's chapters (councils) in the state in the 1930s, 1940s, and 1950s, 3) LULAC elected four New Mexican national presidents and a Tejano living in New Mexico, 4) it was the inclusion of New Mexico that made the league realize its national strength, and 5) LULAC's expansion precipitated the inclusion of Arizona, Colorado, and California.

The inclusion of New Mexico inaugurated significant exchange between Tejanos and Hispanos. *LULAC News* introduced both groups to one another's problems. On a monthly basis the *News* was sponsored by local councils who highlighted their communities: Taos, Santa Fe, Albuquerque, and Las Vegas. Likewise, Hispanos read about Tejanos in El Paso, San Antonio, Laredo, Austin, and Houston. The national presidents also toured other states and reported on their travels. New Mexican Filemón Martínez wrote of his trips to Texas, as did Ezequiel Salinas of Laredo, Texas, who visited New Mexico. In addition, LULAC members also shared stories of their journeys in *LULAC News*. Hispana Fabiola Cabeza de Baca of Santa Fe toured Texas, and J. T. Canales of Brownsville visited Albuquerque and Santa Fe. LULAC members traveled to national conventions in Texas and New Mexico. Santa Fe hosted the 1940 and 1947 conventions, and Albuquerque sponsored the 1942 meeting, which Tejanos attended. Likewise, Hispanos journeyed to national conventions in Texas. For instance, Hispanos, joined by several members from Arizona and California, attended the 1937 Houston Convention.

New Mexicans found LULAC appealing for several reasons. While Hispanos had a long history as a demographic majority, they, like Tejanos, were subordinated by European Americans. Moreover, in the 1920s, Hispanos witnessed an increase in European American political power in the eastern part of the state as white Texans moved in. In the 1930s and 1940s, Hispanos sensed a demographic decline; in Albuquerque, Hispanos became a minority by 1950. Hispanos sensed European American encroachment and organized LULAC in response.

The first connection between LULAC and New Mexico occurred in 1929 and involved Hispano Filemón Martínez. Originally from the Mora/Colfax county-line area, Martínez's family once owned Charlotte Lakes, south of Springer. His grandfather was Father Antonio José Martínez's brother. Filemón graduated from New Mexico Normal University in Las Vegas and became a teacher and principal. In 1925 he joined the insurance business and moved to El Paso. In 1929, he attended the city's first LULAC meeting and met Ben Garza, first president of LULAC. In 1930, Martinez left for Santa Fe.

In May 1933, Martínez was appointed as the special organizer of New Mexico by Mauro M. Machado and in 1934, Benigno C. Hernández was also appointed. From 1936 to 1938, Martínez served as state organizer and became national president from 1938 to 1939. From 1941 to 1942, he acted as New Mexico regional governor. Expansion into New Mexico must be attributed to Martínez who, by 1938, was called the "father of Lulackism" in the state. By June 1939, 24 councils had been organized or reinstated. Also during his presidency, Colorado joined the league and several councils were formed in Arizona and California. . . .

Albuquerque men began by sponsoring an annual banquet/dance and soon had 40 members. Founded on 20 January 1934 as Council 34, by August 1937, *LULAC News* reported the city had the "strongest council in Lulackdom." . . .

Albuquerque's membership was middle class. As sociologist E. B. Fincher noted, "In membership, Lulac represents a somewhat privileged group, for it is distinctly middle class in composition, and admittedly is made up of men of prominent [sic] in diverse professions . . . persons truly cosmopolitan and capable not only of bringing honor to their race but to all humanity." . . .

Council presidents in the 1930s included postmaster Magdaleno C. Gonzales, known as M. C. Gonzales, (not to be confused with LULAC founder and Tejano of the same name), Emilio D. Chávez, Melitón F. Otero, Onofre F. Sandoval, and I. V. Gallegos. In 1937, officers included a real estate agent, a druggist, a businessman, a banker, and a judge. Members included elected political figures Orlando Ulibarri, A. Patsy Vigil (a man), Dennis Chávez, and Benjamín Osuna. Some members were University of New Mexico (UNM) graduates.

By 1934, the LULAC constitution provided for Ladies LULAC, composed of separate women's chapters. They were active in Texas. New Mexican women initially organized ladies auxiliaries in Albuquerque, Santa Fe, and Las Vegas, although the constitution allowed for ladies' chapters, not auxiliaries. Albuquerque women formed an auxiliary around January 1935, but they did not become Ladies LULAC Council 17 until 1939. In 1939, they had 75 members, perhaps the largest women's council.

. . . Women joined LULAC for many of the same reasons men did. Antoinetta Martínez, wife of Filemón, wrote about "lady LULACers": "They think that the future of Lulackism does not depend only in what the men are doing but also in the part that the women will play." . . . Women may have formed auxiliaries because when males established chapters, they organized men first, and men may have believed women should be in auxiliaries. Women may have sought to support spouses and fathers, or LULAC men may have suggested an auxiliary. Filemón Martínez organized no women's councils; chapter-organizing was largely gender-segregated and in the pre–World War era women organized only in the state's three major cities. Later, Albuquerque, Santa Fe, and Las Vegas each shed their auxiliary status and became Ladies LULAC chapters. In Santa Fe, men reported they were "willing to see that their wives install a ladies council." The women's councils were also middle class and included professionals. Apparently, this middle class was absent in other New Mexican towns and villages and no Ladies LULAC could be sustained.

Albuquerque presidents included Ysabel Armijo, Jennie M. Gonzales, Celia Baca de Redman, and Dell Baca, who was single.

Women members acted independently, but cooperated in joint endeavors. Albuquerque President Ysabel H. Armijo wrote a letter to the director of the state's National Youth Administration protesting a 1939 *Collier's* article portrayal of Hispana girls in Capitán in southern New Mexico. She explained, "We feel it our duty as representatives of the Spanish and Latin women, we should protest against the defamatory things said of our native girls." Hispana Secretary of State Elizabeth F. Gonzales addressed the chapter on women in politics. And in January 1935, auxiliary officers and Council 34 signed a resolution favoring a UNM law school. The two councils sponsored joint activities, including a youth chapter and a LULAC Educational Loan Fund. Both councils helped administer the Barelas Community Center, although documents suggest the men founded it. It is unclear if the women's contribution to the founding simply went undocumented.

Besides sponsoring joint activities, women also organized separate efforts. In 1939, the Albuquerque ladies council established the youth council, Junior LULAC. Ranging in age from 10 to 17, members included the children of Albuquerque LULAC men and women's councils. Secondly, women organized the Rhythm Band of Children ages 5–10. The band participated in the Highway 66 parade and included girl band members featured as Miss Spain, Miss Mexico, and Miss Colombia. Finally, Council 17 contributed $200 to the LULAC Educational Fund of New Mexico. These activities suggest women had different ideals from the men; children were one of their primary concerns. But like the men, they too fostered gender-typed behavior for girls and boys.

Differences between Texas men and New Mexico men are revealed by a comparison of the issues addressed by the Albuquerque men's and women's councils with those in San Antonio, Austin, and other Texas towns. Between 1934 and 1943, Albuquerque LULAC focused on three issues: the celebration of the Coronado Cuarto Centennial, the establishment of Hispano/Latin American studies, and the founding of the Barelas Community Center in Albuquerque. In contrast, Tejanos played no central role in the Texas Centennial and spent little effort influencing, collaborating with, or fighting the University of Texas or other colleges. They did, however, establish a LULAC hall in Pecos, Texas, and helped with public housing in San Antonio—though they founded no local community center. . . .

New Mexico LULAC differed from Texas LULAC with regard to class, race, gender, and identity. The Albuquerque councils were more middle class, since their membership included numerous elected political officials, more professionals, and more college graduates. The presence of elected officials in New Mexico made partisan bickering among LULAC members more frequent. The constitution did not permit elected officials to join the league but in New Mexico this stipulation was ignored. Albuquerque had two LULAC members run for Bernalillo County sheriff with members working both campaigns. Some Hispanos feared LULAC was "just another political trap."

LULAC News produced by New Mexico reveals a middle class consciousness.

In 1950, sociologist John Burma described their ideology. "It is not homogeneous. It has its liberal and its conservative elements: anti-Negro, anti-Semetic [sic], and anti-peon feeling exists on the part of some, while others display complete tolerance." Fincher called it an "organization catering to the somewhat privileged middle class, as compared to the Alianza, Advancement of Spanish Americans, and *Associación Nacional Mexico-Americana*." New Mexico LULAC passed a resolution denouncing the "un-American" activities of the *Congresso* [sic] *de Habla Española* at UNM, an organization that developed in the post–1940 period as pan-Latino, pro-labor, and pro-immigrant, and that fought "double discrimination" against women. New Mexico LULAC rarely discussed the Depression, wages, labor struggles, Mexican immigrants, or land rights. . . . Likewise, Hispanas rarely addressed gender inequity.

Still, this middle class was colonized in both New Mexico and Texas. Burma's 1951 study noted that "the Spanish Americans were severely under-represented in the core business and professional class of New Mexico during the 1930s." This sector paralleled the colonized middle class Tejanos of San Antonio and Texas in general. Despite its more middle class composition, this sector was excluded from European American club life, as were the Tejanos. As women, Hispanas had a larger professional class in New Mexico than they did in Texas. Men in both states were more middle class. A "pattern of social separatism" existed as " . . . two ethnic groups are separated socially by the organization of clubs and societies along ethnic lines." Burma added, "the Spanish-Americans are often ill at ease with the Anglos who look down on them and whose antipathy drives the Spanish-Americans more closely into their own group for appreciation and self-expression." LULAC served this purpose.

Yet, Burma called the Hispano middle class "the most powerful and effective of all comparable Mexican American groupings in the Southwest." New Mexico's membership composition led it to a different course of action. Hispanos had greater access to their state legislature and the university administration. In 1934, Albuquerque men's LULAC appointed a legislative committee. A 1937 La Mesilla LULAC men's resolution sought to petition the state legislature to build a highway from Santa Fe to Las Cruces to El Paso and Mexico City. Hispanos could appeal to numerous Hispano legislators and even a few Hispana legislators. In Texas, Tejanos and Tejanas were at the complete mercy of an all-white legislature and despite the efforts of middle class members like Alonso S. Perales of San Antonio, were unable to get an anti-segregation bill passed.

At the same time there is evidence that Hispanos used LULAC's name for social activities more than Tejanos did; this was a function of class and regional differences. Filemón Martínez criticized LULAC festivities, and in 1940, Dell Baca pressed for more attention to La Raza's problems. Antonio Fernández of Santa Fe wrote, "I realize, of course, that conditions in other communities [read Texas] may be considerably different from those existing here, and that a more militant and combative attitude is necessary at times." He was referring to race conflict in Texas. According to Zeleny, "The most powerful instrument holding back conflict over the 'race-issue' has been strong party organization." Hispano consciousness as exhibited in LULAC dealt with race conflict in a more subtle manner.

Race issues differed in Texas and New Mexico. In Texas, by 1942, 122 school districts in 59 counties had separate schools. Desegregation was the primary emphasis of Texas LULAC in the 1930s whereas segregation was not an issue in Albuquerque or Santa Fe. Segregation was not as institutionalized as in Texas, and it appeared only occasionally. Still, there were signs and ads reading "No Spanish, No Mexicans" and "Anglos Only." In 1948, a Santa Fe English-language newspaper ran an ad reading "For Rent—Anglos Only." A number of Hispanos wrote Senator Dennis Chávez to complain of segregation and discrimination. . . . Nevertheless, in 1952, the city of Albuquerque passed a municipal order banning discrimination in public sites. No Texas city passed a similar order until the 1960s and then only as it related to African Americans.

In southern New Mexico and especially in southeastern New Mexico, where white Texans migrated, segregation was more common. Moreover, the presence of Mexican braceros from 1942 to 1964 may have also stirred racism. In Hurley, theaters were segregated from the 1940s through the 1960s. Christina Durán complained of race prejudice by "ignorant Okies or Texans." Discrimination was prominent in Alamorgordo and in Silver City as revealed by LULAC member Carlos Castañeda's Federal Employment Practices Commission reports. These issues gave rise to local LULAC councils in southern New Mexico. . . .

The ethnic identity claimed by New Mexico LULAC also differed from that claimed by Tejanos. *LULAC News* reveals that Hispanos referred to themselves as Hispanos, Hispanics, Spanish, Latin American, and American. Phillip Gonzales and Joseph V. Metzgar contend that "Mexican" and "Mexican American" were less common in New Mexico, and *LULAC News* confirms this thesis. In Texas, the Tejano LULACers called themselves Mexican, Mexican Texan, Mexican American, Latin American, and Americans, but LULAC members there did not call themselves Hispanos, Hispanics, or Spanish. The Hispano identification with Spain and Latin America related to the lengthy colonial settlements in New Mexico, the preservation of the Spanish language, and extensive non-contact with European Americans until after World War II. According to scholar John Chávez, LULAC "abandoned" the Spanish language, but such was not the case in Texas and even less so in New Mexico. Hispanos, like Tejanos, had a regionalistic self-awareness. At the time, women did not have a gendered ethnic identity and did not use Hispana or Tejana.

There were also differences and similarities between Hispanas and Tejanas. Both believed in organizing women and that women belonged in the public sphere. They promoted education, voted, paid poll taxes, and sponsored poll tax drives. Both states had some experience with auxiliaries, but only for a short period, and the auxiliaries participated in political issues, not tea parties. In New Mexico, the membership in Albuquerque, Santa Fe, and Las Vegas seemed to include more professionals, including several women officeholders (of which there were none in Texas). The presence of professionals may also explain why New Mexico women and men were involved in more joint endeavors than were women and men in Texas. For instance, New Mexican men and women hosted a regional convention in January 1940, and when committee appointments were made, women were well-represented in all of them. In Texas, women were relegated to "women's work," and women's activities were more separate and excluded by men's LULAC. Both Hispana electoral participation and Hispanas' more middle class status may explain this difference.

Moreover, during the late 1930s and 1940s, Hispanas held several LULAC national positions, including the position of second vice-president general, the highest position a woman could obtain during this era. National officers included Mrs. Joe E. Romero, Las Vegas (1939); Miss Dell Baca, Albuquerque (1942); Mrs. S. J. Apodaca, Albuquerque (1945); and Mrs. Albert Gonzales, Santa Fe (1947). Two New Mexican women also served as trustees of national LULAC: Fabiola Cabeza de Baca Gilbert in 1938–1939 and Mrs. José Maldonado in 1940–1941. Jennie González and Cabeza de Baca Gilbert also served as organizer generals of ladies groups. Tejanas also held these positions, but it is clear that Hispanas became active at the national level sooner than Tejanas.

LULAC's expansion into New Mexico moved the organization's horizon into the Southwest. Despite historians' Tejano-centric treatment of LULAC as a Texas organization, as early as 1940 it had become a southwestern institution. New Mexico's golden years in LULAC were 1938 to 1948, encompassing five national presidencies, expansion into three other southwestern states, the creation of regional governors for four states, the formation of numerous men's and women's councils, and an agenda related to national issues.

The league's work with the Coronado Cuarto Centennial suggests the league's participation in the "Hispanic cultural florescence" in the 1930s and a profound respect for Spanish heritage. LULAC offered a symbolic protest when it withdrew its support of the CCC, but its reinstated support suggested its civic Americanism.

Albuquerque LULAC's work in the founding of the Barelas Community Center suggests that it sought to institutionalize community empowerment. Making the most of a New Deal program, Albuquerque LULAC envisioned Barelas as a training ground for future Hispano leadership and sought to aid the working class community. The league was not estranged from the working class. As a middle class organization, it sought to serve the poor. To aid Barelas, Albuquerque LULAC garnered the resources of the university.

Albuquerque LULAC also initiated the first struggles for Chicano studies in the nation. This research revises our knowledge of the origins of Chicano studies. Scholar Carlos Muñoz identified several early Chicano studies scholars, such as George I. Sánchez, but described no institutional efforts before 1965. LULAC sought to create Hispano/Latin American studies as early as 1939. The connection that LULAC made between Hispanos and Latin America preceded the discussion by contemporary Latino studies scholars.

Women in New Mexico, like those in Texas, played an important part in the activities of LULAC. New Mexican women, as compared to Tejanas, worked in more cooperative endeavors with men, and attained higher positions at the state and national levels at a much faster rate. This occurred despite an auxiliary stage. Yet, feminist ideology critical of men's domination in the league came from a Tejana. New Mexico scholars have recognized Hispanas' unique role in electoral politics, but Hispanas in voluntary organizations require more research. For instance, Sandy

Schackel's *Social Housekeepers: Women Shaping Public Policy in New Mexico, 1920–1940* (Albuquerque, 1992), a discussion of women's organizations, omitted Hispanas, yet Hispanas have a rich volunteerist tradition in the state.

Sociologist Phillip Gonzales has raised the issue of whether or not the Hispanos of the 1930s exhibited "pride without protest." New Mexico LULAC exhibited both ethnic pride and protest. When confronted with blatant race discrimination, New Mexico men and women in LULAC attacked it directly. Race relations in Texas made Tejano and Tejana LULACs more race-conscious, militant, and combative, and class relations in New Mexico made social affairs in LULAC more important. Nevertheless, Albuquerque's middle class and LULAC's liberal politics were highly effective—they recognized the need for Hispano diplomats, lawyers, and community leaders and Hispano institutions like Latin American studies programs and the Barelas Center. Hispanas and Tejanas exerted the pride of their womanhood but with the exception of Dickerson Montemayer, they did not challenge the patriarchal nature of LULAC.

This comparative study of LULAC in New Mexico and Texas reveals the significance of regionalism in understanding Chicano and Chicana politics. Regional differences also existed within New Mexico. New Mexican scholar Erna Fergusson gave attention to the role of Texans in influencing and changing New Mexico in a chapter entitled "Texans Keep Coming." White Texans brought their racist attitudes to New Mexico, making southern and eastern New Mexico more Texan than New Mexican. Likewise, Hispanos and Hispanas imported LULAC, a Tejano and Tejana organization. With it, they fought racial subordination and sought to empower La Raza. As Hispano Arthur Chávez noted, "We have the race issue to work with . . . Texas, our sister and neighbor, is our friend and now, through the LULAC Organization, fraternally our beloved sister. . . ." LULAC, however, proved to be a better brother than a sister to New Mexico.

17

LABOR UNREST AND INDUSTRIALIZED AGRICULTURE IN CALIFORNIA

The Case of the 1933 San Joaquin Valley Cotton Strike

RAMÓN D. CHACÓN

Like fellow Chicano scholars Lea Ybarra and Alex Saragoza, Ramón D. Chacón is a product of the San Joaquin Valley. He initiated his college career at California State University, Fresno, where he received his B.A. in history in 1968. He earned his Ph.D. at Stanford University in 1983. At present he is an associate professor in the History Department of Santa Clara University, where he has been employed for almost twenty years.

Studies that examine labor conflicts on California farms have, for the most part, failed to make the connection between strike activity and the nature of capitalist agriculture. This not only is true of strikes that occurred decades ago, but is also true of those that took place more recently, such as the Cesar Chavez-led strikes of the 1960s and 1970s. This essay will examine one such outbreak, the 1933 San Joaquin Valley cotton strike. The cause of the conflict will be placed in the context of industrialized cotton production in that fertile region and the plight of Mexican workers who harvested the crop.

The cotton strike, which broke out on 4 October 1933, involved from 12,000 to 19,000 workers, paralyzed cotton farming operations in several counties for almost four weeks, and threatened to destroy the state's cotton crop valued at more than $50,000,000. The Cannery and Agricultural Workers' Industrial Union (C&AWIU), a labor organization affiliated with the Communist Party, spearheaded

From *Social Science Quarterly* 65 (June 1984): 336–53. Copyright 1984 by the University of Texas Press. All rights reserved. The original text has been modified. Reprinted by permission.

the organization of the striking cotton pickers, 75 percent of whom were Mexican. The strike was called because the cotton growers rejected the workers' demands for an increase in wages from 60 cents to $1.00 per hundred pounds. Although the C&AWIU finally settled for a wage rate of 75 cents on 26 October, marking the end of the struggle, the strike was considered a victory for the workers.

. . . The purpose of this essay is not to present an overview of the cotton strike. Its objective, rather, is to explain the cause for its outbreak, which was due to the nature of large-scale industrialized agriculture that prevailed in California and denied workers fair wages. Ginning companies, particularly Anderson, Clayton & Co., controlled the financial arrangements of cotton production (including wages and labor) and as a consequence shared much of the responsibility for the strike that unfolded by depriving the work force of a fair wage for cotton picking.

INDUSTRIALIZED AGRICULTURE AND LABOR STRIKES

Agricultural labor strife rocked California farms during the 1930s, and it owed its origins to the large-scale farming operations introduced at the turn of the twentieth century. Industrialized agriculture specializing in one or a few crops increased rapidly in scope and importance during the 1910s under the stimuli of continued urban expansion, more complex market relationships, and notable technological improvements in transportation and in methods of production on the land. Due to the large-scale and specialized nature of the operations, particularly in fruits, vegetables, and certain specialty crops, such as cotton, the usual family labor force of an individual farm operator was often inadequate to meet the demands of periodic labor that accompanied various stages of cultivation and harvest. The development of large-scale agricultural operations demanded the employment of gangs of wage labor, often on a seasonal, periodic, and casual basis, resulting in a departure from the usual ties between those who owned the land and those who worked it. Indeed, a subcommittee of the U.S. Senate Committee on Education and Labor headed by Senator Robert M. La Follette of Wisconsin, which investigated the violation of civil rights of agricultural workers in California during the 1930s, concluded that industrialized agriculture played an important role in causing labor unrest by radically modifying employer-employee relations. . . .

A major factor determining the size and frequency of strikes in agriculture, therefore, was the prevalence of large-scale farms that sought to underpay their labor force to reap greater profits. In testimony presented to the La Follette Committee, Paul S. Taylor, an economist and specialist on agricultural labor, contended that labor unrest was not associated with grower operations that employed a relatively small work force. In Taylor's view, the problem which the committee was investigating "was grounded in the relationship between those who employ large numbers on the land . . . and those who serve them as wage laborers."

Taylor's assessment was well founded, as large-scale farming operations predominated in California. In 1930, 36.7 percent of all large-scale farms in the United

States, those with an annual gross income of approximately $30,000 or more, were located in California. Although these industrialized farms were less than 3,000 in number, or barely 2 percent of all farms in California, "they accounted for more than a quarter of the land in farms, more than a fifth of the harvest crop, two-sevenths of the value of all farm products, and more than a third of all the expenditures of farm labor." . . .

A relationship between labor unrest and industrialized agriculture represented a major characteristic of the San Joaquin Valley. Large farms and a massive labor force, predominantly Mexican, prevailed in this region. During the 1930s, the valley experienced 42 strikes involving thousands of workers.

THE COTTON INDUSTRY

Farm strikes showed a high degree of concentration by crops as well as by geographic areas. Cotton production, for instance, appeared to have attracted considerable labor unrest. Although according to crop, cotton ranked fourth in the number of farm strikes throughout the nation during the 1930s (behind vegetables, peas, and citrus), cotton placed first in the number of strikers with a total of some 48,000. Six major violent strikes in California alone involved approximately 28,000 farm workers. The fact that cotton farms employed more seasonal migratory labor than any other crop in the state accounts in part for the above-mentioned strife.

The frequency and size of cotton strikes in California were attributed to a number of other related factors. One factor, however, that stood out as a cause for conflict concerned the size of the cotton farms and their pattern of labor relations that provoked an unusual degree of labor strife. Farms in California, as noted above, were large, but cotton farms were extraordinarily large-scale. Paul Taylor stated that although California produced less than 2 percent of the nation's cotton crop in 1929, it had 30 percent of the country's large-scale cotton farms. In fact, since the early 1920s, California's cotton farms on the average were the largest in the country. . . .

The underlying factors which specifically provoked labor unrest in the cotton industry . . . were low wages, caused in part by the depression, and a one-sided bargaining relationship. In their efforts to reap great profits, California's cotton producers practiced monopolistic wage setting through regional employers' associations. Because of low wages and a disadvantaged bargaining position, general discontent tended to flare into overt strike action and conflict during periods of depression and wage-cutting. The 1933 San Joaquin Valley cotton strike was a product of these conditions. . . .

THE POWER BROKERS: THE GINNING COMPANIES AND COTTON GROWERS

The valley's cotton growing region was a mammoth zone that spread across six counties, an area 114 miles long, 30 to 40 miles wide, dotted with more than 2,000 farms. Since agribusiness was the basis of wealth for the valley, the larger growers and cotton gin operators were among those who dominated the region politically and economically. . . .

The political and economic influence established by cotton growers and ginners not only exploited farm workers by denying them decent wages and living conditions, but also infringed upon smaller growers who were dependent on the cotton gins for financing the cultivation and harvest of their cotton crop. These large-scale growers who employed a sizable labor force accepted the production and marketing costs of their crops as relatively fixed and rigid but organized together with ginning companies and smaller growers to control wages to reap greater profits. . . .

The smaller farmers, despite the fact they employed little labor, supported the large growers and the ginning companies' wage-setting measures, especially the latter who financed the smaller farmers' cotton crop. . . .

The ginning companies played a major role in causing labor strikes because they controlled the wages that were established for cotton picking and, as noted above, financed the cultivating of cotton. Several large ginning companies in the San Joaquin Valley dominated the ginning and financing operations of the region, among them, Anderson, Clayton & Co., J.G. Boswell Co., the Pacific Cotton Seed Corporation, and the California Cotton Oil Corporation. In the 1930s, Anderson, Clayton & Co. was the dominant cotton ginning company in California and Arizona. . . .

Ginning companies, by means of their financial arrangements, controlled the wage scale for cotton picking in two ways. First, by withholding loans from growers who wanted to pay a wage scale the ginners contended would jeopardize the loan and put the cost of their cotton up too high, the ginners could force the growers to pay a lower wage rate. Second, the smaller growers who were especially dependent on the ginners' financial assistance, in order to obtain a loan, were compelled to deliver their crop as collateral months in advance to the ginning company. Therefore, to make a profit, the small cotton growers were forced to establish a low pay rate for picking cotton since the ginners had already purchased their crop at a prearranged price. This arrangement with ginners left the growers with little room for bargaining about wage rates with workers, and the result was low wages and labor unrest. . . .

Ginning companies and large growers also underpaid and manipulated labor through the establishment of agricultural labor bureaus. One of the essential elements of industrialized agriculture was the need for an abundant pool of seasonal hand labor. To secure an adequate labor supply and establish wage rates in given localities, such as in the San Joaquin Valley, agricultural industries formed labor bureaus. Most prominent in this region was the San Joaquin Valley Agricultural Labor Bureau (SJVALB). . . .

The leaders of these associations, and the major source of their funding, came from the large corporate farms and great processing and credit-financing firms of commanding size. Major agricultural interests controlled these bureaus and used them to impress their policies on other agriculturalists. In the San Joaquin Valley the large farmers and cotton gins, particularly the latter, dominated the SJVALB and controlled the supply, working conditions, and wages of agricultural labor.

F. A. Stewart, an agent for Anderson, Clayton & Co., served on the board of directors of the SJVALB. Participation of large corporations on the boards of labor bureaus reflected their dominance and the important roles such corporations played in the financing of such agencies. The annual budget of the SJVALB increased from $6,500 in 1932–34 to $10,000 in 1937–38. Over a seven-year period from 1932 to 1938, the SJVALB's receipts totalled $57,495. Over half of these funds, $29,605, came from 17 cotton ginning companies. J. G. Boswell Co. and Anderson, Clayton & Co. contributed large sums to the SJVALB; in fact, the latter in various years accounted for one-third of the agency's financial support. Large cotton growers also contributed to the bureau and benefited from its operations. On the other hand, smaller growers profited little from the SJVALB's operations, and their financial contribution was nil.

The La Follette Committee concluded in its investigation that ginning companies and large growers controlled the SJVALB and used their influence to establish the 60 cent wage scale for picking cotton. . . .

Major cotton growers and ginners, through the SJVALB, thus found another means to force individual cotton farmers to pay a lower pay rate for labor whenever their wage rates for picking cotton were above those established by the wage-fixing bureau. Rather than individual growers setting their own wages, the SJVALB now dictated the pay rate for the entire industry. Nevertheless farmers claimed throughout the cotton strike that they maintained a fair level of farm wage rates for labor based on the limit of their ability to pay, a wage rate they asserted was predicated on existing economic conditions. Cotton growers contended that they were unable to pay a higher wage scale in order to convince the general public of the notion that they had consistently sought to pay the maximum possible wages to their farm hands. Yet, the available evidence strongly suggests that cotton growers were able to pay a higher wage scale than the 60 cent per hundred pounds which was established in 1933 by the SJVALB. . . .

. . . Laurence I. Hewes, regional director of the U.S. Farm Security Administration, in testimony before the La Follette Committee, expressed his opinion concerning the farmers' refusal to pay better wages. He contended that the wages paid were "based not on the ability of the industry to pay better wages," but that employers were "more powerful and better organized . . . than the workers" who were "practically defenseless." "An oft repeated statement to the effect that the industry cannot pay higher wages," he stated, "would appear to be lacking in real significance."

Although the depression contributed to declining wages, the wage-cutting measures imposed by growers also contributed to lowering wages for cotton pickers in the San Joaquin Valley. Wages for cotton pickers of the region declined from $1.45 per hundred pounds in 1929 to 40 cents in 1932. The following year the SJVALB established a wage of 60 cents, but as a result of the 1933 cotton strike the pay rate was raised to 75 cents. Wages increased after 1933, reaching $1.00 in 1936 and declining to 80 cents in 1939.

These figures meant that during this period the annual earnings of all farm workers in the state depreciated. According to a report published by the California State Relief Administration, during the years 1930 and 1935 the average annual earnings of the state's migratory farm workers had declined steadily from $381 to $289 and the average amount of employment from 7.5 to 5.9 months. The annual earnings of farm worker families thus dwindled to the point where they were well below the minimum subsistence levels of $780 and $850 established for those respective years. . . .

THE MEXICAN LABOR FORCE

Since the 1910s the majority of California's agricultural labor force was comprised of Mexicans, most of whom had recently immigrated to the United States. . . .

Mexicans also comprised a significant part of the San Joaquin Valley's agricultural work force. A study published in 1928, dealing with the employment of nonwhite labor in California, documented a high concentration of Mexican agricultural labor in the Imperial and Coachella valleys, 75 percent; the southern California region, 84 percent; and the San Joaquin Valley, 56 percent. By 1933 the figure for the San Joaquin had increased to 75 percent. Many Mexicans who worked on the valley's farms were residents of the area. A large number, however, were migrants who traveled throughout the state and often migrated to other states seeking work. These migrants had permanent residences, but their work demanded that they travel with their families, motoring from one labor camp to another following seasonal crops. The great majority of the migratory laborers who moved seasonally into the San Joaquin Valley had permanent residences in southern California. Thus, between 1924 and 1930, a yearly average of 58,000 Mexicans reportedly trekked from the southern part of the state to the San Joaquin Valley principally for the cotton harvest.

Traditionally, or at least until the 1920s, the San Joaquin Valley guaranteed employment to farm workers during the spring and summer months, forcing migrants to return south in the fall. The expansion of cotton cultivation in the valley altered the seasonal labor demands by providing late fall and winter employment in picking and early spring employment in chopping. Migrants followed a labor cycle which guaranteed them employment for certain months of the year at their permanent residence. Then, after the crop season, they journeyed to other regions to find similar employment. . . . With the expansion of cotton production, however, migrants who formerly returned south found that the cotton harvest dovetailed with grape picking. Thus, with the season of employment lengthened into February, many migrants remained in the valley to await the opening of spring employment in preference to returning south. In many cases, after years of following this cycle, workers established a permanent residence in the San Joaquin Valley. . . .

. . . [F]armers considered Mexicans docile, tractable, and therefore capable of being manipulated. As early as 1908, Victor Clark, an economist, contributed to developing this stereotype when he wrote: "The Mexican is docile, fairly intelligent under competent supervision, obedient and cheap. If he were active and ambitious, he would be less tractable and would cost more." . . . One observer noted that the farmer regarded the Mexicans as a "desirable addition to the population, for they were a class of people who would always be content with performing the menial tasks, thus leaving other people free to engage in a higher order of enterprise."

The belief that the Mexican was racially inferior supported the reasoning behind these views. Although the Mexican was regarded as inferior prior to the twentieth century, the influx of Mexican immigration during the 1920s generated new pseudo-scientific explanations which tried to analyze racial differences in the United States. Many Americans, especially farmers, were influenced by these racial explanations and perceived the Mexican as racially different. Growers believed the Mexican possessed unique physical characteristics which were biologically determined and made the Mexican worker well suited for agricultural labor. Employers, for instance, asserted that Mexicans were part Indian and therefore were essentially rural folk, preferred the outdoor environment, and were content working on farms. Growers also stated that Mexicans were small, agile, and wiry and thus had the necessary physical qualities, unlike whites, to do farm work. Employers also asserted that only "niggers and Mexicans" could work in the hot sun because of their dark skin pigmentation. . . .

Mexicans were also regarded as ideal workers because according to growers they did not pose an economic threat to the American farmer like Asians, especially the Japanese, who were engaged in farming in growing numbers. . . .

Finally, growers preferred Mexicans because they regarded them as vulnerable aliens living a short distance from their homeland. Employers rationalized that should Mexican workers cause racial or social problems, or make outrageous demands such as seeking better working conditions, they, unlike other groups, could easily be deported.

These attitudes regarding Mexican workers also prevailed during the San Joaquin Valley cotton strike. As a result, during the course of the strike these preconceived notions that depicted Mexicans as inferior, docile, and subservient influenced growers to take courses of action which they believed would quickly end the strike. Such actions included "Red scare" hysteria tactics, threats to close down the strike camp, racial attacks, and threats of deportation.

Since most of the farm workers were Mexicans, cotton growers and their supporters treated them differently, using racist and xenophobic views to undermine the strike movement. Farmers argued that the Mexicans were "backward," accustomed to a poor standard of living, and therefore did not need wage increases to improve their lot. A cotton farmer made the following statement concerning the backwardness of Mexicans: "Picking cotton, that's their lot. It don't make any difference whether you pay them 15 or 35 cents an hour. Their women wear shoes only when someone will see them. They buy Buicks and don't know how to spend their money intelligently. They're stupid." Moreover, through the press and using the influence of local officials, growers tried to intimidate Mexican strikers by threatening those who engaged in strike action with deportation. . . .

. . . But growers had miscalculated and underestimated the workers' capabilities. The image built by the growers of Mexican workers contrasted sharply with the actual workers they confronted in the strike. The workers refused to be intimidated, and they responded to farmer attacks with violent actions of their own. Thus, the two sides squared off in the fields, using shovels, axe handles, and grape stakes to fight each other and blasts from shotguns and Winchesters as a last resort. The strike left scores of workers wounded and three were killed by growers firing volleys from ambush. The latter were identified, tried, and acquitted by a jury not considered impartial.

Many farmers witnessing strike violence were perhaps forced to modify their previously held views of the docile, tractable Mexican. Indeed, although growers had engaged in vigilante activities to suppress labor movements in the past, the 1933 cotton strike caused such apprehension among farmers that it prompted them to organize vigilante groups. The most important of these groups was the powerful Associated Farmers of California, a statewide organization established in March 1934 to defeat farm labor unionization and the C&AWIU. The cotton strike ended, however, not because of grower violence, vigilantism, or intimidation, but because C&AWIU leaders "concluded that the strike had caused enough suffering and that neither the strikers nor the union could gain anything by prolonging it further." . . .

CONCLUSION

The 1933 San Joaquin Valley cotton strike is a classic case of labor conflict centered in California's core agricultural producing regions. It has the essential ingredients for documenting the conflict that ensues when a highly capitalized industry, controlled by a small group of powerful ginners and growers, not only dominated the production and financing of cotton, but also controlled the work force and the wage rate for labor. More than any labor strike of the 1920s and 1930s, the cotton strike provides documentation establishing a strong connection between industrialized agriculture and labor unrest. Furthermore, the strike demonstrates that far from being passive and docile, as growers maintained, oppressed Mexican workers sought better working conditions and were willing to combat injustice to the point of sacrificing their lives. . . .

18

WOMEN, WORK, AND COMMUNITY IN THE MEXICAN *COLONIAS* OF THE SOUTHERN CALIFORNIA CITRUS BELT

GILBERT G. GONZÁLEZ

Gilbert G. González, the son of Mexican immigrant parents, was raised in southern California. He was awarded a Ph.D. in American history at the University of California, Los Angeles, in 1974. At present Dr. González teaches in the Program in Comparative Culture and Chicano/Latino Studies at the University of California, Irvine. His books include *Chicano Education in the Era of Segregation* (1990) and *Labor and Community: Mexican Citrus Worker Villages in a Southern California County, 1900–1950* (1994). Dr. González's current research focuses on Chicano politics in California during the agricultural strikes of the 1930s.

By the 1930s, hundreds of Mexican communities, ranging in size from the huge urban Los Angeles *colonia* to tiny hamlets hidden within vast agricultural and mining districts, were scattered throughout the Southwest. In 1940 at least two hundred Mexican communities of various sizes sprinkled the central and southern sections of California. "Hardly a town of any size or pretensions," observed Dr. Ernesto Galarza, "—Delano, Hanford, Brawley, Sacramento, San Diego, Fresno—failed to acquire between 1900 and 1940 its Mexican *colonia* on the weathered side of the railroad tracks."

The small-sized rural *colonias* can be appropriately termed villages. The category "village" has not been used previously in the literature on Chicano community history. Yet for countless southwestern Mexican settlements, village is a fitting description. It is particularly appropriate when surveying the history of southern

From *California History* 74 (Spring 1995): 58, 134–35. The original text has been modified. Copyright by the California Historical Society. Reprinted by permission.

California Chicano communities between 1910 and 1950, the formative years in twentieth-century Chicano history. Various forms of village-like settlements formed an integral part of that widely dispersed settlement pattern known as the "*colonia* complex."

This analysis is intended as a historical sketch emphasizing the activities of women within one village form: the numerous southern California citrus-worker villages established between 1910 and 1930 that were home to as many as 35,000 laborers and their families, with a total population of roughly 75,000. Given the wide geographic dispersion of the many villages, it is impossible to examine each in detail. I have therefore chosen as a case study the fourteen citrus-worker settlements in Orange County, a major agricultural region. Ranging in population from three hundred to one thousand, the fourteen settlements are numerically significant, yet manageable enough for drawing out those qualities that distinguished citrus villages.

Conditions of life in the villages varied from merely poor to extremely poor. Few, if any, residents reached the lower rungs of middle-class status, and those who did so were invariably merchants. Picking and packing were the principal (and many villagers would say the only) occupations open to Mexican residents. With yearly family incomes ranging from $600 to $800 (when combining the incomes of all adults and working children), it was virtually impossible to rise far above the subsistence level. Yet, substantial numbers of families were purchasing homes in the tracts. One 1931 survey found that half the families in Placentia "and practically all in Atwood and La Jolla were buying their own homes." Similar figures were reported for La Habra's *Campo Corona* and *Alta Vista* and the Stanton and Independencia villages.

Making ends meet on meager salaries required inventiveness, creativity, and adaptability on the part of the settlers. Examples ranged from the construction of their own homes to the tending of small livestock for food. . . . Unsurprising, the Mexican community did not require a disproportionate share of welfare assistance before the Depression. In 1930, the county dispensed $10,065 "to the needy," of which only $2,107, or about twenty percent, went to Mexicans; the remainder went to Anglo-Americans. An editorial in the *Placentia Courier* congratulated local Mexican communities for their low reliance on relief, stating, "Mexican residents have their own relief organizations which are functioning." A long-time resident confirms that the villagers cooperated to help out those who fell below the minimal income level. . . . Most families purchased staples, such as beans, rice, flour, sugar, coffee, and lard, in bulk. The more important purchases, especially clothing, textiles, and bulk food items, were made in town, usually in the commercial centers of Santa Ana, Fullerton, or Orange. One-hundred-pound sacks of beans or flour, forty-five-pound cans of lard, and five-pound coffee boxes were stored and used daily in food preparation.

Chickens, goats, ducks, and perhaps a pig or two were prevalent in village yards, supplying a principal source for meat. One study found half of the homes in a Santa Ana village had a milk cow. The same study reported that one in five county village families had a goat to provide its milk supply. Where possible, a wide variety of vegetables, including corn, squash, chilies, lettuce, string beans, chayote squash, and cactus, were planted in home gardens. Herbs used for cooking, medicinal teas, and poultices sprouted in lard cans standing in the yards. Other recycled cans held geraniums or mums, and these were separated from cactus or chili plants. The relative geographic isolation of several of the villages, and their inability to meet all their nutritional needs by raising animals and gardening, required purchasing some provisions from grocery trucks that were managed by Mexican merchants who drove through the village once or twice a week. Fresh, cheaper cuts of meat (usually tripe for a weekend *menudo* and pigs' feet for *pozole*), vegetables, fruit, eggs, bread, pastries, and other small items were used by homemakers to fill in for other goods when these were unavailable or too expensive.

Families, particularly the women, institutionalized a pattern of activities in the home, including the tending of vegetable and herb gardens, recycling materials for additional uses, and canning. Pedal-powered sewing machines were a common and much-used household item employed to sew flour, rice, and bean sackcloth into window coverings, quilts, bed sheets, table covers, shoe-pockets, kitchen towels, handkerchiefs, or other needed items. . . . In the villages, shirts, pants, and dresses made from store-bought materials saved considerable expense, and when children outgrew them, clothes were passed on to a younger sibling or to another family. When clothing wore thin, a patch renewed the item's utility. Men also engaged in sewing, but in cases within the sphere of men's employment. . . .

Canning foods, especially cactus, added to the *colonia* residents' cost-cutting, as did the brewing of beer. During Prohibition and afterward, many homes had a brew-pot to ferment hops, malt, sugar, yeast, and water into a tasty, smooth, strong beer. The steady supply of beer was bottled at home and was shared during frequent visits from neighbors, friends, and relatives and for the many birthday, baptism, confirmation, and wedding parties. Brewing was not confined to home use; small-scale bootlegging was also practiced in the villages. At La Jolla, for example, at least eight individuals sold beer. Home-brewing chores were added to the usual house-work, such as meal preparation (this invariably included handmade tortillas), wash-ing, ironing, sewing, housekeeping, and child care. If the woman worked in the packinghouse, cleaned house for a "high-tone" lady, or ran a small store, these were over and above her customary responsibilities at home.

Women were the storytellers, recalling the age-old stories of Mexico, some of which were handed down from pre-Columbian times, and many of which referred to the supernatural. In addition to managing the home, practicing thrift, producing handicrafts, and preserving the oral traditions, women were responsible for reli-gious celebrations, such as *Las Posadas* and the *Dia de la Virgen de Guadalupe* (De-cember 12), as well as for processions, such as for *Dia de Los Muertos* (All Soul's Day) and Sunday church fairs called *jamaicas*. Women, therefore, created and acted with-in the oral and visual cultural life of the camps and in no small measure shaped the material and cultural quality of life, all of which helped to overcome, to some de-gree, impoverished conditions.

Numerous business enterprises operated by women also served the villages. Common enterprises included selling homemade lunches to single workers or preparing foods to sell at *jamaicas*. Occasionally, women ran boarding houses for traveling agricultural pickers and packers. Small family-operated stores selling sundry goods were a common and an accepted sphere of labor for women. The Placentia *Comercial Mexicana*, a store founded in the late 1920s by José Aguirre and operated by Doña Martina Aguirre and her daughter from 1934 until its closing in 1943, provided people with smaller staples. Six small Campo Corona/Colorado stores, one of which was owned by a partnership between a woman and three men, provided villagers with goods. At La Jolla, the local pool hall was owned and operated by a woman, and at the end of the citrus era, a former packer, Irma Magaña, founded Pee Wee's Market, a grocery she ran for nearly twenty years. Villagers had no objections to women operating as merchants, even full-time merchants, as long as they also fulfilled their traditional domestic responsibilities, which they often did while tending store.

In the small homes, the kitchen was the heart, where the family clustered, not only for meals, but for social activities. The kitchen, and therefore the cooking, was almost always the province of the wife or her daughters, who relied on both fresh and processed ingredients. Tortillas, beans, chili sauces, and a variety of dishes, especially those using chicken, were the mainstays of the villagers' diet. Seldom was an evening meal eaten without fresh tortillas. Tortillas could be made from corn or flour; older women preferred to grind lime-soaked corn on stone *metates* (grinders) to prepare the dough for the griddle. Traditions changed over the years, however; flour tortillas, which require less preparation than corn tortillas, became the main homemade variety. Not only were meals served to the immediate family, but when neighbors, relatives, and the children's playmates happened by, as they frequently did, they were welcome to enjoy the family's hospitality.

For large families, washing laundry was not an easy matter, as it was nearly always done by hand. Children's clothing soiled easily in the dirt streets, and pickers' overalls seldom seemed clean. Washtubs, washboards, and long wooden stirring sticks remained constantly damp from their frequent use on back porches. The ashes from wood fires for heating water never seemed to cool completely. Occasionally a family purchased a secondhand electric washing machine, which reduced the chore time somewhat for its owner and for those relatives and neighbors eligible to borrow the machine for the minimal cost of electricity. After drying the laundry on backyard clotheslines, the finer clothing required ironing. The clothes were now ready for the next cycle of wearing, washing, drying, and ironing. Laundry was just one of many areas of villagers' labor that the women shouldered.

Women were frequently employed in the packinghouses, but this required the permission of their parents, or if they were married, their spouses. If they were mothers, child care was indispensable, and was often provided by in-laws (or *comadres*), trusted neighbors, or, if they were willing, their husbands. Many women packed citrus while also raising families and providing and caring for the home. . . . Some women packed on a casual basis, others considered it a full-time occupation. Seldom did women work and live independently. Even if they were single, their wages supported their parents' families, and even packers who were married women often set aside a portion for their parents.

The work was demanding and straining, resulting in a very tired work force at the end of the day. "I mean," recalled Julia Aguirre, "We were exhausted." Legs and backs ached as the day dissolved into the evening hours, when the "second shift" of cooking, washing, and cleaning house took over. Irma Magaña thought back and remembered that after work she, like others, "stayed home, made dinner, did the wash, and made beer for my dad." After years of packing, Angelina Cruz's mother suffered rheumatoid arthritis, a condition that she and several former packers claimed was caused by packing. Other work—the chores at home, especially washing—probably contributed as well to a prevalence of arthritis among former packers. . . .

Packinghouses usually employed a set crew of women year after year, and filled in with replacements when necessary. The packers came to be well known in the houses in which they worked, and, like the men, they quite often moved from Valencia to navel orange-growing areas, and not infrequently into the central California navel region. Following the growing season, a migration of packers paralleled the movement of agricultural pickers. There was no uniform movement of both groups; some made the seasonal trek annually, others occasionally, or seldom, if ever. Yet, migration was not uncommon, and thus it became a fairly accepted part of the citrus worker's life. Rarely, however, did the Mexican pickers and packers venture outside of those communities established for them. Citrus workers moved from citrus village to citrus village when migrating, and when doing so, hired on with foremen or packinghouse managers who knew them well enough. Managers came to know the available and experienced local and distant personnel by hiring them for more than one season. An informal seniority system functioned, and the same work force seemed to reassemble year after year. As in many other occupational lines, packers had a strong respect for their occupation. . . . Those who performed the job well, especially the *cieneras* or *campionas*—those who could pack one hundred boxes—received considerable respect, which translated into a camaraderie enjoyed exclusively by women.

Women packers often earned wages equal to those of men, thereby allowing a measure of economic social independence. Consequently, female packers developed a separate identity from women who remained at home. But, when employed, packers also enjoyed a distinctive social life within the packinghouse. Birthdays, wedding engagements, or other special events were often celebrated in the packinghouse with potlucks and parties. Packers shared information regarding employment through informal grapevines, notifying each other about which packinghouses were scheduled to increase their packing crews. As fictive-kin or as blood relatives, women tended to gather together when seeking employment, when employed, and when traveling to local and distant packinghouses. . . .

Generally, most families in the *colonias* enjoyed sufficient diets, but cyclic unemployment and low wages often depleted precarious food supplies, and many families periodically sank below minimal nutrition standards. In addition, the poor conditions in the villages, dirt streets, lack of flush toilets, and inadequate plumbing and heating prevented basic sanitation practices. Disease and illness found a double entry. Consequently, health problems disproportionately attacked the Mexican communities. One illness, tuberculosis, proved especially deadly, affecting Mexicans three to five times more than the larger community, according to reports. In 1930, forty-four Mexicans died of TB in Orange County between January and September, nearly tripling the death rate outside the Mexican communities. . . .

Death claimed a larger number of Mexican village infants than those in the rest of the towns, illustrated in statistics from 1934, when of Orange County's one hundred infant deaths, sixty were of Mexican children. Other diseases also took their tolls. Trachoma, a contagious eye infection, spread through the Campo Colorado/Corona in 1927, affecting twenty-five children. Meanwhile, only one child in the non-Mexican district of the community was so infected. When serious illness struck, villagers depended on the county hospital; lesser health problems were combated with folk medicines. Women specialized in health care and were knowledgeable about childbirth, as well as the supernatural causes of and cures for illnesses. Villages generally had the services of a *partera* (midwife) and a *curandera* (curer), both of whom practiced a traditional medicine that employed teas, roots, flowers, poultices, leaves, prayers, and charms. These skills were passed on from one generation to the next. . . .

No sooner had the villages constructed a routine than the Depression brought more adversity to an already difficult life. Some families were forced into a relentless, often fruitless, search for survival, causing some fathers to break down and cry unashamed before friends and relatives. . . . Several sources indicate that about forty percent of Mexican families were forced into some form of public assistance. Available credit in village stores was stretched to the limit. At the end of the Depression, Placentia's *Comercial Mexicana* held sixty accounts due, ranging from a few dollars to $60. Only half were ever paid. Other forms of help came from within the community, such as self-help lodges that raised modest funds for destitute families.

Outside of the community, however, the Mexican became a scapegoat for depression-caused troubles. In 1931 and 1932, local and county governments seeking to cut budgets became caught up in the national movement to deport Mexicans. Induced through threats of relief cutoff sweetened with an offer of free transportation to Mexico, about two thousand Mexican immigrants left Orange County. The majority left in nine train loads but some by private car. Families debated whether to leave and instances of sharp conflicts surfaced between those wishing to stay and those willing to repatriate. Compared to other industries, the citrus industry in general was not particularly hard hit by the Depression, but for those workers who declined repatriation, competition from other newly unemployed workers cut into employment opportunities, sending already low wages into a decline. . . .

Mexican residents were the poorest social group in the citrus belt. Yet by pooling their resources, utilizing materials others considered useless, sewing clothes and other items from recycled materials, building their own homes, producing their food, and caring for themselves in a communal fashion, they managed—but never defeated—the formidable limitations of subsistence wages, substandard living conditions, and natural and economic disasters.

The Mexican community knew well that, except for the lowest-paid positions in the sugar refining industry, employment in factories, restaurants, department stores, and shops was closed to all but the dominant community. A lid on their possibility for economic and social progress forced the Mexican community to function as cheap labor. Legal restrictive covenants segregating residential zones mirrored the division of labor. In public parks, swimming pools, theaters, restaurants, bars, dance halls, clubs, and societies, Mexican immigrants and their families were either systematically excluded or segregated. At Anaheim's public park, for example, a corner section with a sign "for Mexican use only" was cordoned off by a chain-link fence. On weekends, a police officer patrolled the grounds, warning potential transgressors to stay within their assigned areas. Cross-cultural dating was out of the question and inter-marriage rare. In sum, the Mexican community was isolated socioeconomically, and subject to the political decision-making of the dominant community. Ironically, the citrus industry at large enjoyed many of its most prosperous years while this social practice was in force.

Most immigrants were strangers to each other, coming from several states in Mexico; yet they founded a dynamic and creative community with distinctive life, organization, traditions, and customs. The old-world heritage of the people provided a firm and trusted foundation for their community life in the United States. The Mexicanized Spanish language, Mexican patriotic and religious observances, and folk art flourished. New cultural patterns in the forms of labor unions, baseball, music, language, American food, customs, patriotic practices, and political action were either selectively integrated or engineered by outsiders into the Mexican atmosphere.

Villages had the qualities of an extended family. The routines of daily life, the rituals of birth, baptism, marriage, and death, the problems of adequate shelter, nutrition, and health care, and even the maintenance of family ties and friendships were neighborhood concerns. One educator who was active in the La Jolla village observed that in "La Jolla a very friendly spirit prevails, because the inhabitants know each other well; many are related. Therefore, there are many good times at home." Residents of the villages verified the observation, contending that the village was home, neighborhood, playground, and social center, within which, as one villager commented, "it seemed everyone was a relative."

In time, an immigrant's extended family network merged with other families. Marriages, baptisms, and close and trusting friendships served to broaden family ties already cemented in *compadrazgo,* or co-parenthood. Thus the La Jolla resident's comment that "everyone was a relative," easily could have applied to the villages throughout the region. Local villages were bound to others in the region through the same kinship and *compadrazgo* system, forming a type of regional network. This local and regional network obtained in other areas of village life, notably in recreation, entertainment, patriotic and religious observances, and unionization. Since villagers knew one another, a locked door was a rarity, and all were welcome to a particular family's celebrations. Life was relatively straightforward and stable, although it was marked by poverty, seasonal unemployment, high incidence of illness, substandard housing, and social segregation from the Anglo-American community.

In spite of their humble conditions, the villagers' lives were ennobled by their efforts, to a degree successful, to create an independent way of life. Chafing under the burdens of segregation and feeling the sting of legal oppression, the residents, women and men, raised themselves above the onerous burdens forced on them by their time and place and constructed their vision of a good society.

19

TEXAS NEWSPAPERS AND CHICANA WORKERS' ACTIVISM, 1919–1974

IRENE LEDESMA

Before her untimely death in 1997, Irene Ledesma was an assistant professor in the Department of History and Philosophy at the University of Texas–Pan American in Edinburg, Texas. A native of Pharr, Texas, she received her Ph.D. from Ohio State University in 1992. Her dissertation is titled "Unlikely Strikers: Mexican-American Women in Strike Activity in Texas, 1919–1974."

During the 1935 organizing of Dorothy Frocks workers in San Antonio, Mexican women, members of the International Ladies Garment Workers Union (ILGWU) advertised for a fund-raising dance in the local labor-union paper. In the advertisement, union leaders described the women workers as "some of the most comely of the female sex to be found anywhere. They are good seamstresses besides." Although the editors of the paper recognized the women's struggle, they portrayed the dance merely as a social event. This incident was not unique. The press image of Mexican women workers frequently diverged from the women's pronouncements and actions. In this article, I would like to show that Texas-press images of Mexican-American strikers depended on Anglo, "American," and male criteria, and therefore touched only peripherally on the women's experiences.

This essay critiques the coverage of strikers in local, labor, and Spanish newspapers during four periods of Chicana labor militancy in El Paso and San Antonio. Coverage of the strikers was tainted by popular notions of gender, class, and ethnicity. The Chicana strikers' situation was often at variance with these images. . . .

Historians have shown little interest in the work experiences of Mexican-American women. They have focused on males or Anglo-American women. In the last twenty years, however, Mexican-American historians have begun to study the union activity of California Mexican-American women. Some described these women as

From *Western Historical Quarterly* 26 (Autumn 1995): 309–31. The original text has been modified.

activists with supportive union leadership. Others showed them as innovative participants in benignly neglectful unions. A few questioned union motives. In Texas, Mexican-American women strikers were as activist and innovative as union members anywhere, despite tremendous odds: hostile owners, city officials, laborites, or a Mexican-American community holding certain expectations of them.

Texas newspapers reported numerous union disputes and constructed images of Chicana strikers. To name four significant examples: In El Paso, in 1919, Mexican laundry women protested the firing of two workers for union activity. During the 1930s, Mexican women in San Antonio—cigarmakers, pecan shellers, and dressmakers—went on strike for higher wages and for improved working conditions. Chicanas also played a significant role in the 1959 Tex-Son strike in San Antonio and the 1972–1974 strike at Farah in El Paso.

The Mexican women strikers in El Paso contended with a particularly antagonistic, Anglo-dominated economy. World War I anti-foreign propaganda and Pancho Villa raids into New Mexico generated hostile anti-Mexican sentiments. Accordingly, in 1919, the Anglo-American population of El Paso generally viewed Mexican immigrants as an alien force. . . .

Organized labor also resented Mexican immigrants. Union officials blamed them for low wages, claimed they took jobs from Americans, and declared that they served as strikebreakers. . . .

When the Mexican women's laundry strike broke out, however, xenophobic labor leaders momentarily stopped their racially based campaigns against the employment of Mexicans. The story of the laundry workers is a good example of how labor leaders seemingly change their attitudes toward Mexican workers. On 24 October 1919, Mexican women workers organized a local of the International Laundry Workers Union. Soon after, the Acme Laundry of El Paso fired two veteran workers—one sorter and one marker—because they were recruiting new members to the union. . . . Within a few days, almost five hundred laundry women walked out of the six laundries in the city.

On the evening of the walkout at Acme, several hundred Mexican laundry women voted to stay out until the company reinstated the two fired workers. Subsequently, William Moran, editor of the labor paper and head of the Central Labor Union (CLU), the labor leadership in El Paso, assumed control of the strike. . . . The CLU leadership takeover reflected a belief generally held among unionists that working women could be dominated by male leaders. The takeover further suggested that Anglo CLU leaders perceived Mexicans as docile people.

From previous experience, labor leaders understood the difficulty of presenting a favorable image of Mexican immigrants to the Anglos in El Paso. Like many Progressive reformers of the era, the editors of the *El Paso City and County Labor Advocate* called on employers to prevent vice among the unmarried Mexican women workers. Labor leaders focused on the low wages of the laundry strikers, asking, "What chance has a girl or woman to live a decent respectable life at the wages of this kind?" . . . As the strike intensified, the paper attempted to counter El Pasoans' notions that Mexicans were morally lax. To do this, they imposed on the public images of the women's vulnerability.

In this attempt to help, the labor leadership itself ignored other roles of the Mexican women unionists. In November, a Texas Welfare Commission study of wages—in a variety of industries—revealed that many of the laundry women supported their families. . . . Despite the report and personal testimony, union leaders continued to portray these workers as women in need of moral protection and guidance. . . . By focusing on working women's alleged immorality and vulnerability, unionists sought to overcome resentment of the image of Mexicans as scabs and cheap labor, an impression that they themselves had cultivated in previous years during anti-alien campaigns. . . .

But union leaders' appeals on the issue of morality posed a problem. When Mexican women strikers positioned themselves at the El Paso–Ciudad Juarez border bridge to prevent Mexican citizens from taking their places, they contradicted union images of vulnerability. Those that remained picketing at plant sites issued verbal threats. . . . Such actions clearly contradicted the prevailing image of these workers as defenseless women. . . .

Laundry owners rallied, turning the tables on their opponents by seizing these negative preconceptions and applying them to union members. The daily press was quick to echo the owners' cause. . . . The *El Paso Herald* added to the negative image by describing strikers as "Mexican girls" who "are enjoying their vacation." . . .

Without evidence, the commercial press disparaged the Mexican strikers by linking them to radical groups. . . . The press gave inordinate attention to materials written in Spanish that had been seized from the Industrial Workers of the World (IWW). The daily papers played up the actions of scab laundry drivers as a first blow against Bolshevism. . . .

The Spanish-language press, with its largely Mexican audience, was enthusiastic, but patronizing, in its portrayal of laundry strikers. . . .

For all its posturing in support of the laundry strikers, *La Patria* was often condescending. . . .

Those civic groups to whom *La Patria* appealed clearly reflected the class interests of the Spanish press and of their own membership. In particular, the Mexican Alliance's denial of rumors that it was contemplating supporting a general strike by Mexican workers showed the members' eagerness to appease the owners. When questioned on the issue, members responded that "they were in full sympathy with the striking girls [but] no proposition of a sympathetic strike by local Mexican workers was favored or had even been considered." Seeing themselves as representatives of El Paso's Mexican community, the Mexican Alliance quickly discounted any connection to extremist actions.

By 1920, many CLU members withdrew into an alliance with a Ku Klux Klan–dominated good-government movement. With this retreat, organized labor and Mexican immigrants lost the opportunity for an alliance. Nativism in the 1920s and bad economic conditions in the 1930s widened the rift. It would not be until the 1950s that organized labor in El Paso allied itself once again with those workers of Mexican heritage.

Labor union activity in the United States increased enormously in the 1930s because of economic conditions and encouragement from the national government

in the form of the Wagner Act. The creation of the Congress of Industrial Organization (CIO) made trade unionism possible to the "unorganizable." In San Antonio,
between 12,000 and 15,000 mainly unorganized pecan shellers worked in the pecan industry. . . . When the CIO began unionizing efforts among the shellers, business and community leaders, who touted the city as a haven of cheap labor and who
relied on bought Mexican votes, worried that the Chicano masses might become
politically conscious.

Conditions and pay in pecan plants in San Antonio early in this century can best
be described as poor, but the economic situation of the 1930s made it worse. . . .

On 1 February 1938, thousands of pecan shellers walked out in protest of yet
another wage reduction. The pecan shellers chose a non-sheller, twenty-three-year-
old Emma Tenayuca, as strike committee chair. . . . Tenayuca had earned the Mexican-American workers' respect through her activities as secretary of the local chapter of the Workers' Alliance. . . .

. . . Refusing to consider the frustrations of a destitute people, the mayor and
chief gave voice to Anglo San Antonians' views of Mexican immigrants as ignorant,
tractable people open to subversive influences.

Daily press accounts of the strike focused on similar allegations about Tenayuca. They centered on Tenayuca's connections to Communism. . . .

In contrast to the obviously hostile attitude of the Anglo press and aggressive
actions of the police, the middle-class Spanish-language paper *La Prensa* expressed
some support for the Mexican strikers. . . .

. . . As had *La Patria* in El Paso in 1919, *La Prensa* offered support only
when the women behaved according to middle-class standards. Additionally, by the
1930s, the owner of the paper, favoring American citizenship, lost interest in returning to Mexico. His editors reflected this shift in mindset by emphasizing that
the Mexican strikers were peaceful, citizenship-worthy people.

The Anglo-labor leadership in San Antonio shared city government fears that
the Mexican masses might revolt. This concern explained the labor paper's lack of
coverage of the shellers' strike. . . .

The Mexican pecan shellers won the dispute. Three Mexican women—Amelia
De La Rosa, Natalia Camareno, and Velia Quinones—served on the committee arranging for an arbitration board settlement that restored wages to pre-strike levels.
Other women did not fare as well. Tenayuca left San Antonio in 1939 when in
August a mob stormed the city auditorium in a successful effort to prevent an Alliance rally. Tired of her protest activities, city leaders advised her to leave or face
the consequences. Pecan-shelling companies reverted to machine labor in 1939 to
avoid paying the wage rates of 25 cents an hour that had been set by the Fair Labor
Standards Act. This measure reduced the work force in the sheds by thousands.

In addition to the 1938 pecan shellers' action, three . . . brief dressmakers'
strikes took place in the decade. . . .

The 1930s pattern of garment strikes continued after World War II. They included much violence, bread and butter demands, and many Mexican-American
women in low-level, union positions. . . .

In the winter of 1959, approximately 185 Chicanas and Anglo women workers at Tex-Son went on strike to protest the company's policy of sending out work to Mississippi. . . . For two years the Chicana strikers picketed Tex-Son. They experienced two violent confrontations with non-strikers and participated in a regional boycott. . . .

The regional boycott of Tex-Son products required an extensive propaganda campaign. The union made appeals for support based on family and motherhood. . . .

. . . Union insistence on portraying the Chicana strikers as mothers, while true to a large extent, placed the women in an extremely limiting role. Women were presented either as bad and promiscuous or as good and virginal. In a period tainted by McCarthyism, images of virginity, motherhood, and peace and quiet worked better for the union than allusions to citizenship.

The commercial media presented a less generous view of the Chicana ILGWU strikers. . . .

. . . Though women pickets continued into the winter of 1962, monetary resources dwindled and the union could provide little support. The women eventually conceded the situation.

The 1972 Farah strike in El Paso was the other major garment dispute in the post-war period. The labor disagreement between Farah Manufacturing Company and the Chicana members of the ACWA [Amalgamated Clothing Workers of America] lasted two years. It centered on an owner determined not to accept the union, and included a nationwide boycott of Farah slacks. The union relied on prevailing ideologies based on ethnicity in garnering support for the women strikers and frequently turned for aid to the Chicano civil rights movement, which had begun more quietly, but lasted longer than the Black civil rights movement. . . .

In their boycott campaign against Farah slacks, union publicists played on the two themes of family and social justice with success. In 1973, the Committee for Justice for Farah Strikers created a Christmas card showing a female child clinging to an adult hand and explaining that her father was a Chicano striker "struggling to attain simple human rights." A union leaflet for shoppers portrayed a young female with arm raised in a clenched fist, representing, the inscription said, a minority group seeking to end its oppression. . . .

In their propaganda against Farah, the union betrayed their basic underlying insensitivity to issues of gender and ethnicity. The inscription on the leaflet of a young woman with raised fist seemed to imply that Chicanos had previously never protested their oppression, although the ACWA itself had led strikes of Chicanas in 1953, 1965, and 1971 in El Paso. Unable to forego its image of workers and unionists as men, the union in the Christmas card poster of 1973 pictured a male hand for the child to hold on to, and the legend discussed the striking parent as "her father." Yet, the majority of workers at Farah and on strike were women. Even the union emphasis on the nuclear family seemed questionable. According to women strikers at Farah, many of them were single female parents with children. . . .

From the beginning, Farah publicly and privately opposed the ACWA with every available means. He humiliated women by making them sweep floors, and he fired others suspected of union activity. To stop the walkout, Farah secured an injunction resulting in the arrests of hundreds. He placed barbed wire fences around his five plants and hired security guards with dogs to protect them. In his most pernicious pronouncement, he used the old charge of subversion, telling the *Los Angeles Times* that the strikers were Communists, and the union "had done him a favor by getting rid of that filth." By quoting Farah, the *LA Times,* long a self-admitted voice for the California elite, continued that policy in Texas. . . .

With their pro-Farah stance, the local press published many of Farah's public statements unchallenged. . . . By accepting uncritically Farah claims and by bypassing the position of the strikers, the press made clear the reality that the latter did not matter politically or otherwise in El Paso. . . .

The ACWA survived Farah's determined efforts to keep the union out because of the tremendous success of the national boycott of Farah pants. Farah stock plummeted from $39.50 in 1972 to $8 in February 1974. The "don't buy" campaign cost the company about $8 million in 1972 and $2.5 million in the last quarter of 1973. After two years, Farah agreed to the original demands for job security, arbitrable quotas, a grievance system, and a company-paid health plan, as well as agreeing to recognize the union and rehire the strikers. . . .

Guided by accepted ideas of gender, class, and ethnicity in American society, Texas newspapers expressed unwarranted assumptions in their representations of the Chicana strikers. The daily, local papers maintained a consistent profile of the strikers as outside mainstream America—as Bolsheviks, Communists, and as evil and filthy foreigners. When the local press was not focusing on the alleged anti-social and anti-American behavior of the women, it tended to ignore them and concentrate on the males instead. San Antonio and El Paso papers emphasized the Mexican heritage of the strikers in negative ways, usually through the comments of company owners or city officials. These papers pictured the Chicanas as lazy, impressionable, and stupid—or simply as "Mexicans." The daily paper's representations illustrated their bonds with Anglo government at the local level.

The daily press did not seem bothered by their contradictory depictions of the strikers. Their efforts *meant* to alienate the women from the rest of the community. At times, the papers portrayed the women as the antithesis of American good. In the next breath, the papers called them gullible and too indolent even to realize the American work ethic. Anglo readers could be comfortable with these representations because they fit into the accepted notion of Chicanas as an alien and unassimilable element. It was [with] this shared understanding with other establishment institutions that the commercial press pushed incomplete images of the striker.

To gain support, the labor press would periodically change its image of the Chicana strikers. It would select what was socially palatable in an effort to make acceptable a group of strikers who stood on the margins of society. In 1919, the 1930s, and 1959, the labor papers overlooked the Mexican heritage of the strikers to stress their American citizenship and their roles as vulnerable women and mothers. In the 1970s, with ethnic movements "in," the ACWA exploited the Chicana identity of the Farah strikers to gain boycott support nationwide.

Labor editors operated with many of the same prejudices as the rest of the community. In 1919, the labor paper pulled back from earlier anti-Mexican diatribes and supported the Mexican women strikers only to retreat into a KKK alliance by 1920. In the pecan strike of 1938, the labor paper, run by AFL leaders, gave coverage only in reaction to CIO interest or involvement in it. Only after World War II did mainstream labor provide less hesitant support to striking Chicanas—and they still continued to create narrow depictions of these women workers.

Spanish-language papers virtually disappeared after World War II, but in the earlier strikes, the papers, caught between their Mexican origins and ties to Chicana strikers and their hopes of becoming Americans, tried to play it both ways by stressing the Mexican heritage of the women in a positive way and at the same time stressing their good behavior. By emphasizing proper behavior, the Spanish press, with its own middle- and upper-class management, clearly exhibited patronizing attitudes towards the strikers as women and as working-class people.

. . . The striking women's often violent responses served to place them beyond the pale of traditional middle-class ideology, and the male hierarchy in the Spanish language press preferred instructing the women on strategy and conduct. Particularly after the 1920s, the middle- and upper-class Mexican immigrant embraced American ideals, and they pushed their ideals on their less well-placed ethnic sisters.

The distorted press portrayals of Mexican-American women strikers contain implications for all women workers. What the papers noted about the women revealed more about the journalists' inclinations and societal expectations of women than any meaningful delineation of the women's experiences. Women never did fit journalists' standards, whether based on class or ethnic definitions—because both or either were seen in male terms. All three press institutions expected certain behavior from women strikers, after having already designated them as the "other." This designation of otherness might well explain women strikers' actions, which are often defined as fierce, aggressive, and extreme. If they were already beyond the rules, why not act that way? For each woman striker, it was another woman striker who acted as her guide. The women's sense of striker solidarity became heightened when the local press, the labor papers, and the Spanish press deemed them as different.

The newspapers in El Paso and San Antonio proved unable to move beyond established notions of gender, class, and ethnicity in their coverage of the Chicana strikers between 1919 and 1974, but in the process, the press provided information on the overwhelming forces the women faced during protest situations. The Chicanas fought not only great opposition from the companies, but a powerful daily press ready to condemn their actions in support of the established order. Even their supporters, the unions and Spanish-language papers, expected certain behavior from them based on each paper's particular agenda in a given period. Despite these complex odds arrayed against them, Chicanas in Texas demonstrated the power of persistence in the battle for labor justice.

PART IV.
THE RISE OF THE
MIDDLE CLASS
1940–1965

Momentous socioeconomic changes in Mexican-American communities were characteristic of the period from World War II to the mid–1960s. These changes were largely a continuation of previous trends, but the war itself was a significant catalyst. Chicano scholars rightly see this conflict as a watershed in Mexican-American history.

The labor needs created by the war meant that the U.S. government would relax its stance on Mexican immigration. In 1942, the governments of Mexico and the United States initiated the Bracero program, whereby Mexican nationals, under contract, were permitted to enter the United States on a temporary basis to perform labor in key areas, predominantly agriculture. Intended as a wartime expedient, the guest-worker agreement proved such a bonanza for American economic interests that Congress regularly extended the program until 1964. Ultimately, three-quarters of the braceros worked in Texas and California; but, as historian Erasmo Gamboa shows in his essay, Mexican nationals were used far beyond the Southwest. During the Bracero program's twenty-two-year existence, nearly five million Mexican nationals were employed. Many of them remained in the United States upon the termination of their contracts, an illegal immigration that swelled the population of Mexican colonias, especially in the 1950s.

Eager to prove their allegiance to their country, Mexican-American youth joined the military in droves in the aftermath of Pearl Harbor. Ultimately, some 350,000 of them served in the armed forces. They fought with distinction in both the European and Pacific theaters. Indeed, they were the most decorated ethnic group on the battlefront, winning seventeen Congressional Medals of Honor during World War II and the Korean War—a contribution that remains one of the least appreciated aspects of their history. As historian Christine Marín illustrates in her essay, Mexican-American participation was not limited to the military front; on the home front, *mujeres* (women) were assiduous in sustaining the troops and picking up the slack in defense and other industries. Inevitably these activities, as historian Vicki L. Ruiz indicates, gave women greater liberties than they ever had before, beginning a trend that would have far-reaching social consequences.

Because the better-paying jobs were in cities, the war stimulated urbanization. By 1950, about two-thirds of all Mexican Americans resided in urban settings. Hence, perhaps the most momentous socioeconomic consequence of the war was the strengthening of the Mexican-American middle class. After the war, their numbers also grew as a result of the G.I. Bill of Rights, which provided servicemen educational subsidies and low-interest business and housing loans.

As important as the material benefits of the war, however, was a new sense of self-confidence that returning servicemen had gained. These veterans were instrumental in forming the Community Service Organization (CSO) in California in 1947 and the American G.I. Forum in Texas in 1948, and reinvigorating LULAC, ethnic organizations which stepped up efforts initiated before the war to gain better treatment for the ethnic community. Graphic illustrations of the continuing plight of ethnic Mexicans in the country during the war were the Sleepy Lagoon case (1942–1943) and the zoot-suit riots (1943) in southern California, both clamorous examples of anti-Mexican sentiment which, as historian Mario T. García argues in his essay, mobilized the entire ethnic community. However, this kind of mobilization was not always possible, for, as musicologist Manuel Peña notes in his essay on Tejano popular culture, the war also accentuated class differences among Mexicanos.

Although Chicano scholarship in the past has generally been critical of LULAC and other middle-class associations, particularly of their assimilationist orientation, these organizations' more positive features are currently receiving belated recognition. During the forties and fifties, for example, both LULAC and the G.I. Forum, as historian Guadalupe San Miguel points out in his essay, were in the forefront of the legal battle to end the educational segregation of Mexican-American children. Thanks to scholars like San Miguel and the brothers Mario and Richard García, leaders of the so-called Mexican American Generation are increasingly seen as precursors of Chicanismo.

20

BRACEROS IN THE PACIFIC NORTHWEST

Laborers on the Domestic Front, 1942–1947

ERASMO GAMBOA

Erasmo Gamboa is Associate Professor in the American Ethnic Studies Department at the University of Washington. A native of Edinburg, Texas, he served in the U.S. Navy in 1962–1966, receiving a Vietnam Service Medal. After military service, he attended the University of Washington, where he earned all his academic degrees, including a Ph.D. in 1984. An outstanding teacher, Dr. Gamboa has written many articles relating to Chicano labor history in scholarly journals.

Between 1943 and 1947, the United States government contracted with approximately 47,000 bracero agricultural laborers in Mexico to work in the northwestern states of Idaho, Oregon, and Washington. Despite the large number, little is known about the experiences of these men. In contrast, the history and administrative details of the agricultural bracero program in California and other southwestern states have been well documented. This essay examines the social and work experiences of the braceros on farms in the Northwest and compares their record with those of braceros elsewhere in an attempt to provide a broader understanding of the national wartime labor program.

During the Second World War, the U.S. War Manpower Commission's call for record-shattering farm production exerted tremendous pressure on an already labor-starved western agricultural economy. One result was a demand for Mexican workers to which Congress responded in August 1942 with Public Law–45 (PL–45), a binational agreement authorizing the importation of agricultural workers from Mexico. Two months later, the Utah-Idaho Sugar Company at Topenish, Washington, announced that 500 braceros would arrive for the October beet harvest.

From *Pacific Historical Review* 56 (August 1987): 378–98. Copyright 1987 by American Historical Association, Pacific Coast Branch. The original text has been modified. Reprinted by permission.

Within a year, Mexican nationals had become a vital mainstay in northwestern farm production; only California recruited more workers. Of the 220,640 laborers who entered the country under PL–45, approximately twenty-one percent were contracted by northwestern farmers.

The braceros' experiences in the Pacific Northwest were shaped by their background, the attitude of growers and northwestern communities, and the federal bureaucracy. Government officials expected the workers to live in tent camps under spartan conditions with few organized social activities. Overall, the men endured much racial discrimination from employers and local communities alike. On the job, they suffered many accidents not only because of their unfamiliarity with farm machinery, but also because farmers had little regard for their safety. As a rule, braceros received low wages, and when they organized strikes to win increases, they encountered quick and sometimes violent resistance from growers and local officials. Although these experiences differ little from those of braceros in the Southwest, the record of the workers in the two regions significantly diverged.

Life was difficult for the braceros because they were young and came from rural areas steeped in traditional Mexican culture. Typical were the eighty men housed at the camp at Lyndon, Washington, where the greater number were between twenty and thirty years of age with only two over forty. For most, their sojourn to the United States would be the first separation from their immediate and extended families which were (and are) so important in Mexican culture. Thus they arrived ill-prepared to cope with the strain of hostile and unfamiliar circumstances and the tensions and emotion surrounding the war effort. Not surprisingly, many men became distraught and feigned illness or wrote to their families asking to be recalled for reasons of supposed sickness or death before the end of their seasonal contracts. In one week alone at Preston, Idaho, twelve men returned home before their contracts had expired. . . . In 1945, the Chief of Operations at Portland reported that ten percent of all braceros contracted to the Pacific Northwest were either missing or had been granted an early repatriation.

Poor living conditions also heightened the desire of many workers to return to Mexico. In the Northwest, the braceros generally lived in mobile tent camps designed to go where needed among the widely dispersed agricultural areas. As a rule, six workers lived together in a 16' by 16' tent furnished with folding cots, one blanket per person, and stove heaters when available. Although each individual was entitled to bring seventy-seven pounds of personal effects from Mexico, in reality most arrived with little more than a change of clothes. Within time, the workers scavenged for discarded crates or boxes and placed them inside the tents for storage and seating. These makeshift creations, along with personal pictures of loved ones, tokens of remembrance, or knick-knacks purchased locally, completed the interior.

During the summer, the men were often driven from the tents by 100 degree temperatures, and in fall and winter, the fabric structures offered little protection from the inclement Northwest weather. Stoves, if provided, were virtually ineffective because the loose sides of the tent allowed heat to escape quite easily. Moreover, the frequent lack of adequate supplies of kerosene, coal, or dry wood meant that the stove heaters were often useless. . . . Although the specter of hypothermia was present, the braceros faced a more serious threat from fires as they struggled to keep warm with the combination of kerosene, old stoves, and highly flammable tents. Besides frequent tent fires, there were also destructive explosions. . . .

In the Northwest, as in California, meals were the source of more discontent and work stoppages than any other single aspect of camp life. In July 1943, Mexicans at the Skagit County camp north of Seattle went on strike in order to call attention to the terrible kitchen services. Workers there started their daily routine with breakfast at 4:30 a.m. Seven and a half hours later, they stopped work to eat a noon lunch consisting of three sandwiches: one contained meat, one egg spread, and another jelly. A sweet roll and half pint of milk were also provided. The camp, improvised at the county grounds, had no refrigeration; therefore by lunch time, the sandwiches, prepared the day before, were unappetizing and the milk was "sour or blinky." The type of sack lunches served in the Northwest were found in most bracero camps throughout the country. Although the men had a strong dislike of white bread and lunch meats, cooks served such sandwiches because they were easy to prepare. In California, camp kitchens continued to serve sack lunches for many years after the war. . . .

Food services were inadequate in other ways. Workers were not provided containers to carry coffee or milk, so they used anything they could find without much thought to sanitation. This doubtlessly contributed to bracero camps in the Northwest having an unusually high incidence of food poisoning. In 1946 in a period of nine months, there were five outbreaks of food poisoning. The most serious outbreak had occurred three years earlier on a hop ranch near Grants Pass, Oregon, where 500 of 511 braceros fell sick and 300 required hospitalization. The Pacific Northwest was not unusual in this respect, for elsewhere gastrointestinal disorders also developed as the most common health problem among Mexican workers.

Leisure time activities, a key to the physical and social well being of most persons, were just as precious to the braceros—yet the men had little to do during their off hours. In most camps, Mexican movies projected outdoors on walls were a bright spot in an otherwise dull routine. Among the films making the rounds of the camps and enjoying great popularity were *Jalisco Nunca Pierde, Huapango, Dos Mujeres, Un Don Juan, Ojos Tapatios,* and *El Héroe de Nacozarí.* . . .

When films were not available, the braceros found other ways to pass time during nonworking hours. On Sundays, they sometimes requested Catholic priests to offer mass in camp. They also frequently pooled their resources to purchase radios or jukeboxes, which they stocked with Spanish records. Others passed idle hours with handicraft work, such as fashioning rings out of scrap pipe or suitcases from discarded wood.

Beyond the limited leisure activities, the social highlight of the year at most camps was the celebration of Mexican Independence. The Office of Labor, in the War Food Administration, sanctioned the festival because officials recognized it as an excellent way to sustain morale and a dedication to task among the imported work force. State farm labor officials also encouraged local communities to cooperate with the celebrations at the labor camps. . . . Independence day festivities in most northwestern camps were largely improvised but still provided a welcomed break from the daily routine. At Wilder, Idaho, for example, the workers organized an impromptu evening dance but because "Mexican senoritas" were not available, some of the men agreed to dress in women's clothes in order to provide partners for the camp population.

Another much-celebrated occasion in the camps was Cinco de Mayo, the anniversary of the defeat of the French in Mexico. At Medford, Oregon, in 1944, more than a thousand attended the celebration, including U.S. Senator Rufus Holman (a member of the Senate Appropriations Committee), the mayor of Medford, members of the chamber of commerce, students in local high school Spanish classes, many farmers with their wives and families, and "several of the local barmaids." . . .

These two celebrations, which brought the braceros and public together, stood in stark contrast to widespread anti-Mexican sentiment usually faced by the workers. In the Northwest, Idaho developed the most notorious reputation for discrimination. Prejudice became so common and deep-seated that in 1946 the Mexican government threatened to forbid its workers to go into the state and two years later made good on its threat. Consequently, Idaho, like Texas, was blacklisted by the Mexican government for its mistreatment of braceros. This action resulted from the blatant racism of some Caldwell and Nampa merchants and businesses. A Mexican government official found that "signs in both Nampa and Caldwell business houses forbid the Mexicans to enter. Seven beer parlors in Caldwell and 11 in Nampa have such signs posted. . . ." The members of the Notus Farm Labor Committee, which had contracted the braceros, denounced the Caldwell Chamber of Commerce for violating the prohibitions against discrimination in PL–45 and cautioned that the practice jeopardized the growers' work force. . . . Few heeded the warning and Mexico put Idaho off limits.

Antipathy against Mexicans developed outside of Idaho as well. In Seattle, the Reverend U. G. Murphey, chairman of the Evacuees Service Counsel which worked on behalf of Japanese Americans relocated in internment camps, was unsympathetic toward the Mexican men, and although PL–45 did not provide for permanent residency, he opposed any settlement of braceros. Meanwhile, the school superintendent at Boardman, Oregon, asked Senator Rufus C. Holman why the braceros in the state could not be conscripted into the military. At Stanwood, Washington, braceros had an altercation with some high school students and a local marshal outside a restaurant resulting in a near "race riot." Not long thereafter, the camp manager at Medford, Oregon, reported that a Mexican national was attacked in public "without provocation" and severely injured by five young men. . . . Such instances were not everyday occurrences, but they did reveal a pattern of racial animosity toward the Mexican workers.

In Idaho the braceros asked I. A. Pesqueira, the Mexican consul at Portland, to intercede on their behalf against the discriminatory practices. It was their protest, coming on the heels of the earlier complaints about conditions in Idaho, that finally resulted in the state being placed off-limits in October 1948 for Mexican laborers. . . .

Braceros faced another severe form of discrimination from health authorities. Some hospitals refused to treat them . . . Sometimes, the workers were denied treatment on racial grounds, while on other occasions health practitioners doubted the men's ability to pay their medical expenses and feared they would be left with outstanding bills. . . .

When medical authorities and community hospitals treated the braceros, the workers usually received minimal attention. On one occasion in 1945, a Mexican worker received a gunshot wound in the abdomen (cause not stated), and died six weeks later. The Agricultural Workers Health Association, which worked with braceros, strongly condemned the doctor who treated the victim. "Burial visually eliminated medical incompetence," stated a spokesperson for the association and "it is indeed unfortunate in such cases that the physician cannot be given as the cause of death." The same year in Idaho, a group of braceros had been summoned to fight forest fires. On the third day a tree fell on one of them, Ramón Carrillo, and injured his leg. He was examined at the hospital in Grangeville, found fit, and returned to duty. Back fighting fires he continued to experience considerable pain in his leg. Six or seven days later, Ramón was examined once more but the doctor found no reason for the suffering. Finally, Ramón made his own way to a nearby War Food Administration office where he explained what had happened. Subsequent x-rays disclosed that Ramón's leg was fractured. Twice, he wrote to the Mexican consul at Salt Lake City to seek compensation for the time lost from work. Then in despair, he sent a letter in Spanish to President Franklin D. Roosevelt. "They do as they please," he complained to the President, "because I cannot speak English." Ramón was more fortunate than another injured worker who died after failing to recover from anesthesia administered to set a fractured arm.

In addition to poor living conditions, discrimination and minimal health care, braceros faced unpleasant and dangerous work conditions because some farmers had little concern for the welfare of the men. At times, growers required that the braceros work during extremely cold weather although the men were not acclimatized and lacked proper clothing. . . .

The growers' lack of concern for the men's welfare was reflected in numerous work-related accidents which resulted from poor safety and the braceros' inexperience with the hazards of working near powerful farm machinery. At Weiser, Idaho, Apolinar Calderón accidentally severed a finger while working on a seed harvester. In Oregon, Primitivo Mosqueda suffered serious injuries to the temporal region, lacerations, and a fractured skull when his head was pinned between two pieces of farm equipment causing "a portion of an end of a bolt to pierce down in the skull to an unbelievable distance." . . . At Kennewick, Washington, Pedro Correa Armenta lost his sight in a work-related accident. Following an unsuccessful operation to restore his vision, he was repatriated to Mexico. Often the braceros were killed or critically injured in accidents while being transported to and from work in open flatbed trucks. . . .

The braceros could legally do little more than complain to Mexican government officials to improve working conditions because their contracts prohibited work stoppages or strikes. In the Southwest these prohibitions kept labor disturbances to a minimum. As Ernesto Galarza noted, dissatisfied workers had but two alternatives: "either shut-up or go back." Doubtlessly, southwestern braceros staged labor protests . . . but no general pattern of strikes emerged. In the Northwest, on the other hand, braceros were constantly on strike, and this made the region unique among other parts of the country.

Just months after the braceros arrived in the Northwest, they initiated the first strike and established a pattern that continued until PL–45 expired in 1947. At Burlington, Washington, a local Mexican American convinced the braceros to halt work because farmers were paying higher wages to Anglos doing similar work. The growers ended the work stoppage by reminding the Mexicans that strikes were prohibited under the terms of their contract and by giving the Mexican American a "friendly warning against inciting a riot in a government camp." The "instigator" at once left and the workers returned to their jobs.

Most bracero strikes were not so easy to put down. Idaho, which had the lowest wage scales and the most recalcitrant farmers, experienced many serious labor disturbances despite the state legislature's approval, in February 1943, of a strong measure to curb labor unrest. The law prohibited union organizers from entering, without the owner's consent, "any ranch, farm, feeding and shearing plant or other agricultural premise" to solicit members, collect dues, or promote a strike. Picket lines and consumer boycotts were also illegal.

The law notwithstanding, in June 1944 the braceros at Preston, Idaho, went on strike over wages. "Those breaking their contracts," warned the growers, "would be taken out to the road where they would be out on their own, the proper immigration authorities would be notified, they would be picked up by these authorities, placed in jail to await court action; in the meantime while awaiting for court they would have to work for 90 days without compensation, except board and room." Under this threat, the braceros resumed work. However, five months later, the same workers struck again over wages, and this time they sought the Mexican consul's assistance. The farmers responded with violence and ended the strike. . . .

The longest and best coordinated work stoppage involved more than 600 braceros from four camps near Nampa, Idaho, in June 1946. The timing of the walkout was critical to the growers primarily because their crops were ready for harvest and because prisoners of war, who had earlier been used as agricultural workers, were no longer available. The strike was in protest to a higher wage scale in the western part of Canyon County where growers had to compete with Oregon farmers. Government labor officials described the walkout as a "general strike," because it included the four camps and the men were demonstrating in the streets of Nampa in open defiance of the growers. In an attempt to control the strike, a Spanish-speaking farm labor supervisor negotiated with the braceros until they finally agreed to call off the strike on the promise that the Mexican consul would push for a hearing before the county wage stabilization board.

Twelve days later, the workers and growers got an opportunity to testify before the wage board. The braceros presented their case for a uniform wage of $.70 an hour. The growers responded that some workers were paid as much as $.75 because they were skilled "American laborers" employed year around, but as for the braceros, they were paid adequately at a $.60 rate. In the end, the growers convinced the hearing examiners to rule that "there was no evidence presented that warranted a change, either increase or decrease, in the existing scale."

The Mexican consul, in a move to force an increase in wages, threatened the growers: "Considering that ample opportunity has been given Farmers Associations [of the] Nampa District to revise discriminatory attitudes toward contracted Mexican Nationals, please proceed to remove workers at your earliest convenience unless seventy cents per hour prevailing wage in nearby areas is recognized before Monday, July 22nd." . . . The labor dispute ended, however, without either an increase in wages or repatriation. Although made uneasy by the consul's threat and the braceros' "extremely rebellious attitude," the growers persuaded local law enforcement officials to break the strike by arresting the strikers on spurious felony charges. . . .

The pattern of labor unrest among braceros in the Pacific Northwest must be seen in light of circumstances peculiar to the region and the men's motive for coming to the United States. They came to earn sufficient money to take back to Mexico but this was not always possible because of working conditions or low wages. Most braceros left terrible living conditions in Mexico, yet the tent camps left much to be desired and the food was deplorable. When the workers protested, northwestern farmers searched for another source of cheap labor.

The expiration of PL–45 in April 1947 gave growers added reason to stop bringing braceros in the Pacific Northwest. The new legislative authorization for the bracero program, PL–40, contained major administrative changes, including payment by employers of all transportation costs from Mexico. As a result, braceros were replaced by Mexican American workers on northwestern farms, although southwestern states continued to recruit Mexican nationals in record numbers until 1964.

As in the Southwest, the war caused the northwestern agricultural economy to boom. Growers faced critical labor shortages that could be met only through the use of cheap imported Mexican workers. These men came with their civil rights formally protected by contract, but no sooner were they on northwestern farms than employers set aside the agreement. The braceros sought to improve their wages and treatment on and off their jobs, but the federal government, which had authority over any violation of the workers' contracts, offered them little support. . . .

21

MEXICAN AMERICANS ON THE HOME FRONT
Community Organizations in Arizona during World War II

CHRISTINE MARÍN

Christine Marín is Curator/Archivist of the Chicano Research Collection, Department of Archives and Manuscripts in the Hayden Library at Arizona State University, Tempe, Arizona. Her publications include *Latinos in Museums: A Heritage Reclaimed* (1998) and "The Power of Language: From the Back of the Bus to the Ivory Tower," in *Speaking Chicana: Voice, Power, and Identity,* edited by D. Letticia Galindo and María Dolores Gonzales (1999). Ms. Marín is a member of the Society of Southwest Archivists and the Western Historical Association.

The Mexican American experience in Arizona during the World War II period can be studied from new perspectives and viewpoints. Other than its main importance in the social history of ethnic minorities in the Southwest, it can be placed in the context of United States social history. It can certainly be placed in the context of Mexican American, or Chicano/a history, since World War II was a major turning point for Mexican Americans.

It is generally accepted by Chicano/a historians that World War II provided a variety of opportunities for changing and improving the economic and social conditions of Mexican Americans. Life outside the barrio during wartime exposed soldiers to new experiences. The G.I. Bill of Rights provided them opportunities for higher education, job training, business and home loans. Other Mexican Americans, however, continued to struggle with the common and prevalent evils of racism and discrimination in their communities. Mexican Americans were still segre-

From *Perspectives in Mexican American Studies* 4 (1994): 75–92. *Perspectives* is published by the Mexican American Studies and Research Center at the University of Arizona. The original text has been modified. Reprinted by permission.

gated in theaters and restaurants, and barred from public swimming pools, dance halls, and other establishments. Inferior education or lack of educational opportunity for Mexican Americans remained a deep-seated problem in Arizona.

No attempt is made here to analyze the military history of Arizona's role in World War II. Instead, this essay is an attempt to explain how Mexican Americans organized themselves within their own communities to become important, patriotic contributors to the American war effort. It also shows that Mexican Americans in Phoenix and Tucson supported each other's efforts to combat racism while helping win the war for all Americans. This wartime activism was prevalent in other Mexican American communities throughout the state as well.

There are some problems, however, in writing about Mexican American participation on the home front in Arizona during the war. For example, one cannot build on previous literature, since little has been written on this topic. Most Arizona historians or scholars have virtually ignored the history of Mexican Americans during this important period. In essence, they have completely failed to recognize a valid, fascinating, and viable aspect of Arizona history.

Other historians, like Gerald D. Nash of New Mexico, considered the World War II period as a turning point in the Southwest. Nash believes the war transformed the American West from a "colonial economy based on the exploitation of raw materials into a diversified economy that included industrial and technological components." His contention is that this changed economy encouraged the influx of larger numbers of ethnic minorities in the West, especially Mexican immigrants and African-Americans, thus diversifying the ethnic composition of the region.

Arizona was organized as a territory in 1863 and admitted to the Union as the forty-eighth state in 1912. Its population on April 1, 1940, according to the Sixteenth Census, was 499,261. Three major race classifications were distinguished in the Sixteenth Census tabulations, namely "White," "Negro," and "other races." Persons of Mexican birth or ancestry who were not American Indian or of other non-White races were classified as "White" in 1940. Thirty percent of Arizona's population was represented by persons of Mexican descent. Urban areas such as Tucson and Phoenix reflected a growing trend during this period. The urban population of Tucson in 1940 was 36,818; approximately 12,000 individuals were Mexicans and Mexican Americans. The total population of Phoenix numbered 665,414, of which roughly 15,000 were of Mexican descent.

Mexican Americans in Phoenix at this time lived in the same barrios they traditionally lived in when Anglo-American speculators, carpetbaggers, and entrepreneurs arrived in 1867. This area was near the south side of the Salt River. The land was undesirable to Anglos, mainly because of occasional heavy flooding and its proximity to unsightly railroad tracks. By 1930, the large Mexican barrio had been split into two distinct sections. The poorer district, bounded by Washington, Sixteenth, and Twenty-fourth streets and the river, contained a shack town of the poorer Mexicans, and a "7-Up Camp," a block of shacks along the north side of the railroad tracks housing hundreds of Mexican families. The second section of this same barrio was located between Second and Fourth Avenues, south of Madison Street. By 1940, this same large barrio consisted of smaller barrios from within, such as "Cuatro Milpas," "Little Hollywood," and "Golden Gate." Here, Mexicans and Mexican Americans owned small businesses, stores, houses, and built and attended their own churches. They generally lived apart in poverty from the Anglo residential areas and pockets of Anglo growth and business and economic development, which were further north of the barrio. In 1941, the Phoenix Housing Authority built three separate low-income housing projects with a $1.9 million New Deal grant from the federal government. The developments were the Marcos de Niza Project for Mexicans and the Matthew Henson Project for African-Americans, both located in south Phoenix. The housing project for Anglos, named for the Phoenix flying ace of World War I fame, Frank Luke, Jr., was built in east Phoenix. These housing units were to accommodate six hundred low-income families who lived in substandard dwellings in the same area. Segregated housing, however, reflected the thinking of city officials and leaders who were slow to eliminate other forms of discrimination in their town.

The Mexican American community of Phoenix readily supported the war effort almost immediately after war was declared late in 1941. The *Leñadores del Mundo* (Woodmen of the World), an active Mexican fraternal and life insurance society, sponsored the "Diamond Jubilee" to show Mexicano support for the war effort and for President Roosevelt. The festival and dance were held at the meeting hall of the Leñadores on the president's birthday, January 30, 1942.

Other *mutualistas,* such as the *Alianza Hispano-Americana,* the *Club Latino Americana,* and *La Sociedad Mutualista Porfirio Díaz,* were also active in Phoenix and throughout the state during this period. The Alianza Hispano-Americana was a fraternal insurance society that was first organized in Tucson in 1894. Like other mutual-aid societies in Arizona, the AHA offered low-cost life insurance and social activities to its members. Mutual-aid societies provided essential support for Mexicanos in the fight against racism and discrimination. Many proved to be the sources of cultural, social, and religious cohesion in Mexicano communities.

The coming of World War II saw the establishment of war-preparedness programs and training schools. The National Youth Administration (NYA) was one such New Deal program. The NYA was initiated on June 26, 1935, and provided for the educational and employment needs of America's youth. Two statewide National Defense training schools were set up under the NYA in Arizona. The training school for boys was in Tempe; the girls' school was located in Coolidge. Established in Pinal County in 1926, Coolidge is approximately 30 miles south of Phoenix. Tempe, at this time, was a small farming and livestock-raising community with a population of about 3,000. It was just nine miles east of Phoenix, along the Salt River.

Tempe educators and city leaders were targets of Mexicano opposition to racism and discrimination in three separate incidents in 1912, 1925, and 1946. Mexicanos settled in what is now Tempe in 1865, when the Ft. McDowell military post was established. The early settlement of San Pablo, later known as "Mexican Town" by the Anglos of Tempe, was already firmly established in 1874. The town itself was later incorporated as "Tempe" by the Anglos in 1895. Just after Arizona statehood in 1912, Mexicanos became the center of controversy, when they learned they could not claim title to the lands which they had legally lived on and developed, because their farms and homes were in what was called "Section 16." This area, which under the new Constitution of Arizona and its precedent Organic Act, was a school section, and thus not subject to permanent settlement. Consequently, the Mexicanos lost their land.

From 1914 to 1926, only Mexican children attended the Eighth Street School. In 1915, the Tempe School District made an agreement with the Arizona State Teachers' College (now known as Arizona State University) that allowed them to use Eighth Street School as a University Training School to establish Americanization programs for the segregated Mexican children in the first through third grades. The agreement lasted until 1950–51, when the primary students moved to the nearby Wayne Ritter School. In 1925, Adolfo "Babe" Romo, whose family settled in the area in the 1800s, filed a lawsuit (now known as the "Landmark Case") on behalf of his children who were attending the segregated Eighth Street School. In October 1925, Superior Court Judge Joseph Jenckes ruled the Romo children could attend the Tenth Street Grammar School. The following Monday morning, several Mexican children attended school there. However, the enrollment at the Eighth Street School was completely Mexican American until 1945. The third racial incident involved the desegregation of Tempe Beach, the city's public swimming pool. Tempe Beach was opened in 1923, and did not admit Mexicans. It was not until 1946 that the Tempe Chamber of Commerce agreed to admit Mexican Americans to Tempe Beach in response to legal pressures from Mexican American veterans from Phoenix who formed the Tony F. Soza Thunderbird Post 41 of the American Legion.

Another kind of pressure was applied to Arizona's Governor Sidney P. Osborn to integrate the training schools of the NYA in 1941. Led by Vicente Alfaro, a respected member of Tucson's Mexican American community, parents demanded that their children be allowed to participate in the NYA's resident vocational training school programs. The schools in Tempe and Coolidge provided classroom instruction to develop clerical and library skills among the girls, and enabled boys to learn and improve machine skills and welding techniques. Students also received civil defense training and learned about community safety. The training schools sought boys and girls from nearby communities, and many Mexican American youngsters from Tucson applied.

The training schools brought problems as well as opportunities to Arizona. The problems were racial, and opportunities were denied to the Mexican American youngsters. They were subjected to segregated classes and ethnic slurs. Anglo youngsters refused to interact with them, and they questioned them about their loyalties to America. The Coolidge training school director refused to accept Mexican American girls into the program because "Spanish Americans were not fit for employment in National Defense work," and felt that "it was utterly useless for them to start receiving instruction" there. Alfaro wrote letters to Governor Osborn requesting that he put an end to these biased practices. He cited President Franklin D. Roosevelt's pledge to be a "good neighbor" with Latin America in order to improve relations between countries as an example for Osborn to follow. In his reply to Alfaro, however, Osborn was not convinced he was the individual who could create change. Instead, Osborn reminded Alfaro that the NYA was a "federal set-up and one with which the governor, or no state official [sic], [had] anything whatever to do. It [was] certainly under the control and management of the United States government." There is nothing in the documentation to show that the matter was ever resolved. However, the Governor did ask Jane H. Rider, the Arizona administrator of the NYA, to investigate Alfaro's complaints. The record, however, is neither clear nor complete, and contains no reply to his request. Nor is there correspondence from the Governor to Vicente Alfaro regarding the incidents of racism in Tempe.

Mexican American youths were targets of racism in the copper mining community of Morenci, located approximately 250 miles southeast of Phoenix. Again, the Governor's lack of action disappointed the Mexican Americans who sought his help. This time, however, several Mexicano leaders from Phoenix, who were active sponsors and organizers of the city's only Mexican American Boy Scout troop, appealed to Governor Osborn in the spring of 1942 to use his powers to change the long-standing segregation policy of two Morenci facilities: the Morenci Club, and the Longfellow Inn.

Morenci was established as a mining camp in 1884. Bitter labor strikes and racial conflicts involving Mexicano miners and the Phelps Dodge Copper Corporation have occurred in the Clifton-Morenci mining districts since the late 1800s. Morenci is located in Greenlee County in southeastern Arizona, near the New Mexico border. The Morenci Club, owned by the Phelps Dodge Copper Corporation, offered recreational facilities to Anglos only. The Longfellow Inn was a restaurant in the community. Boy Scout Troop 134, with S.A. Morales, William R. Sanchez, S.G. Murillo, and Alberto Montoya as its leaders, planned on attending a two-day Music Clinic at the Morenci Club. Here, the group was to learn about the use of instruments and musical arrangements in the performance of musical events for their communities. Young boys and girls would sing and play patriotic music, and hear various groups perform. But their attendance and participation at the event was called off when the Scout leaders read in a local newspaper publicizing the event that "the Morenci Club and Longfellow Inn are not open to Spanish-American people." The article warned: "Please caution your students on this as we do not wish anyone to be embarrassed." Outraged at such blatant and open racism aimed at the young Boy Scouts—who symbolized the youth and democracy of the United States —the scout leaders sent a signed petition to the governor so that he could respond to their concerns. In the petition they cited the humiliation, embarrassment, and shame felt by the boys in the troop. They reminded Governor Osborn that these boys were American citizens who were entitled to fair, honest, and democratic treatment in their own state. Scout leaders also asked the governor to issue an official public apology in the form of a statement in the Morenci and Phoenix newspapers in order to expose the shabby treatment of these young boys. The apology never came from Governor Osborn.

Despite this racist atmosphere, other Mexican American youths in Phoenix participated in a wartime activity that involved the country at large. When the Standard Oil Company challenged all neighborhoods in July of 1942 to gather much-needed rubber for its war efforts, the youngsters from the Marcos de Niza housing project combed their Phoenix neighborhood for anything made of rubber. Gathering discarded tires and other materials, their final accumulation of rubber totaled more than 2,200 pounds, surpassing what was gathered by other youth groups in the city. Their "prize" for this accomplishment was a picnic/party, where they were treated to pies, sherbet, cakes, candy, sandwiches, and other refreshments. Rogelio Yanez, the U.S. Housing Authority's Mexican American representative for the Marcos de Niza housing project, worked with various mutualistas such as the Leñadores del Mundo, and the Alianza Hispano Americana, to sponsor and pay for the party.

Other mutualistas such as the Club Latino Americana and La Sociedad Mutualista Porfirio Díaz were instrumental in organizing Mexican American cotton pickers during a drastic shortage of farm labor in the Salt River Valley's cotton fields in Phoenix. This labor shortage served as the catalyst for the Mexican American community to become united with the larger Anglo community in an emergency harvest of cotton. In October 1942 the Victory Labor Volunteers responded to the call.

Long-staple cotton was desperately needed to make parachutes, blimps, and gliders for the troops overseas. These volunteer labor groups organized spontaneously and comprised members of civic clubs, women's social clubs, churches, and garden and veterans groups within the Anglo segments of Phoenix. The volunteers were headed by an informal committee whose sole interest was doing emergency war work whenever it was needed. Citizens throughout the city were encouraged to volunteer for a minimum of a half-day each week to harvest the cotton crop. They were paid three dollars per 100 pounds for long-staple cotton, and $1.50 per 100 pounds for short-staple cotton. Volunteers registered with cotton canvassers at the Phoenix Chamber of Commerce office, or at nearby U.S. Employment Service offices.

The Spanish-language newspaper in Phoenix, El Sol, ran a lengthy advertisement in its October 9, 1942, issue calling for the Mexican American community to participate in a patriotic show of Mexicano unity and become cotton pickers. Women and school children were encouraged by various mutualistas to participate in the picking and bagging of cotton, and the Phoenix Union School system permitted students to be absent from classes one day a week to do so. Transportation was provided by the city on a daily basis from various pickup locations within the Mexican American barrios of Marcos de Niza, Golden Gate, Riverside, Cuatro Milpas, and East Lake. Transportation trucks also left from neighborhood locations such as Conchos Grocery, Washington Elementary School, and the Friendly House. These trucks carried Mexicanos from residential areas near Fourteenth Street and Henshaw Road; Ninth Street and Washington; and East Lake Park to the cotton fields located in the valley. It was estimated that within a three-week period, 5,000 Mexican American workers—men, women, and children—harvested over 35,000 pounds of long-staple cotton for the nation's war effort. Thus, this cotton harvest emergency brought a rare opportunity for Mexicanos and Anglos to share equally in a patriotic, community effort during a tense and difficult labor and cotton shortage.

These two examples of Mexican American participation in Anglo-dominated activities may provide insight into how Mexican Americans created their own separate support systems in times of crisis, while co-existing with Anglos in meeting a larger demand. A national wartime emergency required and enabled these two groups to organize within their own communities and work together towards a larger common goal. The goal was met, even though the two groups stayed within their own social boundaries and worked separately. The tremendous responses to these critical emergencies also showed how the war briefly united Phoenicians, who crossed ethnic lines in order to meet economic challenges. In these examples, each group contributed equally to a vision of American unity and American victory, but did so separately, a point which should be emphasized.

In the early stages of the war, several military installations and air bases were established in the Phoenix area. Latino cadets undergoing training nearby were welcomed and honored by the Mexican American community with testimonial dinners, dances, social gatherings, and community meetings between February 17 and March 10, 1942. These cadets came from Mexico, Brazil, Cuba, Costa Rica, Honduras, Nicaragua, and Guatemala. They symbolized Latin American friendship and support of the United States in wartime. Mexican American alumni from the Spanish Club of Phoenix Community College, "Los Ositos," helped in sponsoring and arranging dinners, receptions, and honoring the cadets throughout the Mexican American community. The cultural ties that the community shared with these cadets reinforced feelings of ethnic and cultural pride.

Mexican Americans in Phoenix participated in other war-related community projects. American citizenship classes were taught by the bilingual staff of the Friendly House, a social service center formed to provide for the needs of the Mexican and Mexican American community. Classes on the Constitution were held on a daily basis at the Friendly House, and were also available in the evening. Members of the Spanish-speaking community felt they were helping in the war effort by studying to become American citizens. Obtaining American citizenship may have been an accepted way for Mexicanos to show their patriotism and loyalty to the United States and the war effort. It was, therefore, a unique opportunity for the Mexican American community to be accepted into the larger American society that still maintained racist policies and traditions.

Mexican American boys were encouraged to become involved in Boy Scout activities. Since it was felt that the American character was formulated and developed through the scouting organization, Mexican Americans believed that their youths could be molded into productive, patriotic, and loyal Americans, eager to support their country in times of war. Early enrollment numbered over 25 boys who became active in Troop 47, the only Spanish-speaking troop in Phoenix. . . .

Mexican Americans . . . needed their own heroes and heroines who could personalize and simplify the larger wartime struggle. The Mexican Americans in these communities proved themselves to be such homefront heroes and heroines, meeting the challenge to advance the Allied cause, while retaining the morale of their communities through social and cultural activities.

In spite of the culture clashes with Anglos, and the prevalent racism and prejudice against them, the Mexican Americans shared with the larger society the intent to win the war abroad. Unfortunately, however, this shared goal of victory during wartime was not enough to break all the existing racist barriers. The Mexican American soldiers fighting overseas for democracy left behind those in their hometowns to struggle for this same goal in Arizona. Mexican men, women, and youths . . . created their own separate American home front activities in their own communities. They left behind a legacy which is manifested in a cultural and ethnic pride that can be defined simply as "Mexican Americanism."

This form of nationalism, pride in one's ethnicity and cultural history, coupled with the patriotism of Mexican Americans, convinced many of them that racism was un-American and unpatriotic. These individuals took on the responsibility of eradicating it from this country.

The Mexican American soldier was the cultural and historical symbol of Americanism and social equality. At home, the Mexican Americans were the brave patriots who remained loyal to America as they sacrificed their loved ones for freedom and democracy. Such a sacrifice is the legacy the Mexican Americans of the 1940s leave behind for the rest of us to acknowledge and remember.

22

A PROMISE FULFILLED
Mexican Cannery Workers in Southern California

VICKI L. RUIZ

Vicki L. Ruiz received her Ph.D. in 1982 from Stanford University, where she studied under Albert Camarillo. She was born in Georgia of mixed parentage, her mother being Mexican, and attended Florida State University. Dr. Ruiz is chair of the Department of Chicana/o Studies at Arizona State University. Previously she was at the Claremont Graduate School, where she was Andrew W. Mellon Professor in the Humanities and chair of the History Department. Her most recent work is *From Out of the Shadows: Mexican Women in Twentieth-Century America* (1998).

Since 1930 approximately one-quarter of all Mexican women wage earners in the Southwest have found employment as blue collar industrial workers (25.3% [1930], 25.6% [1980]). These women have been overwhelmingly segregated into semi-skilled, assembly line positions. Garment and food processing firms historically have hired Mexicanas for seasonal line tasks. Whether sewing slacks or canning peaches, these workers have generally been separated from the year-round, higher paid male employees. This ghettoization by job and gender has in many instances facilitated labor activism among Mexican women. An examination of a rank and file union within a Los Angeles cannery from 1939 to 1945 illuminates the transformation of women's networks into channels for change.

On August 31, 1939, during a record-breaking heat wave, nearly all of the four hundred and thirty workers at the California Sanitary Canning Company (popularly known as Cal San), one of the largest food processing plants in Los Angeles, staged a massive walk-out and established a twenty-four hour picket line in front of the plant. The primary goals of these employees, mostly Mexican women, concerned not only higher wages and better working conditions, but also recognition

From *Pacific Historian* 30 (Summer 1986): 50–61. The original text has been modified. Reprinted by permission of the author.

of their union—the United Cannery, Agricultural, Packing and Allied Workers of America, Local 75—and a closed shop.

The Cal San strike marked the beginning of labor activism by Mexicana cannery and packing workers in Los Angeles. This essay steps beyond a straight narrative, chronicling the rise and fall of UCAPAWA locals in California. It provides a glimpse of cannery life—the formal, as well as the informal, social structures governing the shop floor. . . .

During the 1930s, the canning labor force included young daughters, newly married women, middle-aged wives, and widows. Occasionally, three generations worked at a particular cannery—daughter, mother, and grandmother. These Mexicanas entered the job market as members of a family wage economy. They pooled their resources to put food on the table. "My father was a busboy," one former Cal San employee recalled, "and to keep the family going . . . in order to bring in a little more money . . . my mother, my grandmother, my mother's brother, my sister and I all worked together at Cal San."

Some Mexicanas, who had worked initially out of economic necessity, stayed in the canneries in order to buy the "extras"—a radio, a phonograph, jazz records, fashionable clothes. These consumers often had middle-class aspirations, and at times, entire families labored to achieve material advancement (and in some cases, assimilation), while in others, only the wives or daughters expressed interest in acquiring an American lifestyle. One woman defied her husband by working outside the home. Justifying her action, she asserted that she wanted to move to a "better" neighborhood because she didn't want her children growing up with "Italians and Mexicans."

Some teenagers had no specific, goal-oriented rationale for laboring in the food processing industry. They simply "drifted" into cannery life; they wanted to join their friends at work or were bored at home. Like the first women factory workers in the United States, the New England mill hands of the 1830s, Mexican women entered the labor force for every conceivable reason and for no reason at all. Work added variety and opened new avenues of choice.

In one sense, cannery labor for the unmarried daughter represented a break from the traditional family. While most young Mexicanas maintained their cultural identity, many yearned for more independence, particularly after noticing the more liberal lifestyles of self-supporting Anglo co-workers. Sometimes young Mexican women would meet at work, become friends, and decide to room together. Although their families lived in the Los Angeles area and disapproved of their daughters living away from home, these women defied parental authority by renting an apartment.

Kin networks, however, remained an integral part of cannery life. These extended family structures fostered the development of a "cannery culture." A collective identity among food processing workers emerged as a result of family ties, job segregation by gender, and working conditions. Although women comprised seventy-five percent of the labor force in California canneries and packing houses, they were clustered into specific departments—washing, grading, cutting, canning, and packing—and their earnings varied with production levels. They engaged in piece work while male employees, conversely, as warehousemen and cooks, received hourly wages. . . .

Standing in the same spots week after week, month after month, women workers often developed friendships crossing family and ethnic lines. While Mexicanas constituted the largest number of workers, many Russian Jewish women also found employment in southern California food processing firms. Their day-to-day problems (slippery floors, peach fuzz, production speed-ups, arbitrary supervisors, and even sexual harassment) cemented feelings of solidarity among these women, as well as nurturing an "us against them" mentality in relation to management. They also shared common concerns, such as seniority status, quotas, wages, and child care.

Child care was a key issue for married women who at times organized themselves to secure suitable babysitting arrangements. In one cannery, the workers established an off-plant nursery, hired and paid an elderly woman who found it "darn hard . . . taking care of 25 to 30 little ones." During World War II, some Orange County cannery workers, stranded without any day care alternatives, resorted to locking their small children in their cars. These particular workers, as UCAPAWA members, fought for and won management-financed day care on the firm's premises, which lasted for the duration of World War II. Cooperation among women food processing workers was an expression of their collective identity within the plants.

At Cal San many Mexican and Jewish workers shared another bond—neighborhood. Both groups lived in Boyle Heights, an East Los Angeles working-class community. Although Mexican and Jewish women lived on different blocks, they congregated at street car stops during the early morning hours. Sometimes friendships developed across ethnic lines. These women, if not friends, were at least passing acquaintances. Later, as UCAPAWA members, they would become mutual allies. . . .

. . . [T]he cannery culture appeared unique in that it also included men. Comprising twenty-five percent of the labor force, men also felt a sense of identity as food processing workers. Familial and ethnic bonds served to integrate male employees into the cannery culture. Mexicans, particularly, were often related to women workers by birth or marriage. In fact, it was not unusual for young people to meet their future spouses inside the plants. Cannery romances and courtships provided fertile *chisme* [gossip] which traveled from one kin or peer network to the next.

The cannery culture was a curious blend of Mexican extended families and a general women's work culture, nurtured by assembly line segregation and common interests. Networks within the plants cut across generation, gender, and ethnicity. A detailed examination of the California Sanitary Canning Company further illuminates the unique collective identity among food processing workers. Cal San, a one plant operation, handled a variety of crops—apricots and peaches in the summer, tomatoes and pimentos in the fall, spinach in the winter and early spring. This diversity enabled the facility, which employed approximately four hundred people, to remain open at least seven months a year.

Female workers received relatively little for their labors due to the seasonal nature of their work and the piece rate scale. In the Cal San warehouse and kitchen departments, exclusively male areas, workers received an hourly wage ranging from fifty-eight to seventy cents an hour. On the other hand, in the washing, grading, cutting and canning divisions, exclusively female areas, employees earned according to their production level. In order to make a respectable wage, a woman had to secure a favorable position on the line, a spot near the chutes or gates where the produce first entered the department. . . . Although an efficient employee positioned in a favorable spot on the line could earn as much as one dollar an hour, most women workers averaged thirty to thirty-five cents. Their male counterparts, however, earned from $5.25 to $6.25 per day.

Though wages were low, there was no dearth of owner paternalism. Cal San's owners, George and Joseph Shapiro, took personal interest in the firm's operations. Both brothers made daily tours of each department, inspecting machinery, opening cans, and chatting with personnel. Sometimes a favored employee—especially if young, female, and attractive—would receive a pat on the cheek or a friendly hug; or as one informant stated, "a good pinch on the butt."

While the Shapiros kept close watch on the activities within the cannery, the foremen and floor ladies exercised a great deal of autonomous authority over workers. They assigned them positions on the line, punched their time cards and even determined where they could buy lunch. Of course, these supervisors could fire an employee at their discretion. One floor lady earned the unflattering sobriquet "San Quentin." Some workers, in order to make a livable wage, cultivated the friendship of their supervisors. One favored employee even had the luxury of taking an afternoon nap. Forepersons also hosted wedding and baby showers for "their girls." While these "pets" enjoyed preferential treatment, they also acquired the animosity of their co-workers.

The supervisors (all Anglo) neither spoke nor understood Spanish. The language barrier contributed to increasing tensions inside the plant, especially when management had the authority to discharge an employee for speaking Spanish. Foremen also took advantage of the situation by altering production cards of workers who spoke only Spanish. . . . In general, low wages, tyrannical forepersons, and the "pet" system prompted attempts at unionization. In 1937 a group of workers tried to establish an American Federation of Labor union, but a stable local failed to develop. Two years later Cal San employees renewed their trade union efforts, this time under the banner of UCAPAWA-CIO.

The United Cannery, Agricultural, Packing and Allied Workers of America has long been an orphan of twentieth-century labor history even though it was the seventh largest CIO affiliate in its day. Probable reasons for this neglect include the union's relatively short life—1937–1950—and its eventual expulsion from the CIO on the grounds of alleged communist domination. UCAPAWA's leadership was left-oriented, although not directly connected to the Communist Party. Many of the executive officers and organizers identified themselves as Marxists, but others could be labeled New Deal liberals. As one UCAPAWA national vice-president, Luisa Moreno, stated: "UCAPAWA was a *left* union not a communist union." Union leaders shared a vision of a national, decentralized labor union, one in which power flowed from below. Local members controlled their own meetings and elected their own officers and business agents. National and state offices helped coordinate the individual needs and endeavors of each local. Moreover, UCAPAWA's deliberate recruitment of Black, Mexican, and female labor organizers and subsequent unionizing campaigns aimed at minority workers reflected its leaders' commitment to those sectors of the working-class generally ignored by traditional craft unions. . . .

In California, UCAPAWA initially concentrated on organizing agricultural workers, but with limited success. The union, however, began to make inroads among food processing workers in the Northeast and in Texas. Because of its successes in organizing canneries and packing houses, as well as the inability of maintaining viable dues-paying unions among farm workers, union policy shifted. After 1939, union leaders emphasized the establishment of strong, solvent cannery and packing house locals, hoping to use them as bases of operations for future farm labor campaigns. One of the first plants to experience this new wave of activity was the California Sanitary Canning Company.

In July 1939, Dorothy Ray Healey, a national vice-president of UCAPAWA, began to recruit Cal San workers. Healey, a vivacious young woman of twenty-four, already had eight years of labor organizing experience. At the age of sixteen, she participated in the San Jose, California, cannery strike as a representative of the Cannery and Agricultural Workers Industrial Union (C&AWIU). Healey had assumed leadership positions in both the C&AWIU and the Young Communist League. . . .

The Shapiros refused to recognize the union or negotiate with its representatives. On August 31, 1939, at the height of the peach season, the vast majority of Cal San employees left their stations and staged a dramatic walk-out. Only thirty workers stayed behind and sixteen of these stragglers joined the picket lines outside the plant the next day. Although the strike occurred at the peak of the company's most profitable season and elicited the support of most line personnel, management refused to bargain with the local. In fact, the owners issued press statements to the effect that the union did not represent a majority of the workers.

In anticipation of a protracted strike, Healey immediately organized workers into a number of committees. A negotiating committee, picket details, and food committees were formed. The strikers' demands included union recognition, a closed shop, elimination of the piece rate system, minimal wage increases, and the dismissal of nearly every supervisor. Healey persuaded the workers to assign top priority to the closed shop demand. The striking employees realized the risk they were taking, for only one UCAPAWA local had secured a closed shop contract. . . .

Early in the strike, the unionists extended their activities beyond their twenty-four hour, seven days a week picket line outside the plant. They discovered a supplementary tactic—the secondary boycott. Encouraged by their success in obtaining food donations from local markets, workers took the initiative themselves and formed boycott teams. The team leaders approached the managers of various retail and wholesale groceries in the Los Angeles area urging them to refuse Cal San products and to remove current stocks from their shelves. If a manager was unsympathetic, a small band of women picketed the establishment during business hours. In addition, the International Brotherhood of Teamsters officially vowed to honor the strike. It proved to be only a verbal commitment, for many of its members crossed the picket lines in order to pick up and deliver Cal San goods. At one point Mexicana union members became so incensed by the sight of several Teamsters unloading their trucks that they climbed onto the loading platform and quickly "depantsed" a group of surprised and embarrassed Teamsters. The secondary boycott was an effective tactic—forty retail and wholesale grocers abided by the strikers' request.

Action by the National Labor Relations Board further raised the morale of the striking employees. The NLRB formally reprimanded the Shapiros for refusing to bargain with the UCAPAWA affiliate. However, the timing of the strike, the successful boycott, and favorable governmental decisions failed to bring management to the bargaining table. After a two and a half month stalemate, the workers initiated an innovative technique that became, as Healey recalled, "the straw that broke the Shapiros' back."

Both George and Joseph Shapiro lived in affluent sections of Los Angeles, and their wealthy neighbors were as surprised as the brothers to discover one morning a small group of children conducting orderly picket lines on the Shapiros' front lawns. These malnourished waifs carried signs with such slogans as "Shapiro is starving my Mama" and "I'm underfed because my Mama is underpaid." Many of the neighbors became so moved by the sight of these children conducting what became a twenty-four hour vigil that they offered their support, usually by distributing food and beverages. And if this was not enough, the owners were reproached by several members of their synagogue. After several days of community pressures, the Shapiros finally agreed to meet with Local 75's negotiating team. The strike had ended.

A settlement was quickly reached. Although the workers failed to win the elimination of the piece rate system, they did receive a five cent wage increase, and many forepersons found themselves unemployed. More importantly, Local 75 had become the second UCAPAWA affiliate (and the first on the west coast) to negotiate successfully a closed shop contract.

. . . In late 1940, Luisa Moreno, an UCAPAWA representative, took charge of consolidating Local 75. Like Dorothy Healey, Moreno had a long history of labor activism prior to her tenure with UCAPAWA. As a professional organizer for the AF of L and later for the CIO, Moreno had unionized workers in cigar making plants in Florida and Pennsylvania.

Luisa Moreno helped insure the vitality of Local 75. She vigorously enforced government regulations and contract stipulations. She also encouraged members to air any grievance immediately. On a number of occasions, her fluency in Spanish and English allayed misunderstandings between Mexicana workers and Anglo supervisors. Participation in civic events, such as the annual Labor Day parade, fostered worker solidarity and union pride. The employees also banded together to break certain hiring policies. With one very light-skinned exception, the brothers had refused to hire blacks. With union pressure, however, in early 1942, the Shapiros relented and hired approximately thirty blacks. By mid–1941, Local 75 had developed into a strong, united democratic trade union and its members soon embarked on a campaign to organize their counterparts in nearby packing plants. . . .

The success of UCAPAWA at the California Sanitary Canning Company can be explained by a number of factors. Prevailing work conditions heightened the union's attractiveness. Elements outside the plant also prompted receptivity among employees. These workers were undoubtedly influenced by the wave of CIO organizing drives being conducted in the Los Angeles area. One woman, for example, joined Local 75 primarily because her husband was a member of the CIO Furniture Workers Union. Along with the Wagner Act, passage of favorable legislation, such as the Fair Labor Standards Act, the Public Contracts Act, and the California minimum wage laws (which set wage and hour levels for cannery personnel), led to the rise of a strong UCAPAWA affiliate. Workers decided that the only way they could benefit from recent protective legislation was to form a union with enough clout to force management to honor these regulations.

World War II also contributed to the development of potent UCAPAWA food processing locals, not only in southern California, but nationwide. To feed U.S. troops at home and abroad, as well as the military and civilian population of America's allies, the federal government issued thousands of contracts to canneries and packing houses. Because of this increased demand for canned goods and related products, management required a plentiful supply of content, hard-working employees. Meanwhile the higher-paying defense industries began to compete for the labor of food processing personnel. Accordingly, canners and packers became more amenable to worker demands than at any other time in the history of food processing. Thus, during the early 1940s, cannery workers, usually at the bottom end of the socio-economic scale, had become "labor aristocrats" due to wartime exigencies. . . .

Of course, the dedication and organizing skills of UCAPAWA professionals Dorothy Ray Healey and Luisa Moreno must not be minimized. While Healey played a critical role in the local's initial successes, it was under Moreno's leadership that workers consolidated these gains and branched out to help organize employees in neighboring food processing facilities. The recruitment of minority workers by Healey and Moreno and their stress on local leadership reflect the feasibility and vitality of a democratic trade unionism.

Finally, the most significant ingredient accounting for Local 75's success was the phenomenal degree of worker involvement in the building and nurturing of the union. Deriving strength from their networks within the plant, Cal San workers built an effective local. The cannery culture had, in effect, become translated into unionization. Furthermore, UCAPAWA locals provided women cannery workers with the crucial "social space" necessary to assert their independence and display their talents. They were not rote employees numbed by repetition, but women with dreams, goals, tenacity, and intellect. Unionization became an opportunity to demonstrate their shrewdness and dedication to a common cause. Mexicanas not only followed the organizers' leads but also developed strategies of their own. A fierce loyalty developed as the result of rank and file participation and leadership. Forty years after the strike, Carmen Bernal Escobar emphatically declared, "UCAPAWA was the greatest thing that ever happened to the workers at Cal San. It changed everything and everybody."

. . . [T]he UCAPAWA movement demonstrates that Mexican women, given sufficient opportunity and encouragement, could exercise control over their work lives, and their family ties and exchanges on the line became the channels for unionization.

23

AMERICANS ALL

The Mexican American Generation and
the Politics of Wartime Los Angeles, 1941–45

MARIO T. GARCÍA

Mario T. García is Professor of History and Chicano Studies at the University of California, Santa Barbara. Born in El Paso, he received his education in California schools, including his Ph.D. at the University of California, San Diego, where he worked under Ramón Ruiz. He has written a great many articles and books on Chicano/a history. His books include *Desert Immigrants: The Mexicans of El Paso, 1880–1920* (1981) and *Mexican Americans: Leadership, Ideology, and Identity, 1930–1960* (1990).

World War II was a major political watershed for Mexican Americans. They fought for democracy abroad and struggled for the same goal at home. The war revealed the political coming of age of first generation American-born Mexicans, the sons and daughters of the immigrant masses who crossed the border during the early decades of the century. The war also created a more propitious climate for reforms. Astute Mexican American leaders, utilizing the stated democratic goals of the conflict, promoted for the first time on a large scale the integration of Mexican Americans into the mainstream. These leaders were the vanguard of the Mexican American Generation. This is a case study of such generational leadership.

THE MEXICAN AMERICAN GENERATION

A political generation can be defined by shared experiences and consciousness more so than by precise age grouping. For the Mexican American Generation, these expe-

From *Social Science Quarterly* 65 (June 1984): 278–89. Copyright 1984 by the University of Texas Press. All rights reserved. The original text has been modified. Reprinted by permission.

riences and consciousness derived from growing up during the Great Depression and maturing by World War II. Aware of and experiencing the historic racism directed at Mexicans in the Southwest, the Mexican American Generation organized community movements throughout the region in its attempt to rectify the contradictions affecting Mexican American life. A few favored socialist alternatives, but most Mexican American leaders remained committed or at least temporarily reconciled to American capitalism. They absorbed the idealistic reform spirit of the New Deal and the vision of a new order propagandized by this country's participation in the war. They accepted reform either because it fit well with their political beliefs or because they understood that there were limits to social change at the time. United in a common front against racism, both Mexican American middle- and working-class leaders shared reformist objectives. Reform, not revolution, characterized the Mexican American Generation.

Pursuing new political initiatives, the Mexican American Generation broke with the immigrant experience in consciousness while upholding a tradition of ethnic defense. By 1940, moreover, the majority of the Mexican origin population in the United States possessed American citizenship. Politics for them meant the politics of citizenship, not the politics of Mexico, still of interest to immigrants. More Americanized than their parents and with a sense of permanently residing in the United States, Mexican Americans struggled for integration rather than separation from American society. Consequently, they demanded civil rights for all Mexican Americans. The Mexican American Generation believed in democracy and sought peaceful reforms through pressure group politics and the electoral process. Not tied to the ethnic nationalism of immigrant politics, Mexican Americans advocated alliances with Anglo American sympathizers, but recognized that ethnic politics could also be effective. Finally, the Mexican American Generation combated identity problems by promoting a pluralistic world view that stressed coexistence between the material and political rewards of the "American Dream" and the preservation of their parents' culture.

THE COORDINATING COUNCIL
FOR LATIN-AMERICAN YOUTH

In Los Angeles with its thousands of Mexican Americans, organizations such as the Coordinating Council for Latin-American Youth symbolized this Americanized reform-minded political generation. Founded in 1941 as a response to growing youth alienation in the barrios, the Council was one of the first significant efforts at community organizing by young Mexican American professionals. Distinctly middle-class, the Council was led by executive secretary Manuel Ruiz, Jr. A dynamic and articulate bilingual attorney, Ruiz had been among the first Mexican Americans to receive a law degree from the University of Southern California. By 1941 he headed a successful law firm specializing in international commerce. Able to function in both Mexican and Anglo circles, the Council's core of activists stressed ethnic cooperation by including representatives of Anglo organizations concerned with juvenile issues. Both liberal and conservative Anglo leaders recognized the importance of endorsing middle-class Mexican American reformers to undermine the possible appeal of "radicals." As political liberals, Council members relied more on convincing the power structure of the value of reforms than on arousing mass demonstrations of civil discontent. The Council believed in elite leadership and in the responsibility of the small Mexican American middle class to uplift their poorer constituents.

YOUTH WORK

In its reform program, the Council adopted youth work as its priority. Yet juvenile issues composed only one facet of the problems affecting the Mexican origin community. To combat delinquency, changes had to be also made in education, housing, jobs, and political participation. The Council did not see delinquency as the only issue, but it did believe the issue could be used to attack other problems. Consequently, between 1941 and 1945, the years of the Council's most active phase, it pressed forward vigorously to address some of the chief concerns of the Mexican American community.

The Council established and operated two youth clubs close to the predominantly Mexican origin section of East Los Angeles. Here, both boys and girls engaged in a variety of activities. By 1945 the Council sponsored 14 youth groups throughout Los Angeles as well as in San Fernando, Canoga Park, and Pacoima. The Council regarded athletics as a means to build character and as a deterrent to antisocial acts. Hence, the Council in conjunction with the Mexican Athletic Association of Los Angeles also supported youth teams in a variety of sports.

To complement these programs, the Council provided counseling services to youth, especially gang members. In this effort, the Council received aid from the Los Angeles County Board of Supervisors, which assigned several probation officers to work full-time in Council activities. Through conferences in East Los Angeles, the Council called attention to the problem of delinquency and offered advice to Mexican origin parents and Mexican organizations as to how best to aid in rehabilitating youth. . . .

EDUCATIONAL REFORM

Next to youth work, the Coordinating Council worked on educational reforms. It believed education to be the principal means for young people to achieve social, cultural, and economic integration. Yet it also recognized that the majority of Mexican Americans as a predominantly poor population faced obstacles in the public schools. Hence, the Council sought to create awareness among educators, superintendents, politicians, and parents about the specific language and cultural setting in which Mexican origin children lived, and about their special school problems. Council members spoke at school assemblies and at PTA meetings, and conferred with teachers and parents on how best to educate Mexican American students. The

Council consistently stressed the public school's responsibility for a successful integration of Mexican American children.

Consequently, the Council struggled to desegregate the so-called "Mexican schools." Faced with the immigration of thousands of Mexicans into the American Southwest, by the turn of the century school authorities in the region had established a dual public school system. . . .

Not segregated by law, the Mexican schools were in fact segregated due to housing patterns and the lack of economic and residential mobility among Mexican Americans. In many cases school officials citing language differences segregated Mexican origin students until they could adequately speak and write English. Ironically, most children never left the Mexican schools even after they learned English. The alleged health hazard posed by Mexican origin children was also used to justify separation. California segregated Mexican American pupils not only on these arguments but on section 8003 of the Education Code that read:

> The governing board of any school district may establish separate schools for Indian children, excepting children of Indians who are wards of the United States government and children of all other Indians who are descendents of the original American Indians of the United States, and for children of Chinese, Japanese, or Mongolian parentage.

Under this section, certain school districts separated Mexican Americans on the ground that they were part Indian, along with language and health rationalizations.

The Coordinating Council initiated in 1945 a campaign to repeal section 8003. In Los Angeles, it acquired the support of key officials and organizations including Mayor Fletcher Bowron. "We hold that segregation prevents assimilation," Ruiz put the case to authorities, "thereby defeating the purpose of this nation's good neighbor policy. Mexican American pupils in many instances have been required to attend school in dilapidated structures, far from their homes. In some cases, where no facilities for segregation were available, they have been excluded from classes entirely." The Los Angeles system mixed students more, although with increasing segregation patterns. However, in such surrounding areas as Orange County, Carpinteria, Oxnard, Montebello, and El Monte, officials widely segregated Mexican origin pupils. . . .

To reach into Sacramento, Ruiz and the Council gained the support of State Senator Jack B. Tenney of Los Angeles County and Assemblyman William H. Rosenthal of the 40th District, Los Angeles. Both agreed to sponsor the fight for the repeal of section 8003. Ruiz also obtained the backing of Governor Earl Warren, as well as other state officials. . . .

The Assembly repealed section 8003 in 1945, but opponents stalled it in the Senate. In the meantime, the Coordinating Council helped desegregate the El Monte School District on a local basis. Together with the Federation of Hispanic American Voters and LULAC, the Council met with Mexican origin parents of children attending El Monte schools. Persistent and effective, this Mexican American coalition pressured school officials to agree in May 1945 to integrate Mexican American children into the non-Mexican schools during the next academic year. *Aristo,* the Council's newspaper, hailed the desegregation victory and hoped that it would stimulate action where similar humiliating conditions existed. The newspaper correctly reminded its readers that only through pressure exerted by Mexican Americans themselves had desegregation in El Monte been achieved. . . .

A year later the Council supported successful legal efforts by Mexican origin parents in Orange County to desegregate local schools on the basis of the Fourteenth Amendment to the Constitution of the United States, which mandates the equal protection of the laws. In the Westminster case, a U.S. district court ruled illegal the segregation of Mexican American children on the grounds of language difference. Buoyed by the victory in Orange County, the Council in 1947 achieved the repeal of section 8003. Hence, in a two-year period the Council had helped gain three significant breakthroughs in the struggle to desegregate Mexican schools in southern California. Clearly, these successes did not eliminate de facto segregation nor did they eradicate inferior education. Still, they constituted important political initiatives by Mexican American leaders. Mexican Americans in southern California had served notice they would no longer accept second-class status in the schools for their children.

JOB OPPORTUNITIES

Job opportunities also concerned the Coordinating Council. The growth of war-related industries in Los Angeles after the attack upon Pearl Harbor moved the Council to take steps to insure that both Mexican Americans and Mexican nationals would have access to such employment. Apprehensive over equal opportunity, the Council learned that some plants discriminated against persons of Mexican origin. The Council in October 1941 publicized that it would investigate cases of job discrimination in war-related industries. Ruiz in an interview with *La Opinion,* the Spanish-language daily in Los Angeles, urged victims of such discrimination to contact the Council. . . .

The Council protested job discrimination against persons of Mexican origin, especially non-citizens, to both the state and federal government. Ruiz singled out contractors on public housing projects who refused to hire Mexican nationals. The contractors claimed they had no choice because of a state labor code making it a crime to contract non-citizens for public works. Ruiz countered that according to emergency provisions of the same labor code non-citizens could be hired for such jobs in time of war. He called upon the state commission to act on the matter. Receiving no response, Ruiz took his case to the federal War Production Board and requested clarification of federal statutes to allow employment of non-citizens during war. The council also issued resolutions in 1942 stressing both the importance of employing alien workers in war production and the ideological contradictions of excluding them. . . .

In agreement, President Roosevelt in the summer of 1942 redefined policy toward the employment of alien labor. Refusal to hire aliens in war industries was discriminatory. Aliens could work both in war and non-war industries except on classified contracts. Although it could not take sole credit for this victory, the Council had assisted in bringing attention to the issue.

In Los Angeles, the Council helped train persons of Mexican origin for war-related employment. With the National Youth Administration (NYA), it disseminated information on NYA job training centers in East Los Angeles. Here, Mexican origin youth could acquire free training in a variety of industrial skills while receiving approximately $25 a month.

More importantly, the Council contributed in founding the Pan American Trade School. Largely through the Council's efforts in cooperation with the Los Angeles city schools and appropriate state and federal agencies, the school opened for vocational classes in April 1943. . . . While this type of job training maintained Mexican origin workers in blue-collar occupations, still the school aided in creating opportunities in skilled trades: jobs, for the most part, previously unavailable to this population.

ANTI-DEFAMATION

The Coordinating Council further worked to mitigate anti-Mexican sentiments in Los Angeles due to increased wartime racial tensions. It frequently sent representatives to conferences on race relations to interpret the problems of Mexican Americans. The Council refuted anti-Mexican statements made by individuals, organizations, and especially by the news media. Fearing that any attempt to classify Mexicans as people of color might subject them to "legal" forms of discrimination and segregation, the Council rejected any implication that Mexicans were not white. The Council's insistence that Mexicans were white also appears to have stemmed from the historic ambivalence and insecurity of Mexicans on both sides of the border concerning their racial status. These feelings often led to a denial of possessing Indian blood. The Council believed that any attempt to place Mexicans in a racial category other than white to be racist and divisive. . . .

The Council particularly protested about the way the *Los Angeles Times* often insinuated that most Mexican origin youths belonged to delinquent gangs. This practice became an explosive issue during the "Sleepy Lagoon Case" of 1942 and the "Zoot-Suit Riots" the following year when hundreds of white servicemen rampaged in downtown Los Angeles attacking Mexican origin individuals dressed in "zoot suits." Ruiz personally defended many of the riot victims. The Council blamed the news media for inciting the crisis and called upon President Roosevelt and the federal government to moderate the "attitudes of [the] local press which has openly approved these riots and is treating the news in a way that is definitely inflammatory."

POLITICAL ACTION

While the Council's activities were not overtly political, they still constituted political action. The Council as a political pressure group mediated between the Mexican origin community and the Anglo power structure. Influential Anglos recognized

Council members as spokespersons for the Mexican origin community. The Council also engaged in electoral politics. It supported in 1942 the unsuccessful campaigns of two members who ran as "Roosevelt Democrats": Eduardo Quevedo for the 40th Assembly District and Fred Rubio for the 51st Assembly District. Three years later the Council again aided Quevedo's candidacy, this time for a seat on the Los Angeles city council. . . . Defeated in his bid, Quevedo believed that his campaign had helped unify the Mexican origin community and urged the Council to continue raising political consciousness.

The Council further realized the importance of organizing a unified front among Mexican Americans in Los Angeles, or at least those of similar convictions. With this in mind and aware of postwar problems facing Mexican Americans, the Council assembled on 7 October 1945 a Postwar Congress. . . . The Congress called for a variety of reforms: the creation of an independent nonpartisan political action committee to advance the interests of Spanish-speaking people; nondiscrimination in employment and preferential hiring of war veterans; a state and federal Permanent Fair Employment Practices Commission; a federal Full Employment Bill; CIO and AFL organization of Mexican origin workers; the reintegration of returning Latin American veterans; health programs to eliminate the high rate of communicable diseases among those of Mexican origin in Los Angeles; increased hiring by state and local governments of Spanish surnamed persons; social security as well as other federal labor standards for farm workers, including child labor laws; and that eligible Spanish-speaking citizens be encouraged to take the civil service examinations in law enforcement.

MEXICAN AMERICAN IDENTITY

Besides trying to meet the economic and political needs of the Mexican origin population in Los Angeles, the Council dealt with identity and the definition of what it meant to be an American of Mexican descent. Hence, Council members contributed to the making of a particular Mexican American generational world view. World War II served as a decisive watershed in this ideological process. Mexican Americans during the war repeatedly pledged their allegiance to American democratic values and to Mexican American support in the struggle against fascism. Moreover, the Council upheld the American system and looked toward integration. In their approach to integration, Council members shunned identification as a minority. For them the concept of a minority meant separation. After all, the ideology of wartime America stressed the equality of all Americans. To label someone a minority, Ruiz suggested, stigmatized them as different and made them defensive.

Desiring integration, Council members in forming their world view unfortunately drew distinctions between Mexican Americans and Afro Americans as a way of trying to avoid the stigma of racial inferiority imposed on blacks. Disregarding the fact that both groups suffered from racial discrimination, Council leaders stressed that while Afro Americans had been legally excluded from their rights Mexican Americans had not, implying that no basis for political unity existed. The Council focused on ethnic rather than racial discrimination. Ruiz, for example, refused to discuss Mexican Americans on the basis of race. He insisted that Mexicans were white and hence no different from other ethnic groups such as the Irish, Italians, or Germans.

To overcome the ambiguity of identity, Council members acknowledged that Mexican Americans were first and foremost American citizens. At the same time, they called on Mexican Americans to be proud of their ethnic origin. The Council argued for a pluralistic approach to ethnicity in American life and stressed that integration could be accompanied with degrees of cultural retention.

CONCLUSION

The Coordinating Council by the postwar period ceased to function. Just as the war provided Mexican American reformers with greater political leverage, its conclusion and the postwar economic recession in turn weakened . . . that leverage and momentum. According to Ruiz, moreover, the Mexican origin community in Los Angeles had become even more dispersed, a disadvantage for effective organizational work, and its leaders more interested in electoral politics. The Council apparently also suffered from lack of financial resources. Finally, Council leaders allowed younger returning Mexican American GIs to carry the organizational load.

The Council achieved modest reforms, but its importance transcends concrete accomplishments. The Council and indeed the Mexican American Generation throughout the Southwest symbolized larger changes affecting the Mexican origin population in the United States. Immigrant enclaves were being transformed into Mexican American communities. More Americanized Mexicans shifted loyalties away from Mexico and to the United States. The immigrant dream of one day returning to Mexico—the "Mexican dream"—now became for Mexican Americans the dream of a good life north of the border, the "American dream." . . .

Yet the Council and the Mexican American Generation could only accomplish so much. Poverty continued to coexist with progress. Mexican Americans continued to face discrimination and slower rates of mobility. While the Council had hopes for a pluralistic society under capitalism, race and class discrimination together with cultural prejudice retarded the integration and assimilation of Mexicans. Mexican American middle-class leaders failed to appreciate the intransigence of race and class barriers.

Still, despite this myopic consciousness and the limits of what San Miguel (1982) calls the "politics of accommodation," the Council aided in making life slightly better for some Mexican Americans. As part of a historical process of change, the Council's reform struggles served notice that Mexican Americans would no longer accept second-class citizenship. One hundred years after the Anglo conquest of the Southwest, a political generation of Mexican Americans demanded not reannexation to Mexico, but democratic rights and full integration into the U.S. body politic. The expectations and frustrations resulting from this change in political consciousness would ignite more intense struggles in succeeding decades.

24

FROM *RANCHERO* TO *JAITÓN*
Ethnicity and Class in Texas-Mexican Music
(Two Styles in the Form of a Pair)

MANUEL PEÑA

A native of Weslaco, Texas, Manuel Peña has a Ph.D. in anthropology (folklore and ethnomusicology) from the University of Texas at Austin. He did his fieldwork in the Lone Star State, investigating Texas-Mexican music, the subject of his most important works, *The Texas-Mexican Conjunto: History of a Working-Class Music* (1985) and *Música Tejana: The Cultural Economy of Artistic Transformation* (1999). Dr. Peña's teaching career has been spent in both Texas and California. He is currently Professor of Music at California State University, Fresno.

The purpose of this essay is to provide an interpretive summary of certain musical developments among Texas-Mexicans, or *tejanos*. It is the result of several years of fieldwork research related to two popular musical styles that were forged by tejano musicians during and after World War II. The styles are known as *orchesta tejana,* or simply *orquesta,* and *norteño.* Among tejanos the latter is more commonly referred to as *conjunto,* and that is the label that will be used here. . . .

The essay focuses mainly on the period 1935–1965, with particular emphasis on the decade or so after the war. Additionally, my primary interest is to explain the dynamics that sustained the conjunto-orquesta relationship, particularly the series of contrasts the two musics came to articulate and, indeed, embody: working vs. middle class, ethnic resistance vs. cultural assimilation, continuity vs. change, and folk vs. "sophisticated." Moreover, underlying these contrasts, or oppositions, was what I propose to be the key factor operating in the emergence of both conjunto and orquesta—namely, the shift in tejano society from a Mexicanized, rural, folk, and proletarian group to a class-differentiated, urban, and increasingly American-ized and literate population. . . .

CONJUNTO:
"A FOLK MUSIC OF THE PEOPLE"

. . . Briefly, the development of conjunto music was, in every sense of the concept, a folk phenomenon. . . . Without exception, its contributors had two characteristics in common: they were totally or for the most part illiterate, and they belonged to a proletarian class. In short, conjunto musicians were members of a society that was characterized by strong folk elements: a deep oral tradition, a lack of socioeconomic differentiation, a collective sense of ethnic identity, and a relative isolation from other groups. . . .

The mid-1930s . . . marks the juncture when the modern conjunto first emerged. The history of the ensemble and its style can be divided into two phases. The first is represented by those musicians who established themselves before the war—"los músicos viejos," as accordionist Narciso Martínez called them. The sec-ond phase belongs to "la nueva generación," under whose direction the music reached stylistic maturity.

Of the many musicians who contributed to the creation of the emergent style, three first-generation accordionists stand out in a retrospective assessment. These are Narciso Martínez (unanimously called "el primero"), Pedro Ayala, and Santiago Jiménez. . . .

The second generation of musicians included a number of outstanding per-formers, accordionists in particular, but, again, three of the latter may be acknowl-edged in this brief sketch. In the order of their rise to prominence, they are: Valerio Longoria, Tony de la Rosa, and Paulino Bernal. Longoria's accomplishments are many, but among the most notable is his introduction in 1947 of two vocal genres into the conjunto—the *canción ranchera* and the bolero (the latter, again, consider-ably simplified, or "rancheroized"). His most important contribution, however, was his enlistment of the modern drum set, in 1949. . . .

Tony de la Rosa is known for his superb polkas, which featured an extremely staccato style on the accordion and a considerably slower tempo than hitherto com-mon. . . .

This brings us, finally, to the last and most famous exponent of conjunto music during its formative years—Paulino Bernal. El Conjunto Bernal is generally recog-nized as the "greatest of all time," as one orquesta musician described it. The group draws the praise of other musicians (and laymen) because, first, it was able to syn-thesize the stylistic elements that had been coalescing around the accordion en-semble since Martínez's initial emphasis on the treble end. Second, Bernal succeeded in attracting the best musicians available in the tradition, an accomplishment that enabled the group to bring the kind of finesse to the music that was unmatched before or after. Lastly, El Conjunto Bernal launched several innovations of its own—

for example, the introduction of three-part vocalizations (1958) and the chromatic accordion (1964). In fact, in the mid–1960s two such accordions were featured. In sum, El Conjunto Bernal represented the apex of the conjunto tradition; no other group since then has been able to duplicate its innovative spirit.

Indeed, since the experiments of Paulino Bernal the music has remained virtually static, especially with respect to its most unique and characteristic genre—the *canción ranchera* in polka tempo. The question, of course, is why conjunto suddenly reached such a stylistic dead end. In other words, how could a vital, unfolding tradition do such a drastic about face after El Conjunto Bernal became so rigidly conservative? . . .

ORQUESTA MUSIC: SQUEEZED BETWEEN RANCHERO AND "HIGH CLASS"

Although the modern orquesta tejana was originally patterned after the American swing bands of the 1930s and '40s, it did have important precursors, both in Texas-Mexican and Mexican music. . . .

It was . . . in the 1930s that more permanent and better organized wind orquestas—the new type, modeled after the American big bands—began to appear with increasing frequency. On the basis of informants' reports and the course that orquesta music subsequently took, it is clear that the new orquestas articulated the strategies of a nascent group of Texas-Mexicans, usually upwardly mobile, who wanted to distance themselves from the mass of proletarian workers, and who desired at the same time to imitate the lifestyle of middle-class America. Highly symbolic of this desire . . . was the demand for American music, which was generously represented in the orquesta repertories. . . .

By the mid–1930s several well established orquestas were playing in cities like San Antonio, Corpus Christi, Kingsville and in the Rio Grande Valley. These were the immediate predecessors of the modern orquesta tejana, as it came to be known by the 1950s. The man who more than anyone else was responsible for the creation of an orquesta tejana style began his professional career in the early 1930s. It was in 1932 that Beto Villa, Narciso Martínez's counterpart in the orquesta tradition, organized his first group. . . .

. . . [T]he concept of *lo ranchero* has been firmly linked historically to the ideology of romantic nationalism, or *mexicanismo* . . . To grasp the concept's significance in tejano (as well as Mexican) culture, we need, first, to understand that the bulk of Mexican society has traditionally been folk and agrarian, and only in recent times has it moved forward with "modernization." Second, ever since romantic nationalism first made its appearance in Mexico (after the expulsion of the French), it has been endemic among Mexicans, manifesting itself in numerous facets of national life. Particularly germane for this discussion is the heavy commercialization since the 1930s of some of the symbols of that nationalism, as capitalists began to convert them into profitable mass commodities, principally through radio and film. It was, in fact, in the 1930s that the ranchero label was first attached to the Mexican *canción*.

Moreover, it is evident that such labeling was a conscious effort by commercial promoters to capitalize on the ideology of romantic nationalism.

The symbols I refer to belong to the vast collective consciousness that is Mexico's cultural heritage, symbols that have been selectively chosen for exaltation as representative of the glory of Mexico's history and culture. A number of these symbols have long enjoyed currency—for example, the Virgin of Guadalupe and the familiar Aztec warrior—but two encompass the concept of lo ranchero especially well, although they have become somewhat stereotyped. These are the *charro/vaquero* figure, which symbolizes the arrogant manliness (machismo) of the Mexican male, and the person of the *campesino,* which signifies the humble but perseverant spirit of that same Mexican.

These last two have been singled out for intensive exploitation in both music and film (often simultaneously) since the 1930s. As a result of this commercial exposure, the twin symbols of the charro and campesino have succeeded admirably in imparting to the concept of lo ranchero its visual substance. The one's dauntless machismo and penchant for action coexists with the other's stoicism and humility, which actually border on inertia and diffidence. But this juxtaposition creates tension, as the two symbols, representing opposite qualities, pull in different directions. . . .

On this side of the border the ambiguities attached to lo ranchero are compounded by the pressures for assimilation and conformity. For example, to espouse lo ranchero, as many Chicanos do through their advocacy of *música ranchera,* is to overvalue their Mexican "roots": to ennoble the culture of pastoral, agrarian life, which is presumed unspoiled by social snobbery. Yet, this mystified vision can quickly turn into disillusion when jarred by the reality of modern life, especially in the United States, where the campesino (the sleeping man with the wide-brimmed sombrero) is a stereotype for fatalism and laziness. Thus, to the "progressive" Mexican-American the negative side of lo ranchero is never completely hidden. It lies ready to spring into consciousness to transform nostalgia into rejection, for the romanticized rancho also happens to harbor the *arrancherado*—the "low-class," coarse, excessively Mexicanized peon who cannot possibly appreciate the subtleties of modern, civilized life. There is an apt folk expression that captures the acculturated Mexican-American's indignation: "Mexico, recoge a tu gente" [Mexico, pick up your people]. An appeal is made in this well-worn refrain for Mexico to reclaim its vagabonds, who are a source of embarrassment to the "respectable" Mexican-American.

Yet, despite the paradox, if there is one encompassing musical symbol among Texas-Mexicans, it is that conveyed by música ranchera (as is true among Mexicans generally, for that matter). A sound that spans several styles, música ranchera compresses a wide range of feelings and attitudes into a single esthetic moment. People immediately recognize a ranchero sound, whether it be interpreted by a conjunto, orquesta, or any other group, although it is true that some types of ensemble are considered more "naturally" ranchero than others—for example, the conjunto and the mariachi. But invariably, the music stirs vaguely defined but deeply experienced feelings of *mexicanismo*—or, in other words, romantic nationalism.

Thus, *ranchera* music has always been an integral part of Texas-Mexican musical consciousness, even among the upwardly mobile urbanites. That fact was never lost on Beto Villa and other orquesta musicians. Consequently, even in the immediate post-war years, a ranchero style was cultivated by all but the most Americanized (i.e., culturally assimilated) orquestas. . . .

But the negative side of lo ranchero was not lost on orquestas either, and it helps explain why orquesta musicians were so caught up in what one of them called "lo moderno"—the modern, which on closer examination turns out to be a code phrase for the assimilation of middle-class elements, not only from American bands, but from similarly situated groups in Mexico. Thus, in comparing conjunto and orquesta music, one prominent musician observed that while conjunto was the music of the farmworker, "the so-called upper crust demanded big bands and sophisticated music"—i.e., foxtrots, boleros, etc.

However, the orquesta tejana was also powerfully affected by developments in conjunto music, and it was never able to free itself completely from the latter's influence. Indeed, one of the problems we face in analyzing orquesta as a cultural expression is its extreme stylistic fluctuations—its many faces, as it were. To a far greater extent than any of the other musics that influenced it, orquesta tejana has always been a multidimensional musical expression, as even a cursory listening of the recordings made since the 1940s will reveal . . . [U]nlike conjunto, which adhered to a strongly homogeneous style, orquesta encompassed a broad spectrum of styles, only one of which, properly speaking, stamped the "tejana" label on it.

Thus, most orquestas attempted to amalgamate any number of disparate types of music, including those associated with the big American dance bands (e.g., foxtrots, swings, etc.), Mexican and Latin American dance bands (boleros, danzones, mambos), and, of course, the ranchero, regional style of the conjunto. Within this spectrum of styles and genres there were some orquestas—particularly the most culturally assimilated and middle-class oriented—that emphasized cosmopolitan music. They played, in the words of working class tejanos, "música mas *jaitona*" ("more high-toned music"). However, the most commercially popular were those that, like Beto Villa's, succeeded in accommodating both the ranchero and the "sophisticated," or "high class." . . .

In a retrospective assessment it is clear that Isidro López was the man most responsible for setting in motion the final shift of orquesta music toward that of conjunto. However, that shift did not proceed in an uninterrupted sweep—an indication of the conflicting currents that determined the course of orquesta music. Thus, Little Joe, who most personifies the next phase of orquesta tejana, and Sunny Ozuna, who also ranks among the leading personalities, began their careers in pursuit of the exploding rock and roll market of the late 1950s. . . .

Clearly, what was taking place among the Mexicans in Texas was the inexorable assimilation of American culture, as Richard García so cogently demonstrates in his essay, "The Mexican American Mind: A Product of the 1930s" (1983). The post-Depression babies—the first generation of Mexicans to enjoy a measurable upgrading in their education—were responding to the pressures of cultural assimilation, even if the barriers that effectively prevented them from complete integration into American society (i.e., through "primary" associations achievable principally through intermarriage) remained firmly in place. With cultural assimilation came a desire to adopt the lifestyles of American mass society. . . . In short, they demanded the amenities of middle-class citizenship. Lastly, among the symbols that signified upward mobility was music—specifically music that approximated the ideal of mainstream American life.

. . . [T]here have been two discernible (and contradicting) trends in orquesta tejana music since its inception. One is obviously ranchero and heavily influenced by the conjunto style. The other is difficult to classify neatly, since it has always aimed at amalgamating a number of disparate styles. We may, however, label it collectively (as I have done) as "sophisticated," "cosmopolitan," or "modern." Or, we may follow the native, working-class usage and call it "high class" or "jaitón"— terms that I heard many times while growing up in Texas in the 1950s. In either case, some orquestas have not hesitated to shift back and forth between ranchero and jaitón. . . .

. . . [B]eginning in the early 1970s the orquesta tejana witnessed a major resurgence and burst of innovation that has been unrivalled before or after. It is probably not premature, then, to label the 1970s as the "golden age" of orquesta tejana music. . . .

Since about 1978 orquesta music has witnessed considerable stylistic retrenchment, as well as a decline—though *not* a demise—in its popularity. But, as one orquesta musician put it, "Conjunto music has its epochs, we have ours. We'll come back." Renamed *La Onda Chicana* ("The Chicano Wave"), it has held its ground into the 1980s, thanks largely to the efforts of the indefatigable Little Joe Hernández.

AN INTERPRETIVE SUMMARY

Now that I have traced the evolution of conjunto and orquesta, I would like to add a few comments on the social and cultural variables that were present at the inception of these two styles, and the possible relationship between these and the emergence of the two ensembles.

First, as a number of researchers have observed, tejano society experienced important—if not dramatic—socioeconomic changes during World War II. Indeed, the war ought to be considered a threshold for Texas-Mexican society. This was a period when the process of urbanization was greatly accelerated, when the native born for the first time outnumbered the immigrants, and when tejanos began to be absorbed into the American political economy in occupations that offered some upward mobility. In addition, thousands of young men fought in the war, and they returned to civilian society with a new sense of purpose that contributed to the redefinition of citizenship, not only for them but for many other Mexican-Americans as well. In sum, these tejanos demanded—with some success—equal treatment in housing, education, employment, and so forth. But success had its ramifications for the structure of tejano society. Among other things, homogeneity of class gave way to differentiation, and its attendant distinctions (e.g., "clean" vs.

"dirty" occupations). In short, the war changed the makeup of tejano society in an irrevocable way, presenting it with a set of challenges it had never before faced.

Perhaps the most far-reaching consequence of the changed nature of Texas-Mexican society was the increasing disparity in cultural assimilation between the middle and working classes, a disparity that was reflected in the undeclared rift that developed between them. For example, even the old ethnic solidarity was called into question by upwardly mobile tejanos who were caught up in the assimilation of American middle class ideology. It is important to note, however, that despite the internal changes in tejano society that emerged during World War II, the formidable ethnic boundary that separated tejano and Anglo remained, posing a nearly insurmountable obstacle against the complete structural (i.e., marital) assimilation of tejanos into Anglo-American society.

It was against this backdrop of *internal* socioeconomic differentiation and *external* ethnic segregation that orquesta and conjunto were cast. Here it is worth recalling James Ackerman's comments on style formation as a response to the challenges of an age. These remarks are eminently applicable to the emergence of conjunto and orquesta. For what tejano society witnessed was a fundamental shakeup of its infrastructural composition, along with a high degree of social upheaval. . . . [T]his social upheaval could not be negotiated without profound cultural dislocation. This dislocation, expressible in terms of social uncertainty and conflict, necessitated solutions. This is where conjunto and orquesta fulfilled their design: they were cultural solutions to infrastructurally generated problems.

In the case of conjunto, we can explain its emergence in this way: In the face of an unsympathetic middle class that saw the working class (both native and immigrant) as an impediment to the acceptance of Mexicans into American society because of its alleged "backwardness," the less acculturated workers felt obligated to respond in kind and to elaborate cultural strategies in their defense. These strategies were intended to defend and also legitimize working class existence and cultural sovereignty. Thus, if upwardly mobile tejanos were critical of working class lifestyles, then the latter countered with its own ridicule. Middle-class oriented people were considered *agringados* (gringoized Mexicans), or worse, *agabachados,* an even more caustic epithet for Mexicans who were seen by traditional (usually) working class people as snobs who pretended to be what they were not. Worst, in so doing they not only demeaned themselves, but also committed the contemptible act of denying their true cultural heritage—their *mexicanismo.* . . .

. . . [I]t was out of this clash between change and continuity, between cultural assimilation and ethnic resistance, and between middle and working class ideology that conjunto music derived its cultural energy and symbolic power. By balancing innovation with tradition—by being subjected to changes strictly at the hands of working-class artists—conjunto music, as a symbolic expression, negotiated through esthetic means the conflicts and uncertainties that its constituency was experiencing in the socioeconomic sphere. In sum, the creation of this unique artistic expression was a symbolic solution to the conflicts I have outlined. Lastly, once the original conflict between proletarians and their middle class antagonists was mediated musically—that is, once conjunto music was seen as consummated—

further innovation came to a halt. In short, as an esthetically satisfying expression, reflective of working class sentiments, conjunto music was considered "perfected" by its practitioners. . . .

A similar case can be made for orquesta. Just as the stylistic maturation of conjunto signified a working class response to the challenges posed against it by the changing conditions of its existence, so did orquesta likewise correspond to the Texas-Mexican middle class's search for an appropriate expressive (artistic) response to its own emergence as an ideological bloc in tejano society. On the one hand, orquesta—at least in its first phase, up until 1965—was clearly an alternative mode of artistic expression to conjunto. . . .

Yet, the unavoidable reality of interethnic conflict and the subordination of Mexicans generally—especially before the civil rights gains of the 1960s—made middle class status for Texas-Mexicans a rather precarious proposition. Quite simply, the upwardly mobile tejanos were caught on the horns of a dilemma. On the one hand, they aspired to be American, though Anglo society did not welcome them into its midst. On the other hand, a retreat to the cultural position of the traditional proletarian class was out of the question, because the middle class's ideology, which was shaped, paradoxically, by American middle class institutions such as the schools, clashed at many points with the ethnic culture of traditional tejano society. The middle class's position can be summed up succinctly: socially and culturally it lived in a state of contradiction.

Musically, this state of contradiction was mediated—and reflected—by orquesta's extreme variations in style. For the sake of analysis, these variations may be reduced conceptually to simple bi-musicality, with American styles on one side and Latin ones on the other. Moreover, the bi-musicality was an extension of middle class tejanos' increasing biculturalism, a biculturalism that straddled the interethnic boundary between Mexican and Anglo life experiences. Beyond bi-musicality there was also pervasive bilingualism and ambiguous attitudes about family, religion, and traditions generally—all a commentary on the contradictory position of the middle class. (Ambiguity crept into working class life as well, but with far less unsettling results.) In short, the upwardly mobile tejano was caught in a bicultural bind that promoted considerable social stress. I suggest that the stylistic flip-flopping orquestas engaged in—their struggle to mediate the differences between the Mexican and traditional vs. the American and "modern"—was a manifestation of that stress. . . .

POSTSCRIPT:
TWO STYLES IN THE FORM OF A PAIR

From the 1960s to the 1980s, orquesta and conjunto embarked on a strongly convergent course, as two factors combined to blur the original social distinctions between the two ensembles. First, the surrender of many acculturating tejanos to the attraction of American pop music stripped the orquesta tejana of many of its former supporters, as these were coopted by the various styles in the "mainstream" market.

Second, the Chicano movement of the sixties and seventies, with its essentialist ideology of ethnic solidarity based on "the roots of Chicano culture" and its disdain for middle-class and acculturative expression, forced the orquesta to "go ranchero," in order to appeal to "born-again" Chicanos looking for their "roots." But in doing so, orquestas like Little Joe y la Familia (now going by the label "la Onda Chicana") encroached on the ranchero domain of the conjunto, resulting in an orchestral sound that at times differed little from that of the conjunto.

Thus, by the late 1970s it was possible for American music journalists to lump conjunto and orquesta under one rubric, that of *música tejana*. The classification was justified, as by then the similarities between the two musics were readily acknowledged by most performers in either tradition. It was also recognized by the people themselves, who often referred to the two styles as "música tejana." In short, the musics had become twin forms—what, paraphrasing Eric Satie's title, we might call "two styles in the form of a pair."

Beginning in the mid-eighties, yet more transformations ensued in the field of Texas-Mexican music, resulting in the almost total demise of the orquesta. These transformations are explored in the book *Música Tejana* (Texas A&M University Press, 1999), but they are attributable to social, economic and ideological changes sweeping through the Hispanic communities of the Southwest, in which the process of "postmodernization" weakened the strongly symbolic charge of musics like orquesta. Even the more strongly grounded conjunto was symbolically weakened, as it was increasingly challenged by a much more commoditized music that went by the name of "Tejano," as exemplified by the late Selena, La Mafia, Emilio Navaira, El Grupo Mazz and dozens of their epigones. In the wake of the commercial explosion of Tejano (driven by the suddenly active big labels like EMI Latin), the orquesta tejana, with its always tenuous social base, was overwhelmed. By the late 1990s, it had faded from the social memory, its former cultural power barely recalled by members of what we may call the "Post-Chicano Generation."

25

THE STRUGGLE AGAINST SEPARATE AND UNEQUAL SCHOOLS
Middle Class Mexican Americans and the Desegregation Campaign in Texas, 1929–1957

GUADALUPE SAN MIGUEL, JR.

Guadalupe San Miguel, Jr., received his Ph.D. in social education history from Stanford and now teaches in the History Department at the University of Houston. A specialist on the history of Mexican-American education, Dr. San Miguel has written extensively on the subject. His works include *"Let All of Them Take Heed": Mexican Americans and the Quest for Educational Equality in Texas* (1987).

Since 1929 Mexican American organizations, headed by middle class leaders, have played a significant and increasing role in challenging discriminatory school policies and practices. Led and inspired by the League of United Latin American Citizens (LULAC) and the G.I. Forum, the challenge to education has been essentially a liberal one. As most liberals, Mexican Americans have perceived discrimination, segregation, inferior schools, and culturally biased curriculum and instructional practices as problems incidental to education, not as specific manifestations of systematic structural inequality. As a result, they have not sought the improvement of the existing educational structure by eliminating those barriers which limit Mexican American access to and participation in that system. Hence, the challenge to education has been limited to abolishing segregated schools and student assignment and classification policies which serve to increase segregation. The following essay is a history of this campaign to eliminate the segregation of Mexican American children

From *History of Education Quarterly* 23 (Fall 1983): 343–59. Copyright by History of Education Society. The original text has been modified. Reprinted by permission.

in the Texas public schools. . . . The period to be covered will be between 1929 and 1957. The year 1929 marks the period during which the League of United Latin American Citizens . . . , the first statewide civic organization of Americans of Mexican descent, was organized in Texas. In the latter year [1957] the last of a series of desegregation cases filed by the Mexican American community was won. . . . The campaign to desegregate the public schools by Mexican American organizations from 1929 to 1957 has not received the scholarly attention it deserves. This essay will hopefully contribute to [closing] this gap in the history of American minority groups by describing and tracing the nature of this campaign against separate and unequal schools for Mexican Americans in Texas.

Prior to 1929, the Mexican community in Texas did not effectively and collectively challenge discriminatory public policies and practices. Although there were sporadic local efforts aimed at eliminating specific types of discriminatory treatment, especially in the public schools, and journalistic exposes of deprivations of civil liberties of the Mexican communities in south Texas by Anglos, the Mexican community lacked forceful and articulate spokespersons. There are several reasons for this lack of collective effort to influence discriminatory educational policy by the Mexican community. The primary reason for this condition was that there was no statewide organization of Mexican Americans to articulate the group's interests, develop collective positions on important issues confronting the community, or bring pressure on local and state school officials. . . .

Secondly, and perhaps a more important reason for the lack of collective action on the part of Mexicans, the Mexican community had not been integrated into the American system; that is, it had not been socialized into accepting the legitimacy of American social, economic, and political institutions, including public schools. The Mexican community in general did not speak English, nor did they necessarily attempt to participate in the established institutions of this country. In many cases, as the history of the campaign to eliminate segregation in the schools will illustrate, local and state officials sought to exclude or limit participation of those Mexican Americans willing to participate in the existing institutions.

During the 1920s, a fundamental shift in ideological and organizational orientation occurred within the Mexican communities of south Texas which significantly affected the social and cultural development of the overall Mexican population. In response to the deteriorating social and economic conditions caused by the growing anti-Mexican feeling among Anglos in Texas, the first generation of Mexicans born or raised in the United States founded new types of organizations in the communities of south and central Texas. Comprised largely of the college trained, the small businessman, and the skilled craftsman, that is, the incipient Mexican American middle class element, these new organizations formed to eradicate social injustices, to ensure just treatment of the Mexican population under the law, and, most importantly, to promote the integration of the Mexican population into the existing social, economic, and political structures of the American society. The formation of the Order Sons of America in the early 1920s, the League of United Latin American Citizens . . . in 1929, and, later, the G.I. Forum in 1948, represented a significant departure from the founding of traditional protective and mutual benefit organizations for a number of reasons. First and foremost was the basic shift from largely protective and self-help to assimilative activities. . . .

Another reason why these new organizations represented a significant departure from the past concerned their membership. The *mutualista* organizations of the past welcomed both Mexican immigrants and Mexican citizens of the United States. The Order Sons of America and LULAC, on the other hand, initially limited . . . membership to U.S. citizens of Mexican ancestry. Alonso S. Perales, one of the founders of LULAC, stated that only by using the rights they had as citizens could the socioeconomic problems of all the Mexicans living north of the border be solved. . . .

In pledging allegiance to the United States government, the middle class Mexicans in these organizations also de-emphasized dependence on the mother country for moral sustenance. Instead of looking to Mexico for guidance, advice, and intellectual nourishment, the middle class now looked to the political and ideological institutions of the United States. As the LULAC Constitution stated, the organization was formed to "define with absolute and unmistakable clearness our unquestionable loyalty to the ideals, principles, and citizenship of the United States of America." To achieve this end, LULAC adopted English as the official language of the organization and pledged "to learn and speak and teach [the] same to our children."

The middle class Mexicans, as Americans of Mexican descent and conscious of themselves as an emerging middle class, assumed the responsibility of educating, protecting, and incorporating the Mexican population into the dominant institutions of their country. But the integration of the Mexican population into the mainstream of Anglo social, political, and economic life was not to be achieved at the expense of their cultural background. The Mexican American middle class was not calling for the total assimilation into Anglo cultural society, as has been suggested by some authors. Integration into Anglo-American political and social life was to be a selective process. . . . Cultural pride was not to be neglected either. . . . The English language and Anglo American political and social customs were to be learned, but not at the expense of the Spanish language and the Mexican customs. Cultural pride, retention of the Spanish language, and the physical and cultural defense of the Mexican heritage were as much goals of the new organizations as were the acquisition of the English language, the training for citizenship, and the struggle for equality for the residents of Mexican ancestry.

Education in the eyes of many was to play an important role in the general strategy of incorporating Mexicans into the dominant institutions of the land. Most importantly, especially in the initial stages, education was also to assist in the enlargement of this particular group of individuals who would eventually lead this historic mission of incorporating Mexicans into the mainstream American life. Thus, from its founding, one of the major goals of these new organizations was to promote education for organizational growth. . . .

. . . [M]ost LULAC members agreed that education was important for elevating the general socioeconomic and political condition of the Mexican community. Yet, they also believed education would do more than elevate the status of the community. It would increase the size of the middle class within the Mexican community. By receiving more education, especially higher education, the Mexican middle class would enlarge itself as a class. This enlargement of the educated and upwardly mobile elements within the Mexican community would ensure the continued existence and further growth of organizations such as LULAC by providing them with future leaders and members. But in order to achieve more schooling, it was necessary to struggle against obstacles impeding the educational progress of Mexicans. For this reason, their struggle became two-fold. On the one hand, they had to modify existing discriminatory educational policies and practices in order to improve the accessibility to more and better schooling for Mexicans. On the other hand, they had to go among their own people and disseminate their faith in public education. To a large extent, LULAC members believed that the problem confronting the Mexican community consisted both of Anglo prejudice as well as Mexican American inaction. "The problems with which they and their racial brothers are faced in Texas and the United States," one observer commented, "have been created quite as much by their own deficiencies as by the deficiencies of the Anglo-American in his dealings with them." With respect to education, LULAC believed that Mexicans had to adopt the national language, treasure public schooling and learn to demand equal treatment in schools. . . .

The G.I. Forum was ideologically similar to LULAC. Politically liberal, highly patriotic, and pragmatically oriented, it espoused LULAC's faith in the power of education. . . . Fighting discriminatory school policies occupied much of their time. In general, the G.I. Forum promoted more and better education for Mexican Americans and fought against the provision of separate and inferior schooling.

. . . The primary target of LULAC's and the G.I. Forum's reform activities centered on challenging the legality and practice of separate and unequal schooling for Mexican American students. School segregation of Mexican Americans and denial of access to elementary and secondary education were perceived by most leaders to be the major obstacles to educational equality. Most importantly, separate and inferior schools for Mexicans was symbolically the most vicious manifestation of the denial of educational opportunity and the most visible aspect of discriminatory treatment in the public schools; it was also the most personal reminder of institutional racism.

The initial response by Mexican American organizations to discrimination and segregation in the public schools began several months after the founding of LULAC in 1929. At first, their efforts were aimed at challenging the legality of using national origin as a basis for providing separate and inferior schools for Mexicans. For example, in 1930, a group of Mexican American parents with the professional, financial, and organizational support of LULAC filed a suit against the Del Rio Independent School District in Southwest Texas. In this court case the community sought to prove that the local school officials of Del Rio, Texas, segregated school children of "Mexican and Spanish descent" from the school children of all other white races in the same grade. Although the Texas Court of Civil Appeals agreed in theory that "school authorities had no power to arbitrarily segregate Mexican children, assign them to separate schools, and exclude them from schools maintained for children of other white races, merely or solely because they are Mexican," in practice it did not find the Del Rio school officials guilty of such actions. Lacking financial resources, an adequate professional staff, and an atmosphere conducive to legal change, LULAC lessened its stress on legal challenges to segregation and instead emphasized other measures. Informal consultations and persuasion was strongly emphasized as a more effective strategy for changing conditions in the public schools. . . .

The soft approach to education reform was illustrated in 1939 during Ezequiel Salinas' term as state president of LULAC. In that year he took several steps to improve the deplorable condition of Mexican children in the public schools. As president of LULAC, he voiced the concerns of Mexican children in school to the state superintendent of public instruction, L. A. Woods, and encouraged him to take action against local school districts. He also appeared before an education conference attended by 100 school superintendents of Texas and spoke in favor of eliminating racism and distortions of Mexicans in the history textbooks. Before his term expired, Salinas worked and supported a Works Project Administration school construction project aimed at solving overcrowded conditions in the public schools of Hondo, Texas. In certain cases where the local school officials failed to eliminate discriminatory educational practices, LULAC conducted boycotts of the public schools and established temporary bilingual schools in the community.

During the 1940s organizational efforts at challenging discriminatory educational policy increased. These new efforts were influenced by two federal court cases declaring that segregation based on national origin was unconstitutional, by administrative responses of different state agencies to the segregation of Mexican American children, and by the emergence in 1948 of the G.I. Forum, a militant and vocal Mexican American veteran's organization.

On April 8, 1947, in response to a California Federal District Courts case which found segregation of Mexican students to be unconstitutional, the Attorney General of Texas, Price Daniel, issued a legal opinion forbidding the separate placement of Mexican children in the state's public schools. . . . But the legal opinion on segregation was ineffective for no mechanism to secure compliance was established nor guidelines for implementing these steps provided to local school officials.

Consequently, additional legal efforts aimed at the establishment of the unconstitutionality of segregation practices were pursued by LULAC. In 1948, it filed a desegregation suit aimed at clarifying the constitutional issues involved in the segregation of Mexicans in the public schools. In *Delgado v. Destrop* [sic] *Independent School District,* the parents of the school aged Mexican American children charged that school officials in four communities in central Texas were segregating Mexicans contrary to the law. As in the case of California, the United States District Court, Western District of Texas ruled that the placing of students of Mexican ancestry in different buildings was arbitrary, discriminatory, and illegal. . . .

Of additional significance, especially for the continued anti-segregation efforts of LULAC and the G. I. Forum, was the stipulation by the District Court that permanently restrained and enjoined the local school boards and the superintendents

> from segregating pupils of Mexican or Latin American descent in separate schools or classes within the respective school districts of said defendants and each of them, and from denying said pupils use of the same facilities and services enjoyed by other children of the same age or grades. . . .

Exception, however, was granted in cases where children did not know English and were placed in separate classes on the same campus for the first grade only. The placement of non-English speaking students in separate classes would be determined on the basis of "scientific and standardized tests, equally given and applied to all pupils." The sanctioning of segregation of Mexican American children in the first grade "solely for instructional purposes" weakened the potential impact of this federal decision. . . .

In response to the *Delgado* case, the State Superintendent of Public Instruction and the Texas State Board of Education issued regulations regarding the illegality of discriminatory school practices such as segregation. The new instructions to the school districts stipulated that segregation as mandated by the State Constitution and by judicial and legislative decree only applied to blacks and not to members of any other race. . . .

Besides increasing public awareness of existing patterns of racial discrimination and segregation in schools and filing legal challenges, the Mexican American middle class also attempted to document the extent of segregation in Texas during the late 1940s and early 1950s. . . .

. . . On May 8, 1950, Gus Garcia of G.I. Forum and George I. Sanchez of LULAC appeared before the State Department of Education and discussed the continued existence of segregation despite the *Delgado* case. They recommended that a state policy of desegregation be declared and that the appropriate mechanisms be established to ensure the implementation of that policy. In response to Garcia's and Sanchez's presentation, the State Board of Education issued a "Statement of Policy Pertaining to Segregation of Latin American Children." This policy recognized the illegality of segregation, but it asserted the right to local districts to handle the complaints and grievances of local citizens alleging discriminatory treatment. . . .

The State Board of Education's desegregation policy led to the creation of an elaborate bureaucratic redress mechanism whereby Mexican Americans could voice their complaints to their local schools. If these local school officials failed to eliminate segregation, the Mexican American community could appeal to the State Department of Education, which would then investigate the charges and issue an opinion. The entire process, which was challenged by Mexican Americans in 1952, was tedious, time consuming, extremely bureaucratic, and intended to impede efforts to eliminate school segregation of Mexican American children. . . . Of the handful of cases heard by the Commissioner of Education, little was done to eliminate the assignment of Mexican American children to separate schools or classes. . . .

While willing to abide by the State Board's administrative remedies, the Mexican American organizations did not hesitate on taking recalcitrant school districts to court, although they preferred not to. . . .

Approximately 15 cases of discrimination in the public schools were filed during the first seven years of the 1950s. Although some of these were dismissed by the courts for various reasons, the decisions reached in all of the desegregation cases supported the Mexican American community's claims of discrimination based on national origin. The nature of the arguments made by school officials favoring separate classes for Mexican American children and [by] community persons favoring the elimination of segregation in the grades is best illustrated in the Driscoll case of 1957.

. . . The finding of discrimination against Mexican Americans in the public schools in Driscoll, Texas was welcomed by LULAC and the American G.I. Forum. Unfortunately, the federal district court's rulings on the unconstitutionality of segregation in Driscoll and other Texas cities had little impact on local school practices. Local school districts managed to circumvent the findings of segregation based on national origin by formulating and implementing creative discriminatory practices which maintained and in some cases strengthened school segregation. The mid and late 1950s can probably be called the era of subterfuges, since it was during this period that a multitude of evasive practices, e.g., "freedom-of-choice" plans, selected student transfer and transportation plans, classification systems based on language or scholastic ability, and others, were utilized by local school districts to maintain segregated schools. Although some small school districts, e.g., Driscoll, did eliminate separate schools for Mexican Americans, the LULAC and the G.I. Forum leaders perceived further litigation to be futile since "there were so many subterfuges available to bar effective relief." No further desegregation litigation was initiated by LULAC or American G.I. Forum until political and economic circumstances changed in the late 1960s.

Results were disheartening three decades after the first desegregation case was filed in 1930. As late as 1968, a nationwide survey on the education of Mexican Americans in the Southwest reported that while ethnic isolation of Mexican Americans in general was high, it was most pronounced in Texas. Approximately 40 percent of the Mexican school age population was attending schools which were 80 percent or more Mexican American. Segregation thus continued to be a way of life for many Mexican American students in Texas. . . . Yet, despite setbacks, Mexican American organizations like LULAC and the G.I. Forum between 1929 and 1957 played an extremely important role in challenging existing patterns of educational inequality at the local and state level. They were instrumental in filing complaints against segregation practices, in encouraging the Mexican community to take advantage of the public schools, and most importantly, in establishing the unconstitutionality of discriminatory practices based on national origin. Encountering racism, indifference, and hostile attitudes, Mexican American organizations, led by middle class members, played an important role in keeping the spirit of resistance alive within the barrio by struggling for equal access to public schooling. Guided by the ideals of political liberalism, Mexican American leaders demonstrated a commit-

ment to American institutions and to their eventual improvement. While the incul-
cation of liberal thought among Mexican American leaders can be considered a
positive step forward in that it inspired individuals to challenge existing patterns
of educational inequality, it was also a negative ideological development. Solutions
framed within the context of political liberal thought served to deflect serious analysis of the source of inequality in the society. Failure to raise basic questions concerning the nature of existing social, economic, and political institutions and the role
they play in maintaining and perpetuating inequality also tended to limit the number of possible strategies for dealing with the issues of segregation and school discrimination. In essence, efforts to use the legal system to dismantle school segregation failed to bring about substantive changes. . . .

PART V.
CHICANISMO AND
ITS AFTERMATH
1965–2000

The Delano strike launched in 1965 by César Chávez (1927–1993) in the vineyards of the San Joaquin Valley opened up a new chapter in Mexican-American history. The momentous event is a harbinger of the Chicano movement, the Mexican-American civil rights movement, which would reverberate in Mexican-American communities throughout the remaining years of the twentieth century.

The Chicano movement spanned the decade 1965–1975. The political activism of these years was influenced by contemporary protest movements, especially the Black civil rights movement and, to a lesser extent, the anti-war movement spawned by American involvement in Southeast Asia. Most of all, though, it was the culmination of political agitation within Mexican-American communities that can be traced back for decades.

The farmworkers' movement is a case in point. Efforts to organize *campesinos* (farmworkers) can be traced back to the turn of the century. Despite overwhelming odds, given the enormous discrepancy in power between agribusiness and impoverished and often illiterate migratory laborers, efforts to improve conditions in the fields were initiated time and again. The establishment of the Bracero program, however, effectively ended the attempt to create agricultural unions since braceros were essentially used as strike-breakers. Significantly, it was only in 1965, the year after the guest-worker program was terminated, that Chavez initiated his famous strike. He was aided by Dolores Huerta, who, as historian Richard García convincingly argues in his essay, was in many ways a better symbol of Chicanismo than Chávez himself.

The most dynamic element within the Chicano movement was represented by students, who surfaced as a militant force after the 1968 high school walkouts in East Los Angeles. It was youths who introduced the element of cultural nationalism, demanding the liberation of the Southwest, which they claimed as Aztlán, the Chicano homeland. It was students, too, as political scientists Carlos Muñoz and Mario Barrera assert in their essay, who became the backbone of La Raza Unida Party (LRUP), a political party predicated on the ideals of Chicanismo. The movement, however, was much larger than the student component. The working class, especially in the urban centers of California and the Southwest, was equally committed to Brown Power. Hard-won reforms were often the results of tireless efforts by barrio organizations, some of them, like the Brown Berets, as radical in their demands as were the students. Finally, the movimiento had a middle-class component. Admittedly the great majority of the middle class maintained a distance from La Causa or was even opposed to it. However, whatever long-term benefits were achieved, as political scientist Maurilio Vigil indicates in his essay, were often products of middle-class agitation by organizations like the Mexican American Legal Defense and Educational Fund (MALDEF).

With the sole exception of women's liberation, all the civil rights movements of the sixties were initially dominated by men. The Chicano movement was typical in this respect. By about 1970, at the height of political radicalism, mujeres began to assert themselves, soon creating a distinct Chicana presence within the larger movimiento. In the long run, the Chicana movement—like feminism in general—was more successful in consolidating the gains made during the turbulent decade than was its male counterpart. Anthropologist Alma García, in an oft-quoted essay, traces the early trials and tribulations of Chicana feminism.

By 1975, LRUP was in shambles and Chicano militancy was quickly falling out of fashion. Momentum was clearly spent. The end of the war, police repression, War on Poverty reforms, and a multitude of other factors created an entirely new political climate, underscored by Republican ascendancy in national politics during the eighties and into the nineties. The legacy of Chicanismo, however, was a lasting one. Occasionally it would surface, as sociologist Mary Pardo shows, in organizations like Mothers of East Los Angeles (MELA). A grassroots women's group, MELA waged a long but ultimately successful campaign in the late 1980s to protect the rights of barrio residents. The old Chicano spirit was evident, too, as the nineties drew to a close, when disparate Mexican-American communities throughout the United States closed ranks in defense of the rights of Mexican immigrants.

As anthropologist Leo Chávez illustrates in the concluding essay, the most striking issue to surface at the end of the twentieth century was the same as that in the beginning of the century: immigration. The Mexican-American population mushroomed during the years surveyed in this section, a demographic shift that can be attributed mainly to a sharp increase in the immigrant population. By the end of the twentieth century, 38 percent of the Mexican-origin population in the United States was foreign-born. The *causes* of Mexican immigration are relatively clear: the economic disparity between the United States and Mexico and the immense population explosion south of the border. The *consequences* of this massive international migration—the subject of an intense immigration debate in the United States as the new millennium begins—remain a mystery. How will these immigrants impact established Mexican-American communities? More generally, what effect will they have on American society? Will these newcomers be absorbed in the same way as others have been in the past? Objects of hope in some quarters and trepidation in others, only the immigrants themselves can provide answers.

26

DOLORES HUERTA
Woman, Organizer, and Symbol

RICHARD A. GARCÍA

Richard A. García received his Ph.D. from the University of California, Irvine, in 1980. At present, he is Professor of History at California State University, Hayward, where he teaches a variety of courses on ethnicity, including Mexican-American history. A visiting professor of history at Santa Clara University in 1989 and 1990, Dr. García has written a number of books and articles on Chicanos. His *César Chávez: A Triumph of Spirit* (1995) was co-authored with Richard Griswold del Castillo.

In 1962, Dolores Huerta co-founded the United Farmworkers union with Cesar Chavez. Since then, she has been called the unsung heroine, *La Pasionaria,* a humble woman, a non-traditional Mexicana, a union leader, and a great negotiator. She has even been compared to a Mexican revolutionary. Yet, despite being in the public sphere for two and a half decades, she is still not well known by most people and is still even an enigma for those who do know her. While tomes have been written on Cesar Chavez, almost nothing has been written about Huerta. Her appearance is familiar, but not her persona. All of these different thoughts and perceptions were in the air when Dolores Huerta spoke at a meeting that I attended in 1990 in California, at Santa Clara University, where she had been asked to speak in support of unionizing employees because she was a woman leader, an organizer, and a symbol of justice and fairness. . . .

After being formally introduced, Huerta began by speaking about her experiences with the union, about the poor and the farmworkers, and about the obligations of employers to their employees. As she spoke she began to sway the crowd with her message and her quiet, personal, but forceful, rhetorical tone. When she finished her short talk, the audience felt touched by her personality, her self-confidence, and her simple, powerful oratory. This was not the charismatic and dynamic oratory of Luisa Moreno or Emma Tenayucca [usually spelled Tenayuca].

From *California History* 72 (Spring 1993): 56–71, 97–98. The original text has been modified. Copyright by the California Historical Society. Reprinted by permission.

Above all, the audience was not barraged with facts and figures in the manner of Chavez; it was engaged by Huerta's theme. Afterward, we not only remembered it, but we felt it. She had touched our moral sensitivity and our hearts, not just our heads or emotions as Moreno or Tenayucca would have done.

Huerta's main point was clear and unadorned: that all persons should be treated fairly, that all should share equally in the goods and services of American society, and that all should have a voice in determining their own lives. Above all, she said that each of us had responsibility for the other. Her message was so simple that no one could argue against it. . . .

Later, as I remembered her talk, two statements by the philosopher and literary critic Richard Rorty—about the self and change—came to mind, putting Dolores Huerta and the meeting in some perspective. Rorty has written that the new self in the post-modern world is best perceived as a "picture of a centerless web of beliefs and desires" and "the only thing that can displace an intellectual world is another intellectual world—a new alternative, rather than an argument against an old alternative." In her public work as an organizer and in her private life, Dolores Huerta represents this "centerless web" of beliefs and desires. In this essay I will explore three textual categories: Huerta as the self-confident woman, as a skillful organizer, and as a philosophical symbol of justice. I suggest that Dolores Huerta has a strong sense of herself in a psychological, rather than in an ideological, way. She also uses Saul Alinsky's basic assumptions that empowerment of the poor is fundamental, that the poor must determine their own issues, and that a mass organizational drive for power is basic. Moreover, it seems clear that Huerta is not driven by specific ideological concerns, but by her general commitment to justice and fairness. Together, her beliefs and actions suggest that Huerta functions as a symbol of the "New *Mestiza*," as writer Gloria Anzaldúa has posited: a woman *sin fronteras* (without borders).

THE WOMAN: "BE YOURSELF"

Dolores Huerta is a complicated person who is constantly at odds with Cesar Chavez. . . . Both are stubborn and opinionated. Indeed, Huerta is notorious in the union for her combativeness. Her strong personality and independence have spelled constant conflict with her two husbands. . . .

Dolores married twice and engaged in a third live-in arrangement. From these three relationships, she has had eleven children. Motherhood, however, has not tempered her union activity. As she acknowledges, "the time I spend with my kids is very limited." Sometimes she is separated for months at a time from her children. Several writers have pointed out that Dolores is tough, competitive, individualistic, and very skilled. In many ways she lives in the space between the traditional woman's role and the radical feminist one. Huerta represents the New Mestiza that Gloria Anzaldúa has described, the woman who lives on the border between tradition and non-tradition, and between the accepted and the non-acceptable. . . .

. . . Huerta's inner strength comes from her sense of personal inviolability of the

kind that philosopher John Rawls has suggested, or the personal interiority that
Simone de Beauvoir has explored. . . .

   . . . This is what is appealing to farm working women, and urban Mexican
American women, regardless of age. She appeals to women because of her strength,
her aggressiveness, and her independence from men, but not in the feminist or lesbian ideological senses. It is simply in Huerta's manner of not having to use the feminine mystique. It is her air of personal strength, of assertive nature, and her disdain
of the need for any mystique that caused long-time organizer and labor leader Bert
Corona to call her too aggressive. . . . Huerta's independence, self-confidence, and
aggressiveness is what young Chicanas—the feminist and nationalistic activists of
the Chicano youth movement—have been looking for since the 1960s. . . .

   Ironically, even though in her everyday family life and in her organizational
work Huerta is the "new woman," in public she has acted and has been perceived as
the woman behind leader Cesar Chavez. Chavez, it seems, has had a tight rein on
his lieutenants, even on his equals like Huerta. Dolores Huerta, however, has by her
life example broken from the images of the traditional mother and wife or the woman activist behind the scenes, and has also broken from the Mexican male's sexist
perception that independence and sexuality are wrong and not culturally acceptable. . . . She has fractured the hegemonic Mexican and American womanly and
familial ideas, without becoming an ideologue of feminism. . . .

   . . . She grew up assuming that women and men were equal, as she constantly
saw the strength and activism of her mother, who on her own became a business
entrepreneur, independent from men. She also saw and experienced the ideal of
equality in America, where ethnicity was not a barrier. As she writes: "I was raised
with two brothers and a mother, so there was no sexism. My mother was a strong
woman and she did not favor my brothers. There was no idea that men were superior. I was also raised in Stockton in an integrated neighborhood. There were Chinese, Latinos, Native Americans, Blacks, Japanese, Italians, and others. We were all
rather poor, but it was an integrated community so it was not racist for me in my
childhood." Huerta perceived and interpreted the world as egalitarian, both within
and beyond the ethnic group. She felt free to be herself, worked hard to succeed in
school, and believed that she could participate in life as actively as her mother had.
She especially saw how her mother, a divorced woman, had, without the help of a
man, worked hard and started a successful restaurant and a hotel. . . .

   Overall, Huerta emerged from a communal atmosphere that fostered self-secu-
rity, self-esteem, and self-respect, in a place where ethnic commonalities were not
barriers. She grew up without a "them/us" complex, and with a strong belief in success, individualism, and hard work, and a strong sense of herself. Without realizing
it, she, like Emma Tenayucca, grew up with a middle-class mentality, if not necessarily in a strictly middle-class home. She reflected such values of stability, tradition, and Americanism that she briefly joined the Republican party in her twenties.
In fact, her Americanism was so pronounced that, as she remembers, she "thought
Fred Ross from the Community Service Organization (CSO), who was a Saul Alinsky organizer, was a Communist, so I went to the FBI and had him checked out. I
really did that. I used to work for the Sheriff's Department. See how middle-class I

was. In fact, I was a registered Republican at the time [the late fifties]." "But," she says, "I don't think I was ever really a cop-out." Despite her middle-class life, she remembers having friends who were *pachucos.*

Paradoxically, within this comfortable life and the consciousness of suburbia and of the possibility of "making it," Dolores Huerta experienced psychological anomalies and moments of ambiguity. . . . As she matured, she began to notice the poor on the streets, and to realize that most of the poor were the "out crowd" of her high school clubs. She specifically remembers being "crushed" when the legitimacy of her high school essays was questioned because they were so well written. The teacher thought someone else was writing them for her. "That really discouraged me," she said, "because I used to stay up all night and think, and try to make every paper different, and try to put words in there that I thought were nice."

As she matured, consequently, Huerta began to see life through a different lens, not because of the absence of personal freedom—because she did not feel she lacked freedom for herself—but because of overall injustice she had witnessed toward herself, to her Mexican friends, and to poor people at large in America. In short, she began to see the paradoxes of equality and justice, equality and class. . . .

At this same time, her 1950 marriage to her Irish sweetheart—which had taken place after high school—was failing, and her role as a mother to several children was unfulfilling. In addition, her college education, with the goal a teaching credential, no longer provided her with adequate intellectual or personal stimulation. During the 1950s, even teaching and helping children did not satisfy her. As she writes, "I felt I had all of these frustrations inside me . . . I was frustrated. I had a fantastic complex because I seemed to be out of step with everybody and everything. You're trying to go to school and yet you see all of these injustices. It was just such a complex." . . . Remembering her mother's constant advice—which would become almost a philosophical axiom—that she should always "be yourself," she began to shift to viewing her life with a new perspective, a new gestalt.

Consequently, in 1955, Huerta began to try to change the direction of her life. Armed with a high school and community college education that made her more educated than most women of the fifties, and certainly most Mexican women, she was also driven by a strong belief that individuals can change their lives and the lives of others. Hearing the Alinskian call for radicalism in the voice of Fred Ross, she joined the Community Service Organization (CSO). She had decided then to put herself at the service of others as an organizer and negotiator. . . .

. . . To Huerta, the world of the CSO, and later the farmworkers union, was no different from any sector of business. They needed well-organized executive managers who wanted to succeed. In the era of Eisenhower, when women were still considered "the second sex," Dolores Huerta accepted this calling as a woman who felt equal to men and free of a sense of inferiority about her ethnicity.

THE ORGANIZER: "PURSUING JUSTICE"

In 1955 Dolores Huerta responded to Fred Ross's CSO inquiry to become an organizer. Such involvement offered her an avenue to serve the poor, a notion she had acquired from her mother's example and tutoring. She also joined the CSO because it provided her with an avenue to "making it," albeit as a political organizer and not in mainstream America. Additionally, it coincided with her philosophical axiom, "be yourself." . . . With this new commitment to a life of social and political service, Huerta made a personal, moral, and political choice. She thus embarked on what Sidney Hook has described as a tense relationship between pragmatism, as in Huerta's choices for doing right, and a tragic sense of life, the consequences of that choice. . . .

In 1955, Huerta faced a complex moral dilemma. Her conflict of values was clear: betterment for herself or betterment for justice. The choice was between one ethical good and one personal right. I would suggest that in the persona of Dolores Huerta the classic American moral conflict was evident: the choice between two acclaimed values, individualism and equality. But, avoiding the binary choice, she instead chose the bridge between them: justice. . . . Huerta's choice put her into a world of sacrifice for the right of others, but at the expense of her own life's plans.

By doing this, Huerta relinquished the opportunity for "making it" in the ordinary American middle-class world of the 1950s and therefore had to endure the consequences, although she never changed her decision. As a result, she has endured the criticism of her father for failing her wifely and motherly duties, the criticism for two failed marriages, and the anger of middle-class women who berated her for neglecting her children when she entrusted them to communal parents while she went on organizing trips that often lasted months at a time. Huerta also endured resentment of male farmworkers and tolerated Chavez's constant anger at her independence. Above all, she had to put up with conditions of poverty for herself and her children. She often did not have money for milk or food. Her economic circumstances worsened when, in 1962, she moved from a relatively comfortable administrative position with the Community Service Organization to work as the powerful but still impoverished vice-president and principal director of negotiations for the Farmworkers Organizing Committee. . . .

Huerta finds organizing an enjoyable, creative process that gives her intellectual and personal fulfillment. Simply put, she admitted, "I like to organize." "My duties," she says, "are policy making like Cesar Chavez. It is the creative part of the organization. I am in charge of political and legislative activity. Much of my work is in public relations." All her work, regardless of whether it is policy-making, political and legislative activity, or public relations, is based on her four philosophical axioms that are both ends and means: first, to establish a strong sense of identity; second, to develop a sense of pride; third, to maintain always the value of service to others; and fourth, to be self-reflective and true to oneself. For Huerta, all organizing and leadership work had to be imbued with these principles as means and ends. Above all, she believes in psychological strength and strives to inspire the Mexican community, politicians, and the poor in general not to be afraid to deal with issues. As she put it, *"que no fueran miedosos"* (do not be afraid of anything). . . .

She believes that the equal participation of women in an organization is vital. Among the critical reasons, she emphasizes, is that "the participation of women has helped keep the movement nonviolent." According to Huerta, women are more patient, while men seem to be "separate, but equal." For Huerta, women's leadership complements men's, and therefore gender equality and justice are not only to be pursued goals but must be nurtured and practiced in daily organizing activities. Equality, for Huerta, is intertwined with justice and gender, but the core of her philosophy remains freedom of self through choice. Again, it is her mother's lesson emerging—"be yourself."

Dolores Huerta's ideas are rooted in numerous traditions. In many ways, Huerta's conceptualization of "be yourself" is a Durkheimian one; that is, it stresses the individual's freedom and morality, but the individual is tied to a responsibility to the community and a consciousness of collectivity. . . . In addition, Huerta's emphasis on the idea that organizers and leaders do not just give to the workers in the tradition of liberal-welfarism or lead the workers in the Marxist-Leninist tradition, coincides with Saul Alinsky's philosophy of organizing. Also, knowingly or not, her beliefs reflect philosopher John Rawls's ideas that justice conveys a philosophical core of individual inviolability, a doctrine of fairness, and a method of contractarianism. . . .

. . . Huerta, in a Rawlsian fashion, is calling for the poor to sit side-by-side with the rich and in a contractual relationship, to make the choices of what primary goods and services are to be distributed (i. e., liberties and economic, personal, intellectual, and political freedoms), and to determine the opportunities that must be made available to achieve better employment positions, income, and wealth.

Huerta combines this philosophy—which politically rests on the New Deal era and the New Left ideals of the radical 1960s—with the basic Alinskian concepts of developing mass organizations, community and self-empowerment, and self-commitment and self-responsibility by the communal members. Huerta clearly links the New Deal policies of justice and fairness with the 1960s ethnic youth rebellion for a new contractualism and redistribution of the primary goods and services of the society. . . .

While Chavez is more directly concerned with building the union and getting people's commitment to specific union activities such as boycotts, Huerta is not always directly attempting to build a commitment to the farmworkers union as she supports other causes. With her Jeffersonian, Rawlsian, and Alinskian beliefs, she reaches out to people with a simple message that can provide a new alternative intellectual world, as Rorty suggests. Hers is not an ideological message, nor does she advocate a structural revolution. She is simply calling for a new moral commitment based on a new sense of individual responsibility. Her new vision of justice calls for this alternative intellectual world to be used as an ideal plan of action. It is in the philosophical tradition of pragmatic self-discovery. . . .

THE SYMBOL

. . . Clearly, Dolores Huerta is a unionist, but more. She is ethnic, but more. She is liberal, but more. She is a communal conservative, but still more. In short, . . . we cannot rely on the familiar categories to characterize or understand Huerta. She is all of these things, but she still retains her individuality. She is marked by all the personal and symbolic attributes applied to her—feminist, nationalist, humble, aggressive, non-traditional, and *pasionaria*—but her specificity is in their overlapping and in the way she responds to events and issues. Further, it is difficult to place Huerta as a symbol of any single intellectual or philosophical tradition because she works with the constantly changing material of issues and crises, as determined by people in different communities. She is constantly revitalized by, as well as revitalizing, the present temporal issues and discursive events. Thus, in many ways she is more important, I suggest, than Chavez himself, who has continued to speak and work within the one tradition of unionism. . . .

At the core, I suggest that Huerta's cause is societal openness, universal equality, and a new humanism based on justice. Huerta is, I suggest, a symbol of openness—of not closing knowledge into truths, not compartmentalizing life, and not establishing divisions of ethnicity. And as justice is at the crossroads of freedom and equality, Huerta is a Rortyian self, constantly fracturing ascribed categories of life, a woman at the crossroads of femininity and masculinity, as well as of liberalism, conservatism, socialism, and nationalism.

Overall, she is a woman, an organizer, and a symbol of what Gloria Anzaldúa has called the New Mestiza, *sin fronteras*—without boundaries or borders. . . .

27

LA RAZA UNIDA PARTY AND THE CHICANO STUDENT MOVEMENT IN CALIFORNIA

CARLOS MUÑOZ, JR., AND MARIO BARRERA

Political scientists Carlos Muñoz, Jr., and Mario Barrera are two of the most respected scholars in the field of Chicano/a studies. In fact, they shared the distinction of being the National Association of Chicana and Chicano Studies (NACCS) Scholar of the Year in 1999. Members of UC Berkeley's renowned Ethnic Studies Department, both have had distinguished careers as activists and educators. Born in El Paso and raised in East Los Angeles, Muñoz received his Ph.D. in government from the Claremont Graduate School in 1973. Barrera, from Mission, Texas, earned his Ph.D. from UC Berkeley in 1970. Muñoz's *Youth, Identity, Power: The Chicano Movement* (1989), a participant history of the Chicano student movement, is a minor classic. Barrera has written two seminal books: *Race and Class in the Southwest: A Theory of Racial Inequality* (1979) and *Beyond Aztlán: Ethnic Autonomy in Comparative Perspective* (1988). In recent years, Dr. Barrera has increasingly devoted his time to the relationship between film and ethnic studies, while Carlos Muñoz has continued a life-long commitment to the cause of civil rights.

THE ORIGINS OF LA RAZA UNIDA PARTY

Youth of Mexican descent in the United States were deeply affected by the politics of the times during the turbulent decade of the 1960s. Those who were college and university students during that time were exposed to the civil rights movement, the farm worker struggles for unionization, and the protest movement against the war

From *Social Science Journal* 19 (April 1982): 101–19. The original text has been modified. Reprinted by permission of JAI Press.

in Vietnam. They were also strongly influenced by the Black Power movement that stressed pride in black culture and black control of community institutions.

During this time Chicano student activists became involved in the organization and implementation of electoral campaigns for local candidates and in the development of new grassroots community organizations, as well as in the revitalization of traditional ones. As their level of political consciousness and militancy grew, however, they became more and more critical of the old guard Chicano political leadership and organizations. They began to perceive the need for alternative institutions and organizations and to call for a new and more radical direction in Chicano politics.

Many of the student activists who participated in community politics came to be influenced by the symbolism and teachings of Rodolfo "Corky" Gonzales, leader of Denver's Crusade for Justice. Gonzales became the leading exponent of a Chicano nationalist ideology, and in 1969 his organization hosted the first annual Chicano National Liberation Youth Conference that brought together thousands of activist youth and students from all over the country to discuss, debate, and develop a plan for action for the fast rising Chicano Power movement in the United States. It was at that conference that the concept of an independent Chicano political party was first raised.

Among the dominant themes of the Chicano Youth Liberation Conference were the necessity for community control of institutions and the creation of alternative institutions. The two major political parties had been denounced as not responding to the needs and aspirations of the Chicano community. The new political party was first launched in Texas, where it grew out of a student-based organization called MAYO (Mexican-American Youth Organization). . . .

. . . A MAYO national conference in Mission, Texas, in December of 1969 put top priority on the formation of the party, and MAYO chapters became active in the organization of party chapters throughout the state in the ensuing years. By 1971, La Raza Unida had largely supplanted MAYO as the student activist organization and focus of activities. Organizational work for the party also began in other areas, particularly in Colorado and in California.

LA RAZA UNIDA IN CALIFORNIA

Although the greatest concentrations of Chicanos in California are in the southern part of the state, it was in the north that the first La Raza Unida chapters were formed. The Oakland-Berkeley Chapter had its first organizational meeting on November 22, 1970. . . .

. . . By the end of 1971, chapters of La Raza Unida had been formed throughout the state, at the initiative of local organizers rather than as part of a coordinated, centralized effort. The resulting organizational fragmentation was to characterize the party during its brief but intense existence.

The organizers of the California branch of the party threw themselves into a variety of political activities during 1971. Regional conferences were held in both northern and southern California in order to discuss platform and strategy and to stimulate the formation of new chapters. A major effort was launched to register voters with La Raza Unida. According to state law, a minimum of 66,334 persons would have had to register as La Raza Unida members for the party to gain official ballot status. A number of local elections were contested by candidates of La Raza Unida, although the official designation could not appear on the ballot. . . .

The year 1972 was . . . important for La Raza Unida because of the state-wide and national conferences that took place then. A state-wide meeting was held in San Jose in April of 1972, at which a wide variety of issues were discussed. The creation of a state-wide organization aimed at eliminating regional antagonisms was discussed, but it was eventually decided to remain with the existing three-part regional organization, divided into northern, central, and southern parts of California. In July of the same year, some five hundred persons gathered for a second state-wide meeting in Los Angeles. Ideological tensions within the party were clearly evident, with debates taking place as to the proper amount of emphasis to place on electoral activity, and also as to whether the party would be exclusively Chicano in composition or should aim at a broader Latino and Third World constituency. The second issue was resolved in favor of remaining focused on the Chicano community, but the first issue was to continue plaguing the party in the future.

In September of 1972, a climactic event took place in the history of La Raza Unida Party, not only for California but for the organization as a whole. The first national convention of the party was held in El Paso that month in order to try to create a national organization, and to determine the role of La Raza Unida in the 1972 election. Much of the activity of the convention was overshadowed, however, by the struggle for the national leadership of the party that took place between Jose Angel Gutierrez and Rodolfo "Corky" Gonzales, the leader of the party in Colorado.

The tension between the two men had surfaced during the debates on what emphasis to place on electoral activity that occurred prior to the convention. Those favoring a more radical politics tended to support Gonzales because of his emphasis on ideology as opposed to electoral activity, while those who tended to support Gutierrez did so largely because of his non-ideological approach, more in line with the electoral politics orientation that had succeeded in South Texas. . . .

On the surface the national convention was a huge success, with hundreds of delegates in attendance from throughout the Southwest and Midwest. Underneath the activity and enthusiasm, however, lurked seemingly irreconcilable divisions that were to loom larger and larger as time went on. The struggle for leadership between Gutierrez and Gonzales represented several different things at the same time. It was certainly a personal struggle between two charismatic leaders, each with a devoted following and a strong feeling for power. The contest also represented a certain amount of regionalism, with the delegates from Texas and Colorado equally desirous of having the party's leadership vested in their home states. At a more fundamental level, however, the choice between the two men reflected a divergence in ideological and strategic thinking that was becoming more evident throughout the party. "Corky" Gonzales, a dramatic figure with his all-black outfit and his coterie of ever-present bodyguards, had been moving away from the narrowly cultural Chicano nationalism of which he had originally been the high priest. His ideological statements now were interspersed with themes of internationalism and class conflict, and at least lip service to the women's movement and the struggle against sexism.

Jose Angel Gutierrez, on the other hand, remained steadfast in his orientation. He favored a focus on local issues specific to the Chicano community and argued against diffusing the thrust of the movement by emphasizing international issues. His style remained pragmatic and largely nonideological, at least in the sense of lacking a structured and broadly encompassing ideology. His appeals were still largely nationalistic, and he paid little attention to issues of class or sexual oppression.

In the contest for selection of a national chairman, Gutierrez had an advantage in that he had been the inventor of the model that others were attempting to copy elsewhere, and in the end he was selected by the convention and Gonzales was named vice-chairman. The show of unity which followed the election was only show, however, and the national organizational structure that was formed at the convention, *El Congreso de Aztlan,* failed to materialize because of the continuing personal and ideological divisions within the party. . . .

The California delegation to the national convention was divided in its loyalties. The division between Gutierrez and Gonzales was reflected within its ranks, with the San Francisco Bay Area delegates and part of the Los Angeles delegation supporting Gonzales, and southern California and the rest of the Los Angeles delegates going to Gutierrez.

The saga of La Raza Unida in California had largely played itself out by the end of 1973. The frustrations of the electoral campaigns, the ideological divisions within the party, and other factors analyzed in a later section of this article, had combined to undermine many of the state's chapters and to seriously weaken the others. . . .

THE STUDENT ROLE IN LA RAZA UNIDA

The full extent of student participation in California's version of La Raza Unida Party has generally not been fully appreciated. It would not be an exaggeration to say that La Raza Unida in this state was largely an outgrowth of the Chicano student movement and that its internal workings were for the most part shaped by students, friends of students, and faculty.

The Los Angeles City Terrace Chapter, to which Raul Ruiz belonged, had a membership which was about 30 percent student. Many of the members who were not students at the time either had been recently or were connected with colleges in some way. Raul Ruiz, their most prominent member, was a college instructor, and his campaign manager was a student. The East Los Angeles Chapter, also among the most active, was formed out of an independent studies class at California State University at Los Angeles and was originally overwhelmingly student in composition. Later on, more community people were to join, but the tone continued to be set by students. About half of the Oakland Chapter's members were students, and some of the other members were college instructors. In Orange County the membership was about 80 percent student. In the San Jose Chapter, another important chapter in a major urban area of Chicano concentration, the proportion of students was also about 80 percent. The Riverside–San Bernardino Chapter was approximately 30 percent student, and the majority of its original organizers were students. A heavy student representation thus characterized most La Raza Unida chapters in California with some exceptions, such as Union City and La Puente. . . .

Students were significant in La Raza Unida chapters not only in terms of their proportion of the membership, but in terms of the kinds of roles they occupied within the organization. In most of the chapters mentioned above, students dominated in the leadership roles, in part because they had more time than non-students to devote to the work of the party. Students, then, were located in organizational positions that allowed them to play a directing role in La Raza Unida and to influence decisively the ideological orientation and the strategies and tactics of the various chapters. Students were the ones who were also involved in the work of the chapters in a relatively continuous manner. . . .

Why is it that students were so heavily represented in the formation of La Raza Unida Party in California? The answer to this question is closely tied to the existence of a strong and vigorous Chicano student movement at the time. Through their involvement in campus politics students had been in a certain sense put in motion, and the very dynamics of that motion tended to propel them beyond the confines of the campus, not only in La Raza Unida but into other organizations as well. The student movement, in other words, had served as an agent of mobilization. The urge to become involved in off-campus politics was strong in Chicano students precisely because many had ambivalent feelings about being on campus in the first place. Chicano students could not help but be aware that they were a small and relatively privileged group as compared to most of their friends and acquaintances from the barrio and from high school. Although they still identified strongly with the Chicano communities from which most of them came, being on campuses where they formed a small proportion of the student body and where they were usually physically removed from the barrios produced feelings of guilt and isolation. "The community" and people who were active in the community were idealized, and the feeling that Chicano students should be working in the communities was perennially expressed at MEChA meetings and in Chicano Studies classes. La Raza Unida was one avenue for realizing these objectives, and its nationalistic thrust provided an almost tailor-made vehicle for feelings of integration and solidarity with the community. . . .

The large proportion of students in the California version of La Raza Unida Party had important consequences for the workings of the party. Certain characteristics of students were clearly assets to the party, while others were liabilities; and most of the respondents were keenly aware of both. Typically, the evaluation of student participation in La Raza Unida tends to be ambivalent. On the positive side there is agreement that the party benefited from the energy that students were able to put into organizational work. Given that their schedules were generally more flexible than those of working people, and that they usually had few family obligations, students were able to devote more of their time to party work. They were also relatively mobile, and thus able to attend out-of-town conferences and workshops. Students had a great deal of enthusiasm, at least in the early stages, and this was important for developing a new organization. Students also had certain types of skills to contribute. They had greater writing skill than most community people, an ability helpful in drafting resolutions, publicity, and announcements. Many of them were also articulate and could function as spokespersons for the party. Often they were knowledgeable about national and international issues; their knowledge broadened the information base of chapters.

On the other side of the question, a number of disadvantages of having such heavy student representation have also been noted by respondents from the different chapters. While some students were or had recently been active in other political organizations, generally they lacked experience and in-depth knowledge of the local political system in which they tried to operate. Students tended to be more rhetorical and theoretical in their statements; at times community people felt that students were talking down to them. Some were perceived as participating in La Raza Unida only for college credit they could receive. There was also a generation gap that made it difficult for college students to communicate with older people in the community. In some chapters many of the students were not from the local communities and had difficulty establishing ties and feelings of rapport with local residents. Students were often perceived by community people as transient and somewhat unreliable. This tended to be more true for University of California students, who often came from other parts of the state, than for students at the community or state colleges. . . . Student participation, then, posed somewhat of a dilemma. Indispensable to the formation of the party, students also brought with them a host of characteristics which, if not sufficiently counterbalanced, created weaknesses within the organization.

Sexism within the party also posed a dilemma for party unity. Women were an important component of most La Raza Unida chapters in California. In the San Jose and City Terrace chapters, for example, half or more of the members were women. In the Oakland and Riverside–San Bernardino chapters the proportion of women was about one third, and it was about one fourth in the East Los Angeles and Orange County chapters. Interviews with women members of La Raza Unida indicate that important problems existed in dealing with the role of women in the party, just as they did in the Chicano student movement as a whole. Women were generally assigned to handle routine tasks within the organization, and in most chapters it appears that few efforts were made to encourage women to assume leadership positions. Men tended to dominate ideological discussion within the meetings of the chapters in a manner that many women found difficult to deal with. . . .

IDEOLOGY AND STRATEGY

The model that was developed in Texas was that of a third party based on ethnic identification and cutting across class lines. The concept of "La Raza" was intended as a broad designation that could bring together those people whose origins could be traced to the blending of Indian and European peoples in Mexico and other Latin American countries. Within the Texas context "La Raza" is a common term of self-designation among the Spanish-speaking people, virtually all of whom are Mexican in origin. The concept of a party called La Raza Unida was thus in essence that of a party based on identification as a national minority, and the ideology was thus broadly nationalistic in tone. Self-determination was an important part of the concept, self-determination interpreted not as secession from the United States but as the gaining of control of existing institutions and the creation of new ones where necessary.

In California the ideological currents then flowing in the Chicano student movement blended in well with this ideological thrust. The student movement was basically nationalist in its orientation, and the idea of forming an alternative political party based on the Chicano community had broad appeal to students. In terms of ethnic identification most of the chapters of La Raza Unida in California unambiguously identified as Chicano, with the partial exception of some Bay Area chapters such as Oakland, where a broader Latino identification responded to the large numbers of persons from Central America in the area.

When it came to translating the concept of an ethnically based party into a working reality, however, some very fundamental problems were immediately uncovered. The Texas model was based on a region of the country where Chicanos were the overwhelming majority of the population and where the takeover of local political power by mobilizing the vote was a real possibility. In California, however, there are few analogous situations. . . . A strategy based on such an approach soon encountered frustration. The drive to place La Raza Unida on the state-wide ballot never came close to realization. By January of 1974, only slightly more than 20,000 registrations had taken place, with over 66,000 needed to quality for official party status. The campaigns for state-wide office also came to little, as typified in the highly publicized races of Raul Ruiz for the State Assembly. The possibility still remained that Raza Unida candidates could play the "spoiler" role and shake up the Democratic Party to some degree, but this in itself was not enough to sustain interest and commitment.

Given this situation, other strategic orientations emerged within the party and led to open conflicts over strategy within chapters and at regional conferences. The major school of thought opposing the emphasis on registration and campaigns had several components. One was that the chief focus of effort should be on increasing the levels of information and awareness of political issues on the part of the Chicano population, that is, "raising the level of political consciousness." . . .

Behind these strategic differences lay even more fundamental divisions on basic political ideology. . . .

Side by side with the dominant nationalist ideology existed a more radical, Marxist-oriented ideological tendency, unevenly represented in the different chapters. The Riverside–San Bernardino–Upland Chapter had little or no Marxist influence, as was generally true of the "inland" chapters, those away from the large coastal cities. The Oakland Chapter, on the other hand, had a fairly strong left orientation, including some independent socialists and several members of the Socialist Workers Party. The San Jose Chapter had a minority of Marxists, with the students more inclined towards left ideology than the nonstudents. The Labor Committee of the Los Angeles area, a chapter which was not confined to a small geographical area but which recruited from the entire Los Angeles region, was the only predominantly Marxist chapter in the state. . . .

Ideological debate between the more Marxist and more nationalistic party members tended to center upon several key issues. The more radical members were more often in favor of broadening the scope of the party to include non-Chicanos. . . . Marxists also argued for more attention to international issues, and particularly to anti-imperialist struggles in other countries, such as Vietnam. . . . Nationalists, on the other hand, wanted to maintain a narrower focus on local issues. . . .

Radical members of the party also tended to favor the more consciousness-raising approach to political work and to de-emphasize the winning of electoral contests. The more radical members were more inclined to drag their feet on the registration drive, which all chapters were supposed to push, and to feel that the political campaigns were "reformist" and "unrevolutionary."

The Marxist tendency added one other component which the nationalist orientation lacked. It provided a fundamental critique of American capitalism and insisted that the problems of Chicanos addressed by Raza Unida, such as poverty, political powerlessness, racism, and cultural intolerance, were unlikely to find solutions within the existing structure of society. The nationalist tendency never tied its analysis of Chicano problems to the broad workings of the American political economy and never called for a fundamental restructuring of society. . . .

THE DECLINE OF LA RAZA UNIDA

By 1973, La Raza Unida Party was already in a state of decline. Some chapters, particularly in Los Angeles, maintained some level of activity through 1975 but were much reduced in numbers. After 1975, the few chapters which still claimed to be in existence were essentially skeleton chapters. The decline of the party in California can be traced to several powerful trends which combined in a disastrous way.

One reason for the decline clearly lay in the failure to achieve state-wide ballot status, a difficult task given California's tough requirements for new parties. The party had invested a considerable proportion of its resources in the registration drive, and its failure could not help but have a profound demoralizing effect. This demoralization was compounded by the emotional letdown after the frantic activities of 1972, a presidential election year.

An even more fundamental factor in the decline of the party was the division which had taken place at the 1972 national conference in El Paso. The struggle between the backers of Jose Angel Gutierrez and "Corky" Gonzales had resulted in some very basic antagonisms within the party, and the California delegation had been split in its loyalties. . . .

The failure of the electoral campaigns which various Raza Unida chapters mounted in 1971 and 1972 also contributed to demoralization, especially for the dominant nationalistic sector of the party. The disappointing showings in most of the campaigns left that sector with no viable or even plausible strategy. . . .

A related factor was the co-optative response of the Democratic Party leadership, some of whom had become concerned about La Raza Unida incursions into the traditionally Democratic Chicano vote. The Raul Ruiz campaigns in Los Angeles had attracted more attention, and it was no coincidence that in 1972 the Democratic Party elected five Chicanos to State Assembly seats, up from two in the previous election. This had the effect of defusing La Raza Unida's most potent appeal to Democratic voters, the lack of representation of Chicanos in high elective office.

Another basic cause for the decline of La Raza Unida has been completely missed by analysts of the party. The fact, little appreciated to this day, that La Raza Unida in California was fundamentally a product of the Chicano student movement meant that its fortunes were closely tied to the campus-based movement. The overall decline of the student movement inevitably meant a decline in its off-campus extension. As students turned their attention elsewhere, the party lost its most dynamic component and entered its precipitous decline. . . .

CONCLUSION

. . . Despite these limitations, the experience of La Raza Unida in California was valuable in providing concrete political experience to many new activists. Significant networks developed from it, and skills gained in party work have been applied in many other contexts. La Raza Unida Party should thus be seen as part of a long tradition of Chicano political activism and resistance dating back to the mid-nineteenth century. This tradition has encompassed forms of political struggle ranging from electoral politics to union organizing to armed uprisings. Hopefully the continued study and analysis of such experiences will contribute to building political movements that can more effectively break through the limitations with which we have become so familiar, and point the way to more fundamental solutions to our seemingly intractable social problems.

28

THE ETHNIC ORGANIZATION AS AN INSTRUMENT OF POLITICAL AND SOCIAL CHANGE
MALDEF, a Case Study

MAURILIO VIGIL

Maurilio E. Vigil is Professor of Political Science at New Mexico Highlands University in Las Vegas, New Mexico. A native of Las Vegas, he
received both his B.A. and M.A. at New Mexico Highlands before moving on to the University of New Mexico, where he earned a Ph.D. in
1974. His many books include *Los Patrones* (1980), *The Hispanics of
New Mexico* (1986), and *Hispanics in Congress* (1996). Dr. Vigil has contributed chapters to several other books, and his articles are to be found
in a wide variety of journals.

. . . Hispanic organizations have been the vanguard of the Hispanic struggle for
social, political and economic opportunity in the United States. They have been
active in every arena—social, legal, political, religious, business, and professional—
and at every level of government in order to address the problems and concerns of
Hispanics.

There are two general functions performed by ethnic organizations. One is the
advancement of group consciousness which leads to greater cohesion and political
power; the other function is the provision of goods and services which address the
needs and concerns of the minority. . . .

Hispanic organizations, contrary to common assumptions, have been numerous, but have faced inherent obstacles in advancing the interests of Hispanics. Difficulties can be attributed to the dearth of knowledged and skilled leadership, limited
fiscal resources, and a constituency not always attuned to participatory democracy.
In recent years all of these deficiencies have been partially corrected, and some

From *Journal of Ethnic Studies* 18 (Spring 1990): 15–31. The original text has been modified. Copyright
by Bureau for Faculty Research, Western Washington University. Reprinted by permission.

Hispanic organizations have begun to make significant progress. One such organization is the Mexican-American Legal Defense and Education Fund, more commonly known by its acronym, MALDEF. MALDEF is probably the most important contemporary Hispanic organization. Viewed with the dual function framework, it can be said that MALDEF has addressed the problems, needs, and concerns more than any other contemporary Hispanic organization. Its sponsorship of litigation and lobbying activity have produced marked changes in such areas as education, employment and political participation for Hispanics. Its lawyers and leaders, who are Hispanics, have enhanced group consciousness and pride in the fight for their own rights and those of other Hispanics, thus promoting Hispanic cohesion and solidity.

SCOPE OF THE STUDY

Prior studies of Hispanic organizations have largely focused on general trends or patterns of organizational activity, or have provided classifications of the types of Hispanic organizations, with brief descriptions or profiles of specific organizations. In reviewing some of these organizations and in speculating on their importance, I have analyzed some specific Hispanic organizations, particularly those in the Mexican-American community. In conjunction with this type of effort and in the interest of providing a more significant evaluation and analysis, this study of MALDEF will focus on its history, structure, activities and accomplishments. . . .

HISTORICAL BACKGROUND, OBJECTIVES, AND ORGANIZATIONAL STRUCTURE OF MALDEF

The Mexican-American Legal Defense and Education Fund is a private, non-profit organization founded in 1967 by a small group of Hispano attorneys who sought to create an instrument to protect by "legal actions and legal education" the constitutional rights of Mexican-Americans. From a single office, the organization has expanded to include a national office headquartered in downtown Los Angeles, California, and four regional offices in San Francisco, Chicago, San Antonio, and Washington. It also maintains a program office in Sacramento, California. The organization consists of and is administered by a 36-member Board of Directors, mostly Hispanos, and includes attorneys, law professors, law school deans, judges, public officials, businessmen, journalists, educators, and other community leaders.

Although MALDEF maintains its staff of attorneys in each regional office, their work is aided by members of the organization and by a national network of referral lawyers from private law firms, corporations, and businesses who provide *pro bono* services and make in-kind contributions. MALDEF operations are funded by a variety of sources, including foundations (such as Gannet, GTE, Walt Disney, Kaiser, and General Electric) and private corporations (such as Allstate Insurance, AT&T,

AMOCO, Anheuser-Busch, Bank of America, Chevron, Coca-Cola, IBM, Levi Strauss, NBC, Quaker Oats, and Sears Roebuck). Also included are several labor unions and many individuals. Its operating budget in 1988–89 was $3.5 million. . . .

A . . . recent MALDEF publication states its broad objective . . . as being "to promote and protect the civil rights, of Hispanics living in the United States." The publication also adds that Mexican-Americans can "no longer accept discrimination in a society that boasts of equality for all its residents" and that accordingly MAL-DEF "has been at the forefront of civil rights litigations, setting precedents in many cases and establishing new systems to elect officials, hire employees and educate our children."

MALDEF has employed several strategies in its effort to accomplish its goals. These have included litigation, advocacy, educational outreach, law school scholarships, and leadership development. The most important strategy is the "litigation program" designed to implement legal action to eliminate discriminatory practices. The procedural strategy has been to initiate "class action" suits, with one or more Mexican-Americans representing a larger group. MALDEF has been especially interested in pursuing cases which reverse previous discriminatory practices and set new precedents. In addition to sponsoring (initiating) litigation, MALDEF has also participated in cases as "intervenor," that is, as an outside interested party and through *amicus curiae* (friend of the court) briefs. In substantive cases, MALDEF's objective has been to select cases where there are traditional barriers and violations, such as abridgment of civil rights, inequalities in educational opportunities, discrimination in employment and education, police brutality, political exclusion in voting and electoral laws, and inequities in public services. Recently it has taken up equitable enforcement of immigration legislation. In the past, MALDEF's efforts were directed on behalf of Mexican-Americans, and while this Hispanic sub-group is still its most important constituency, MALDEF does represent the broader Hispanic community, including documented and undocumented aliens. It coordinates efforts with other organizations such as the Puerto Rican Legal Defense and Education Fund. MALDEF litigation and advocacy programs are divided into three main areas: education, employment, and political access. It has also been involved in immigration, policy, and leadership issues.

MALDEF'S EDUCATION PROGRAM

Recognizing that education is the key to political, economic, and social opportunity for Hispanics and alarmed at the extremely high dropout ratio among Hispanics (estimated at 51 percent), MALDEF has addressed educational problems and barriers to education. Among these are segregation of schools, biased testing procedures, inequities in public school finance or resource allocation, and failure of the school systems to address language problems of Hispanic students. MALDEF's first significant legal victory was in education through the case of *Phyler v. Doe* (1982). MALDEF argued that the Texas law which permitted exclusion of children of undocumented illegal aliens from Texas public schools was a violation of the equal protection clause of the 14th Amendment. The U.S. Supreme Court affirmed MALDEF's position and ordered an end to the exclusionary process.

An example of MALDEF's anti-segregation effort was the lawsuit waged in 1986 against the San Jose, California schools (*Vasquez v. San Jose United School District*). MALDEF charged that the school district discriminated against Hispanic students by means of segregation. Initially U.S. District Judge Robert Peckham ruled against the Hispanics, saying that while the district was ethnically imbalanced, the school board had acted "without segregative intent." An appeal to the U.S. 9th Circuit Court of Appeals overturned Peckham's ruling, saying that the school district "had intentionally kept Hispanic students segregated since 1962." After the two-week hearing, the Court ordered the school to end segregation over a five-year period, cease school closures in Hispanic neighborhoods, and directed it to institute bilingual education and dropout prevention programs. The Court also appointed an official monitor to assure compliance with the order. In the same year in Denver, MALDEF attorneys worked with school officials to develop a desegregation plan and an early childhood bilingual program.

MALDEF's efforts to secure more equitable allocation of school finance have yielded results. In 1986 MALDEF filed a lawsuit against the Los Angeles United School District (*Rodriguez v. Los Angeles Unified School District*) seeking fairer allocation of school funds in areas with predominantly low-income minority student populations. The suit alleged that poor and minority students receive a substantially inferior education than their Anglo counterparts in Los Angeles schools because of differences in allocation of funds which result in poorer facilities and more limited instructional staff in the minority schools. . . .

In another case involving school finance, MALDEF supported the claims of undocumented aliens to a free public education in Texas. In this case, the school board of Tyler, Texas tried to charge the children of illegal Mexican aliens for their education received in Tyler public schools. The board was acting in conjunction with a 1975 Texas state law which stipulated that local school districts could not receive state funds to finance the education of children of illegal aliens. The law allowed school districts to bar attendance altogether, or to charge the parents for the education.

Accordingly, the Tyler, Texas school board decided to charge the parents of some 40 Mexican children the sum of $1,000 per year per child. Poor and unable to pay the $1,000, all of the children dropped out of school. MALDEF filed suit on behalf of sixteen of those children, claiming the law violated the equal protection clause of the 14th Amendment of the U.S. Constitution. The state opposed the suit, arguing that any person who is in the state illegally is technically not within the state's jurisdiction; thus, the 14th Amendment did not apply. The Supreme Court in 1982 ruled in favor of MALDEF and the Mexican children, stating that the children of illegal aliens have an inherent right to free public education which is considered a basic national policy.

MALDEF has also been an advocate of laws which would provide language assistance such as bilingual education for Hispanic students. In the case of *Gomez v. Illinois State Board of Education*, MALDEF sought enforcement of laws requiring provision of bilingual education to English language handicapped students. The U.S. Circuit Court of Appeals ruled on January 30, 1987 that the state of Illinois is required by law to assure that the Transitional Bilingual Education Act was implemented in a way to assure that Hispanic children are not deprived of equal educational opportunity. Similar efforts in bilingual education were pursued in Texas and California.

In higher education, MALDEF has sponsored litigation aimed at assuring desegregation, the adoption of equitable testing admission standards and professional school entrance requirements. MALDEF has sought to discourage use of standardized tests such as ACT and SAT as admission criteria for Hispanics because that group has historically performed poorly in those tests in comparison to anglo students. The tests are viewed as culturally biased. . . .

MALDEF EMPLOYMENT PROGRAMS

Hispanics have suffered every conceivable form of discrimination, exploitation, harassment, and abuse in the work place. They have been denied employment opportunity and job security. As former U.S. Senator Dennis Chavez once said, "Hispanics are the last to be hired and the first to be fired." Beyond the basic privilege of employment, Hispanics have often had to settle for the lowest paying jobs and in some cases the most physically arduous. They have often been denied job training and other opportunities to develop job skills that would ensure their advancement and promotion to higher paying and managerial positions. Even if they achieved equal training and experience, Hispanics have been denied "equal pay for equal work." As employment itself dictates other facets of one's life—where one lives, where one's children attend school, the availability (or lack thereof) of parks, recreation, and other similar amenities—one can appreciate that unemployment or underemployment is responsible for the harsh social conditions imposed on Hispanics. It is not surprising, therefore, that one of MALDEF's main thrusts has been in employment. MALDEF has addressed employment problems through "litigation, negotiation and advocacy."

MALDEF has sponsored or assisted in presenting the case for several Hispanics involved in litigation which has challenged discriminatory patterns in hiring and promotions. In 1985–86 a class action law suit was filed against San Antonio's largest grocery chainstores, the H. E. Butt Company. The court adopted a consent decree requiring annual goals for promoting Hispanics into supervisory positions. The court also approved establishment by the Butt Company of a $250,000 scholarship fund to prepare Hispanics for new jobs. In a similar case filed against the Ralph's supermarket chain in southern California, the company agreed to hire Hispanics in their 120 stores in proportion to their availability (about 20 percent) in the workforce. In still another case involving a grocery chain (*Ballesteras v. Lucky Stores, Inc.*), MALDEF and Hispanic employees won a settlement providing for a ten-year hiring and promotion plan. . . .

In a multi-state case MALDEF gained a settlement in a discrimination suit filed against the western region of the National Park Service (NPS). The agreement called for the NPS to develop an affirmative action law aimed at hiring and promoting Hispanics at all levels of employment throughout the western region of the NPS (California, Arizona, Nevada, Hawaii, and Guam). Hispanics, who held 5.0 percent of the 2,500 jobs in the region, were expected to improve to 28 percent of blue collar, 5.3 percent professional, 7.6 percent administrative, and 11 percent of technical jobs. NPS was asked to augment the bilingual capacity for serving the Hispanic public. An added benefit was that the higher percentage of Hispanics and bilingual staff in the NPS work force would enhance service to Hispanics using the national parks. . . .

In Los Angeles, MALDEF prepared a report for the Los Angeles Police Commission in 1986 which documented and described the hiring and promotional practices of the Los Angeles Police Department for the previous ten years. In March, 1987 the Los Angeles Police Commission adopted most of MALDEF's recommendations, including the increase in hiring goal for Hispanics from 22.5 to 30 percent. . . .

The enactment of the Immigration Reform and Control Act of 1986 (IRCA) has presented new challenges and a host of new problems for Hispanics and MALDEF. The overzealousness of employers in complying with the part of IRCA requiring employers to verify the citizenship or resident status of employees has, as MALDEF anticipated, resulted in arbitrary firings and refusal to hire Hispanic citizens or legal (documented) Hispanic aliens. MALDEF has addressed the problems caused by IRCA through an education campaign and through litigation.

In the fall of 1987 MALDEF launched a Fair Employment Campaign to publicize the anti-discrimination provisions of IRCA. Using articles, letters, seminars, and presentations, MALDEF explained the provisions of IRCA pertaining to employer responsibilities, while cautioning against discriminatory practices against Hispanics, which were also outlined in the provisions of IRCA.

MALDEF has filed many charges on behalf of clients (both citizens and documented "legal" aliens) before the Office of Special Counsel of the Immigration and Naturalization Service (INS) claiming discrimination due to the new law. . . .

MALDEF'S POLITICAL ACCESS PROGRAM

Hispanics, except for those in New Mexico, have historically avoided political involvement. There has generally been low registration and turnout by Hispanics. This has been reflected in the comparatively small number of Hispanic elected officials. Hispanic leaders and organizations have long recognized, however, that active participation in the political process, beginning with registration and voting and extending into office-holding and other forms of electioneering, is essential for the future progress of the minority group. Politics is seen as the means by which Hispanics can begin to influence or participate in the decision-making process that leads to public policies in education, employment, housing, and civil rights which Hispanics need for future progress. For far too many years, discriminatory electoral arrangements and apathy have kept Hispanics out of the voting booth and left them without effective representation in capitols, courthouses, and city halls. Accordingly, MALDEF has made the elimination of barriers to the political process a top priority in its litigation and advocacy programs.

MALDEF has engaged in various lawsuits involving voting rights violations, including arbitrary and restrictive registration requirements, denial of bilingual ballots, and explicit voting procedures in conflict with the Voting Rights Acts of 1965, 1970, and 1975.

The major portion of MALDEF's litigation and intervention activities has been directed at apportionment, districting, and gerrymandering problems. At-large election systems have especially been targeted because of their discriminatory effect on Hispanic representation in city councils, school boards, and county commissions.

Shortly after the 1982 redistricting of the Los Angeles City Council, the U.S. Department of Justice filed suit, and MALDEF intervened in the case of *United States and Carrillo v. Los Angeles,* arguing that the districting plan gerrymandered the Hispanic vote. MALDEF presented evidence, showing that in over 100 years only two Hispanics had been elected to the city council, despite the fact that Hispanics had been increasing in numbers until, after 1980, they constituted one-third of the population. The suit resulted in the creation of a second predominantly Hispanic district in northeastern Los Angeles and consolidated Hispanic strength in the San Fernando Valley when the city council adopted a new districting plan in July 1986.

In a follow up lawsuit to the city council action, MALDEF filed a similar lawsuit in August, 1988 against the Los Angeles County Board of Supervisors, charging the county with discrimination against Hispanics in its 1981 reapportionment plan. The suit charges that the districting plan, which does not contain a single "Hispanic district," effectively disenfranchises the two million Hispanics in Los Angeles County who make up 28 percent of its population. The present districting scheme splits up the Hispanic population concentrations in East Los Angeles and the San Fernando Valley. MALDEF argues that at least three supervisor districts could be created, encompassing the areas with Hispanic concentration. . . .

The most publicized victory was the case of *Gomez v. City of Watsonville.* In that case MALDEF challenged the at-large voting scheme which had denied Hispanics representation in the city council, despite the fact that they comprise 49 percent of the population. In July, 1988 the Ninth Circuit Court of Appeals found that the at-large mayoral and city elections impermissibly diluted the voting strength to Hispanics in Watsonville in violation of Section 2 of the 1975 Voting Rights Act. In one year MALDEF won a total of five cases in Texas, one in New Mexico, and one in California, involving challenges to at-large voting systems. . . .

OTHER MALDEF PROGRAMS

In addition to the primary programs in education, employment, and political access, MALDEF has sponsored other programs to advance the interests of Hispanics. MALDEF's *Immigrants Rights Program* has involved monitoring the implementation of IRCA and ameliorating its negative effects on the Hispanic community. Long opposed to the Immigration Reform Act, MALDEF was concerned about discrimination by employers against "foreign looking" legal immigrants and Hispanic American citizens. MALDEF provided a toll free immigration Hot Line Project in 1987 designed to provide general information to employers and employees on IRCA. During its operation, the Hot Line handled nearly 10,000 inquiries pertaining to many facets of IRCA, with the largest volume involving personal problems associated with it.

As complaints of employment discrimination stemming from the act appeared, MALDEF began to intervene on behalf of employees. In most instances it was a matter of contacting employers and clarifying the law, but in others litigation became necessary. MALDEF also provided data on IRCA's adverse employment effect on Hispanics to the U.S. General Accounting Office responsible for monitoring its effort. MALDEF has also challenged INS's arbitrary policy of using "general warrants" to enter workplaces in order to find illegal aliens. In the case of *Molders v. Nelson*, a case which will have long-reaching implications for INS procedures in enforcing IRCA, a San Francisco federal district court issued an order restricting INS's use of such blanket warrants. . . .

Undoubtedly MALDEF's activities on behalf of legal and illegal immigrants will expand as the full implementation of IRCA begins to take effect. . . .

MALDEF's *Policy Analyst* program has involved an effort to monitor and lobby for policies that are of direct benefit to Hispanics. Among recent activities are efforts to defeat English-only proposals in various states and Congress. In California, MALDEF has lobbied for legislation that would require school boards with over 1,000 students to elect school board members by single-member district. MALDEF's *Law Scholarship* program has resulted in the awarding of ten scholarships nationwide to promising Hispanic law students. The *Leadership Program* has involved MALDEF in offering leadership classes to about 1,000 mid-career Hispanic professionals. Additionally, MALDEF has sponsored efforts to assure a more effective census for 1990 by its "Make Yourself Count!" slogan and has also tried to involve parents in their children's education through its "parent leadership program." . . .

SUMMARY AND RETROSPECTIVE

Education, employment, and political participation have been the main thrust of MALDEF's efforts on behalf of Hispanics, since they are crucial to the future of Hispanics in American society. The American historical legacy for Hispanics has largely meant political exclusion and subordination, inequities in educational opportunity, discrimination in employment, and prejudice in the social environment. . . . As Hispanics begin to avail themselves of the advantages of the triad of opportunities in political participation, education, and employment, they will begin to reverse past patterns of prejudice and stereotype in the social environment to which they have fallen victim in the past. Through its central role in pursuing change in the three areas of concern to Hispanics, MALDEF has placed itself squarely in the vanguard of the Hispanic struggle.

29

THE DEVELOPMENT OF CHICANA FEMINIST DISCOURSE, 1970–1980

ALMA M. GARCÍA

Alma M. García is Associate Professor of Sociology and Ethnic Studies at Santa Clara University. Dr. García has served as chair of the National Association of Chicana and Chicano Studies (NAACS). She is the editor of *Chicana Feminist Thought: The Basic Historical Writings* (1997). Her current research project is a book to be titled *Latinas in Higher Education*. Born in El Paso, Texas, she comes from a family of scholars; her brothers are historians Mario and Richard García.

Between 1970 and 1980, a Chicana feminist movement developed in the United States that addressed the specific issues that affected Chicanas as women of color. The growth of the Chicana feminist movement can be traced in the speeches, essays, letters, and articles published in Chicano and Chicana newspapers, journals, newsletters, and other printed materials.

During the sixties, American society witnessed the development of the Chicano movement, a social movement characterized by a politics of protest. The Chicano movement focused on a wide range of issues: social justice, equality, educational reforms, and political and economic self-determination for Chicano communities in the United States. Various struggles evolved within this movement: the United Farmworkers unionization efforts; the New Mexico Land Grant movement; the Colorado-based Crusade for Justice; the Chicano student movement; and the Raza Unida Party.

Chicanas participated actively in each of these struggles. By the end of the sixties, Chicanas began to assess the rewards and limits of their participation. The 1970s witnessed the development of Chicana feminists whose activities, organizations, and writings can be analyzed in terms of a feminist movement by women of color in American society. Chicana feminists outlined a cluster of ideas that crystal-

From *Gender & Society* 3 (June 1989): 217–38. The original text has been modified. Reprinted by permission of Sage Publications.

lized into an emergent Chicana feminist debate. In the same way that Chicano males were reinterpreting the historical and contemporary experience of Chicanos in the United States, Chicanas began to investigate the forces shaping their own experiences as women of color.

The Chicana feminist movement emerged primarily as a result of the dynamics within the Chicano movement. In the 1960s and 1970s, the American political scene witnessed far-reaching social protest movements whose political courses often paralleled and at times exerted influence over each other. The development of feminist movements has been explained by the participation of women in larger social movements. [Anna] Macias, for example, links the early development of the Mexican feminist movement to the participation of women in the Mexican Revolution. Similarly, [Jo] Freeman's analysis of the white feminist movement points out that many white feminists who were active in the early years of its development had previously been involved in the new left and civil rights movements. It was in these movements that white feminists experienced the constraints of male domination. Black feminists have similarly traced the development of a Black feminist movement during the 1960s and 1970s to their experiences with sexism in the larger Black movement. In this way, then, the origins of Chicana feminism parallel those of other feminist movements. . . .

DEFINING FEMINISM FOR WOMEN OF COLOR

. . . In the United States, Chicana feminists shared the task of defining their ideology and movement with white, Black, and Asian American feminists. . . .

Chicana, Black, and Asian American feminists were all confronted with the issue of engaging in a feminist struggle to end sexist oppression within a broader nationalist struggle to end racist oppression. All experienced male domination in their own communities as well as in the larger society. . . .

Among the major ideological questions facing all three groups of feminists were the relationship between feminism and the ideology of cultural nationalism or racial pride, feminism and feminist baiting within the larger movements, and the relationship between their feminist movements and the white feminist movement.

CHICANA FEMINISM AND CULTURAL NATIONALISM

Throughout the seventies and . . . eighties, Chicana feminists have been forced to respond to the criticism that cultural nationalism and feminism are irreconcilable. In the first issue of the newspaper, *Hijas de Cuauhtemoc,* Anna Nieto Gomez stated that a major issue facing Chicanas active in the Chicano movement was the need to organize to improve their status as women within the larger social movement. Francisca Flores, another leading Chicana feminist, stated:

> [Chicanas] can no longer remain in a subservient role or as auxiliary forces in the [Chicano] movement. They must be included in the front line of communication, leadership and organizational responsibility. . . . The issue of equality, freedom and self-determination of the Chicana—like the right of self-determination, equality, and liberation of the Mexican [Chicano] community—is not negotiable. Anyone opposing the right of women to organize their own form of organization has no place in the leadership of the movement.

Supporting this position, Bernice Rincon argued that a Chicana feminist movement that sought equality and justice for Chicanas would strengthen the Chicano movement. Yet in the process, Chicana feminists challenged traditional gender roles because they limited their participation and acceptance within the Chicano movement.

Throughout the seventies, Chicana feminists viewed the struggle against sexism within the Chicano movement and the struggle against racism in the large society as integral parts of Chicana feminism. . . .

Cultural nationalism represented a major ideological component of the Chicano movement. Its emphasis on Chicano cultural pride and cultural survival within an Anglo-dominated society gave significant political direction to the Chicano movement. One source of ideological disagreement between Chicana feminism and this cultural national ideology was cultural survival. Many Chicana feminists believed that a focus on cultural survival did not acknowledge the need to alter male-female relations within Chicano communities. For example, Chicana feminists criticized the notion of the "ideal Chicana" that glorified Chicanas as strong, long-suffering women who had endured and kept Chicano culture and the family intact. To Chicana feminists, this concept represented an obstacle to the redefinition of gender roles. Nieto stated:

> Some Chicanas are praised as they emulate the sanctified example set by [the Virgin] Mary. The woman *par excellence* is mother and wife. She is to love and support her husband and to nurture and teach her children. Thus, may she gain fulfillment as a woman. For a Chicana bent upon fulfillment of her personhood, this restricted perspective of her role as a woman is not only inadequate but crippling.

Chicana feminists were also skeptical about the cultural nationalist interpretation of machismo. Such an interpretation viewed machismo as an ideological tool used by the dominant Anglo society to justify the inequalities experienced by Chicanos. According to this interpretation, the relationship between Chicanos and the larger society was that of an internal colony dominated and exploited by the capitalist economy. Machismo, like other cultural traits, was blamed by Anglos for blocking Chicanos from succeeding in American society. In reality, the economic structure and colony-like exploitation were to blame.

Some Chicana feminists agreed with this analysis of machismo, claiming that a mutually reinforcing relationship existed between internal colonialism and the development of the myth of machismo. According to [Adaljiza] Sosa Riddell, machismo was a myth "propagated by subjugators and colonizers, which created damaging stereotypes of Mexican/Chicano males." As a type of social control imposed by the dominant society on Chicanos, the myth of machismo distorted gender relations within Chicano communities, creating stereotypes of Chicanas as passive and docile women. At this level in the feminist discourse, machismo was seen as an Anglo myth that kept both Chicanos and Chicanas in a subordinate status. . . . While some Chicana feminists criticized the myth of machismo used by the dominant society to legitimate racial inequality, others moved beyond this level of analysis to distinguish between the machismo that oppressed both men and women and the sexism in Chicano communities in general, and the Chicano movement in particular, that oppressed Chicana women. According to [Mirta] Vidal, the origins of a Chicana feminist consciousness were prompted by the sexist attitudes and behavior of Chicano males, which constituted a "serious obstacle to women anxious to play a role in the struggle for Chicana liberation."

Furthermore, many Chicana feminists disagreed with the cultural nationalist view that machismo could be a positive value within a Chicano cultural value system. They challenged the view that machismo was a source of masculine pride for Chicanos and therefore a defense mechanism against the dominant society's racism. Although Chicana feminists recognized that Chicanos faced discrimination from the dominant society, they adamantly disagreed with those who believed that machismo was a form of cultural resistance to such discrimination. Chicana feminists called for changes in the ideologies responsible for distorting relations between women and men. One such change was to modify the cultural nationalist position that viewed machismo as a source of cultural pride.

Chicana feminists called for a focus on the universal aspects of sexism that shape gender relations in both Anglo and Chicano culture. While they acknowledged the economic exploitation of all Chicanos, Chicana feminists outlined the double exploitation experienced by Chicanas. Sosa Riddell concluded: "It was when Chicanas began to seek work outside of the family groups that sexism became a key factor of oppression along with racism." . . . Thus, while the Chicano movement was addressing the issue of racial oppression facing all Chicanos, Chicana feminists argued that it lacked an analysis of sexism. . . .

CHICANA FEMINISM
AND FEMINIST BAITING

The systematic analysis by Chicana feminists of the impact of racism and sexism on Chicanas in American society and, above all, within the Chicano movement was often misunderstood as a threat to the political unity of the Chicano movement. As Marta Cotera, a leading voice of Chicana feminism, pointed out:

> The aggregate cultural values we [Chicanas] share can also work to our benefit if we choose to scrutinize our cultural traditions, isolate the positive attributes and interpret them for the benefit of women. It's unreal that *Hispanas* have been browbeaten for so long about our so-called conservative (meaning reactionary) culture. It's also unreal that we have let men interpret culture only as those practices and attitudes that determine who does the dishes around the house. We as women also

have the right to interpret and define the philosophical and religious traditions beneficial to us within our culture, and which we have inherited as our tradition. To do this, we must become both conversant with our history and philosophical evolution, and analytical about the institutional and behavioral manifestations of the same.

Such Chicana feminists were attacked for developing a "divisive ideology"—a feminist ideology that was frequently viewed as a threat to the Chicano movement as a whole. As Chicana feminists examined their roles as women activists within the Chicano movement, an ideological split developed. One group active in the Chicano movement saw themselves as "loyalists" who believed that the Chicano movement did not have to deal with sexual inequities since Chicano men as well as Chicano women experienced racial oppression. According to Nieto Gomez, who was not a loyalist, their view was that if men oppress women, it is not the men's fault but rather that of the system.

Even if such a problem existed, and they did not believe that it did, the loyalists maintained that such a matter would best be resolved internally within the Chicano movement. They denounced the formation of a separate Chicana feminist movement on the grounds that it was a politically dangerous strategy, perhaps Anglo inspired. Such a movement would undermine the unity of the Chicano movement by raising an issue that was not seen as a central one. Loyalists viewed racism as the most important issue within the Chicano movement. . . .

Chicana feminists were also accused of undermining the values associated with Chicano culture. Loyalists saw the Chicana feminist movement as an "anti-family, anti-cultural, anti-man and therefore an anti-Chicano movement." Feminism was, above all, believed to be an individualistic search for identity that detracted from the Chicano movement's "real" issues, such as racism. . . .

The ideological conflicts between Chicana feminists and loyalists persisted throughout the seventies. Disagreements between these two groups became exacerbated during various Chicana conferences. At times, such confrontations served to increase Chicana feminist activity that challenged the loyalists' attacks, yet these attacks also served to suppress feminist activities.

Chicana feminist lesbians experienced even stronger attacks from those who viewed lesbianism as a divisive ideology. In a political climate that already viewed feminist ideology with suspicion, lesbianism as a sexual lifestyle and political ideology came under even more attack. Clearly, a cultural national ideology that perpetrated such stereotypical images of Chicanas as "good wives and good mothers" found it difficult to accept a Chicana feminist lesbian movement.

Cherríe Moraga's writings during the 1970s reflect the struggles of Chicana feminist lesbians who, together with other Chicana feminists, were finding the sexism evident within the Chicano movement intolerable. Just as Chicana feminists analyzed their life circumstances as members of an ethnic minority and as women, Chicana feminist lesbians addressed themselves to the oppression they experienced as lesbians. As Moraga stated:

My lesbianism is the avenue through which I have learned the most about silence and oppression. . . . In this country, lesbianism is a poverty—as is being brown, as

is being a woman, as is being just plain poor. The danger lies in ranking the op-
pressions. The danger lies in failing to acknowledge the specificity of the oppression.

Chicana, Black, and Asian American feminists experienced similar cross-pres-
sures of feminist-baiting and lesbian-baiting attacks. As they organized around feminist struggles, these women of color encountered criticism from both male and
female cultural nationalists who often viewed feminism as little more than an "anti-
male" ideology. Lesbianism was identified as an extreme derivation of feminism. A
direct connection was frequently made that viewed feminism and lesbianism as
synonymous. Feminists were labeled lesbians, and lesbians as feminists. Attacks
against feminists—Chicanas, Blacks, and Asian Americans—derived from the existence of homophobia within each of these communities. As lesbian women of color
published their writings, attacks against them increased.

Responses to such attacks varied within and between the feminist movements
of women of color. Some groups tried one strategy and later adopted another. Some
lesbians pursued a separatist strategy within their own racial and ethnic communities. Others attempted to form lesbian coalitions across racial and ethnic lines. Both
strategies represented a response to the marginalization of lesbians produced by
recurrent waves of homophobic sentiments in Chicano, Black, and Asian American
communities. A third response consisted of working within the broader nationalist
movements in these communities and the feminist movements within them in order to challenge their heterosexual biases and resultant homophobia. . . .

Chicana feminists as well as Chicana feminist lesbians continued to be labeled
vendidas or "sellouts." Chicana loyalists continued to view Chicana feminism as associated, not only with melting into white society, but more seriously, with dividing
the Chicano movement. Similarly, many Chicano males were convinced that Chicana feminism was a divisive ideology incompatible with Chicano cultural nationalism. Nieto Gomez said that "[with] respect to [the] Chicana feminist, their credibility is reduced when they are associated with [feminism] and white women." She
added that, as a result, Chicana feminists often faced harassment and ostracism
within the Chicano movement. Similarly, Cotera stated that Chicanas "are suspected
of assimilating into the feminist ideology of an alien [white] culture that actively
seeks our cultural domination."

Chicana feminists responded quickly and often vehemently to such charges.
Flores answered these antifeminist attacks in an editorial in which she argued that
birth control, abortion, and sex education were not merely "white issues." In response to the accusation that feminists were responsible for the "betrayal of [Chi-
cano] culture and heritage," Flores said, "Our culture hell"—a phrase that became a
dramatic slogan of the Chicana feminist movement.

Chicana feminists' defense throughout the 1970s against those claiming that a
feminist movement was divisive for the Chicano movement was to reassess their
roles within the Chicano movement and to call for an end to male domination.
Their challenges of traditional gender roles represented a means to achieve equality.
In order to increase the participation of and opportunities for women in the Chicano
movement, feminists agreed that both Chicanos and Chicanas had to address the

issue of gender inequality. Furthermore, Chicana feminists argued that the resistance that they encountered reflected the existence of sexism on the part of Chicano males and the antifeminist attitudes of the Chicana loyalists. Nieto Gomez, reviewing the experiences of Chicana feminists in the Chicano movement, concluded that Chicanas "involved in discussing and applying the women's question have been ostracized, isolated and ignored." She argued that "in organizations where cultural nationalism is extremely strong, Chicana feminists experience intense harassment and ostracism." . . .

CHICANA FEMINISTS AND WHITE FEMINISTS

It is difficult to determine the extent to which Chicana feminists sympathized with the white feminist movement. A 1976 study at the University of San Diego that examined the attitudes of Chicanas regarding the white feminist movement found that the majority of Chicanas surveyed believed that the movement had affected their lives. In addition, they identified with such key issues as the right to legal abortions on demand and access to low-cost birth control. Nevertheless, the survey found that "even though the majority of Chicanas . . . could relate to certain issues of the women's movement, for the most part they saw it as being an elitist movement comprised of white middle-class women who [saw] the oppressor as the males of this country." . . .

Chicana feminists adopted an analysis that began with race as a critical variable in interpreting the experiences of Chicano communities in the United States. They expanded this analysis by identifying gender as a variable interconnected with race in analyzing the specific daily life circumstances of Chicanas as women in Chicano communities. Chicana feminists did not view women's struggles as secondary to the nationalist movement but argued instead for an analysis of race and gender as multiple sources of oppression. Thus, Chicana feminism went beyond the limits of an exclusively racial theory of oppression that tended to overlook gender and also went beyond the limits of a theory of oppression based exclusively on gender that tended to overlook race.

A second factor preventing an alliance between Chicana feminists and white feminists was the middle-class orientation of white feminists. While some Chicana feminists recognized the legitimacy of the demands made by white feminists and even admitted sharing some of these demands, they argued that "it is not our business as Chicanas to identify with the white women's liberation movement as a home base for working for our people."

Throughout the 1970s, Chicana feminists viewed the white feminist movement as a middle-class movement. In contrast, Chicana feminists analyzed the Chicano movement in general as a working-class movement. They repeatedly made reference to such differences, and many Chicana feminists began their writings with a section that disassociated themselves from the "women's liberation movement." Chicana feminists as activists in the broader Chicano movement identified as major struggles the farmworkers movement, welfare rights, undocumented workers, and prison rights. Such issues were seen as far removed from the demands of the white feminist movement, and Chicana feminists could not get white feminist organizations to deal with them. . . .

Chicana feminists continued to stress the importance of developing autonomous feminist organizations that would address the struggles of Chicanas as members of an ethnic minority and as women. Rather than attempt to overcome the obstacles to coalition building between Chicana feminists and white feminists, Chicanas called for autonomous feminist organizations for all women of color. Chicana feminists believed that sisterhood was indeed powerful but only to the extent that racial and class differences were understood and, above all, respected. . . .

30

MEXICAN AMERICAN WOMEN GRASSROOTS COMMUNITY ACTIVISTS

"Mothers of East Los Angeles"

MARY PARDO

Mary Pardo received her Ph.D. in sociology at the University of California, Los Angeles. She teaches courses on the Chicana and contemporary issues and research methods in Chicana/o studies in the Department of Chicana/o Studies at California State University, Northridge. Her most recent work is *Mexican American Women Activists: Identity and Resistance in Two Los Angeles Communities* (1998).

The relatively few studies of Chicana political activism show a bias in the way political activism is conceptualized by social scientists, who often use a narrow definition confined to electoral politics. Most feminist research uses an expanded definition that moves across the boundaries between public, electoral politics and private, family politics; but feminist research generally focuses on women mobilized around gender-specific issues. For some feminists, adherence to "tradition" constitutes conservatism and submission to patriarchy. Both approaches exclude the contributions of working-class women, particularly those of Afro-American women and Latinas, thus failing to capture the full dynamic of social change.

The following case study of Mexican American women activists in "Mothers of East Los Angeles" (MELA) contributes another dimension to the conception of grassroots politics. It illustrates how these Mexican American women transform "traditional" networks and resources based on family and culture into political assets to defend the quality of urban life. Far from unique, these patterns of activism are repeated in Latin America and elsewhere. Here as in other times and places, the

From *Frontiers: A Journal of Women's Studies* 11 (1990): 1–7. The original text has been modified. Reprinted by permission.

women's activism arises out of seemingly "traditional" roles, addresses wider social and political issues, and capitalizes on informal associations sanctioned by the community. Religion, commonly viewed as a conservative force, is intertwined with polities. Often, women speak of their communities and their activism as extensions of their family and household responsibility. The central role of women in grassroots struggles around quality of life, in the Third World and in the United States, challenges conventional assumptions about the powerlessness of women and static definitions of culture and tradition.

In general, the women in MELA are longtime residents of East Los Angeles; some are bilingual and native born, others Mexican born and Spanish dominant. All the core activists are bilingual and have lived in the community over thirty years. All have been active in parish-sponsored groups and activities; some have had experience working in community-based groups arising from schools, neighborhood watch associations, and labor support groups. To gain an appreciation of the group and the core activists, I used ethnographic field methods. I interviewed six women, using a life history approach focused on their first community activities, current activism, household and family responsibilities, and perceptions of community issues. Also, from December 1987 through October 1989, I attended hearings on the two currently pending projects of contentions—a proposed state prison and a toxic waste incinerator—and participated in community and organizational meetings and demonstrations. The following discussion briefly chronicles an intense and significant five-year segment of community history from which emerged MELA and the women's transformation of "traditional" resources and experiences into political assets for community mobilization.

THE COMMUNITY CONTEXT:
EAST LOS ANGELES RESISTING SIEGE

. . . [I]n March 1985, when the state sought a site for the first state prison in Los Angeles County, Governor Deukmejian resolved to place the 1,700-inmate institution in East Los Angeles, within a mile of the long-established Boyle Heights neighborhood and within two miles of thirty-four schools. Furthermore, violating convention, the state bid on the expensive parcel of industrially zoned land without compiling an environmental impact report or providing a public community hearing. According to James Vigil, Jr., a field representative for Assemblywoman Gloria Molina, shortly after the state announced the site selection, Molina's office began informing the community and gauging residents' sentiments about it through direct mailings and calls to leaders of organizations and business groups.

In spring 1986, after much pressure from the 56th assembly district office and the community, the Department of Corrections agreed to hold a public information meeting, which was attended by over 700 Boyle Heights residents. From this moment on, Vigil observed, "the tables turned, the community mobilized, and the residents began calling their political representatives and requesting their presence at hearings and meetings." By summer 1986, the community was well aware of the prison site proposal. Over two thousand people, carrying placards proclaiming "No Prison in ELA," marched from Resurrection Church in Boyle Heights to the Olympic Street bridge linking East Los Angeles with the rapidly expanding downtown Los Angeles. This march marked the beginning of one of the largest grassroots coalitions to emerge from the Latino community in the last decade.

Prominent among the coalition's groups is "Mothers of East Los Angeles," a loosely knit group of over 400 Mexican American women. MELA initially coalesced to oppose the state prison construction but has since organized opposition to several other projects detrimental to the quality of life in the central city. Its second large target is a toxic waste incinerator proposed for Vernon, a small city adjacent to East Los Angeles. This incinerator would worsen the already debilitating air quality of the entire county and set a precedent dangerous for other communities throughout California. When MELA took up the fight against the toxic waste incinerator, it became more than a single-issue group and began working with environmental groups around the state. As a result of the community struggle, AB58 (Roybal-Allard), which provides all Californians with the minimum protection of an environmental impact report before the construction of hazardous waste incinerators, was signed into law. But the law's effectiveness relies on a watchful community network. Since its emergence, "Mothers of East Los Angeles" has become centrally important to just such a network of grassroots activists including a select number of Catholic priests and two Mexican American political representatives. Furthermore, the group's very formation, and its continued spirit and activism, fly in the face of the conventional political science beliefs regarding political participation.

Predictions by the "experts" attribute the low formal political participation (i.e., voting) of Mexican American people in the U.S. to a set of cultural "retardants" including primary kinship systems, fatalism, religious traditionalism, traditional cultural values, and mother country attachment. The core activists in MELA may appear to fit this description, as well as the state-commissioned profile of residents least likely to oppose toxic waste incinerator projects. . . . However, these women fail to conform to the predicted political apathy. Instead, they have transformed social identity—ethnic identity, class identity, and gender identity—into an impetus as well [as] a basis for activism. And, in transforming their existing social networks into grassroots political networks, they have also transformed themselves.

TRANSFORMATION
AS A DOMINANT THEME

From the life histories of the group's core activists and from my own field notes, I have selected excerpts that tell two representative stories. One is a narrative of the events that led to community mobilization in East Los Angeles. The other is a story of transformation, the process of creating new and better relationships that empower people to unite and achieve common goals.

First, women have transformed organizing experiences and social networks arising from gender-related responsibilities into political resources. When I asked the women about the first community, not necessarily "political," involvement they could recall, they discussed experiences that predated the formation of MELA. Juana Gutiérrez explained:

> Well, it didn't start with the prison, you know. It started when my kids went to school. I started by joining the Parents Club and we worked on different problems here in the area. Like the people who come to the parks to sell drugs to the kids. I got the neighbors to have meetings. I would go knock at the doors, house to house. And I told them that we should stick together with the Neighborhood Watch for the community and for the kids. . . .

Part of a mother's "traditional" responsibility includes overseeing her child's progress in school, interacting with school staff, and supporting school activities. In these processes women meet other mothers and begin developing a network of acquaintanceships and friendships based on mutual concern for the welfare of their children. . . .

Each of the cofounders had a history of working with groups arising out of the responsibilities usually assumed by "mothers"—the education of children and the safety of the surrounding community. From these groups, they gained valuable experiences and networks that facilitated the formation of "Mothers of East Los Angeles." Juana Gutiérrez explained how preexisting networks progressively expanded community support:

> You know nobody knew about the plan to build a prison in this community until Assemblywoman Gloria Molina told me. Martha Molina called me and said, "You know what is happening in your area? The governor wants to put a prison in Boyle Heights!" So, I called a Neighborhood Watch meeting at my house and we got fifteen people together. Then, Father John started informing his people at the Church and that is when the group of two to three hundred started showing up for every march on the bridge.

MELA effectively linked up preexisting networks into a viable grassroots coalition.

Second, the process of activism also transformed previously "invisible" women, making them not only visible but the center of public attention. From a conventional perspective, political activism assumes a kind of gender neutrality. This means that anyone can participate, but men are the expected key actors. In accordance with this pattern, in winter 1986 an informal group of concerned businessmen in the community began lobbying and testifying against the prison at hearings in Sacramento. Working in conjunction with Assemblywoman Molina, they made many trips to Sacramento at their own expense. Residents who did not have the income to travel were unable to join them. Finally, Molina, commonly recognized as a forceful advocate for Latinas and the community, asked Frank Villalobos, an urban planner in the group, why there were no women coming up to speak in Sacramento against the prison. As he phrased it, "I was getting some heat from her because no women were going up there."

In response to this comment, Veronica Gutiérrez, a law student who lived in the community, agreed to accompany him on the next trip to Sacramento. He also mentioned the comment to Father John Moretta at Resurrection Catholic Parish. . . .

The next juncture illustrates how perceptions of gender-specific behavior set in motion a sequence of events that brought women into the political limelight. Father Moretta decided to ask all the women to meet after mass. He told them about the prison site and called for their support. When I asked him about his rationale for selecting the women, he replied:

> I felt so strongly about the issue, and I knew in my heart what a terrible offense this was to the people. So, I was afraid that once we got into a demonstration situation we had to be very careful. I thought the women would be cooler and calmer than the men. The bottom line is that the men came anyway. The first times out the majority were women. Then they began to invite their husbands and their children, but originally it was just women.

Father Moretta also named the group. Quite moved by a film, *The Official Story*, about the courageous Argentine women who demonstrated for the return of their children who disappeared during a repressive right-wing military dictatorship, he transformed the name "Las Madres de la Plaza de Mayo" into "Mothers of East Los Angeles."

However, Aurora Castillo, one of the cofounders of the group, modified my emphasis on the predominance of women:

> Of course the fathers work. We also have many, many grandmothers. And all this IS with the support of the fathers. They make the placards and the posters; they do the security and carry the signs; and they come to the marches when they can.

Although women played a key role in the mobilization, they emphasized the group's broad base of active supporters as well as the other organizations in the "Coalition Against the Prison." Their intent was to counter any notion that MELA was composed exclusively of women or mothers and to stress the "inclusiveness" of the group. All the women who assumed lead roles in the group had long histories of volunteer work in the Boyle Heights community; but formation of the group brought them out of the "private" margins and into "public" light.

Third, the women in "Mothers of East L.A." have transformed the definition of "mother" to include militant political opposition to state-proposed projects they see as adverse to the quality of life in the community. Explaining how she discovered the issue, Aurora Castillo said,

> You know if one of your children's safety is jeopardized, the mother turns into a lioness. That's why Father John got the mothers. We have to have a well-organized, strong group of mothers to protect the community and oppose things that are detrimental to us. You know the governor is in the wrong and the mothers are in the right. After all, the mothers have to be right. Mothers are for the children's interest, not for self-interest; the governor is for his own political interest.

The women also have expanded the boundaries of "motherhood" to include social and political community activism and redefined the word to include women who are not biological "mothers." At one meeting a young Latina expressed her solidarity with the group and, almost apologetically, qualified herself as a "resident," not a "mother," of East Los Angeles. Erlinda Robles replied:

> When you are fighting for a better life for children and "doing" for them, isn't that what mothers do? So we're all mothers. You don't have to have children to be a "mother."

At critical points, grassroots community activism requires attending many meetings, phone calling, and door-to-door communications—all very labor-intensive work. In order to keep harmony in the "domestic" sphere, the core activists must creatively integrate family members into their community activities. I asked Erlinda Robles how her husband felt about her activism, and she replied quite openly:

> My husband doesn't like getting involved, but he takes me because he knows I like it. Sometimes we would have two or three meetings a week. And my husband would say, "Why are you doing so much? It is really getting out of hand." But he is very supportive. Once he gets there, he enjoys it and he starts in arguing too! See, it's just that he is not used to it. He couldn't believe things happened the way that they do. He was in the Navy twenty years and they brainwashed him that none of the politicians could do wrong. So he has come a long way. Now he comes home and parks the car out front and asks me, "Well, where are we going tonight?"

When women explain their activism, they link family and community as one entity. Juana Gutiérrez, a woman with extensive experience working on community and neighborhood issues, stated:

> As a mother and a resident of East L.A., I shall continue fighting tirelessly, so we will be respected. And I will do this with much affection for my community. I say "my community" because I am part of it. I love my "raza" [race] as part of my family; and if God allows, I will keep on fighting against all the governors that want to take advantage of us.

Like the other activists, she has expanded her responsibilities and legitimated militant opposition to abuse of the community by representatives of the state.

Working-class women activists seldom opt to separate themselves from men and their families. In this particular struggle for community quality of life, they are fighting for the family unit and thus are not competitive with men. Of course, this fact does not preclude different alignments in other contexts and situations.

Fourth, the story of MELA also shows the transformation of class and ethnic identity. Aurora Castillo told of an incident that illustrated her growing knowledge of the relationship of East Los Angeles to other communities and the basis necessary for coalition building:

> And do you know we have been approached by other groups? [She lowers her voice in emphasis.] You know that Pacific Palisades group asked for our backing. But what they did, they sent their powerful lobbyist that they pay thousands of dollars to get our support against the drilling in Pacific Palisades. So what we did was tell them to send their grassroots people, not their lobbyist. We're suspicious. We don't want to talk to a high-salaried lobbyist; we are humble people. We did our own lobbying. In one week we went to Sacramento twice.

The contrast between the often tedious and labor-intensive work of mobilizing people at the "grassroots" level and the paid work of a "high salaried lobbyist" represents a point of pride and integrity, not a deficiency or a source of shame. If the two
groups were to construct a coalition, they must communicate on equal terms.

. . . Throughout their life histories, the women refer to the disruptive effects of
land use decisions made in the 1950s. As longtime residents, all but one share the
experience of losing a home and relocating to make way for a freeway. . . .

The freeways that cut through communities and disrupted neighborhoods are
now a concrete reminder of shared injustice, of the vulnerability of the community
in the 1950s. The community's social and political history thus informs perceptions
of its current predicament; however, today's activists emphasize not the powerlessness of the community but the change in status and progression toward political
empowerment.

Fifth, the core activists typically tell stories illustrating personal change and a
new sense of entitlement to speak for the community. They have transformed the
unspoken sentiments of individuals into a collective community voice. Lucy Ramos
related her initial apprehensions:

> I was afraid to get involved. I didn't know what was going to come out of this and
> I hesitated at first. Right after we started, Father John came up to me and told me,
> "I want you to be a spokesperson." I said, "Oh no, I don't know what I am going to
> say." I was nervous. I am surprised I didn't have a nervous breakdown then. Every
> time we used to get in front of the TV cameras and even interviews like this, I used
> to sit there and I could feel myself shaking. But as time went on, I started getting
> used to it.
>
> And this is what I have noticed with a lot of them. They were afraid to speak
> up and say anything. Now, with this prison issue, a lot of them have come out and
> come forward and given their opinions. Everybody used to be real "quietlike." . . .

People living in Third World countries as well as in minority communities in
the United States face an increasingly degraded environment. Recognizing the threat
to the well-being of their families, residents have mobilized at the neighborhood
level to fight for "quality of life" issues. The common notion that environmental
well-being is of concern solely to white middle-class and upper-class residents ig-
nores the specific way working-class neighborhoods suffer from the fallout of the
city "growth machine" geared for profit.

In Los Angeles, the culmination of postwar urban renewal policies, the growing Pacific Rim trade surplus and investment, and low-wage international labor
migration from Third World countries are creating potentially volatile conditions.
Literally palatial financial buildings swallow up the space previously occupied by
modest, low-cost housing. Increasing density and development not matched by
investment in social programs, services, and infrastructure erode the quality of life,
beginning in the core of the city. Latinos, the majority of whom live close to the
center of the city, must confront the distilled social consequences of development
focused solely on profit. The Mexican American community in East Los Angeles,
much like other minority working-class communities, has been a repository for
prisons instead of new schools, hazardous industries instead of safe work sites, and

one of the largest concentrations of freeway interchanges in the country, which transports much wealth past the community. And the concerns of residents in East Los Angeles may provide lessons for other minority as well as middle-class communities. . . .

Mexican American women living east of downtown Los Angeles exemplify the tendency of women to enter into environmental struggles in defense of their community. Women have a rich historical legacy of community activism, partly reconstructed over the last two decades in social histories of women who contested other "quality of life issues," from the price of bread to "Demon Rum" (often representing domestic violence).

But something new is also happening. The issues "traditionally" addressed by women—health, housing, sanitation, and the urban environment—have moved to center stage as capitalist urbanization progresses. Environmental issues now fuel the fires of many political campaigns and drive citizens beyond the rather restricted, perfunctory political act of voting. Instances of political mobilization at the grassroots level, where women often play a central role, allow us to "see" abstract concepts like participatory democracy and social change as dynamic processes.

The existence and activities of "Mothers of East Los Angeles" attest to the dynamic nature of participatory democracy, as well as to the dynamic nature of our gender, class, and ethnic identity. The story of MELA reveals, on the one hand, how individuals and groups can transform a seemingly "traditional" role such as "mother." On the other hand, it illustrates how such a role may also be a social agent drawing members of the community into the "political" arena. Studying women's contributions as well as men's will shed greater light on the networks dynamic of grassroots movements. . . .*

---

*Postscript: In 1992, the final defeat of the proposed prison resulted from sustained political battles at several levels: mass community protests in the streets, litigation in the courts, and lobbying within the legislature.

31

SETTLERS AND SOJOURNERS
The Case of Mexicans in the United States

LEO R. CHÁVEZ

Leo R. Chávez is an associate professor in the Department of Anthropology in the School of Social Sciences at the University of California, Irvine. His academic focus has been Mexican immigration, and his *Shadowed Lives: Undocumented Immigrants in American Society* (1992) has been acclaimed as one of the best works on that subject. Born in Alamogordo, New Mexico, Dr. Chávez was raised in southern California. He received his Ph.D. in anthropology from Stanford University in 1982. He has been a research associate at both the Center for U.S.-Mexican Studies at the University of California, San Diego, and El Colegio de la Frontera Norte in Tijuana.

This paper examines recent empirical data collected from undocumented immigrants in San Diego, California. Its purpose is to: (a) explore the complexity of the undocumented population; (b) introduce the concept of the "binational family"; and (c) examine the implications of the long-term residence of undocumented immigrants in the United States.

There are two reasons for this examination. . . .

Because past research has focused on the temporary migration of single, undocumented workers, we know less about the behavior of undocumented families who fall out of the migrant stream. . . .

The data presented here attempt to fill in part of this gap. By focusing on the differences between single migrants and those who live with their families in the United States, we can begin to suggest the factors influencing undocumented migrants to abandon a pattern of return migration and to become long-term residents of the United States. . . .

The second reason for this examination is a concern for the implications of settlement by undocumented immigrants. . . . [W]e find two competing views. On

Reproduced by permission of the Society for Applied Anthropology from *Human Organization* 47 (Summer 1988): 95–108. The original text has been modified.

the one hand, the "assimilationist" view asserts that over time immigrants take their place in American society. The road to integration may be rocky, with immigrants taking available low-skilled and unskilled jobs, but eventually they will experience both economic and social mobility. This model has been based largely upon the experiences of European immigrants.

The counter view is one of conflict and non-assimilation. It asserts that immigrants who are racially and/or culturally distinct—specifically Asians, Blacks and Latin Americans—will face obstacles to their integration into American society. Instead of eventual social and economic mobility, such immigrants and their offspring will be relegated to a second-class status characterized by poverty and social problems, in particular juvenile delinquency and other criminal activities.

The data examined here suggest that policies which fail to consider the complexity of the undocumented population may unintentionally contribute to undocumented settlers and their families falling into the less desirable conflict/non-assimilation scenario presented above. . . .

METHODOLOGY

Between March 1981 and February 1982, a research team for the Center for U.S.-Mexican Studies at the University of California, San Diego, gathered data on the characteristics of undocumented and legal Mexican immigrants. Personal in-home interviews were conducted with 2,103 adults (aged 17 or older) born in Mexico who were living or working in San Diego County at the time of the fieldwork.

The sampling methodology employed was considered carefully since interviewing a "representative" sample of Mexican immigrants—in San Diego County or elsewhere in the United States—presents special difficulties of access and identification because of the large proportion of undocumented migrants in this population. To date, the most successful approach for overcoming these special problems has been a "snowball" sampling procedure, in which each successive respondent is a relative or friend of a previous interviewee who provides the interviewer with the necessary introductions and assistance in making contact with other members of his or her kinship/friendship network. The San Diego study utilized this methodology. . . .

The interview schedule consisted of both closed questions (in which the responses are anticipated) and open-ended questions. The latter questions allowed for in-depth probing and follow-up questioning. Responses to open-ended questions were recorded exactly as stated by the interviewees and were later classified into response categories, a method which allowed for the gathering of extensive qualitative data. Interviews averaged about two hours in duration. . . .

The original study focused on individuals. . . . However, the focus of the present work is on households. Household is defined in relation to residence, that is, those who co-reside in a particular place. . . .

In order to compare the behavior and attitudes of singles to that of migrants living with their families in the United States, households will be classified on the basis of composition into three categories: (a) non-family households, or households comprised of singles; (b) simple family households; and (c) complex family households.

Non-family households are made up of individuals ("solitaries") who are not related to one another through marriage or a parent-child bond. These individuals live either alone or with a sibling, other relatives or friends. Included in this category are individuals who live at their place of work, such as live-in maids and farmworkers who live on or near farm premises. Such individuals are single, or if married are not living with their spouse and family, who typically reside in Mexico.

Simple family households are composed of married couples without children, married couples with children, and single parents with children. *Complex family households* include both extended and multiple families. Extended families consist of relatives other than the head of the household's spouse and/or children. Additional relatives may be single or married and not living with spouse and/or children. Households with multiple families include various combinations of two or more families (that is, individuals related by marriage or a parent/child bond).

SOCIOECONOMIC CHARACTERISTICS

Similarities and predictable differences in the age-sex structure of household members in San Diego compared to data collected in the 1980 U.S. Census suggest that the sampling procedure employed in this study identified a population that is similar to that of undocumented immigrants in the country generally. . . .

In general, undocumented interviewees can be characterized as relatively recent arrivals (although 9.6% had been in the U.S. ten years or longer) who lack English language skills, received a limited education, and have low incomes. Their legal counterparts had been in the U.S. for a much longer period, have received about the same level of education, have greater English language skills, and earn slightly more money.

MIGRATION PATTERNS:
SINGLES COMPARED TO FAMILIES

Table 3 [omitted] presents information on age, marital status, whether spouse and/or children accompanied the migrant, and outcome of each migration to the United States for undocumented heads of household (which includes 95 female heads of household). The median age for the interviewees on their first migration was 22 years and the median length of residence in the U.S. was one year. About a third were married (35.6%) and almost as many had children (31.9%). Over half (57.0%) brought their spouse or child(ren) with them, which indicates that some individuals migrated with children but not necessarily with spouses.

As for the outcome of the first migratory experience, 38.1% returned to Mexico voluntarily, 11% were returned to Mexico by the INS, and 50.8% were still on their first migration. Importantly, almost four times as many undocumented migrants returned to Mexico voluntarily than at the hands of the authorities. Interestingly, the proportion of migrants still in the U.S. is similar to the proportion who brought their spouse or children to the United States.

With each succeeding migration, migrants are more likely to be married and have children. However, migrants with multiple migrations are increasingly less likely to migrate with their spouses and children and are more likely to return to Mexico. Importantly, the proportion of those who brought their spouse or children at each succeeding migration continues to be similar to the proportion of migrants who were still in the United States.

These data indicate that two significant patterns are occurring. On the one hand, there are the migrants with multiple migrations who maintain their family and household in Mexico: the traditional return migrant. On the other hand, there are the migrants who bring their families with them and who are more likely to continue their residence in the United States. This latter pattern is examined further after first noting the behavior of female interviewees.

Focusing only on the migratory patterns of female heads of households reveals some important differences with the general pattern. Focusing on their first migratory experience, women were generally older than the general undocumented population when they migrated, were less likely to be married, but more likely to have children. About the same proportion of women as men migrated with spouse or child(ren), but women interviewees stayed in the U.S. longer and were much more likely to still be in the United States. Women with two or more migrations exhibited patterns similar to their male counterparts.

Table 4 [not included here] compares the outcome of migrations for interviewees who migrated with spouse and/or child(ren) with interviewees who left their spouse and/or child(ren) in Mexico. The association between the two variables is highly significant. Examining the first migration, migrants with families were much more likely to still be residing in the United States compared to those who migrated alone (63.8% to 39.5%). On the other hand, those who migrated alone were much more likely to have returned to Mexico after their first migration (60.5% to 36.3%). This pattern continues in succeeding migrations. In short, migrating with a family appears to influence continued residence rather than returning to Mexico.

Examining the types of households formed by undocumented migrants approaches the question of settlement from a different perspective. When we correlate household composition with the length of time the migrant has been in the United States, a definite pattern emerges. . . . [H]ouseholds composed of single migrants tend to be associated with interviewees who have been in the U.S. for a relatively short period of time. The first year of residence in the United States is clearly a "fishing expedition." The undocumented migrant either resides at work, alone or with other single individuals in non-family households. Or, the migrant might live with relatives in an extended or multiple family household. Less than a quarter of the undocumented migrants who have been in the U.S. a year or less live in simple family households.

Over time, undocumented immigrants tend to reside less in households which appear to be transitory, that is, made up of single migrants. Households composed of simple families, particularly those comprised solely of parents and children, appear to be formed only after an initial period of time has been spent in the United States. Family formation can occur either through a single person marrying while in the United States or through an already existing family being brought from Mexico.

The most significant change in household composition and structure appears to occur after one year of residence in the United States, when the proportion of simple family households rises from 22% to 42.4% and a corresponding decrease occurs in households comprised of singles. This change in household structure is related to a process of selection which occurs during migration (as discussed above), resulting in most undocumented migrants (singles) returning to Mexico after about a year of residence in the United States. As a consequence, for those migrants who remain, the temporary nature of the residence begins to dissolve into a more long-term settlement, as reflected in the composition of their households. Simple family households increase in importance the longer the migrants reside in the United States.

MIGRANT VIEWS
OF CONTINUED U.S. RESIDENCE

Differences in migratory and household patterns exhibited by single migrants and migrants with families are also reflected in responses to a series of questions concerning the migrants' ties to Mexico and their future residence intentions. Asked if they had a house in Mexico where they could live permanently, almost all (90.3%) of the 148 singles responded affirmatively, compared to only about half (56.0%) of the 233 interviewees living in simple family households. Of the 155 interviewees living in complex family households, 68.8% indicated that they had a house in Mexico where they could live permanently.

Those interviewees who indicated they had a house in Mexico were then asked, "Is your principal place of residence your house in Mexico or your house in the United States?" Singles overwhelmingly (80.8%) responded "Mexico," while a majority of interviewees living in single family households (68.5%) and complex family households (68.7%) considered their principal house to be in the United States.

This difference in residence preference between households comprised of singles and those comprised of families is underscored in responses to the question, "Do you intend to live permanently in the United States?" Most of the informants living in family households (simple = 71.2%; complex = 61.9%) desired to live permanently in the United States, a commitment few of the interviewees living as singles (25.4%) were willing to make. . . .

As these data make clear, individuals living as singles and migrants living in households composed of families exhibit distinctive views on their residence preferences. Undocumented singles remain committed to their household and residence in the place of origin. In contrast, migrants with families in the U.S. express a commitment to continue residing in the United States.

Whether or not a migrant remits money also indicates the strength of his or her ties to a household in Mexico. Singles (81.1%) were much more likely to send money to Mexico than interviewees living in complex family households (70.6%) or in simple family households (63.0%). Such complex family households are often a combination of recent arrivals and longer-term residents, which is reflected in the responses. In all three types of households, the majority indicated they remitted money to family in Mexico, which indicates both the continued commitment to assisting economically needy relatives and the pragmatic strategy of maintaining a link (as "social insurance") to family whose assistance may be required should the migrant be apprehended and deported back to Mexico.

The reasons given by interviewees for coming to the U.S. shed some light on residence preferences and patterns. Similar proportions of interviewees living as singles (55.2%), in simple family households (50.9%) and in complex family households (54.7%) stated they migrated for economic reasons, such as not enough work in Mexico, low wages in Mexico, higher wages in the U.S. or they were unemployed. However, a clear difference emerges in the proportions of interviewees who cited the need to assist their parents economically as their motivation for migrating (singles = 21.0%, in simple family households = 3.1%, complex family households = 5.4%). Either interviewees living in family households migrated initially for other reasons, or, with their families now in the United States, they no longer believed their purpose for being in the U.S. was to support a family in Mexico.

The data suggest strongly that undocumented migrants living as singles in the U.S. essentially remain members of their household in Mexico. Indeed, their very presence in the U.S. can be interpreted as part of a strategy of household survival that includes diversifying sources of income. Micro-level analysis of the communities which send migrants to the United States have shown that one way of adapting to economic uncertainty is to develop as many sources of income as possible, including sending a household member to work in a nearby urban center or, if family resources permit, to the United States. For such households the selling of their labor resources is not restricted to national boundaries, but responds to the demands of an "international labor market."

Undocumented singles are important to the international labor market. They make up a significant part of the migrant stream that flows from Mexico to the United States and back again. But the families headed by undocumented immigrants appear to be on a different course. They are not directed by membership in a household in Mexico. Their strategies are for survival of the household as constituted in the United States. They no longer participate in a pattern of voluntary return migration. Many appear to be in the process of "falling out," or have "fallen out," of the migrant stream, at least in their view of themselves and their place in the world. For many, they are no longer "birds of passage" but rather settlers who will continue to reside where their family has been relocated. . . .

THE BINATIONAL FAMILY

Based upon the above discussion, the presence of long-term undocumented residents necessitates a broader conceptualization of undocumented families. The term "undocumented" is inappropriate when focusing on families and households. Popular terms such as "undocumented family" and "illegal alien family" are generalities which disregard the fact that many of these families have at least one child who was born in the U.S. and is therefore a citizen. Out of 603 households headed by undocumented immigrants in the San Diego sample, 42.1% contained at least one member who was a citizen by birth in the United States. This proportion compares favorably with similar data collected in Texas.

A more accurate term for families comprised of members of different nationalities and mixed immigration status (some members undocumented Mexicans and others U.S. citizens) is "binational family." Within a binational family, status differentiation among members exists on the basis of rights and privileges in the larger society accorded on the basis of political status (citizen or undocumented).

The age structure of undocumented immigrants indicates that the formation of binational families is fairly predictable. Undocumented immigrants who leave the migrant stream are in the early years of family formation, with a large proportion of the adults between 20 and 29 years of age. Focusing on the children (14 years old and under) in households headed by undocumented interviewees provides further evidence that undocumented settlers are in the early childbearing years: 46% of the children were five years old or younger. Consequently, the chances that a family headed by an undocumented immigrant will have a child born in the U.S. increase the longer that family resides in the United States.

The evidence also indicates another pattern that is important for considering the future of long-term undocumented residents: many eventually become legal residents. Of the 151 legal interviewees who had a previous history of migration to the U.S., 59.4% were at one time undocumented migrants.

A number of possibilities exist for undocumented immigrants to legalize their status. Current immigration policy has an established set of preferences under which aliens can apply to immigrate. Within this system, preference is given to the immediate relatives of U.S. citizens and legal residents who are attempting to reunite with their families. In addition, aliens with labor skills for which there is a need in the U.S. also receive preference. Within binational families, children born in the U.S. who are 21 years old can sponsor their parents' immigration. Undocumented children could also eventually legalize their status through petition by a U.S.-born sibling or through marriage to a U.S. citizen. In short, long-term undocumented residents, especially those who migrate as children, are not forever relegated to an undocumented immigration status.

Finally, both legal and undocumented immigrants often live in households which include friends or other relatives. Almost half (47.3%) of the households with families that were headed by undocumented immigrants (N = 369) included friends or relatives. Many (20.4%) of the family households headed by legal immigrants (N = 465) also contained relatives who have joined the household. . . .

CONCLUSIONS

Contemporary trends in Mexican migration to the United States indicate that greater attention must be paid to the complexity of the undocumented population. Consequently, researchers are increasingly distinguishing between the undocumented who continue a tradition of temporary labor migration from those who become long-term residents of the United States. This work has attempted to contribute to our understanding of the process of settlement by undocumented immigrants. . . .

The examination revealed observable differences in migration patterns and residence intentions. Single migrants were likely to be temporary workers in the U.S. labor market. They viewed their jobs as temporary and were likely to return to Mexico after a brief stay in the U.S., which they did not consider to be their permanent residence. They maintained a strong social and economic relationship to their place of origin.

In contrast, undocumented immigrants living with their families in the U.S. were likely to view their job as relatively secure and desired to continue residing in the United States. For many undocumented, the formation of a family in the United States begins a process which leads to eventual settlement.

A major implication of undocumented immigrants residing on a long-term basis in the U.S. is that families often include children who are U.S. citizens by birth. Families which include both undocumented members and U.S. citizens are here referred to as binational families. Given that the undocumented are a demographically young population, the formation of binational families is fairly predictable.

Managing to reside in the U.S. on a long-term basis does not imply that undocumented immigrants will experience an easy integration into American society. Many laws either explicitly or implicitly restrict undocumented immigrants from using social services. However, the presence of binational families complicates the issue of access to social benefits. For example, binational families are often caught in a dilemma created by the interplay of their social and political characteristics with policies defining access to social services and education. Such policies often do not account for the dual nationality and dual immigration status found in binational families.

The data presented here also have implications for what constitutes a "resident" of a community, a term which is legally ambiguous and yet often a part of the eligibility requirements for social services. When considering residency, policy-makers at all levels of government should take into consideration that: (a) long-term undocumented residents often intend to continue residing in the United States; (b) the formation of binational families creates strong social ties to the U.S.; (c) undocumented immigrants increasingly work in jobs which are year-round rather than seasonal in nature; (d) the lack of evidence on the voluntary return migration of long-term undocumented residents and their children; and (e) the possibility that many long-term undocumented residents will eventually legalize their status. These factors suggest that a failure to plan for the social integration of binational families is shortsighted at best, and at worst undermines society's interest in providing the foundation for all members to make the maximum contribution to their communities.

In sum, many of the undocumented who are long-term residents of the U.S. must be considered "immigrants" rather than "migrants." This is especially true for those who have taken the crucial step of forming a family in the U.S., either by marrying here or by bringing their family from Mexico. Such families will not necessarily follow previous migration patterns based upon the mobility of a single individual. There is scant evidence that most such families would willingly return to Mexico after a brief "season" in the United States. Many will remain in the U.S. unless they are apprehended and returned to Mexico by INS authorities. Even then, these families will have incentives to return to the home, community and equity (both economic and social) they have built up, sometimes over several years, in the United States.

BIBLIOGRAPHIC ESSAY

—◄〇►—◄〇►—◄〇►—

A variety of historiographic essays are available to students who want an overview of the mushrooming studies of the Mexican-American past. Since a complete listing of review articles is impossible here, only historiographic material published in the nineties will be included in this initial paragraph. These are the most useful: Rodolfo Acuña, "The Struggles of Class and Gender: Current Research in Chicano Studies," *Journal of Ethnic Studies* 19 (Spring 1990): 135–38; Antonia I. Castañeda, "Gender, Race, and Culture: Spanish-Mexican Women in the Historiography of Frontier California," *Frontiers* 11, no. 1 (1990): 8–20, and "Women of Color and the Rewriting of Western History: The Discourse, Politics, and Decolonization of History," *Pacific Historical Review* 61 (November 1992): 501–33; Ernesto Chávez, "Culture, Identity, and Community: Musings on Chicano Historiography at the End of the Millennium," *Mexican Studies/Estudios Mexicanos* 14 (Winter 1998): 213–35; Arnoldo De León, "Texas Mexicans: Twentieth-Century Interpretations," in *Texas through Time: Evolving Interpretations,* ed. Walter L. Buenger and Robert A. Calvert (College Station, Tex., 1991); Arnoldo De León and Carlos E. Cuéllar, "Chicanos in the City: A Review of the Monographic Literature," *The History Teacher* 29 (May 1996): 363–78; Sarah Deutsch, "Gender, Labor History, and Chicano/a Ethnic Identity," *Frontiers* 14, no. 2 (1994): 1–22; Jorge Durand and Douglas S. Massey, "Mexican Migration to the United States: A Critical Review," *Latin American Research Review* 27 (Spring 1992): 3–43; John A. García, "Ethnic Identity Research and Policy Implications for Mexican Americans," in *Mexican American Identity,* ed. Marta E. Bernal and Phylis C. Martinelli (Encino, Calif., 1993); Mario T. García, "Family and Gender in Chicano and Border Studies Research," *Mexican Studies/Estudios Mexicanos* 6 (Winter 1990): 109–19; Jeffrey M. Garcilazo, "Chicano Labor Historiography and the Persistence of Common Labor," *Mexican Studies/Estudios Mexicanos* 14 (Summer 1998): 441–49; Juan Gómez-Quiñones, "Questions Within Women's Historiography," in *Between Borders: Essays on Mexicana/Chicana History,* ed. Adelaida R. Del Castillo (Encino, Calif., 1990); Gilbert G. González and Raúl Fernández, "Chicano History: Transcending Cultural Models," *Pacific Historical Review* 63 (November 1994): 469–97; Richard Griswold del Castillo, "Chicano Historical Discourse: An Overview and Evaluation of the 1980s," *Perspectives in Mexican American Studies* 4 (1993): 1–25; David G. Gutiérrez, "Significant to Whom? Mexican Americans and the History of the American West," *Western Historical Quarterly* 24 (November 1993): 519–39; Pierrette Hondagneu-Sotelo, "New Perspectives on Latina Women," *Feminist Studies* 19 (Spring 1993): 193–205; Gregorio Mora, "New Directions in the Chicano History of California," *Mexican Studies/Estudios Mexicanos* 14 (Summer 1998): 451–70; Alex M. Saragoza, "Recent Chicano Historiography: An Interpretive Essay," *Aztlán* 19 (1988–1990): 1–78; and Zaragoza Vargas, "*Obreros y Sindicatos Chicanos:* Varieties of Chicano Working-Class History," *International Labor and Working-Class History* 45 (Spring 1994): 108–19.

There are several general works on the Mexican-American population. They include Lester D. Langley's *MexAmerica: Two Countries, One Future* (New York, 1988) and Peter Sperry's controversial and polemical *Mexican Americans: The Ambivalent Minority* (New York, 1993). However, there is an increasing tendency to look at Mexican Americans within the context of the larger Hispanic community. The best of these studies is Earl Shorris, *Latinos: A Biography of the People* (New York, 1992); the least insightful is L. H. Gann and Peter J. Duignan, *The Hispanics in the United States: A History* (Boulder, Colo., 1986). Other pan-Latino works include Harold J. Alford, *The Proud Peoples: The Heritage and Culture of Spanish-Speaking Peoples in the United States* (New York, 1972); Ilan Stavans, *The Hispanic Condition: Reflections on Culture and Identity in America* (New York, 1995); and Thomas Weyr, *Hispanic U.S.A.: Breaking the Melting Pot* (New York, 1988). A more scholarly approach is provided by Frank Bean and Marta Tienda, *The Hispanic Population of the United States* (New York, 1987). *Americanos: Latino Life in the United States,* preface by Edward James Olmos, introduction by Carlos Fuentes (Boston, 1999), is celebratory, but the photography is stunning.

Textbooks have been prepared from a variety of historical points of view. The pioneering work, the foundation upon which all subsequent authors build, is Carey McWilliams, *North from Mexico: The Spanish-speaking People of the United States,* 3d ed. (Westport, Conn., 1990 [originally published in 1949]). Moderate interpretations include Matt S. Meier and Feliciano Ribera, *Mexican Americans, American Mexicans: From Conquistadores to Chicanos,* 2d ed. (New York, 1993 [1972]), a well-written and comprehensive survey; and Julián Samora and Patricia Vandel Simon, *A History of the Mexican-American People,* 2d ed. (Notre Dame, Ind., 1993 [1976]), which is uneven and poorly edited. Rodolfo Acuña, *Occupied America: A History of Chicanos,* 3d ed. (New York, 1988 [1972]), is widely hailed as the bible of Chicano studies. The militant perspective is also reflected in F. Arturo Rosales, *Chicano! The History of the Mexican American Civil Rights Movement* (Houston, 1997), which has a broader scope than its title suggests; and two works that aim at a high school audience: Luis F. Hernández, *Aztlán: The Southwest and Its People* (Rochelle Park, N.J., 1975), and Carlos M. Jiménez, *The Mexican American Heritage,* 2d ed. (Berkeley, 1994 [1992]). In their comprehensive survey *North to Aztlán: A History of Mexican Americans in the United States* (New York, 1996), Richard Griswold del Castillo and Arnoldo De León stress the heterogeneous nature of the Mexican-American community; however, as the title of their book indicates, they continue to accept the basic tenets of the Acuña perspective. Manuel G. Gonzales, *Mexicanos: A History of Mexicans in the United States* (Bloomington, Ind., 1999), a synthesis of Chicano scholarship, attempts to reconcile militant and moderate perspectives.

A number of anthologies on various aspects of the Mexican-American experience have been published in recent years. *Chicano Studies: Survey and Analysis* (Dubuque, Iowa, 1997), edited by Dennis J. Bixler-Márquez et al., has a concise and informative introduction by Carlos F. Ortega relating the history of Chicano studies programs. Zaragoza Vargas, ed., *Major Problems in Mexican American History* (Boston, 1999), contains both primary and secondary sources. Among readers of a more specific nature are Alma M. García, *Chicana Feminist Thought: The Basic Historical Writings* (New York, 1997), and José "Pepe" Villarino and Arturo Ramírez, eds., *Aztlán: Chicano Culture and Folklore* (New York, 1998). A broader approach, as the title indicates, is taken by *The Latino/a Condition: A Critical Reader* (New York, 1998), edited by Richard Delgado and Jean Stefancic. Older but still valuable is David J. Weber's *Foreigners in Their Native Land: Historical Roots of the Mexican Americans* (Albuquerque, 1973), a minor classic which combines documents with a narrative history.

The remainder of this essay will survey some of the better book-length studies since the seventies. The first generation of Mexican-American scholars who turned to the study of their community came out of the Chicano movement. Their work reflected the militant nationalist perspective best exemplified by historian Rudy Acuña—a historical orientation stressing cultural conflict between dominant Anglos and subjugated Chicanos. Taught almost exclusively within Chicano studies programs in this early period, and thus catering to student activists, it is hardly surprising that the dominant view of Chicano history would stress Anglo oppression and Mexican resistance. An outstanding example of this genre is Robert J. Rosenbaum, *Mexicano Resistance in the Southwest: "The Sacred Right of Self-Preservation"* (Austin, 1981). Southern Methodist University historian John R. Chávez has written a more sophisticated variation of this militant perspective, *The Lost Land: The Chicano Image of the Southwest* (Albuquerque, 1984). Other recent works that stress exploitation are Martha Menchaca, *The Mexican Outsiders: A Community History of Marginalization and Discrimination in California* (Austin, 1995); Rodolfo Acuña, *Anything but Mexican: Chicanos in Contemporary Los Angeles* (New York, 1997); Leticia M. Garza-Falcón, *Gente Decente: A Borderlands Response to the Rhetoric of Dominance* (Austin, 1998); Edward J. Escobar, *Race, Police, and the Making of Political Identity: Mexican Americans and the Los Angeles Police Department, 1900–1945* (Berkeley, 1999); and F. Arturo Rosales, *¡Pobre Raza! Violence, Justice, and Mobilization among México Lindo Immigrants, 1900–1936* (Austin, 1999).

Ideological underpinnings for these "counter-hegemonic" interpretations came from left-wing intellectuals from the West and the Third World who were critical of capitalism and white imperialism. Particularly fruitful were the ideas of Frantz Fanon, Antonio Gramsci, Herbert Marcuse, and Albert Memmi. Perhaps the most influential intellectual mentor, however, was Robert Blauner, a sociologist at the University of California at Berkeley who popularized the internal colony model. (For Blauner's views, see especially *Racial Oppression in America* [New York, 1972].) Carlos Muñoz, Mario Barrera, Tomás Almaguer, and other Chicano scholars made internal colonialism the cornerstone of their interpretations. Rudy Acuña found it to be the ideal vehicle for explaining the oppression of the Chicano. This paradigm, "the quintessential victimization framework," according to historian Alex Saragoza, clearly became the dominant ideological model in Chicano historiography during the seventies. Before too long, however, the limitations of an approach that reduced Mexican-American history to a simple "good guys versus bad guys" perspective became obvious.

By the end of the seventies, Chicano historians began to branch out in new directions. Inspired by scholars like E. P. Thompson and Herbert Gutman, some of them were attracted to the "new urban" history. The first Chicano studies of urbanization were made by Albert Camarillo, *Chicanos in a Changing Society: From Mexican Pueblos to American Barrios in Santa Barbara and Southern California, 1848–1930* (Cambridge, Mass., 1979), and Richard Griswold del Castillo, *The Los Angeles Barrio, 1850–1890: A Social History* (Berkeley, 1979). Though the first was more innovative than the second, both studies were products of exhaustive archival research and made use of non-traditional historical sources. These pioneering community studies were followed in the eighties by numerous others, among them Ricardo Romo, *East Los Angeles: History of a Barrio* (Austin, 1983), and Gilbert Miguel Hinojosa, *A Borderlands Town in Transition: Laredo, 1755–1870* (College Station, Tex., 1983). A recent example of this approach is Douglas Monroy, *Rebirth: Mexican Los Angeles from the Great Migration to the Great Depression* (Berkeley, 1999). These urban studies not only provided a much-needed corrective to the almost exclusive emphasis that ethnic historians had placed on rural settings, but at the same time they effectively demolished the myth that the barrio was nothing more than a human cesspool breeding crime and despair and ultimately giving rise to a permanent underclass.

The mid–1980s saw Chicanos—and increasingly Chicanas—explore a variety of other new subjects and approaches. Committed to an interdisciplinary approach from the outset, Chicano historians came under the sway at this time of a variety of influences from traditional and non-traditional fields, notably cultural and feminist studies. Soon their work was on the cutting edge of scholarship dealing with race, class, gender, and sexuality. That fresh perspectives were emerging trends became patently manifest in 1987 when a half-dozen path-breaking Chicano works were published. Among the most notable of these studies were David Montejano, *Anglos and Mexicans in the Making of Texas, 1836–1986* (Austin, 1987), which explored the complex relationship between class and ethnicity in southern Texas; and Vicki L. Ruiz, *Cannery Women/Cannery Lives: Mexican Women, Unionization, and the California Food Processing Industry, 1930–1950* (Albuquerque, 1987), the first book published by a self-professed Chicana historian, an examination of mujeres and the creation of working-class culture. However, perhaps the best example of the new orientation in the study of the Mexican-American past was a work by historian Sarah Deutsch, a "Chicana" author from outside the ethnic community: *No Separate Refuge: Culture, Class, and Gender on an Anglo-Hispanic Frontier in the American Southwest, 1880–1940* (New York, 1987). From a variety of perspectives, Deutsch examined the lives of Hispanas during a crucial period of their history. Like David Weber and Leonard Pitt before her, the young Rhodes scholar, an "outsider" with impeccable credentials, was instrumental in providing greater credibility to the emerging field of Chicano history.

The best scholarly studies during the decade were those that were able to transcend the limitations of the 1970s perspectives that tended to see a monolithic ethnic community. Clearly, Mexican Americans differed with respect to age, sex, race, religion, class, region, political views, and a multitude of other features. During this period, no ethnic scholar did more than Mario T. García to establish the existence of a variety of Chicano communities, in the process rehabilitating the Mexican-American middle class which had been relegated to *vendido* (sellout) status by Chicano scholar-activists of the preceding decade. This revisionist perspective stressing a generational model was first expressed by Mario García in his *Desert Immigrants: The Mexicans of El Paso, 1880–1920* (New Haven, Conn., 1981), and later fully articulated by his brother, Richard García, in *Rise of the Mexican American Middle Class: San Antonio, 1929–1941* (College Station, Tex., 1991). The decade of the eighties, then, witnessed the rise of alternate ideological perspectives as well as alternative methodologies.

The 1990s saw the emergence of Chicano studies as a field of study with a solid reputation among all but the most traditional members of the academic community. Although nowhere near as great as the number of works on African Americans or Native Americans, the volume of scholarly studies on Mexican Americans increased substantially by the end of the millennium, when it became almost impossible to keep up with the growing literature. Among historians, the most prolific scholars have been Arnoldo De León, from Angelo State University; Richard Griswold del Castillo, from California State University, San Diego; and Juan Gómez-Quiñones, the dean of Chicano history, from the University of California, Los Angeles. More important than the volume of productivity, the level of scholarship has reached unprecedented heights, as is reflected in the number of ethnic scholars, both in and out of Chicano Studies departments, who have won prestigious academic awards. Given the limitations of space, only a few of them can be mentioned here. Like Sarah Deutsch before him, Ramón Gutiérrez, author of *When Jesus Came, the Corn Mothers Went Away: Marriage, Sexuality, and Power in New Mexico, 1500–1846* (Stanford, Calif., 1991), one of the few Chicanos attracted to colonial history, has looked at the Mexican community in New Mexico with fresh eyes and from a variety of perspectives. His award-winning volume is especially insightful on sexuality and ethnicity.

The search for ethnic identity was a major concern of the nineties. David G. Gutiérrez was masterful in his treatment of the subject in *Walls and Mirrors: Mexican Americans, Mexican Immigrants, and the Politics of Ethnicity* (Berkeley, 1995), which focused on southern California. This work was especially notable in that it addressed a key area neglected by Chicanos previously: the relationship between immigrant and native-born Mexicans in the United States. Perhaps the most meticulously researched book on the topic of identity is *Becoming Mexican American: Ethnicity, Culture, and Identity in Chicano Los Angeles, 1900–1945* (New York, 1993), by George J. Sánchez. Like David Gutiérrez, Sánchez was mentored by Albert Camarillo at Stanford University. Other significant works on ethnic identity are Douglas Monroy, *Thrown among Strangers: The Making of Mexican Culture in Frontier California* (Berkeley, 1990); Karen Isaksen Leonard, *Making Ethnic Choices: California's Punjabi Mexican Americans* (Philadelphia, 1992); and Lisbeth Haas, *Conquests and Historical Identities in California, 1769–1936* (Berkeley, 1995).

Racism continues to fascinate scholars, as it has from the very beginning. Virtually all of the books mentioned in the previous paragraph touch upon this sensitive subject. But several authors deal with it at length. Here, too, as with other major areas of inquiry, we see a more nuanced analysis than was possible before. For example, in *Racial Fault Lines: The Historical Origins of White Supremacy in California* (Berkeley, 1994), sociologist Tomás Almaguer finds that while racial minorities in the Golden State were all subjected to discrimination by Anglos in the late nineteenth century, the degree varied according to the group. Mexicans, he concludes, were treated less badly than African Americans, Asians, and certainly Native Americans, who were often victims of genocide. Another recent work that questions the traditional view of complete subjugation of the Mexican in the nineteenth century is Armando C. Alonzo, *Tejano Legacy: Rancheros and Settlers in South Texas, 1734–1900* (Albuquerque, 1998), a well-researched study of land transfer in the Lower Rio Grande Valley. Given the Southern origin of much of the Anglo-Texan population and the legacy of the Alamo, conventional wisdom holds that Tejanos have historically received the worst treatment among Mexican Americans; thus Alonzo's research should inspire heated debate in Chicano circles for some time to come.

Since, with few exceptions, Chicanas began to receive their doctorates in history only during the previous decade, it is not surprising that in the nineties the history of mujeres was not given the attention it merited. The premature deaths of two promising historians, Magdalena Mora in 1981 and Irene Ledesma in 1997, were a major blow given the small community of Chicanas trained in the discipline. Clearly, the greatest single area of Chicano historiography in need of further research is the history of mujeres, both immigrant and native-born. Nevertheless, a meaningful start on Chicana historiography was made, especially as the decade drew to a close. Pierrette Hondagneu-Sotelo, a sociologist, looked at the recent history of Mexican immigration from a woman's perspective in *Gendered Transitions: Mexican Experiences of Immigration* (Berkeley, 1994). *Mexican American Women Activists: Identity and Resistance in Two Los Angeles Communities* (Philadelphia, 1997), by Mary S. Pardo, is a fine monograph on both urban and women's history. While narrower than its title would suggest, Vicki L. Ruiz's *From Out of the Shadows: Mexican Women in Twentieth-Century America* (New York, 1998) is a valuable supplement to Martha Cotera, *Diosa y Hembra: The History and Heritage of Chicanas in the U.S.* (Austin, 1976), and Alfredo Mirandé and Evangelina Enríquez, *La Chi-*

cana: The Mexican-American Woman (Chicago, 1979), two impressionistic and dated but still useful studies. Emma Pérez's long-awaited *The Decolonial Imaginary: Writing Chicanas into History* (Bloomington, Ind., 1999) has a strong feminist and theoretical framework.

Another crucial area where Chicano historiography has been deficient recently is immigration. To find the best survey on this topic by a historian, one has to go back to Lawrence A. Cardoso, *Mexican Emigration to the United States, 1897–1931* (Tucson, 1980); though an even better study of the Great Migration is Mark Reisler's deeply researched *By the Sweat of Their Brow: Mexican Immigrant Labor in the United States, 1900–1940* (Westport, Conn., 1976). Historians Francisco E. Balderrama and Raymond Rodríguez look at one specific aspect of immigration in *Decade of Betrayal: Mexican Repatriation in the 1930s* (Albuquerque, 1995). As well, the works of the historians David Gutiérrez and Arturo Rosales cited above are provocative studies of immigrants. The greatest amount of work of late on immigration, however, has come not from history but from other social sciences. Leo Chávez, an anthropologist, has written a perceptive study of illegal immigrants, *Shadowed Lives: Undocumented Immigrants in American Society* (Fort Worth, 1992). An earlier anthropological study that must be mentioned is Robert R. Alvarez, Jr., *Familia: Migration and Adaptation in Baja and Alta California, 1800–1975* (Berkeley, 1987), a compelling narrative. Useful anthologies include *Between Two Worlds: Mexican Immigrants in the United States,* ed. David G. Gutiérrez (Wilmington, Del., 1996), and *Crossings: Mexican Immigration in Interdisciplinary Perspectives,* ed. Marcelo M. Suárez-Orozco (Cambridge, Mass., 1998).

Labor history, another subfield of social history, remains popular. Agricultural labor, in particular, has appealed to Chicano students recently. Among the most distinguished works are those of Dennis Nodín Valdés, *Al Norte: Agricultural Workers in the Great Lakes Region, 1917–1970* (Austin, 1991); Emilio Zamora, *The World of the Mexican Worker in Texas* (College Station, Tex., 1993); Devra Weber, *Dark Sweat, White Gold: California Farm Workers, Cotton, and the New Deal* (Berkeley, 1994); Gilbert G. González, *Labor and Community: Mexican Citrus Worker Villages in a Southern California County, 1890–1950* (Urbana, 1994); Camille Guerin-Gonzales, *Mexican Workers and American Dreams: Immigration, Repatriation, and California Farm Labor, 1900–1939* (New Brunswick, N.J., 1994); and especially Neil Foley, *White Scourge: Mexicans, Blacks, and Poor Whites in Texas Cotton Culture* (Berkeley, 1998). Winner of prestigious prizes from both the Organization of American Historians and the Western History Association, Foley's volume is one of the finest books published by a historian in recent years. Industrial labor has attracted less attention, but there is one outstanding study on the subject: Zaragoza Vargas, *Proletarians of the North: A History of Industrial Workers in Detroit and the Midwest, 1917–1933* (Berkeley, 1993). Jeffrey Garcilazo has mined a wealth of information on Mexican railroad workers for his forthcoming work *Traqueros: Mexican Track Workers in the United States, 1870–1930*. A particular aspect of railroad labor is covered by Barbara A. Driscoll, *The Tracks North: The Bracero Program of World War II* (Austin, 1999). For a broad synthesis of the contributions made by Mexicans to U.S. economic development, see Juan Gómez-Quiñones, *Mexican American Labor, 1790–1990* (Albuquerque, 1994), which has excellent bibliographies.

Probably the most prolific scholarly investigations in the nineties have been done on political history. The Chicano movement, in particular, has seen increased interest, beginning with the publication of Carlos Muñoz's *Youth, Identity, Power: The Chicano Movement* (New York) in 1989. Muñoz's main thesis, that students were the backbone of the movimiento, has generally been sustained by Armando Navarro in *Mexican American Youth Organization: Avant-Garde of the Chicano Movement in Texas* (Austin, 1995) and *The Cristal Experiment: A Chicano Struggle for Community Control* (Madison, 1998); and rejected by Ignacio M. García in *United We Win: The Rise and Fall of the Raza Unida Party* (Tucson, 1989) and *Chicanismo: The Forging of a Militant Ethos* (Tucson, 1997). Still another participant history is Ernesto B. Vigil, *The Crusade for Justice: Chicano Militancy and the Government's War on Dissent* (Madison, 1999). The best insider view, however, is found in José Angel Gutiérrez, *The Making of a Chicano Militant: Lessons from Cristal* (Austin, 1999). Mario T. García has continued his study of the Mexican-American Generation in *Mexican Americans: Leadership, Ideology, and Identity, 1930–1960* (New Haven, Conn., 1991). More specialized studies on the middle class include Henry A. J. Ramos, *The American G.I. Forum: The Pursuit of the Dream, 1948–1983* (Houston, 1998), and John R. Chávez, *Eastside Landmark: A History of the East Los Angeles Community Union, 1968–1993* (Stanford, Calif., 1998). The indefatigable Juan Gómez-Quiñones provides a panoramic overview in two volumes, *Chicano Politics: Reality and Promise, 1940–1990* (Albuquerque, 1990) and *Roots of Chicano Politics, 1600–1940* (Albuquerque, 1994).

The works of Vargas and Nodín Valdés listed above reflect another important historiographic trend of the nineties: the tendency to move beyond the Borderlands. Given the present demographic shift, the Midwest in particular has inspired scholarly investigation. Other monographs that concentrate on this region are Juan R. García, *Mexicans in the Midwest, 1900–1932* (Tucson, 1996), and Dennis Nodín Valdés, *Barrios Norteños: St. Paul and Midwestern Mexican Communities in the Twentieth Century* (forthcoming). Regrettably, however, no one has followed up on Louise Año Nuevo Kerr's early explorations of Mexican communities in Chicago. A significant consequence of the emerging interest in Chicanos beyond the Borderlands is that midwestern academic presses have begun to compete with southwestern academic presses for Chicano manuscripts.

Finally, students wishing to survey the most important journal articles and doctoral dissertations by Chicanos and Chicanas after 1965 may want to consult the extensive bibliography in my textbook, *Mexicanos*.

INDEX

◄○►◄○►◄○►

MANUEL G. GONZALES is Professor of History at Diablo Valley College in Pleasant Hill, California. A specialist in both modern Europe and the American Southwest, he has been teaching the history of Mexicans in the United States since 1971. Dr. Gonzales received a Ph.D. in modern Italian history from the University of California at Santa Barbara in 1972. He was a visiting professor of Chicano history in the Ethnic Studies department at UC Berkeley in 1993. He has published three books: *Andrea Costa and the Rise of Socialism in the Romagna* (1980), *The Hispanic Elite of the Southwest* (1989), and *Mexicanos: A History of Mexicans in the United States* (1999).

CYNTHIA M. GONZALES is an Education Specialist at Ygnacio Learning Center in Walnut Creek, California. A credentialed instructor, she has been teaching K–12 students since 1969. Ms. Gonzales received a B.A. in history from the University of California at Santa Barbara in 1966 and an M.A. in educational administration from St. Mary's College of California in Moraga in 1996. She was Director of Education at Walnut Creek Hospital from 1985 to 1998.